The Taste of Wine

The Taste of Wine

The Art and Science of Wine Appreciation

SECOND EDITION

Emile Peynaud

with the assistance of
JACQUES BLOUIN

translated from the French by
MICHAEL SCHUSTER

with a foreword by
MICHAEL BROADBENT, M.W.

John Wiley & Sons, Inc.
New York • Chichester • Brisbane • Toronto • Singapore • Weinheim

Originally published in French. Copyright © Bordas, Paris 1983

English translation copyright © 1987, 1996 by Michael Schuster

Published by John Wiley & Sons, Inc.

Library of Congress Cataloging-in-Publication Data
Peynaud, Emile.
    [Goût du vin. English]
    The taste of wine: the art and science of wine appreciation / Emile Peynaud ;
with the assistance of Jacques Blouin; translated from the French by Michael
Schuster; with a foreword by Michael Broadbent. —2nd ed.
      p.   cm.
    Includes index.
    ISBN 0-471-11376-X (cloth: alk. paper)
    1. Wine tasting. I. Blouin, Jacques. II. Title.
TP548.5.A5P4813 1996
    641.2'2—dc20   96-24181

Contents

Foreword

MICHAEL BROADBENT, M.W.

Peynaud is a legend in his own lifetime. Not an original phrase, but nontheless apt.

The reader will note that I refer to the author not as Professor Peynaud or as Emile: The first is magisterial and has a formal, somewhat over-respectful, connotation; the second is over-familiar, and I hesitate to take such a liberty. In England the use of the surname alone has a lordly ring. It is one of respect. That's how I think of him and always refer to him and so, I believe, do many other admirers and disciples the world over.

Two or three years ago, I forget exactly, I was sent an unedited translation of three major chapters of Peynaud's *Le Goût du Vin*. The American publisher asked if the translation was any good and whether there was a market in England for the book. Looking back at the translation now I see it was a bit stilted, but I replied that technically it seemed quite accurate and that, despite a somewhat vested interest in the subject matter as the author myself of a long-running series of books on winetasting, I would be the first to buy it. My reasons were twofold: First, my own knowledge of the French language is shamefully limited—it would be helpful to have a translation; second, from my gleaning of the original and from the drafts I was sent to examine, Peynaud seemed to have a singular ability to explain complicated matters succinctly, with directness, patience, and refreshing humility. I also discovered, to my slight surprise and great delight, that Peynaud had a deft touch and a gentle sense of humor.

My own interest in the subject began in the early 1950s. As a young wine merchant organizing tastings and teachings, I found no written work in the English language on tasting. So I wrote, at one sitting, a pamphlet for the senior staff at Harvey's of Bristol on the technique of tasting. This was produced in 1962 and was serialized in English, French, and Italian wine trade journals. It was first published as a book in 1968. Now I mention this because although, even by this time, there were many books on wine, they dealt almost exclusively with the broader elements: the history of wine, how it is made and where. Yet wine *tasting* was so basic; surely an understanding of this should precede all the generalities. Subsequent researches revealed that there had been some exploratory French texts. Amerine and Roessler had produced their somewhat complicated monograph for the University of California in 1959. Since then, as we all know, there has been a flood of books on wine, not quite as vast as the ocean of cookbooks, but enough to glut the market and exhaust the reader; and many, alas, have been unoriginal in concept and expression.

But what makes for a "good" wine book? There is the vexed question: Is it more satisfactory to employ a professional writer who has, to a greater or lesser extent, researched his subject and who produces a work of some literary merit; or to learn first-hand from the pen of a man who is a thorough master of his subject, an authority but perhaps lacking some polish and style? The English authors who pioneered wine writing included Sir Edward Barry in 1775, Alexander Henderson (1825), and Cyrus Redding (1833). They tended to be learned men but, with the odd exception, not in the business of making or selling wine.

Earlier this century the writers were largely amateur, slight, superficial, and romantic. The pendulum has swung a little too far: Recent wine books have focused more on facts and figures provided by wine professionals. Peynaud's work catches the balance neatly as it swings back, combining technique with humanity, hard facts with authority, clarity, and style.

A quick flip through the pages will reveal some figures and graphs and charts which, at first sight, look daunting. Don't be put off. I have no head for figures. I find the supporting text direct and lucid, the diagrams merely expressing words in a more visual, more mathematical way. In other instances, an elaborate chart may be reproduced only to demonstrate a system or method that Peynaud subsequently dismisses as pedantic and full of shortcomings.

Which brings me to the nub of the book. Peynaud takes nothing for granted. He tells us much about the nature and origins of taste. Most important of all, he manages to explain the background with patience and clarity. He is patently a practical man and a great teacher, an academic who puts his knowledge to work, an authority of immense stature who has the unusual ability to talk, and write, simply and directly.

Peynaud is intensely human; he allows himself an occasional sly dig at, for example, those who rely overmuch on those who taste by numbers on elaborate but limiting statistical methods, on the use of algebra rather than words. But we must bear in mind that Peynaud is French. He is a Bordelais, born and bred. His working life has been spent mainly in France, principally in Bordeaux. Latterly he has been much in demand to advise in other areas and other countries; indeed, years of his official retirement have been packed with work and with travel. He, and we, benefit from what he has seen and learned away from his beloved Bordeaux, but *Le Goût du Vin* was originally written in French for a French audience and, despite his peripatetic experience, has a distinctly French flavor—I avoid going as far as to say a Bordeaux bias. This is the archetypal French approach to wine. And as, dare I say it, the wines of France stand supreme, we have every reason to respect this approach.

Knowledge is one thing, understanding is another. Peynaud has both and helps us with both. He encourages us to flex our imaginations and, above all, to choose words carefully and to *use* them.

On the subject of words, I must praise Michael Schuster for his English text. It is no mean feat, for translating a book on tasting is not like translating a novel. A literal word-for-word equivalent does not give the flavor of the original, and as is well known to wine buffs—and as I found with the foreign translations of my own work—descriptive wine words and phrases have to be translated by someone who appreciates and understands their underlying meaning. I admitted earlier that my French is less than perfect, and it is quite likely that some lofty soul with greater command of the language will find something to disagree with. But, for what it is worth, I think that Schuster has done full justice to Peynaud.

This book will go down in the literature of wine simply as "Peynaud on Wine." We are the richer for him, and for it.

Translator's Note

However accurate the translator attempts to be, all translation remains an approximation, a compromise between a strictly literal (and perhaps stilted) rendering, and one which is faithful to the spirit rather than the letter of the original, but which reads more fluently. In this case, rather than trying to imitate the author's style in English, I have made clarity my main object. Indeed, Emile Peynaud's own generous advice to me was to "adapt as you need to for English."

A particular problem in this book is that in many cases there is no single equivalent English word for a specific French wine term, especially where there is no context. The word *moelleux* is an obvious example. Where it refers to red wine it means primarily **softness** and richness of texture; where it refers to white wine it indicates a degree of **sweetness** in taste. Some words, such as *rancio*, have no English equivalent whatsoever; others (many of them technical), though translatable, sound so odd in an English context that they are best left in French once their meaning is clear. Where words have been left in French I have also glossed them separately or included a translation in parentheses. Eighteenth- and nineteenth-century French wine terms have simply been rendered into a modern English equivalent. If there is room for argument between native speakers over the meaning of words they use to describe wine, there is certainly room for argument over translation. I have tried to give the most useful English option.

There are three people to whom I would like to say a special thank you for their help in this project: to the author himself, who kindly clarified many technical and vocabulary problems; to Michel Bernard, chemist and translator, whose generous advice was invaluable throughout; and finally to Naomi Good and Frances Andersen, my editors, whose suggestions and corrections added so much to the clarity and polish of this text. Any mistakes that remain, however, are entirely my own.

MICHAEL SCHUSTER

Preface

In November 1960, as a young agronomist, I was discovering the rules and rituals of winetasting on the "Monday Courses" given at the Bordeaux Institute of Oenology. For twelve years Emile Peynaud had been at the head of what was France's first school devoted to the subject of tasting. His combination of the practical and scientific fundamentals of modern oenology (chemistry, microbiology, technology) with the act of considered tasting has left its mark on generations of oenologists, winemakers, sommeliers, and informed amateurs. Using a well-defined vocabulary as the link, Peynaud's teaching combined the subjective description of wine with well-established scientific principles in what constituted the first global approach to winetasting. It remains the foundation of the subject today.

In the spring of 1966, at Clos Vougeot in the heart of Burgundy, several hundred wine specialists (myself and my former tutor at Montpelier, Georges Marteau, included) were witness to a remarkable performance, glass in hand, by Jules Chauvet and Louis Orizet. Their dazzling verbal improvisations in describing the subtleties of bouquet yielded by Pinot and Chardonnay, with references to fine leather from Russia and Morocco for example, or bold images borrowed from painting and music, left the non-Burgundian portion of the audience amazed. There remained something to be said, however, and later on this specifically Burgundian tradition of analyzing aromas and their persistence was complemented by the notation more typical of Bordeaux, based on the summary of a wine's structure and shorn of anything that might be judged excessive—more rational if less imaginative. Bordeaux and Burgundy: two completely contrasting styles of wine, two complementary approaches to the same discipline. In the final analysis the enjoyment of wine stems from paying attention to all its characteristics, a global analysis.

The first edition of *Le Goût du Vin* made its appearance in December 1980, a book that was both erudite yet accessible to a wide readership, as beautifully illustrated as it was scientifically documented. Peynaud's clear, precise prose eschewed esoteric jargon and by increasing our understanding of winetasting it enhanced our appreciation of wine. It was *the* book for a generation of professional tasters, and the time has come to update it. There are new vineyards, new vintages, new clonal varieties, and new marriages of grape and soil. There is a fresh generation of professionals, and tastes have changed as a function of fashion and marketing.

When, in the spring of 1995, Peynaud suggested I collaborate with him on the new edition of *Le Goût du Vin*, all these memories surfaced along with those of three decades of tasting and teaching tasters. Working year in, year out with wines from all the Bordeaux vineyards supplemented my early tasting experience, at the same time adapting it to new technology and to economic and social pressures. Thanks to the Bordeaux Institute of Oenology, led by Jean Ribéreau-Gayon and Emile Peynaud (succeeded by Pascal Ribéreau-Gayon, Pierre Sudraud, and many others) Bordeaux practices have served as models for the whole world, from the borders of the Gironde to the extremities of the southern hemisphere.

This new edition of *Le Goût du Vin* is not just a simple reprint, but neither is it a completely new set of theories and practice. For if, over twenty years, our understanding has evolved and our habits have changed, the mechanisms of our senses have remained the same. The pleasure we derive from the good things in life remains a question of personal education. This edition aims to reaffirm what is constant and to update where there is something new to be said. Good tasting is, above all, a sum of accurate perceptions. To taste is to see, smell, savor, and articulate one's impressions based on accumulated experience; thus everyone tastes according to his ability, his knowledge of viticultural geography, historical background, and so on. Wine is a reflection of the people who make it, and if history records the Sumerians of four thousand years ago as drinking wine "like river water," our century will go down on record as combining a scientifically based understanding of wine with a hedonistic idealization of it in the written word. Without the words with which to describe our sensations, our senses would be but illiterate organs.

Every wine lover knows that pleasure is increased by understanding, and that the only real satisfaction is an intellectual one. Before turning the pages of this book, consider what Pierre Poupon had to say: "The word 'taste' signifies more than just one of our five senses. It also describes the ability to discern what is beautiful and to enjoy it. Taste, in effect, becomes part of the intellect."

JACQUES BLOUIN

Preface to the First Edition

To the Amateur

You, dear drinker, are the most important link in the chain. You pay for the wine, you support the winegrowers, you cheerfully help consume what we produce. Whether you are a seasoned toper, an occasional bibber, or, preferably, an enlightened amateur, you will find food for thought in this book.

If you are from a traditional wine-producing country you carry the responsibilities imposed by an established wine culture. You may, however, come from a country that has only recently been making wine; in either case you both reflect and influence the quality of your country's wines. In one sense you "fashion" that quality, for if there are bad wines it is because there are indiscriminate drinkers.

The wine you drink is the wine you deserve. It is up to consumers to discourage bad winemaking: the quality of wine will improve when they make up their minds to drink better wine and when they are also prepared to pay for that extra quality.

If you are French you are possibly an advocate of drinking in quantity with traditional Rabelaisian extravagance, but statistically you are not a connoisseur. Remember, 60 percent of the best French wines are exported. Your wines may be of international standing, but it is well known in the wine trade that as a Frenchman your general knowledge of wine is below average and that you are a provincial drinker.

If you are one of those who drinks and extols the virtues of

French wines from beyond the confines of France, I take my hat off to you; we owe our reputation to your forefathers. Keep your own cellar stocked in turn and bequeath it to your children in the certain knowledge that our great wines are made with you in mind.

This book will, I hope, teach the amateur to understand wine better and to appreciate it more. Knowing what to drink is based on knowing how to taste, and considered tasting teaches not only how to perceive with our senses but how to interpret those perceptions. Good wine encourages drinking in moderation, while alcoholism is the consequence of swigging a poor product. Drink less but be fastidious in your choice; every time you purchase an inferior bottle you compromise the reputation of good wine in general.

I would also like this book to teach you to talk about wine. Drinking should not be a solitary pleasure but a mutual one; if a wine is good say so in your own way. There are few pleasures which lend themselves so well to discussion as those shared sipping good wine, glass in hand. You will see that this is a school where progress is rapid.

TO THE WINE PRODUCER

Of all wine-related occupations yours is the best. You need to be a farmer, viticulturist, winemaker, cellarmaster, and salesman. The wine you produce is a reflection of yourself, the fruit of your land, and your labor; but you also have a responsibility to the wider image of wine which is influenced by the impression your product creates. You can make one of the most fascinating and refined of delicacies— or just a dull and disappointing beverage.

The vine and wine make substantial and manifold demands on you and you must be skilled in numerous different fields. Viticulture is essentially agricultural and, as such, subject to the vagaries of the weather. The quantity and quality of the harvest are difficult to predict and the revenue they will yield even more so. Were it not for a pejorative ring in the context I would call vinification industrial in character, for it is essentially the processing of an agricultural product. The cellar care of wine, on the other hand, is more of a craft; not, however, one of trial and error, for as a winemaker you will keep up with advances in oenology and in consequence your work will become yearly more exacting. Last but not least of your requirements is a good head for business. You need to be a company director, executive manager, and financial adviser all rolled into one. Yours is an all-embracing occupation. For you tasting should be a constant means of quality control. Whatever your kind of wine you need to learn to taste well, for there is always room for improvement, improvement which is difficult to achieve if the only wines you taste are your own. Take whatever opportunity you can to taste further afield, outside your own cellar, beyond your own region and appellation, in other countries if possible. Such encounters are often a salutary experience.

This book will furnish you with a systematic approach to tasting, suggest some new ideas, and possibly inspire a new passion for your own wine. A good taster invariably produces a better wine because he makes it to his own liking. Olivier de Serres said: "A man who makes good wine is considered a good man." In other words, such wine needs to be earned. How many mediocre wines would disappear from our shelves if only those who made them knew how to taste properly!

To the Wine Merchant

You may be a third- or fourth-generation member of a traditional wine merchant's business, a trade stretching back a century or two. It is thanks to you that the names and reputation of our French wines have spread throughout the world. Yet now and again the very appellations which owe you so much have turned against you. For times change and the growers forget that the wines themselves did not create the trade and that the expansion of the vineyards was only as rapid as the merchants' conquest of the markets. Equally, tradition is a cumbersome burden in family businesses and it is often difficult for long-established houses to change their ways. For generations the traditional wine merchants have taught newcomers the trade. I myself learnt to taste with a merchant, and from the very beginning managed first the classification of wines and then their production. For you wine merchants, then, this book may have little to offer. It may, nonetheless, remind you of all that modern technology has brought to bear in a field richly imbued with inherited know-how.

More likely you are one of those merchants who has adopted a more modern approach to commerce. You will have studied marketing and reorganized your distribution chain; you want a shorter period of prebottling cellar maturation and a faster stock turnover. You may be a broker, intermediary between producer and trade, adviser to both; or an agent, a salesman, a retailer, a supermarket drinks manager, a restaurateur, or a wine waiter. Among you are those who make the final sale to the customer and, whatever your place in the supply chain, you should remember that the wine you have sold will be consumed by the person who has paid for it. Thus it would seem only fair and wise for you to know how to taste and assess it yourself beforehand.

This book will help you do so by boosting your confidence and extending your vocabulary. In this way you personally become a guarantor of quality by only selling those wines you would be happy to drink yourself—surely one of the most reliable and pleasant ways of doing business.

TO THE OENOLOGIST

To you I speak as a longstanding practitioner for whom the aim of oenological research has been to explain the tastes in wine as well as to make a better product. I have always felt that wine is not there just to be swilled and swallowed but to be sipped and savored. Some of you will have been taught oenology with very little tasting; indeed, the syllabus leading to the 1955 oenology diploma seems to have been devised by teetotalers! Were they unaware that tasting is essential to good vinification, as well as to cellar care, clarification, analysis, and stabilization? How many are the oenologists who must have learned, and possibly forgotten, the biochemistry of fermentation without ever having learned how to taste. In their first jobs they will have found themselves in an unfamiliar world of professional tasting with a misleading trial-and-error approach, and the extent to which they have succeeded will have depended more or less on natural talent. Subsequently, the teaching of tasting has developed considerably and since 1975 the Bordeaux Institute of Oenology has even offered a University Diploma in Tasting (Diplôme Universitaire d'Aptitude à la Dégustation: DUAD).

Oenology and tasting *are* linked. Having taught both at university I am not sure whether I have contributed most by making tasting an introduction to oenology or oenology an introduction to tasting. That is for the oenologists to decide themselves; after all, tasting is their sphere, their specialty, and where wine knowledge is concerned they hold sway. It is also their responsibility to organize the tasting groups of local viti-vinicultural trade unions, administrative bodies, and wine businesses.

This book has been written in several registers: in textbook language for the oenologist, in simpler paraphrases for the amateur. It has benefited from the considerable theoretical knowledge that oenology has to offer and also from the direct "glass in hand" experience of practical winemakers.

Believe me, it is now up to oenologists to annex and develop the field of tasting; future generations of great tasters will rise from the ranks of the oenologists.

EMILE PEYNAUD

O n e

The Science and Practice of Winetasting

SOME DEFINITIONS

Definitions are unavoidable; each word needs its meaning explained, and its usage defined, so that a dictionary of technical terms becomes both a foundation and a safeguard. To start with, we need basic definitions. Winetasting is both an ancient art and a modern science. As a science it forms part of the broad field of measurement and interpretation of sensation, tempting one to make its vocabulary that of sensory analysis, but this is inimical to the spirit of tasting whose mode of expression is as ancient as the advent of quality wine. The language of tasting, which is continually evolving, was at first very regionalized. When one compares the opinions of early tasters they were many and various, and sometimes contradictory. Gradually, however, definitions have been standardized. According to one historian, it was in 1312 that Philippe le Bel set up an amateur group called Les Courtiers-Gourmets-Piqueurs de Vin (The Brokers-Gourmets-Tasters of Wine), forerunners of our professional tasters. This Parisian group is still in existence today. The noun *dégustateur* was first defined in 1793 as "one whose profession is to taste wine." *Gourmet* was synonymous with *dégustateur* but preceded it. The verb *déguster* (to taste) made its first formal appearance in 1813.

1

The definition which the Larousse dictionary gives is fairly restrictive: *déguster* means "to evaluate with one's sense of taste the flavor and qualities of solid or liquid food"; our other senses are ignored here.

In more recent times the Association française de Normalisation (the French Standards Association) has defined tasting as "an operation consisting of trying, analyzing, and evaluating the organoleptic and more particularly the olfactogustatory characteristics of a product."

Le Conseil international de la Langue française (International Council for the French Language) repeats this definition and adds: "It can be more or less detailed and analytical, as when it aims to break down the characteristics into basic elements, in order to link a particular taste with an identifiable substance or group of substances (analytical tasting). On the other hand it can be all-embracing by simply expressing the pleasure or displeasure experienced (hedonistic tasting)."

Oenologists distinguish four phases of the act of tasting: sensory examination, describing what the senses have perceived, comparison with recognized standards, and reasoned judgment: "Winetasting is to taste a wine with care in order to appreciate its quality; to submit it to examination by our senses, in particular those of taste and smell; to try and understand it by discovering its various qualities and defects and putting them into words. It is to study, analyze, describe, define, judge and classify." (Ribéreau-Gayon)

Too technical a vocabulary and circumlocutions are often primary obstacles to communication. For the sake of clarity I will stick to the simple words "tasting" and "taster" for the activity and the person.

For the purist, tasting and sensory analysis are not exactly synonymous. Winetasting is a particular example of the more general examination which is called sensory analysis, defined by Depledt of the Institut national de la Consommation (National Consumer Institute) as: "All the methods and techniques which we employ in using our senses to perceive, identify, and appreciate the so-called organoleptic properties of food and other objects." In effect, the taster is carrying out a sensory analysis without knowing it.

Texts such as these clearly show that winetasting is at once an art and a science, both difficult, that its vocabulary is often esoteric, and that the winetaster is a professional. For the amateur who might be put off by such definitions, suffice it to say that tasting is also part of general drinking know-how, and that it could also be described as "the period of time between picking up a glass and the moment when the taste of the wine disappears after swallowing." From the length of this period, which varies according to the drinker's preferences, and from the size of each mouthful of wine taken, one can tell, without his knowing, how discriminating a palate he has, even the extent of his general connoisseurship. Show me how you drink and I will tell you who you are. A harsh test for some.

What distinguishes the considered act of tasting from the simple reflex act of drinking is that in tasting one's approach is systematic and one's impressions must be coordinated.

Winetasting is the rationalization of an epicurean activity. To be appreciated, wine demands attention and contemplation; and the appeal of tasting is enhanced if one can analyze it. Countless pleasures are wasted through ignorance and a want of skill and attention.

Winetasting is an exercise in moderation and common sense. Whether as a notional, creative act of imbibing or as a slow prelude to drinking proper, it teaches a thorough acquaintance with one's senses and how to use them, it promotes the close examination of one's reactions and feelings, and, finally, it encourages sobriety. Poupon's definition of tasting elevates it to the realm of a discipline: "Tasting is a way of life. We taste everything that comes into contact with our senses, be it a work of art, the present moment, the reality of existence; objects, people, the arts, love, life." Looked at in this way, tasting is a means of perceiving and understanding the outside world; it presupposes a state of mind that is constantly receptive to sensation.

There is a big difference between drinking and tasting. Good wines and great wines are not drinks which are simply swallowed; one savors them. Their attraction is not that of a thirst quencher, drunk in great drafts merely to refresh one's throat with a pleasant, tactile liquid sensation; nor is it simply that of the gentle warming sensation provided by an alcoholic drink.

Drinking wine and deriving pleasure from it is not an instinctive activity. It has its own techniques which need to be learned and its appeal is on a quite different level from that of the monotonous flavor of manufactured drinks. To anyone who cares to look for them wine provides an infinite variety of natural flavors and aromas. It is complex, multifaceted, and never tastes quite the same, for the occasion changes, the accompanying food differs, and the mood of the drinker may also vary.

Fine wines are the product of skill, patience, and hard work by winemakers who have the pleasure of the consumer in mind. To appreciate this pleasure in full demands an effort, and the skill of tasting provides the means. Physical pleasure by itself is enough to satisfy the urge to drink; the act of tasting requires intelligence and competence as well.

THE ROLE AND PURPOSES OF TASTING

Both during the process of making wine and for the purpose of buying and selling it, tasting is essential for assessing quality. If it has always been so traditionally it is even more the case today with the quality stipulations imposed on both AOC wines and many others. Tasting panels are becoming more and more common in modern wine enterprises and their principal role is to evaluate the tasting properties of a wine; for the appreciation of a wine's quality depends above all on how agreeable it is to taste, even if, as we shall see later, there are other aspects to this quality factor. First and foremost, wine should be considered more as a pleasant complement to food than as a thirst-quenching or nutritious drink. If a wine does quench one's thirst (which, in any case, it does only to a limited extent), and if it also contributes nutrients and calories to one's diet that is something of a bonus.

There is also among wines a unique range and hierarchy of quality that is not to be found in any other processed agricultural product. It makes winetasting not only the most worthwhile but also the most difficult and subtle form of professional tasting.

What is the practical purpose of tasting? It is quite simply the basis of all aspects of the wine business in the long chain from cultivating the vine to bringing the wine to the table. At any of these levels tasting is an essential means of examination and quality control, a system that is both swift and sensitive.

For the producer, cellarmaster, or winemaker there is no more rapid and efficient method of following the vinification, judging when to blend, checking quality, and keeping abreast of the aging process. Chemical analysis is a great help, but nothing can replace the instant information yielded by nose and palate. Chemical analysis is slow and highly subdivided, whereas tasting is rapid and global in its assessment. It is an activity that is complete in both physiological and cerebral terms; it is also practical, whatever the circumstances.

The broker (who acts as a commercial intermediary between producer and merchant) tastes as an expert, consultant, presenter, and judge of wine. Having sampled and approved the product before offering it, he can guarantee it once purchased. He knows the wines of his region better than anyone and it is among the brokers that one meets the most competent palates. The merchant tastes his purchases at all stages from blending to bottling. It is only after a final tasting that he puts his label and name on a bottle.

It would be difficult to imagine oenologists who were not also expert tasters, for they are the technicians in charge of the care, presentation, and stabilization of wines. They have the advantage over other professionals of working very closely with wine from vinification through to bottling. Their tasting analyses probe deeper; they can explain a defect and pinpoint its source, trace a wine's past, predict its future.

Restaurant managers and wine waiters need to know not only how to serve wines but also how to purchase and recommend them, tasks which would be difficult if they were not experienced tasters. Finally, at the end of the line there is the wine lover who knows how to taste and how to discuss wine. He appreciates a wine all the more for being able to perceive its qualities and to explain why it is good. For the consumer to be able to tell the difference between two wines and to recognize their difference in quality, he needs to have acquired at least some basic ideas about winetasting. And educating the consumer's palate is one effective way of raising the overall standard of wine production.

Tasting is thus a means to the better understanding of wine. This in turn leads to improvements in vinification, conservation and quality control, and finally to a greater appreciation.

WINETASTING AND OENOLOGY

People have been slow to recognize that tasting as a means to understanding wine is a branch of oenology, and in a way an introduction to it. Indeed, one of the aims of oenology is to explain the taste of wine at the same time as providing the means of perfecting it. I like to begin teaching oenology by tasting, and I consider oenology's basic tool to be the tasting glass. I see the priority thus because it is precisely by tasting that one judges the success of oenology's principal goal, that of improving the quality of wine. Equally, serious tasting is impossible without a certain knowledge of wine (how can one appreciate or assess a product one barely knows?) and wine knowledge is the realm of oenology.

This point of view may seem obvious, but it is new. Many books on oenology, even recent ones, say little or nothing about tasting. For some it is an integral part of wine analysis, but this is not exactly true; analysis illuminates tasting but it is not an end in itself as tasting is. The new approach is due to Jean Ribéreau-Gayon who devoted a chapter to it in his *Traité d'Oenologie* (1947). Progress in oenology has helped refine the mechanisms and define the rules of tasting technique.

Winetasting is often regarded as a part of the geography of viticulture, just a matter of appellations and growths. This approach goes no further than identifying the grape variety and, occasionally, the soil type. This kind of commercial or regulatory tasting becomes much more exacting and precise when backed up by some knowledge of oenology. The taste of wine is too closely linked to its own chemical composition and that of its grape varieties, to vinification techniques and aging processes, for oenology not to be a great help in the field of tasting. So, if the teaching of oenology must begin with winetasting, the teaching of winetasting must touch on winemaking and the composition of wine.

A distinction is usually drawn between tastings by the consumer or wine buff and by the professional. The former is looking above all for pleasure from the tastings which are arranged to take place in conditions where the wines will be seen at their best, served at an ideal temperature, either by themselves or during a meal. The professional tastes in a more critical frame of mind, looking rather for possible faults in the wine, or at least he ought to. Of course, any wine that satisfies the consumer completely must have successfully negotiated several tasting hurdles; nevertheless, the professional needs to be that much more severe in his judgments, and his experience gives him a more profound appreciation than the layman.

Professional tasting is done in several different ways. One standard approach involves assessing a wine's commercial value, attempting to answer the questions: Is this wine typical of its appellation in terms of character and quality? How much can it be sold for? Is it better or worse than comparable wines? This could be called evaluative tasting. The oenologist's approach is more technical. It attempts to describe a wine's taste by way of its composition, analyzing it into simple recognizable flavors; it tries to link a specific flavor to a specific substance, to trace its source to particular conditions of vinification or storage, and to predict the wine's keeping and aging properties. This type of tasting is more analytical than the first and more searching in its conclusions.

It is true that we taste wine from different standpoints, but in the final analysis appreciation is based on knowledge, and people taste as best they can, according to their ability, training, and concept of what makes good wine; that is to say, with that accumulation of wine-related knowledge that every taster inevitably acquires.

WINETASTING AND WINETASTERS

Since wine is made to be consumed and enjoyed, it follows that tasting is the most sensible way to assess its quality. Indeed, tasting is the only means we have of really appreciating it. Whatever our interest in wine, we are all capable of tasting and of being or becoming a taster in our own way. A little attention and an effort to register one's impressions are all that is required for regular drinking to become winetasting. The most difficult aspect of tasting, and one not within everyone's grasp, is describing sensations and making appropriate judgments.

In wine-producing countries the professional assessment of wines is entrusted to tasters with considerable practical experience. The informed opinion of such experts is considered more valuable than that given by a group of amateurs, even selected amateurs, as is the practice in some countries. To be of any real value, a taster must be able to make judgments independent of his personal taste and be able to justify his choice.

Tasting is said to be at once an art and a science; it can be learned, it can be taught. It is also a profession, or part of one, and its apprenticeship consists first of all in acquiring the basic concepts of tasting through a series of appropriate courses and exercises, and then in tasting regularly with experienced tasters who can describe precisely what they perceive. A host of impressions are memorized in this way; it is a veritable education of taste and smell. While an instructor is certainly necessary, what he can communicate to a student in this kind of teaching is inevitably limited. It is a training which demands a great deal of personal effort and perseverance. In the end the taster, apprentice or expert, is alone in confronting the wine and his own sensations, for not everything that can be perceived is communicable and there are always sensations that one has to discover for oneself.

A good winetaster must combine a clear perception of tastes and odors with a well-developed technique; but even more important for this training are the interest and passion that the individual brings to the task. To taste effectively, one must love wine, and to learn to taste it is to learn to love it more. Practically anyone can learn to taste well if he or she is prepared to make the effort: a few years of regular practice are all that is required. The basic senses of taste and smell are the most fairly distributed of man's attributes and most people's sense of smell and taste are sensitive enough; what is usually lacking is the frequent opportunity to taste a large number of different wines.

On this subject I have come across a quotation which I find particularly apt: "There is no man or woman who cannot learn to taste, at least in the long run, given patience, application, willingness, a conscientious approach, complete honesty, and, above all, plenty of experience; the last because obviously one can only recognize those sensations which one has already encountered. This is not to ignore those privileged individuals who are born with the ability to acquire this experience rapidly, given the right circumstances, and who can get the most out of it thanks to a reliable specialized memory."

There are indeed some individuals gifted with an acute sensory discrimination, though it is rare for this gift to relate to all tastes and all odors. Their superior performance also derives from an acquired sensitivity and from a greater ability to identify a particular sensation.

Few people suffer from a physiological inability to smell or taste (anosmia or agustia); if they cannot smell certain odors it is sometimes because they cannot recognize them, and the same goes for tastes. However, the differences in sensitivity to a given taste or smell are quite marked from one person to another. It is not uncommon for there to be a fivefold variation of sensitivity between individuals' thresholds of perception. A reduced sensitivity does not necessarily mean that one cannot taste, but it does mean that the balance of tastes and smells will vary in its concentrations and proportions. If, in an average sample of individuals, 30 percent have a low sensitivity to bitterness, for example, it could be said that they are typical of one-third of the general population in this respect. Their opinion would, however, not be of much use in understanding the reaction of the majority. Obviously, the professional winetaster's sensitivity should be even more acute than that of the majority.

It is difficult to decide to what extent sensitivity of taste is innate and to what extent it is acquired. The expert winetaster's gift may simply come from the fact that he has always been interested in his senses, and has cultivated them for that reason. The paradox of winetasting is that it tends to be an objective method using subjective means. Wine is the object, the winetaster the subject. The human senses are used as the measuring instruments in winetasting: One can establish procedures to ensure they function effectively, improve their accuracy, and avoid sources of error, but the taster remains not only an executant but also a judge. He is able to conjure up images to describe the wine he tastes, something which no instrumental interpretation can replace. His subjectivity is part of his human personality.

The winetaster must be coldly precise in his descriptive analysis, exacting in his approval but warm in his judgment. His critical opinion should be clear, but he need not be afraid to express his pleasure, for the taster's critical function should not inhibit his ability to enthuse about a wine. He should be capable of astonishment and admiration.

By their training, professional tasters and those who write about tasting belong to different "schools," if one can put it quite like that, for most of them have had no formal training and are more or less self-taught. (In fact, tasting schools or training centers are a very recent creation.) Whether drawn from the production or the selling side of the wine business, the expertise of most tasters has been built up within the traditional confines of a winemaking region; their tasting experience is of a general nature and sometimes rather confused. For them wine is too often something subtle, mysterious, and elusive, capable of changing in the glass from one moment to the next.

9

There are, however, excellent self-taught tasters whose well-developed technique is due to an imaginative and perceptive approach, and who, having become skilled in this professional aspect of wine, have gone on to acquire competence and authority.

At the other extreme are those rigidly narrow tasters who use their senses only as a recording instrument and who consider winetasting to be practically a branch of mathematics. The questions they ask are simple and precise, limited to a few of a wine's characteristics. They want categorical answers, "either/or" boxes must be ticked, the wine's quality is briefly represented by a score, and the results are submitted to statistical analysis. Arithmetic decides whether the results are of any value and whether they are significant in a statistical sense.

Between these two styles of winetasting, the empirical and the statistical, there is room for one that is more comprehensive; one which is both analytic and descriptive, which both measures and assesses. This approach describes the organoleptic (taste and odor) characteristics of wine with a rich yet precise vocabulary, also employing scores and grades, and using statistical analysis when necessary. It is more logical, more rigorous than the empirical style I have described; less impersonal and more realistic than trying to describe wine by statistics. It is more oenological and French in character, and it is the method presented in this book; neatly defined as the relationship between man and wine.

This modern method has emerged from the integration of two schools of thought on tasting. It is a synthesis of the Burgundy/Beaujolais school, with its emphasis on the analysis and description of olfactory characteristics, and the Bordeaux school which originally paid more attention to the balance of flavors and weight of the wine on the palate. The first school has to assess wines from a single grape variety with pure, uncomplicated aromas, so they attached more importance to smell and the length and aromatic character of a wine's aftertaste. The Bordeaux school, which dealt with wines from a blend of grape varieties characterized in particular by the quality of their tannins, attached more weight to the wine's structure. This is a personal interpretation, but these observations reflect my own tasting evolution. I have noticed that the Burgundians no longer limit their descriptions to evocations of aroma and bouquet but happily discuss the wines on the palate, too.

USEFUL AUTHORS

Much has been written on how to taste, and knowledge is inevitably disseminated via the written word; the tasting glass and spoken word are by themselves inadequate for progress. Early writers on winemaking were rather circumspect on the subject, as though the art of tasting had arisen by itself. It was at the turn of the century (1906) that Cloquet and Vincens each, independently, devoted a slim volume to the subject. However, it was only in the 1950s that really fundamental ideas began to take shape.

Le Magnen's books of 1949 and 1951 were the first to offer winetasters the physiological and anatomical data and the concepts of sensory stimulation which are the foundations of taste perception. In effect, these works were the starting point for a more methodical approach to winetasting. At the same time, Amerine and his associates published their attempts to codify tests, to improve their accuracy, and to apply statistical methods to quality assessment. Chauvet's publications of 1950, 1951, and 1956 dealt with olfactory sensations in an attempt to probe deeper into odor analysis. There were also some interesting additions and refinements from Klenk (1950), Got (1955, 1958), and Ribéreau-Gayon (1961).

Since then there have been several seminal texts published on winetasting as a science in its own right and with its own technique. Their importance indicates the progress achieved in a field where the subjectivity of sensations and vocabulary makes research difficult and progress painfully slow.

The Centre National de Coordination des Etudes et Recherches sur la Nutrition et l'Alimentation (National Center for the Coordination of Study and Research into Nutrition and Food) has published the report of a scientific conference held in November 1964, entitled *Méthodes subjectives et objectives d'appréciation des caractères organoleptiques des denrées alimentaires*. The chapters on the rational bases for analyzing organoleptic qualities (Le Magnen) and on tasting test methodology (Depledt) may be considered the foundations of winetasting as a science and an art. The report included a technical vocabulary for the organoleptic characteristics of food products in general; the vocabulary relating specifically to wine consisted of about 140 words. It was a start.

The Principles of Sensory Evaluation of Food by Amerine, Pangborn,

11

and Roessler (1965) is a series of extensively researched monographs on the mechanisms of the senses and the factors which influence judgment in tests; it also develops procedures for the statistical exploitation of test results.

Précis d'Initiation à la Dégustation by Puisais, Chabanon, Guiller, and Lacoste (1969) provided professional tasters with a concise study of the theoretical bases of their activity. The book outlines the basic elements of sensory physiology; it analyzes the various sources of stimulation, and shows the principal relationships between organoleptic properties and chemical substances found in wine analysis. Also covered are: tasting technique, the organization of tastings, and the system of marking.

L'Essai sur la Dégustation des Vins by Vedel, Charle, Charnay, and Tourmeau (1972) summarized our knowledge at the time in its chapters on sensations perceived, sensory analysis, tasters, vocabulary. A work of collective authorship, it showed the progress made in devising a commonly accepted tasting technique. It was a milestone in tasting literature.

In quite a different style are the essays of Pierre Poupon who expresses the science of tasting so well in the language of a poet and philosopher. His books conjure up the image of a virtuoso wine-taster contemplating an interior reflection of himself tasting. Poupon creates a wine ethic and a code for wine drinking.

Michael Broadbent's *Wine Tasting, Enjoying, Understanding* first appeared in 1968. Aimed originally at wine merchants, it outlined the rules of the game for discriminating tasting in keeping with the British tradition as discoverers of fine wines. His book ushered in a happy period of literature on winetasting including Max Léglise's *Une initiation à la dégustation des grands vins* in 1976, a little book rich in expertise and humanity in the service of wine. The same year the Americans Amerine and Roessler followed with *Wines, Their Sensory Evaluation*, an objective guide to judging wine with all one's senses, written for the professional and the connoisseur.

Since the first edition of this book in 1980, the winetaster's library has been enriched by numerous works. These can be classified into four groups.

First, there are those books dealing with sensory analysis in general, viewed as a methodology of quality evaluation of all food and drink. These are works of collective authorship, concerned above all with the codification of methods. In 1991 AFNOR (the official French Standards Organization) produced a set of "standards," and in 1990 the Scientific Society for alimentary hygiene, in collaboration with various laboratories of neurophysiology, published a treatise on sensory analysis. Whether either of these are of any practical use to professional winetasters is difficult to say.

After twenty years AFNOR has only just finalized the design of a standard tasting glass, good for nosing wine, but impractical for the purpose of drinking. And codifiers of this kind decline any real discussion of wine: "Wine is subject to cultural influences when made, and it is also shaped by individuals who are part of the same culture; its taste is therefore relative and arbitrary."

Second, in the 1992 issues of *L'Amateur de Bordeaux*, the pens of P. MacLeod and A. Faurion challenged the theories on which the professional lives of myself and others have been based; theories we developed, paradoxically, during the course of our teaching, and which led to the current methods of vinification and to wines whose qualities are universally recognized. We have the greatest respect for basic research while appreciating that it is difficult to reconcile theory with practice. MacLeod and Faurion opined that the microbiologist is not the person best equipped to conduct a wine's fermentation. Perhaps it might also be said that the physiologist is no great help when it comes to making up a commercial blend. Each to his own!

Yet another category is written for a vast public embracing both professionals and amateurs. One might describe these as books to be read "glass in hand." Jacques Blouin's *Guide d'Initiation à la Dégustation* is a logically reasoned handbook on the first steps to the discovery of quality wine, the fruit of thirty years' experience of a group of Bordeaux oenologists and wine buffs. And it is not pure chance that led to the books of Schuster, *Understanding Wine* (1989), and Spurrier and Dovaz, *The Academie du Vin Wine Course* (1984), being translated into French. The French oenologists advise on winemaking, the English professionals on its appreciation in the glass. It is they who have the last word. There are also Buffin's two instruction manuals, generously illustrated with diagrams linking perception, vocabulary, technology, and origins: *Pratique de la Dégustation* (1987) and *Votre Talent de la Dégustation* (1988).

Finally, several novelties deal with vocabulary and language. These are technical reference books or French/English dictionaries, always useful. In 1984, under the promising title of *Les Mots du Vin et de l'Ivresse*, Martine Chatelain compiled a dictionary which managed to combine humor with scientific precision, civilized learning with a love of good wine, the technical side of winemaking with everyday living. And should you want an insight into what the language of wine is all about you could also thumb through *Les Dégustations du Grand Jury* by Jacques Luxey (1975 to 1985). Throughout the innumerable tastings of great wines, Luxey's work is characterized by the quality and experience of his tasters, the excellent tasting conditions, his preparation of samples and corrected scoring system, the latter taking into account the inevitable variance in marks between tasters (high, low, closely grouped, widely spread, sometimes described as "erratic"). The rankings are accompanied by extensive tasting notes. This series, cut short by the death of the author, offers a vast panorama of fine wines sampled between 1975 and 1985.

Thus the winetaster progresses, from one wine to another, from one book to another, his knowledge gaining in breadth and depth. For three decades developments in the science of tasting have concentrated on the mechanisms of taste perception, an extension of Le Magnen's original work, and on establishing a more complete and precise tasting vocabulary, following Vedel's initiative. The art of describing wine has been refined by tasters like Chauvet, Coste, Goffard, and Puisais. At the same time the experimental aspect of tasting has progressed steadily: the influence of external factors, thresholds of perception for tastes and odors and their interaction. The practical application of developments can be seen in the installation of purpose-built tasting centers in wine regions, and the organized teaching of tasting. But there is still a vast amount to do, as much in the field of experimentation as in the training of a body of qualified winetasters.

T w o

The Senses and
How They Work

THE NEUROPHYSIOLOGICAL
MECHANISMS OF TASTING

Obviously, you can taste without understanding the physiological mechanisms involved. However, the taster can avoid errors of perception and the influence of suggestion if he or she has some knowledge of the functioning of taste and odor receptors and of the central mechanism of interpretation, and is aware of the internal and external factors which can affect judgment.

The transmission of a stimulus to the senses via our nervous system, and the response that the brain relays to our consciousness or motor centers, together create a continuous network of information and interpretation which is the very token of our existence: I sense, therefore I am; our consciousness functions precisely because of the host of impressions which surround it. It is also the means by which we understand our environment; we live because of what we see, hear, smell, taste, and touch. Chauchard reminds us of the Latin adage: "What intelligence we have has its source in our senses."

The senses of sight and hearing are highly refined, constantly alert and active; those of taste and smell are "occasional" senses, used only intermittently. It is understandable, therefore, that we are less skilled at tasting and smelling than we are at looking and listening. Smell and taste are senses that need to be alerted before they function; the first is restricted by our respiratory system, the second by our digestive system. The winetaster tries to fool the senses by simulating consumption and by always being particularly attentive. Tasting sets in motion a series of sensory **stimuli**, these being the **sapid** (pertaining to taste) and **odorous** (pertaining to smell) constituents of wine. When present in sufficient quantity certain molecules or fractions of molecules have the property of stimulating the sensitive terminals of our sensory nerve cells. The effect is similar to inserting an electric plug into its socket or switching on an ignition key: an excitation current is passed to the brain.

The synthesis of information from the nerve cells takes place in a specialized zone of the brain, the olfactory cortex, which attempts to decode it, comparing it with information stored in the taster's memory from previous experience. Once a sensation is recognized it can be interpreted and thus becomes a matter of **perception**. The sensation by itself is reflex and unconscious; perception renders it conscious. An unknown sensation cannot be interpreted and either passes unnoticed or, since the brain reasons by analogy, is confused with a similar sensation. The terminology of this process calls for some definitions. The following table includes a schematic outline of our sensory mechanisms:

Schematic outline of sensory mechanisms

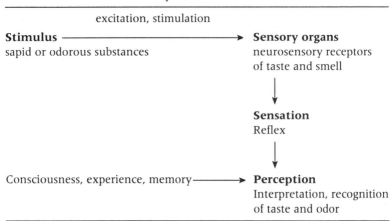

Stimulus: the physical or chemical agent responsible for the stimulation or excitation of specific sensory receptors.

Sensation: a phenomenon resulting from the stimulation of sensory receptors.

Neurons: nerve cells whose endings constitute the sensitive zones throughout the skin and mucous membranes. They send sensory signals to the brain and spinal cord.

Perception: conscious registration of a sensation as a result of interpreting it. For the **sensation** of taste or smell merely to be activated requires a sufficient concentration of a stimulus substance. A greater concentration is required for **perception**, that is, for the stimulus to be recognized, the sensation identified.

The **threshold of sensation** is the weakest concentration of stimulus which will give rise to a sensation; this corresponds to the minimum quantity of a given substance (e.g., sugar for sweetness) needed to produce a sensation which cannot, however, be identified at that level.

The **threshold of perception**, of identification and recognition, corresponds to the minimum quantity of a product required for it to be recognized and identified. For example, 18 percent of people are sensitive to half a gram of sugar (sucrose) per liter in that they notice a sensation; but they can only identify the taste as sweet at a concentration above 1 or 2 grams per liter (1 or 2 g/l).

The **differential threshold** is the name given to the quantity of stimulus that needs to be added to an existing and perceptible amount for there to be a recognizable difference. Take the sweet taste produced by a solution containing 20 g/l of sugar. If, without revealing their order, this is compared with solutions containing 21, 22, and 23 g/l, that is, 5 percent, 10 percent, and 15 percent more concentrated, the variation in concentration between the reference solution and that in which a difference is perceived represents the differential threshold.

Winetasting is based on the assumption that everyone's physiological reaction to given sensation is the same, which is obviously not the case. The thresholds depend on the individual's sensitivity of taste and smell. The determination of these thresholds is one of the factors considered when selecting winetasters. So I am always somewhat surprised at the similar reactions of a group of tasters who finally agree, not so much on the levels of individual flavors but on their balance, and also on the analogies they invoke to characterize odor and aroma. This simply goes to show that trained tasters smell and taste in a fairly similar manner, just as the majority of people see and hear in much the same way.

THE MEASUREMENT OF ORGANOLEPTIC PROPERTIES AND THE SENSES INVOLVED

According to the nineteenth-century chemist Chevreul, the organoleptic properties of any substance are those perceived by our senses, and correspond to the various sensory stimuli inherent in the food, drink, or organic compounds concerned. They derive above all from physical and chemical properties, and they can be measured by physical or chemical means. However, they are called organoleptic only when they have been perceived by the senses.

Take the case of granulated sugar for example. Its physical attributes are those of crystals of sucrose in terms of its form, density, solubility, polarization in solution, etc. Chemically, it is almost pure sucrose: It is a disaccharide in constitution, it hydrolyzes enzymatically or chemically into glucose and fructose, and it caramelizes at high temperature, etc. Nothing in these physical or chemical properties explains why sucrose is sweet to taste; indeed, you have to place some on the tip of your tongue to discover this at all. Sweetness is the organoleptic property of sucrose; it is a true property but one whose reality is only potential until experienced by an individual.

For most people the association between sugar and a sweet taste dates back to earliest childhood, so that the mere sight of sugar conjures up the idea of sweetness. However, it is quite possible to imagine someone who, due to some sensory defect, would be incapable of perceiving sweetness and who would therefore find sugar tasteless. For such a person sugar would have no organoleptic property. While complete inability to taste is rare, individual sensitivity to sweetness and other tastes is generally very variable.

The sweet character of sugar may be undetectable when it is in very dilute solution, below the threshold of sensation, or when it is mixed with a small quantity of a very bitter or acid substance capable of masking it. It may also be concealed if the sweet solution is so hot as to burn the tongue. These examples show that to detect an organoleptic property requires fairly precise circumstances. The conditions must be suitable for tasting, one's sensory sensitivity needs to be not only adequate but also accurate, the organoleptic property itself needs to be sufficiently pronounced to convey a clear impression.

In general, the measurement of organoleptic properties constitutes the first phase of tasting, that of observation and analysis. The second phase involves an assessment of quality.

Sugar will serve again as a reference for distinguishing between objective, subjective, and affective attitudes. To say that it is sweet is an objective statement; sweetness is part of the make-up of sugar. To consider a drink such as a cup of coffee too sweet or not sweet enough is a subjective statement; it is a personal opinion which depends on the tastes and habits of the individual. On the other hand, to insist that sugar and all sweet things are unpleasant is to express an affective opinion. The professional taster must ignore his affective dispositions. He is not being asked whether such and such a wine pleases him; his job is to examine, describe, and assess its positive or negative tasting qualities and to base his conclusions on what he finds. The conclusions will be subjective but they should not reflect his personal taste, or at least as little as possible. This is the major difference between the professional and the amateur whose judgment may be entirely affective.

Winetasting is the interpretation of a sum of sensations perceived either simultaneously or successively. If one drinks or tastes attentively these sensations form a whole. However, the aim of analytic tasting is to distinguish some of the dominant impressions, identifying them where possible.

Several of our senses are used in winetasting. Those of sight, smell, and taste are activated by various sensory stimuli, and the touch- and temperature-sensitive receptors of the mouth are also involved. Finally, there is normal chemical sensitivity, the effects of which vary from slight irritation to actual pain.

When tasting, the sensations perceived with the wine in the mouth should be considered as coming not only from the sense of taste but also from the sense of smell. Indeed, the nose is more involved than the tongue, and the sensations generally described as the "taste" of a substance are in fact perceived primarily by the sense of smell. During tasting, the warmth of the mouth, the movements of the cheeks and tongue, the act of drawing in a little air to aerate the wine, even normal breathing, all these actions combine to drive the volatile elements of the aroma and bouquet up into the nose and so facilitate perception by the sense of smell. The action of swallowing, difficult to avoid when tasting, also contributes to this effect by creating a slight increase in pressure in the mouth.

The role of the nose can be seen at work again when, after tasting and either swallowing or spitting out the wine, you exhale through the nostrils. Then the aroma and bouquet of the wine continue to be sensed for several breaths. This is the aromatic persistence.

It is a simple matter when tasting to exclude the sensations of smell in order to highlight only those that are, in a strict sense, tastes. It is surprising to see just how few sensations are perceived when holding the nose closed, to the extent that one cannot even be sure it is wine one is tasting. A head cold has the same effect as a blocked nose, that of obliterating the sense of smell. In these circumstances most people tend to say they have lost their sense of taste when, in fact, it is the sense of smell they have lost. These simple observations show that the principal sense used in winetasting, and in tasting food for that matter, is the sense of smell. The role of taste is small by comparison. As Brillat-Savarin wrote: "Without the sense of smell which takes place at the back of one's mouth, our sense of taste would be dull and imperfect."

The following table lists the sensations involved in tasting, grouping and classifying them according to a rational terminology. As already mentioned, "taste" in the generally accepted sense of the term includes the odor sensations perceived via the internal nasal (retronasal) passage at the back of the mouth, while taste sensations proper are only those perceived by the tongue. The term "flavor" covers all sensations perceived via nose and mouth during tasting.

Some people would include hearing among the senses involved in winetasting, and indeed the noise of a cork popping or being drawn, the gurgle of wine being poured, the clink of glass, and the effervescence of sparkling wine, are a discreet accompaniment to winetasting. One might even go as far as agreeing with Sallengres that: "Good wine should appeal to the ear through hearing the rep-

The senses used in winetasting

Organ	Sense and sensations	Characteristic perceived		
Eye	*Sight* Visual sensations	Color, clarity, fluidity, effervescence	**Aspect**	
Nose	*Smell* Olfactory sensations (nasal passage)	Aroma, bouquet	**Odor**	**Flavor**
Mouth	*Smell* Olfactory sensations (retronasal passage)	Aroma in the mouth	**Taste**	
	Taste Taste sensations	Savor, taste		
	Reactions of mucous membrane Sensitivity to chemicals	Astringency, causticity, carbon dioxide prickle		
	Tactile sensations	Consistency, liquidity, fluidity, unctuosity	**Touch**	
	Thermal sensitivity	Temperature		

utation of the region it comes from." However, a sense of hearing is not, in fact, essential to tasting; it can even be a hindrance because noise intrudes on the other senses, lessening one's concentration and reducing one's sensitivity. Speaking more generally, there are constant sensory phenomena in our workplaces which interfere with our senses when tasting. Light that is too strong or too weak, and particular colors, for example, can modify our perception of both taste and smell.

THE SENSES: ACUTENESS AND TRAINING

Life begins for us with sensations and the acquisition of perceptions, even before conscious awareness and memory. This is the start of life's apprenticeship, the stage at which there is already an instinctive division between what is pleasant and what is not. Early child-hood is fundamental to the development of our senses; to develop well, each sense requires a proper introductory education and, later on, a more methodical training, for their performance can always be improved. The extent to which different people's senses are developed varies incredibly. Few really know how to look or to listen, fewer still know how to smell or to taste. There are some, however, whose expertise is remarkable.

Say you sharply tap a crystal glass and set it ringing in an adjacent room. For those alert to the sound, it is quite clearly the ringing of crystal, pure and pleasing to the ear. One person, however, says "That's an E." This person has a trained ear, he can distinguish between noise and a musical note; he has perfect pitch.

Similarly, if you offer a group of people a glass of wine and ask them what it smells like, the majority will say "It smells of wine." A few will suggest that it is the pleasing and well-developed bouquet of a mature wine. Eventually, one of the latter may specify "a complex bouquet born of ripe fruit, developed tannin, and old oak casks, with subtle hints of vanilla and various spices, all of which suggest a fine Médoc." This is someone whose training and experience has given him a tasting ability similar to the musician's perfect pitch. As Pierre Poupon puts it: "Nothing can really be appreciated except in its cultural context."

There is a twofold aspect to educating our senses: on the one hand improving sensitivity and accuracy, on the other developing critical faculties. Visual education teaches you how to look at and enjoy the contemplation of a painting for example; aural training teaches you to listen and to experience the emotions evoked by music or poetry; training the palate helps you to smell, taste, and savor what you eat and drink. Much is said about educating the consumer. This is not easy; his senses need training as much as his judgment.

It is obvious that we exploit only a fraction of our sensory potential, doubtless because we have not been trained to do more. I agree with Max Léglise when he speaks of a degeneration of the senses of smell and taste; "In time one ceases to hear cars in the street, passing trains, the clatter of typewriters in a neighboring office, conversation at the next table. A subconscious barrier has been erected and, not surprisingly, the two senses considered the least useful have suffered the most as a result." An increasing indifference and a decrease in usage means we are gradually forgetting how to use our senses. From childhood on, city life cuts us off from the profusion of tastes and smells that occur in nature. Our instinctive curiosity about them is lost, and with it the potential to have our memories and feelings stirred.

The natural consequence of untrained and little used senses is a limiting of opportunity and a loss of sensitivity as the range of tastes and smells one finds acceptable is gradually narrowed down.

The lazy use of our senses means that we accept food which is uniform, neutral, and tasteless. Food manufacturers recognize this and aim to make a product which is the least disagreeable to the greatest number of people. The majority end up only wanting dishes that are bland and reassuring: meat with the least flavor, the most commonplace of cheeses, and the lightest of wines. A far cry from my grandmother's thick Gascon soup and onion omelet, both tasting of wood smoke, and from my grandfather's vigorous, fiery, Tannat-based Madiran.

Winetasting is a remarkable means of training the senses and preventing their decline: It keeps them active and improves their perception. The trained taster is always on the lookout for some unknown odor, some unusual flavor; indeed, his appetite for sensation assumes almost cult proportions. Sensation is a pleasure in itself and the very thought of the wine and his longing for it give the taster real mental and physical pleasure when he is at work. As with any discovery, the successful analysis of a flavor or the identification of a long-sought odor gives a great deal of intellectual satisfaction.

In order to refine and develop our senses we need to use them, and, as with developing muscles, use them to a greater extent than normal. In addition, the winetaster needs to be capable of sustained concentration. Many of the sensations we feel are passive, barely conscious, and we pay them scant attention. In these circumstances it is hardly surprising that the average consumer rarely perceives the differences in quality between wines. The link between sensation and perception is improved by focusing your attention appropriately. In addition, you should be constantly honing your sense of taste and smell by looking for opportunities to taste new things, and by being prepared to try the unusual. Finally, where new flavors are concerned, try to be as open-minded as possible!

CONCENTRATION AND THE ROLE OF MEMORY

"When you taste, ignore the bottle, label, and those around you; concentrate instead on yourself and on forming a clear impression of the developing sensations conveyed by the wine. Close your eyes and use your nose, tongue, and palate to see." So recommends Pierre Poupon. It is the surest method of avoiding errors of judgment due to conditioning and suggestion, the two traps that can catch even the wariest taster.

As a winetaster you must be able to create a sensory void within and around yourself, excluding any superfluous sensations which might distract your attention. Closing your eyes occasionally helps you to think and perceive more clearly, and it is essential to learn to focus on a specific area, not to be distracted, and to commit your senses solely to registering sensations. Too often we eat, drink, and taste without paying any real attention to what we are tasting and smelling, and in such cases we end up noticing practically nothing. Countless sensations pass unremarked as a result of inadequate experience or poor concentration. A practical difficulty during tasting is knowing when to concentrate on what. In effect, your attention needs to be focused on something specific and yet remain sufficiently flexible to notice other sensations as well. Meditation is a useful discipline in this respect.

In order to perceive, your mind must be alert, especially as it is easy to overlook the unexpected. On the other hand, you only recognize what you can put a name to, and for a sensation to have a name you need to memorize its identity at the same time as you register its presence. A lack of concentration means you barely perceive the sensations which are there, or they do not register at all or else you simply do not recognize them.

Tasting is an act of self-examination where the winetaster stands apart from himself, looking on as his mind's eye scans fleeting impressions of wines already tasted, probing his memory for images and reference points.

During tasting, memory is involved in perception, in identification, and in comparative judgment: both the passive, reflex memory and the active, cogitative memory which analyzes perceived impressions. All winetasting implies a comparison. Wines may be next to each other for the taster to compare on the same occasion, an activity based on short-term memory, which may be difficult if there is a large number of samples. Alternatively, the comparisons may be with wines tasted previously, but no longer available or too modified by age, and now only images in the long-term memory; images which memory may have rendered rather hazy and idealized. These are the taster's reference points, constantly being updated.

Comparing past and present sensations is not easy, and demands intense concentration. To start with, a sensation carefully considered is clearer and therefore better memorized. Experience that the taster gains in this way helps him to interpret new sensations later on. Hence the necessity for regular training so that one can memorize a wide variety of distinct sensations and acquire a range of reference points. The tasting knowledge of experienced specialist tasters is irreplaceable because it is based on countless opportunities to compare wines; but it is necessarily subjective as the memories of wines tried will vary according to the individual's training and preferences.

To some extent then, tasting is an exercise in memorizing and recall. The response of the reflex memory is immediate, as when the eye recognizes the written word, but reading is an acquired, not an innate skill. Similarly, winetasting is the ability to "read" a wine. Simple characteristics such as sugar or acid are instantly recognizable, but when the taste features are more complex and subtle, and recognition less sure, then one's memory needs time to recall. Some sensations require a prolonged effort of memory before they can be identified, like trying to put a name to a face you recognize when it is on the tip of your tongue but just refuses to surface. The taster is frequently aware of his inability to describe an impression, even with the taste in his mouth, the smell in his nostrils, and the words on the tip of his tongue. Imagination will sometimes make up for the failure of memory. The taster has only a few seconds to locate within his memory bank the tastes he has on his palate, and often several attempts are needed to find and open the appropriate "memory file."

Regular tasting will mean that identifying sensations eventually becomes largely second nature. As with all training, the winetaster's is based on the acquisition of a wide-ranging body of knowledge. There are wine libraries just as there are book libraries, and just as the literary critic should have read everything so the expert taster should have tasted everything. Wine culture is what the winetaster gains after trying an infinite variety of wines.

ANALYTICAL TASTING VERSUS RECOGNITION

Knowing and understanding an object, be it a face, an odor, or a wine, is based on observation by one's senses; but a single, rapid encounter is inadequate for knowledge in any depth. Thus one comes to understand wine by a thorough and detailed analysis of tastes and smells, and by noting down as many characteristics as possible. Regular and repeated tasting exercises performed with care will provide a sound memory base. If knowledge of something is primarily analytical, recognition is triggered mainly by a total impression.

Pascal describes the latter process: "To a certain extent the object should be grasped and comprehended at a glance, and not by a process of reasoning." This is what is called total perception. The taste image of the wine on your palate is compared with a host of images stored and classified in the mind, and in this case those of wine will be the closest match. In this approach to tasting the winetaster proceeds intuitively; close examination and deductive reasoning are unnecessary as his grasp of the wine is clear-cut and immediate. A single contact with the senses of smell and taste is sufficient to create a well-defined and instantly identifiable image. However, recognition is either immediate or not at all. Some wines, like some faces, are easily remembered, but others, more neutral and unexceptional, make little impression.

The phenomenon of recognition in the cortex is extremely rapid, taking only a fraction of a second. It also constitutes that first, often most distinct, impression which the expert taster rightly tends to rely on. The act of recognition is difficult to describe. In fact, description is unnecessary: One recognizes something first and the words then follow. A tasting note on a wine will no more make it instantly recognizable than a verbal description of somebody's face.

The so-called analytic approach to tasting is based on logic and reasoning. It is knowledge gained by a step-by-step deductive process where the conclusions are slow to appear, taking minutes, sometimes days. I like to make an analogy between winetasting and reading. The taster who has learned how to interpret tastes and smells will size up and appreciate a wine with a sniff and a taste in much the same way that the reader grasps the meaning of a book title, a phrase, or a sign instantly. He can "read" a wine, whereas the layman unfamiliar with the taste alphabet finds such reading difficult. The key to reading wine is knowing by heart the key signs of alcohol, sugar, acid, tannin, and the profusion of wine's odors.

Three

The Visual Aspect
of Wine

Themes color of wine derives from the fact that it absorbs light rays which pass through it in different ways. Red wine appears red because it absorbs other colors, permitting only red light to reach the eye. A white wine appears yellow because it absorbs blues and violets but not yellows. Young red wines show a maximum absorption at 520 nanometers, a wavelength generating the color pure red. As a red wine ages this maximum tends to decrease, corresponding to an increase in yellow hues (see the figure on page 29). Thus the color of wine can be defined by the extent to which it absorbs light rays of different wavelengths. This is known as the absorption spectrum and the instrument which measures the color of wine, its depth and hue, is a spectrophotometer. Red wine is measured across a thin film of liquid at two wavelengths: 420 nanometers in the yellow band and 520 nanometers in the purple band (a nanometer is one-millionth of a millimeter). The **sum** of optical densities (absorbed light) at these two wavelengths gives the **depth** of color, while the **ratio** of yellow to red will indicate the **hue**. The color depth of white wine is measured across a centimeter of wine at a wavelength of 440 nanometers in the yellow band.

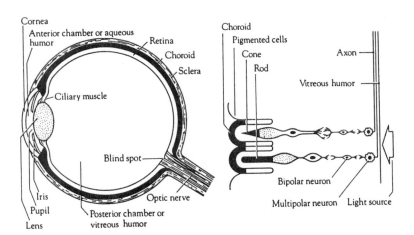

Cross-section of the eye.   Schematic representation of the
                              retina's structure.

Visual sensitivity is limited to light rays with wavelengths between 390 and 820 nanometers. The following table shows the relationship between wavelength (in nanometers), absorbed color,
and perceived color. The colors opposite each other are complementary.

Wavelength	Color absorbed	Apparent color
400–435	Violet	Yellow–green
435–480	Blue	Yellow
480–490	Green–blue	Orange
490–500	Blue–green	Red
500–560	Green	Purple
560–580	Yellow–Green	Violet
580–595	Yellow	Blue
595–605	Orange	Green–blue
605–750	Red	Blue–green

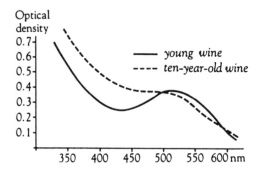

The light absorption spectra of two red wines of different ages.

THE INFLUENCE OF APPEARANCE ON TASTING

The winetaster's eye must be able to interpret the slightest visual clue and it should be as carefully critical of appearance as his nose is of odors. Before tasting, even before smelling a wine, it is normal to examine its appearance, in a clear glass with a light source behind. Sight is the first of our senses to be used in winetasting and there are good reasons for considering the visual aspect of a wine with care. This first phase of tasting conveys much information and it calls for little apparent effort on the taster's part assuming, that is, that he has already examined the appearance of a considerable number of wines. Visual impressions are concerned with limpidity (**dullness** versus **brilliance**) and color (**intensity** and **shade**). Hue and shade can be confusing, and they are not exactly synonymous. For example, yellow is a color or a hue, and there are many shades of yellow.

The appearance of a wine is concerned with other basic information as well: its **fluidity** and **viscosity**; the **visible presence of carbon dioxide**; the level of alcohol as revealed by **capillary action** on the sides of the glass. It also provides a basis for, and lends confirmation to, the judgment of our other senses. A hazy or troubled wine is frequently misjudged on the palate, and color itself gives some indication of a wine's body, its age, health, and maturity.

While depth of color is not really a criterion of quality, it may be a pointer to the wine's structure, its weight and length on the palate. In red wines color and tannin often go hand in hand. If the color is

30

very deep and the wine almost opaque, there is a good chance that it will also be full-bodied, tannic, and abundant in flavor. If, on the other hand, the wine is light in color, it is likely to be lighter in body and shorter on the finish, though it may still be perfectly agreeable given some bouquet and a supple texture.

The hue of a wine is not a criterion of quality either. It relates to age and shows the wine's state of development. Young wines will have a lively purple or ruby-red hue from the anthocyanins in the grape skin. As the wine ages the anthocyanins combine with other components and disappear. As a result, the ruby-red color gradually decreases and takes on a hue described as "brick-red" or "tile-red." It is the condensed tannins that are responsible for this increasingly brown-red color. There is a direct, and hopefully harmonious, relationship between the evolution of color and that of taste. A tile-red color should correspond to a developed bouquet and a flavor softened by age.

Color should always be bright and there will be something wrong with a wine that looks dull. One should be wary of young wines with a noticeably violet hue which are generally heavy, acid, and ordinary; one should also be wary of old wines that are too brown, indicating oxidation or extreme old age. Dark brown is a color appropriate only to dessert wines.

A wine's color has been described as its face, in which age and character can be read. In tasting, judging a wine is made much more difficult if one cannot see it. As proof of this one has only to be shown how easy it is to confuse the identities of a low-acidity white, a rosé, and a red wine with very little tannin, when one cannot see their color! The experiment can be carried out with the help of colored wine glasses, or, even better, with the taster blindfolded. It is an instructive exercise, for this blindman's buff demonstrates to the taster just how soon his judgment becomes uncertain when there are absolutely no reliable clues as to the type of wine or its origin. Lebègue performs the same experiment another way: the taster is confronted with eight glasses of straightforward commercial wines, six red and two white. If, blindfolded, he can identify the two whites, he is either lucky or very experienced.

Sight even has an indirect influence on one's ability to smell. Odors are perceived better when the lighting is good. It is as difficult to appreciate what one is tasting in the obscurity of a wine cellar as it is to appreciate what one is eating in a dimly lit restaurant where the menu can barely be read.

The eye introduces a wine, providing an initial reference point. It is both informative and reassuring actually to see a wine, but it may also be misleading, for the winetaster is easily influenced. The first assessment is based on appearance and appearances are often deceptive.

Max Léglise has written several useful pages about misjudgments based on appearance, habit, or fashion. On the same subject Le Magnen writes: "Colour plays an important part in making food appear appetizing or not, pleasant or unpleasant, edible or otherwise. Colour influences the way we react to smell or taste, but its absence also alters our perception of taste, so colour is in effect part of the taste. There are nauseating colours just as there are nauseating smells." Léglise also makes the point: "Offer people a blue cocktail and you will see them hesitate. Blue is not a customary food colour." Clearly, color has a considerable influence on the appeal of food and drink.

Red and yellow are colors that call to mind various fruits and one would expect drinks, preserves, and sweets of a particular fruit flavor to be the appropriate color. Lemon juice should be yellow, pomegranate juice red, and a strawberry drink also needs to be red in spite of the fact that the natural color of strawberry juice is quite unstable. By the same token a dry white wine is expected to be pale yellow, while a sweet white wine should be golden hued.

The way in which a wine is presented has a persuasive influence on one's reactions. A great wine served in a thick goblet may well be misjudged, while the most basic of wines, served in fine crystal as though just decanted, is easily taken for something better. It is also a simple matter to mislead a taster with false labels, for who would not be fooled, or at least confused, were serious wine lovers to offer them Bordeaux in a Burgundy bottle or vice versa? Is there anybody who does not automatically expect a bottle which cost $25.00 to be better than that bought for $10.00? Another example is the allowance one always makes for venerable old bottles, where respect for fine old vintages prejudices one's critical standpoint.

One of the most revealing experiments on the influence of color is the one outlined by Pierre André. The color of the rosé wines here covers a broad spectrum from pale orange to bright cherry-red. Winetasters tend to make an instinctive association between color and character: "a more deeply colored wine = a more full-bodied wine" and "a paler wine = a lighter, more supple wine."

A group of tasters is given a series of six rosé wines of different colors. They are asked to classify these initially on the basis of color appeal alone, then on the basis of color and taste, and finally, on the basis of taste alone. In the first two cases they can see the wine, in the last case they taste blindfolded so as not to be influenced by appearance. These are the results:

	1st	2nd	3rd	4th	5th	6th
Based on color alone	F	E	B	C	A	D
On tasting, color visible	E	F	B	C	A	D
On tasting, color invisible	C	B	D	A	E	F

The classification based on the first tasting is almost identical to that based on color alone, as if the tasters had, literally, tasted with their eyes. The blind tasting, on the other hand, yields totally different results. The experiment underlines the importance of sight in tasting, and demonstrates that color plays a significant part in the appeal of wines of moderate quality. So long as they look attractive the consumer will be less critical about their flavor, provided they have no obvious defects.

Generally speaking, nonprofessional tasters tend to give more weight to appearance because they can easily find words to describe it from everyday vocabulary. In tasting, however, knowing how to use one's eyes is also to be wary of what they tell you. The art of tasting is also an art of thoughtful observation.

THE PHYSICAL ASPECT OF WINE

The physical aspect of wine is most revealing and an adroit examination of its appearance will tell you a great deal. First your eye considers the liquid's consistency, that of a dilute solution of alcohol. Ten percent to 15 percent of a wine's volume is alcohol, though the proportion is higher for certain fortified dessert wines, such as Vin Doux Naturel, port, madeira, and sherry. Alcohol is an absorptive liquid which spreads and "wets" easily.

Emerging from the same pipette, drops of wine are smaller than those of water because the wine climbs higher up its sides. Based on this principle, an approximate estimation of alcoholic strength has been devised. Its alcohol also makes wine more viscous than water so that it flows more slowly though a very fine tube or a filter, and is slower at penetrating the casks in which it is stored.

Visual examination starts when you pour the wine. It has its own particular way of flowing, it makes an individual liquid sound, it produces a finer mixture with air when it is poured than water does, and the large bubbles rising to its surface last longer. This froth is sometimes colored in very young wines but colorless in old wines.

A lack of fluidity is abnormal and may have several causes. Sometimes a young wine looks thick and oily, flows silently, and makes no froth as a result of a colloidal web which has rendered it viscous and slimy. The mucilage responsible for this comes from the rotting of the grapes or from lactic bacteria coated with polysaccharides (large condensed sugar molecules). This disorder is known as *graisse* (oily disease) where the last drop of wine stretches from the bottle in a thin thread. It is extremely rare today, and would only be encountered where wines had been neglected during malolactic fermentation.

The wine's surface, its "mirror," is examined from above the glass or, better, from a *tastevin* because of its reflective interior. It should always be brilliant though it can be dull or iridescent and occasionally the surface is marred by dust, oil, acetic bacteria, or mycodermic yeast.

The foaming bubbles of carbon dioxide in a glass of sparkling wine are a visual delight in themselves. The profusion of effervescence on pouring, the texture of the resultant *mousse*, the manner in which it subsides, and the vigor of the subsequent sparkle are all telltales of quality for the taster. The initial head of a sparkling wine can be abundant, frothy, made up of large bubbles, evanescent, or persistent. Unlike the head on a glass of beer, however, it should not be too thick, creamy, or stable, but fine and dry, subsiding in a few seconds without ever disappearing completely, so that the surface of the wine is constantly broken by a stream of bubbles. These can be seen emanating from the bottom of the glass, growing in size as they rise to the surface where, after a moment, they burst. The narrow flute is the best glass in which to see this effect.

Bubbles will only form from an active point on any surface, active as a result of, for example, a germ, particle, or scratch on the glass. A sparkling wine will not release its bubbles in a glass which is absolutely inert, cleaned with chromic acid solution (which destroys any organic substance). There are glasses with a deliberately roughened bottom surface which produce an abundant and regular stream of bubbles. Once at the surface such a stream will form a star which then spreads out to the sides of the glass. The collar of bubbles thus formed on the meniscus of the wine is known as the *cordon*. the quality of a sparkling wine can be judged by how fine its bubbles are, the regularity and persistence with which they are released, and how well the *cordon* lasts. However, the slightest trace of detergent or grease on the glass will completely inhibit the *mousse*.

The structure of the *mousse* depends on the constitution of the base wine (on its sparkling potential, due to colloids), and also on the technique of champenization, the length of time it has matured on its yeasts, and, finally, on the temperature of the wine. Champagne *mousse* improves with age. Some wines will liberate their carbon dioxide all at once in large bubbles just like carbonated water; these wines have undergone too rapid a fermentation. On the other hand, the least trace of detergent or grease on the surface of the glass will kill the *mousse* completely.

It sometimes happens that a so-called still (i.e., nonsparkling) wine, close to saturation level in carbon dioxide (1.5 to 2 g/l for example) has a very fine surface *mousse*, and on tasting a prickle is felt on the tip of the tongue. Such a wine, described as slightly sparkling or spritzy, is either still fermenting gently or—sometimes deliberately, as in the case of semi-sparkling wines—retains the carbon dioxide from a previous fermentation. Aeration will partially eliminate the residual gas.

When a glass of wine has just been swirled, one's attention is caught by the streams running down the sides of the glass. A liquid film creeps up the sides, several centimeters above the wine's surface, and then starts to form droplets which fall back in uneven runs. The wine is said to be weeping and the drops are its tears; alternatively, they are called legs, arches, or arcs. According to Amerine and Roessler, this phenomenon is due to the "Marangoni effect," though it was first correctly explained by James Thomson in 1855. Briefly, because alcohol is more volatile than water, a thin layer of more aqueous liquid forms on the surface of the wine and on the sides of the glass moistened by the wine; this fine film has a higher surface tension. Capillary action causes the liquid to rise up the sides of the glass, and the increase in surface tension tends to form tears which eventually flow back down into the wine. The higher the alcohol content of the wine, the more tears there are, and they are generally colorless. These tears are reduced in number or may even be entirely eliminated by detergent residue on the glass surface.

Thomson's explanation, now more than a century old, is the only correct one, so it is surprising to see the formation of these tears still being attributed to glycerol or to "the potency of the wine's oenanthic ethers." Occasionally, one comes across such comments as: "Without being able to prove any direct relationship, there is within any given category of wine a certain correlation between the number of tears and the wine's quality." This myth, carefully fostered by the professionals themselves, dies hard.

I witnessed the following exchange when a number of Canadian students, glass in hand, asked a cellarmaster in the Médoc to explain the tears in the glass:

"It is the glycerin in the wine," he replied.

"So that's how you can recognize a good wine, is it?"

"Exactly."

"And if there are no tears?"

"Then it's not a quality wine."

I could not interrupt and contradict the cellarmaster, but when the Canadians had left I rebuked him for having deliberately misled them. His psychologist's reply was: "The explanation is incorrect but it's such a satisfying one, and anyway, since all wines do have tears . . ."

A simple embroidered falsehood is preferred to the less romantic, and less straightforward, truth; this is doubtless why the myth persists. However, the cellarmaster could have given an even nicer, and less inaccurate explanation by saying: "The tears? They are the spirit of the wine condensing on the glass."

CLARITY AND TRANSPARENCY

Wine is born troubled, emerging from the fermentation vat turbid and charged with foreign matter, consisting of shreds of skin and pulp from the crushed grapes, the results of processes such as flocculation and crystallization, and, above all, the microorganisms which have transformed the must into wine. Each liter of new wine contains billions of yeast cells and bacteria, a liquid that Rabelais described as "autumnal mash," the cloudy, raw, and barely fermented wine drunk at vintage time:

> Jenin, tasting his young wines one evening,
> still hazy and bubbling on their lees.

These coarse particles are the remnants of fermentation which will form the lees of the finished wine and which should eventually be discarded.

Left undisturbed in storage vessels, young wine gradually clears. The particles in suspension settle, starting with the heaviest, and sink slowly to the bottom of the vat or barrel, shallow containers being the most suitable for this process of clarification. However, even after several months wine does not, by itself, acquire sufficient clarity. It does clear but it never becomes brilliant. To achieve a perfect limpidity, fining and filtration are essential as they will rid the wine of those very fine impurities which are the most difficult to eliminate.

Limpidity is measurable. The naked eye can assess the clarity of a wine reasonably well provided the light is adequate and properly directed. An examination made in daylight by a window or against a lighted white background is generally sufficient for the winetaster or consumer. However, it is not a severe enough test for the technician who needs to anticipate, and eliminate, the possibility of a visible deposit, however slight, forming once the wine is in bottle. In the past the cellarmaster would place his tilted glass before a candle flame in the semi-darkness, avoiding any extraneous light. He would move the glass about gently, observing the flame through the wine, and, by refraction, the glass being lit from the side.

A low-power electric light (15 to 20 watts) can be used in a similar, if less romantic, manner, and there are also simple instruments which make the examination more precisely than with a bulb alone. They apply the same principle as that of shafts of light penetrating a dark room and illuminating countless shifting particles of dust, an analogy that is strikingly apt.

As for examining the deposit, we have all probably seen someone grasp a bottle by the neck and either turn it upside down in front of a light to see if any sediment falls back, or simply give it a twist of the wrist to see if the wine turns cloudy as any deposit is disturbed. The naked eye can distinguish between wines of a similar haziness with some precision, but it is not sensitive enough to judge the real state of limpidity; besides, people's visual acuity is very variable. Precise measurements of limpidity are made with a nephelometer or turbidimeter, an instrument which gives a numerical value to the penetration and dispersion of light rays in a wine; alternatively, they are made using a particle counter, an electronic instrument capable of counting solid particles dispersed in a liquid according to their size from a micron (a thousandth of a millimeter) upwards.

Solid particles remaining in a clear white wine after filtering

Particle diameter	Particles per milliliter
4.4	1,600
3.5	2,700
2.2	23,000
1.75	62,000
1.40	339,000
1.25	621,000

However, some particles are a hundred or a thousand times smaller still; these are said to be colloidal. They are too small to precipitate and they do not affect limpidity directly, but in the long term some have the potential to flocculate and form clouds which precipitate and leave a deposit.

In fact, a clear wine can become hazy again quite naturally. The clarity obtained by natural settling or by a clarification procedure is not necessarily definitive. As long as the wine remains unstable, it is susceptible to various changes in clarity affecting both color and appearance; these are known as *casses*. Some fragile wines can become cloudy when exposed to air, others can be similarly affected by light, cold, heat, or microbiological changes, all of which detract from the wine's clarity and quality. The art of *élevage* (conserving and looking after a wine in vat or barrel prior to bottling) is that of ensuring wine does not suffer from any such disorders. A good wine is one which is perfectly clear and whose clarity is permanent. It is only such a stable wine which can develop all its qualities harmoniously as it ages.

The limpidity of a wine is defined as the absence of haze, that is, of particles in suspension. It might be better defined as an acceptable level of visible impurities under analysis because there is no such thing as absolute limpidity in wine.

The following table is a series of adjectives used to describe the state of clarity or cloudiness in a wine. The terms in bold type are the most commonly used and as such are recommended:

State of clarity	State of cloudiness	
bright	barely fermented	dusty
brilliant	**bitty**	**hazy**
clean	blurred	leaden
clear	*casse* (attacked by)	**milky**
crystal clear	**cloudy**	**muddy**
fine	dense	murky
limpid	deposit (light/heavy)	**opalescent**
luminous	dirty	**opaque**
transparent	**dull**	**turbid**
		veiled

Limpidity, transparency, and brilliance may be considered synonymous, as they are in the dictionary. Limpidity and transparency certainly go hand in hand as far as white wines are concerned, but not necessarily in red wines. Depending on its depth of color, a limpid red wine might not be transparent. A limpid wine has brilliance and brightness and it radiates light. The beauty of a wine lies in its color and brilliance. Is not this what Homer meant by "flaming, fiery wine" or what Plato meant by the "visual fire" of wine? Or were these allusions to the fact that wine will catch fire and burn when heated, or even that its spirit kindles in us an inner warmth? The ideas of fire, flame, ardor, and bottled sunshine have often been associated with wine.

In French there is a distinction between *le trouble* and *la turbidité*. *Le trouble* (for which there is no English equivalent in this sense) refers to all the suspended matter in wine which is the cause of *la turbidité* (cloudiness). A state of cloudiness is the optical phenomenon provoked by particles in suspension, or more precisely by their effect on the diffusion of light. In such a case wine is described as blurred or out of focus in the photographic sense of lacking definition. When a wine contains so much suspended matter as to become opaque, this is also due partly to the absorption of light, where the impurities are in effect also acting as a screen.

There are many different ways of describing *trouble* in terms of color and texture. Sometimes it consists of elements visible under a strong light which can variously be described as pinpoints of brilliance, haziness, clouding, flakes, and "beeswings." On the other hand, the terms "milkiness" and "opalescence" refer to a cloudiness caused by particles so fine that they will not precipitate; the specialist calls this colloidal cloudiness.

We have well-established preferences about the appearance of what we drink. We prefer most of our drinks to be clear: Water, wine, beer, and many soft drinks are obvious examples. If any of these are cloudy they are likely to be rejected. They certainly become less attractive to drink, for the lack of clarity suggests they are tainted or have something wrong with them. Probably the most off-putting of all is a deposit lying at the bottom of a glass or bottle. The number of cloudy drinks which we find acceptable is limited, notably to juices from crushed or squeezed fruit, and in this case it is important for the particles to remain in suspension, a condition sometimes ensured artificially by the addition of emulsifiers.

The phrase "as clear as spring water" reflects the appeal of purity. Besides, a cloudy wine never tastes well, for several reasons. If there is a haze and a deposit in a wine that has been in bottle for only a few weeks, or even for two or three years, there is something wrong. Whatever has caused the cloudiness will also have altered the wine's constitution and impaired its quality. Particles in suspension in a cloudy wine affect one's taste buds directly and adversely: The organoleptic qualities are masked by the screen of impurities in suspension and the flavor is distorted. A cloudy wine tastes rough and lacking in harmony. Conversely, the more a wine is clarified, the finer the filtration, the smoother and more supple the wine will taste. Filtration properly carried out does not strip or attenuate a wine; it clears it of internal impurities and improves it. To deny this is to say that a wine's quality is due above all to foreign substances in suspension.

Old red wines provide a further example of the adverse effect of deposit on a wine's taste. The slow formation of sediment is a normal process of aging; indeed, it is inevitable in fine Bordeaux, burgundy, and vintage port after six to ten years in bottle. However, to serve such a wine carelessly, with its deposit unsettled and still mixed up in the wine, would be to ruin it completely; a bit like stirring a cup of Turkish coffee just before drinking. We shall see that before drawing the cork of an old bottle it needs to be stood upright for some time. Decanting, which will be discussed later, is not just a talent peculiar to wine waiters, but a necessity. It separates a wine from its sediment and ensures that it is clear and bright.

COLOR VOCABULARY

Color depends on grape variety, vinification methods, and age. It is such a fundamental factor in the appearance of a wine that it is used by itself to distinguish between types; we talk of red wine and white wine. However, there are no more wines that can truly be called white than there are those which can truly be called red. The former are yellow or golden, the latter purple or ruby.

Words to describe color are the first that a winetaster needs. As we shall see, there are various styles of terminology that can be used to describe the general qualities of a wine. First, there is the precise and concise vocabulary of the expert and qualified taster; this is my preference. A selection of these recommended terms is indicated in bold type. Secondly, there is the vocabulary used by amateurs and those who taste regularly, which is broader and more original, if less precise. Finally, there is the more evocative and imaginative literary style of the wine and food correspondent, the wine critic or the wine buff-cum-writer—wine has always been a felicitous subject for poets.

The oenologist limits himself to noting the **intensity of color**, and the **hue** or **shade**; but *robe*, tone, tonality, and coloration will also be encountered. *Robe* is a term used more frequently in Burgundy and the Loire, although the 1896 *Dictionnaire du Maître de Chai* describes it as a Bordeaux expression. Using the same metaphor, wine is said to have a beautiful *robe* and to be well or badly dressed, or short skirted. One may even hear of two wines of different coloring being compared in terms of fabric or flesh tints.

Color is defined by its intensity, hue, and brilliance. To be seen properly, it requires a light source, a candle flame, or a lighted white background. The conditions under which a wine is observed will modify its appearance, and may be chosen to do so by the observer, but ideally it should be examined in a glass by daylight. The lighting should be neutral if the subtleties and variations of color are not to be distorted, and it should not be too feeble or the colors will seem darker and the hues will be difficult to discern.

A wine will appear darker in a fuller glass or looked at as a wider cross section, and the depth of liquid through which a light source is viewed will affect not only the intensity of color but also its hue. The palest of white wines appears distinctly red when viewed with a strong light behind it shining through 50 centimeters of wine. This seems barely credible but it is the case in experimental glass-bottomed barrels which allow the full depth of the wine to be viewed.

When comparing fine color differences between wines certain precautions are necessary. The wines should be in identical glasses, filled to the same level, and viewed against a white background which is evenly lit. Any light source against which the wines are viewed should come from directly behind the wine, not obliquely or from the side. The color is examined from directly above, looking down through the bowl of the glass and, for comparing pairs especially, with the glasses tilted and adjusted so as to show an equal depth and amount of wine. Daylight may be used in front of a window and when artificial lighting is used it is important to see that it is evenly diffused. The strength of artificial light should be adequate without being too strong, but too little is as bad as too much; neither will allow a proper appreciation of differences in intensity or hue. During the course of a meal lit only by candles, or alternatively only by harsh spotlights, all the red wines tend to look alike. Artificial lighting should be of the neutral "daylight" type; some fluorescent lighting gives a false and unpleasant color impression.

Intensity of color is described by a series of simple adjectives: **pale**, **light**, clear, **weak**, or, on the other hand, **deep, dark, intense,** dense (for a wine with a high optical density), deep, somber, black.

Color is relative. A wine is said to have adequate or inadequate

Color plays an important role in evaluating wines.
Here, four different types of sherry, in four colors, from
Jerez, Andalucía, Spain. (Photo: Copyright 1996 Pedro Coll.)

The "tears" or "legs" which form on the inner surface of the glass are the result of capillary action determined primarily by the concentration of alcohol in the wine. The glass surface is, however, also important, and a trace of detergent will inhibit or eliminate the effect. (Photo: Courtesy of Philip Manor.)

The taster lifts his glass in order to look at the wine against the light. One criterion of quality is the limpidity of the wine. St-Émilion, France, Château Pavie. (Photo: Copyright 1989 Harvey Lloyd.)

Fine glassware enhances the pleasure of fine wine. Nowadays, a glassware set consisting of a water glass, a Burgundy, a Bordeaux, and a champagne flute are all that are normally used. The shape of the glass, the surface area of the wine, and the distance from the surface of the wine to the nose, are all factors that present the same wine with differing intensities of aroma. (Photo: Courtesy of Tiffany & Co., New York.)

color in relation to what is normal for its type. An anemic wine is pale or pallid. A well-structured wine has a fine deep color. A heavy wine is very deeply colored and strongly flavored. *Teinturier* wines are very strongly colored, often made from red-fleshed black grapes, or alternatively they are vinified by a special maceration technique (Spanish *doble-pasta*, for example, corresponds to a concentrated extract from grape skins). Such wines are said to have a color coefficient of 5 or 10 if they still have adequate color when diluted with 5 or 10 times their own volume of white wine. There have always been "black" wines. Hercules emptied amphorae of black wine, and in the eighteenth century the English made a distinction between "claret" and the highly colored "black wine" from Spain and Portugal which they used for blending. In 1714 a Paris merchant had for sale "an excellent Margaux, old, black, and velvety." Here "black" is used to mean very dark in color, and hence the satisfaction of the cellarmaster who, running off his new wine from vat, can describe it as being "black as ink." Some wines are truly black, Pedro Ximénez and laga, for example, made from *arrope*, a must heated to the point of caramelization.

Liveliness is a quality of color related not only to limpidity but also to acidity. A wine may be clear and yet have a color which is lackluster; for a red wine to look lively requires sufficient real acidity.

The following are terms relating to the liveliness or otherwise of color (those in bold type are the most commonly used):

vivid	**dull**
lively	**flat**
clear	doubtful
bright	indistinct
star bright	lackluster
luminous	lifeless
radiant	faded
lustrous	
glittering	

A lively appearance is linked to overall brilliance and certain highlights and tinges which appear in the glass under adequate light: green highlights in young white wines, the greenish cast on an amber background of very old dessert wines, or the brown and orange tints in old reds. As for the iridescence sometimes seen upon swirling a glass of young wine, this may be due to microbiological problems or to crystals of tartrate in very fine flakes.

The hue of a wine may be defined in various ways: first, by the winetaster's eye, an immediate, instinctive general impression, but one which is subjective, and as such liable to error; second, by comparison with a standard color chart such as that of Chevreul; or third, by measuring the wine's absorption of light rays of different frequencies. However, this takes us out of the tasting room and into the laboratory where wines are analyzed by instruments, not appraised by human senses. The winetaster must rely on his own eyesight for interpreting color.

In *Les Mémoires de l'Académie des Sciences,* 1861 (Proceedings of the Academy of Sciences), the chemist Chevreul divided all the colors into seventy-two groups, each of which was subdivided into twenty shades. From this he defined the colors used for dyeing at the Gobelin Tapestry Works, where he taught, as well as the natural colors of various minerals, fruits, and flowers. It was left to Salleron to apply Chevreul's nomenclature to wine at the turn of the century. He demonstrated that a red wine evolved, from youth to old age, through ten distinct color tones:

Violet red
First violet red (amaranth,
  "love lies bleeding")   Red (cherry, safflower)
Second violet red (red currant)   First red (poppy)
Third violet red (crimson)   Second red (fire)
Fourth violet red (ruby, garnet) Third red (scarlet, golden red)
Fifth violet red (cherry)

These definitions are not used any more; the spectrophotometer has replaced the vinicolorimeter's discs of colored satin. Still, I once received a color reproduction of part of Chevreul's range, namely the reds and oranges. An American wine lover wanted to know which of his colors I thought corresponded to the terms: claret, ruby, tile-red, onion-skin, partridge-eye, etc. Put to the test, the variation among my colleagues' answers showed me just how subjective color perception and description are. I was very conscious of how uncertain my own answers were.

WHITES, ROSÉS, AND REDS

Yellows and golds are mainly used to describe the appearance of white wine; the colors of precious stones and various gold ores and alloys offer a wide range of gold and yellow shades from which to choose. According to Max Léglise: "The term **gold** is used for a wine rich in highlights and with a particularly brilliant aspect, and it would be qualified by shades appropriate to the metal. If, despite its brightness, the wine is not noticeably radiant or if it is lacking in highlights, then the description **yellow** is more suitable." Practically all shades of yellow are to be found in white wines (terms most commonly used in bold):

colorless	topaz	bistre
water white	burnt topaz	chestnut
yellow (pale/dark)	**pale gold**	Madeira colored
greeny yellow	**greeny gold**	**maderized**
tawny	canary yellow	gold
copper	**lemon yellow**	old gold
amber	**straw yellow**	reddish gold
brown	straw colored	**golden**
brownish	**golden yellow**	**brownish red**
mahogany	yellowish	russet
caramel	jonquil	dead leaf
walnut stained		

The color of white wine should be appropriate to its type. Though there is a fairly wide tolerance as to what constitutes "pale" in some countries, wines expected to be pale include: dry white Bordeaux, Muscadet, Riesling, *fino* sherry, etc. Others, darker because of their grape variety or method of vinification, are: Gewürztraminer, Chardonnay in Meursault or Montrachet, Jura wines, Spätlese and Auslese wines from Germany, Ste-Croix-du-Mont, Sauternes, and so on.

The oenologists have a confession to make: They have no precise knowledge of which substances are responsible for the color of white wines. It has been attributed to flavones, yellow pigments found widely in flowers and which are also present in grape skins. They are the glycosides (their molecule containing a sugar) of campherol and quercetin. However, the technique for making white wine does not include any maceration of the solid parts of the grape which are rich in these phenolic components, and the pigments of this family are only present in trace quantities, insufficient to account for color in white wine. The same goes for tannins in white wine.

Color evolves. In "reductive" aging, that is, when the supply of air is cut off, wine becomes more golden hued; contact with air, on the other hand, browns the tannins in white wine, turning it first tawny and finally brown. Very old white wines take on a bronze appearance. Paguierre's notes on certain white wines in 1829 are intriguing. He described those of Cérons, Loupiac, and Ste-Croix-du-Mont as being the color of "pale bay leaf." Did the wines then turn greenish brown with age, the color of dried bay leaves?

Wines suffering from oxidative *casse* when exposed to air acquire the color of chocolate or milky coffee and are no longer drinkable. More common are old dessert wines which have become amber-colored, and fortified wines like Madeira which have taken on the dark mahogany hue of an old armagnac. At the El Molino Bodega in Jerez de la Frontera there is an oak sherry butt, signed on one end by Lord Nelson, which, after nearly two centuries, contains a potently aromatic and highly concentrated liquid the color of walnut stain, which was originally a white wine.

A white wine tinged pink is faulty. It will have accidentally acquired a minute quantity of coloring matter from red grape skins or red wine and will therefore contain several milligrams of anthocyanin. It may also have been stored in barrels previously used for red wine. The color can be removed.

Neither true red nor true white, rosé wines come in all the intermediate shades between yellow, russet, and pale red, and it is said of rosés that their color is half their charm. A range of colors is given below:

gray	peony rose	**russet**	**orange hued**
champagne	cherry rose	brownish red	salmon
rosé	raspberry rose	reddish	pink
pale red	carmine rose	apricot	
true rose	**yellow rose**	pale apricot	
violet rose	**orange rose**	**onion skin**	

Gray is used to describe a wine that is barely colored, perhaps one made from the juice of pink grapes. A champagne hue is that of a *blancs de noirs* champagne (a white wine made from black grapes) when very young. The pale rose tint fades and eventually disappears as a result of clarification, second fermentation, and age. Rosés produced by the white-wine vinification method (the juice being run off immediately after pressing) contain 10 to 50 mg/l of anthocyanins (red grape pigments). Rosés macerated on the skins for a short period contain more than 50 mg/l of anthocyanins: These are referred to as *clairet* (pale red), "one-night wines," or "twenty-four-hour wines" (referring to their time in contact with the grape skins). Above 100 mg/l of anthocyanins the wines have a light-red color.

The actual rosé color depends very much on the grape variety. Carignan gives a pomegranate hue, Gamay a cherry hue, Cabernet a raspberry hue reminiscent of the pink of plum blossom, and Grenache a darker color tending toward mauve. With age the wines turn more ripe-apricot in color, then browny orange, and, finally, they become the so-called "onion-skin," typical of Arbois wine made from the Poulsard grape.

The red color of wine is certainly one of its most attractive features since it is red wine that typifies what we mostly think of as real "wine," and the popular symbolism of wine as the blood of the vine is easily understood when one considers its appearance on pouring, its lustrous color in crystal, and the few drops or the stain left at the bottom of one's glass.

Wine is found in practically all shades of red. The palette, reflecting all the reds found in fruit, is vast. The anthocyanins, which so diversely color fruit such as grapes and various flower petals, all belong to the same family. The particular color which anthocyanins give to young wine is a function of the wine's acidity. A high acidity, that is a relatively low pH, gives a marked liveliness to the red in a newly made wine; conversely, a low acidity, a higher pH, renders the wine's appearance less brilliant, its hue more purple.

As a red wine ages the tannins become the dominant influence on color. They combine with the anthocyanins and gradually impart an overall brick or brown tone to the red. Such wines are described as brick-red or tile-red. Extremely old wines retain only the color of pale old polished wood. The following list of colors is not definitive, and the terms apply not only to the full depth of color but also to the

highlights and nuances which a red wine takes on in the glass depending on the way and the light in which it is viewed:

red (pale/dark)	mauve or purplish	**violet**	coffee
reddish	carmine	**brick red**	fire red
true red	**ruby**	blackish	blue
garnet	burnt ruby	**tile red**	**orange** red
partridge eye	**violet red**	pale red	black
chestnut	peony red	pomegranate	bluish
purple	cherry red	vermilion	**brown red**
red	ocher	scarlet	**yellow red**
blood red	crimson purple	red currant	

The precious stones mentioned here, used as vinous metaphors, are
ruby and garnet. Ruby is a dark red, but there are rubies which are
violet hued and others that are rose colored. On one occasion a jew-
eler friend of mine found that 1970 La Lagune resembled a Perpignan
garnet in color, whereas 1966 Pape Clément, a darker wine, looked
more like a Bohemian garnet. The sard (a variety of carnelian),
whose color varies from orange yellow to blood red (*Oxford English
Dictionary*: pale yellow to reddish orange), is used less frequently.

The terms purple and crimson purple are part of the same sort of
poetic language, appearing frequently in wine writing imagery, as in
the expression "the sumptuous color of wine." Wine colors remind
Raymond Dumay of pictures: "The purple in St-Emilion and Pomerol
wines rivals the reds of the draperies in early Flemish paintings,
whereas Médoc wines, the discovery of the 18th century, have chosen the more somber tones of their contemporary Chardin."

Is vermilion used to describe a white wine or a red wine? Probably both. Vermilion may be a warm gold color or else a bright red.
Rabelais wrote of a "vermilion clairet." Wine lees tend more toward
bluish purple. I dislike the terms blue and violet for red wines, often
used in popular fiction to indicate either mediocre wines or those
that are supposed to have been "doctored." Unfortunately, these
colors do exist in wines made from Vitis Labrusca grapes or from
certain hybrid vines. According to a note written at the turn of the
century: "So-called 'blue' wines are to be found primarily on the
banks of the Loire."

So much has been written about the color partridge eye, and

such is the confusion over the term that one dare not use it any more. In early descriptions it refers to a particularly brilliant pale red wine with a suggestion of straw in its color. Larousse defines it as the color of a lightly tinted red wine. Other sources suggest, erroneously it would seem, that it is the appealing color of a white Meursault. In 1915 Verdier applied the term to the blotched appearance of oxidized white wine made from black grapes. In my opinion we must go back to Olivier de Serres at the beginning of the seventeenth century: He describes a partridge-eye wine as *cleret*, the color of an oriental ruby, the equivalent of a lively red. In contrast, the so-called "hyacinth" colored *clairets* are more orange in hue. The hyacinth in question is not the bluish-violet flower but the precious stone which is a reddish-orange color.

The color vocabulary of port is international. White ports are pale white or *branco palido* when young, becoming golden white or *branco dorado* over the years. Young red ports are full or *retinto*, progressing to ruby after eight or ten years, and to tawny or *alourado* after fifteen to twenty-five years. Very old ports are light or pale tawny or *alourado claro*.

Four

The Sense of Smell

OLFACTORY SIGNALS AND THE PHYSIOLOGY OF THE SENSE OF SMELL

The nose and tongue perceive certain properties in the chemical bodies which they encounter, and for this reason smell and taste are known as chemical senses. They react to the molecules in chemical signals, whereas sight reacts to light waves, hearing to sound waves, and touch to physical properties.

We live in a world of molecules. We consume molecules, we live off them, and our senses of taste and smell act as molecule "selectors" as they enter our bodies.

The sense of smell recognizes and classifies volatile products if they are diffused in the air and have a smell. Odors are only detected in a gas state. Tastes are only perceived in a liquid state. The tongue, where the taste organs are located, identifies stable substances provided they are soluble in saliva.

Olfaction is the act of smelling. The organ of smell is located in the upper part of the nose: The olfactory mucosa lies in the upper part of the nasal cavities; the respiratory mucosa, whose function is to filter and reheat the air we breathe, lines the remainder.

Our nose and nostrils as such are not the real organs of smell, but simply guide channels. When we smell a flower or a glass of wine, habit makes us locate the fragrant impression at the end of our nose, at the point where we are actually sniffing, whereas perception in fact takes place 10 centimeters higher, immediately below the brain. Nonetheless, one's nose remains so closely identified with the experience of smell that a taster with a fine sense of smell is said to have a good "nose," and a wine with a pronounced odor is described as intense on the "nose."

In a similar way we perceive aromas in the mouth via the retronasal (oronasal) passage, which explains why it is so easy to confuse taste and smell in food and drink.

The olfactory mucosa is very sensitive and reacts to irritants in the air. These unpleasant sensations are relayed by the trigeminal nerve and are not strictly speaking odors, though they are generally called pungent or suffocating smells. Sulfurous acid in oversulfured wines is an example of this aggressive character, pungent to the point of making one sneeze in a reflex attempt to get rid of the irritation. Alcohol, chlorine, certain esters, and many other volatile substances have a similar effect.

The olfactory mucosa is yellow in color and covers an area of about 1.5 square centimeters. Its surface is covered in olfactory hairs, prolongations of the nerve fibers which cross the mucosa between its supporting cells. All this is permanently bathed in a mucous fluid. The central fibers of the olfactory neurons assemble in small bundles which pass through the finely perforated ethmoid bone and then join up with that part of the brain immediately above, namely the olfactory bulb. There is no olfactory nerve as such; it is the individual neuron which is sensitive. We have approximately fifty million olfactory neurons converging upon some two thousand fiber clusters in the olfactory bulb!

Odor-laden molecules react with the olfactory hairs. The exact mechanism of stimulation in not known, but the sensitivity of the system is staggering if, in fact, very variable. The absolute thresholds of perception vary from 10^7 to 10^{17} molecules per milliliter of air, a range, that is, of one to ten billion! In the case of those molecules to which we are most sensitive, there need only be a few in the nasal cavity, a few per olfactory hair, to produce a sensation. On the other hand, there are considerable variations of sensitivity between individuals as there is a ratio of the order of 1 to 100 between the extremes of concentration perceived. Nor is it unusual to encounter abnormal distributions of sensitivity, where one group of individuals is very sensitive to a given odor, another insensitive, or at any rate 100 to 200 times less so. These natural, inherent sensitivities can be reduced or enhanced depending on one's habits or how much one practices.

The table below gives a number of examples of the thresholds of detection for various substances in wine, whether natural and desirable or fault related (based on various experiments at the Bordeaux Institute of Oenology).

The olfactory sensation thresholds for a number of odorous substances (Expressed in milligrams per liter)

Substance	Specific Smell	Threshold of Detection (mg/liter)	Substrate
Methyl isobomeol	Mold, camphor	30	Water
Geosmin	Dust, vegetable mold	10	Water
Mucidon	Mold, vegetable mold	3.3	Water
2 3 6 trichloroanisol	Mold	0.0001	——
2 4 6 trichloroanisol	Mold	0.03	Wine
2 3 4 6 trichloroanisol	Mold	4	Water
Ethyl acetate	Acescence, nail polish, vinegar	100,000,000	Wine
Hydrogen sulphide	Rotten eggs	800	Water
Methane thiol	Stagnant water, drains	300	Water
Ethane thiol	Onion	100	Water
Ethane thiol	Onion	1,100	Wine
Diethylsulphide	Garlic	6,000	Water
Diethylsulphide	Garlic	15,000	Wine
Hexanol	Vegetal, herbaceous	4,000,000	Wine
Ethyl phenol	Horses, stables	130,000	Water
Ethyl phenol	Horses, stables	440,000	Wine
Methyloctolactone	Coconut, oak	20,000	Water
Vanillin	Vanilla	15,000	Water
Vanillin	Vanilla	105,000	Wine
Vinyl gaiacol	Carnation, clove	32,000	Water
Vinyl gaiacol	Carnation, clove	130,000	Wine

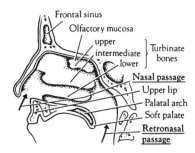

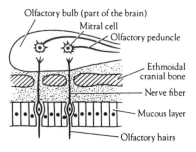

Distribution of the organ of smell, showing the two ways of access to the olfactory mucosa.

Schematic representation of transmission via the olfactory nerve fibers.

The conformation of the receptor system for the sense of smell is such that, with the mucosa located away from the normal air passage and accessible only through a narrow cleft, only a fraction of the odor-laden vapors we breathe actually reaches it unless we are smelling quite deliberately, a fortunate feature which protects us from many a violent odor. It is possible to diminish the intensity of a smell briefly by slowing one's breathing, even stopping for a few seconds, or to eliminate it altogether by holding one's nose. Alternatively, odors can be intensified by inhaling more deeply and repeatedly or by short, sharp sniffing and gentle nosing.

The loss of smell when one has a runny nose is the result of the narrow olfactory cleft being blocked by inflammation and excess mucus, and the tendency in this case is to say that one has lost one's sense of taste. This is because tasting implies smelling as well, though it is not always easy to distinguish the two. Most of the foods we eat emit odors which are drawn into the nostrils when we breathe out and which are consequently a significant aspect of taste, though this effect, linked as it is with breathing, is intermittent. It occurs during chewing and is most marked as one finishes swallowing when the walls of the pharynx act as an extensive evaporating surface.

There are two routes of access to the olfactory mucosa: the **direct nasal route**, where air is drawn in through the nostrils, and the so-called **retronasal route**, where air is drawn up the internal passage connecting the back of the mouth to the nasal channels. The sensation of smell perceived via the nostrils (strict olfaction) depends on how rich in odors the air is immediately above the wine, on how strongly one inhales, and, as we shall see, on technique and glass shape, both of which can enhance the taster's sensitivity. Once sipped, the wine is warmed up and spread around the mouth with the tongue and cheeks; this results in an increased release of aromas which are in turn perceived via the retronasal passage. When one swallows, the movement of the pharynx creates a gentle internal pressure which forces the vapors in the mouth up into the nose, so heightening the olfactory sensations, and it is at this moment, combined with the pleasing tactile sensation of actually swallowing food or drink, that the pleasure of tasting is at its most intense.

The different qualities of individual odors mean one can identify certain substances by their smell, but the relationship between chemical structure and smell is still little understood. Paul Laffort discovered that molecular form is not the key to odor stimulus and, even more surprising, that there are molecules of very different structures which have the same odor. Other characteristics are responsible for triggering the electrical impulse which is interpreted by the brain—molecular size, arrangement, electrical charge, and the way in which a molecule's constituent atoms are grouped. It is thought that each odorous substance specifically stimulates several million different and irregularly distributed olfactory cells, and that it has no effect on several million others. Thus there is a spatial distribution of specific odor-sensitive cells, but equally there are degrees of sensitivity, different frequency bands since, depending on the substance, each olfactory cell reacts differently from its neighbor. The process is extremely complex, involving the integration of messages from a multiplicity of receptors that are irregular in both distribution and sensitivity. These so-called spatiofrequential impulses are integrated and decoded by the olfactory bulb, a veritable computer.

Olfactory sensations are neither stable nor persistent. During a nosing of four or five seconds, corresponding to a slowly drawn breath, a progressive increase in sensation is experienced until an optimum is reached after which the sensation decreases and slowly disappears. The lack of continuity and the fact that one can diminish or augment the sensation, both intentionally or otherwise, all make comparing a series of wines on the nose an arduous task and one that demands an unerring technique from the taster. The same is true when examining a wine on the palate, or, having spat it out, when determining the persistence of the "aroma in the mouth" (*arôme de bouche*) which consists of odors perceived retronasally by the sense of smell. These sensations decrease with each subsequent breath in a series of progressively weaker waves and this fleeting character is an obstacle in trying to measure the aromatic length of a wine.

THE CLASSIFICATION OF ODORS

The olfactory sense is extremely sensitive. If one compares the thresholds of perception in substances that either taste or smell (i.e., the smallest quantity at which they can be perceived), the sense of smell appears ten thousand times more sensitive than that of taste. And yet human olfactory sensitivity does not begin to approach that of many mammals, even less that of some insects, for both of whom it is the primary sense. According to one ethnological hypothesis, when man began to walk upright some of his ability to smell was lost in favor of the senses of sight and hearing.

Nevertheless, our olfactory sensitivity to many chemical substances far exceeds that of laboratory reagents. We can positively smell quantities that are far too small to be weighed or measured, in some cases a mere hundred molecules per milliliter of air suffice.

Our sense of smell is also very versatile. There are many thousand substances that have a smell. Training gives perfumers and tasters a highly developed sensitivity and enables them to detect and identify several hundred different smells. Odors, then, are much more numerous and more complex than tastes proper. The latter can be reduced to a few basic tastes, whereas odors are made up of a considerable number of basic smells.

There have been many attempts at odor classification. Two hundred years ago Linnaeus grouped odors into seven classes; other systems have from six to fourteen different categories. The one we shall use has ten. It is as arbitrary as any of the others, but it has the merit of being fairly comprehensive and, above all, of listing those odors regularly encountered in wines: **animal, balsamic, woody, chemical, spicy, empyreumatic, estery, floral, fruity,** and **vegetal.** A little imagination can find a wide range of rich, complex, and familiar smells in wine.

The **animal** group of smells refers on the one hand to the musky character of some aromatic grape varieties and on the other to the smells of meat, even game, that one finds in some old wines. The **balsamic** group (from the word *balm*) comprises those odors related to pine, resin, and incense smells, and the **woody** group to those deriving from the evolution of tannins or from oak storage casks. **Chemical** odors come from acetic acid and hydrogen sulfide, for example. The **estery** group consists of smells related to acetic esters (ethyl esters and the esters of higher alcohols) and to the esters of fatty acids, all by-products of alcoholic fermentation. A **spicy** bouquet is sometimes found in certain fine wines. The **empyreumatic** group are burnt, smoky, roasted odors. **Floral, fruity,** and **vegetal** categories are very frequently found, though more commonly in young than in old wines. Lime blossom, rose, and vine flowers, black currant, raspberry, and peach, and grassy and herby smells, to name but a few, are all smells regularly encountered in the widely varied bouquets of wine.

Some of the substances in the chemical group, such as alcohol, ethyl acetate, sulfur dioxide, and the like, have a "smell" which is felt as an acrid or pungent sensation at the top of one's nostrils. These are irritants, sensed by the mucosa of the nose rather than detected by the sense of smell proper.

These classifications are convenient rather than scientific. For want of any clearer grouping, and in order to facilitate description, the broad categories are useful. However, they remain an *aide-mémoire* rather than a rational classification.

ODOR-BEARING SUBSTANCES

Wine contains numerous volatile substances which evaporate from its surface when in the mouth or in a glass. These are known as **odorous** or **odoriferous.** Fifty years ago they were grouped under the term *oenanthic ethers,* and they are responsible to a large extent for the agreeable or disagreeable qualities of a wine. We shall see again and again just how important the sense of smell is in judging taste. A good wine is first of all one which has a pleasant bouquet. Great wines are characterized by the intensity and delicacy of their bouquets, what one calls *finesse,* allied to a complexity and individuality which go to make up their distinctive personalities. The bouquets of such wines are regarded in a similar manner to rare and subtle perfumes, so that a connoisseur will admit to getting almost as much pleasure from nosing as from drinking. Indeed, he will devote more time to nosing, as though wanting to put off actually drinking. Our sense of smell is certainly the paramount sense where tasting is concerned, and a quintessential part of wine is its odorous elements.

For a substance in solution to be perceived as having a smell, it needs to be in a volatile state; volatility is as important as the power of the aroma. There are some substances which are very aromatic when dispersed in the air we breathe, but which have little smell in solution because of their low volatility.

When you pour wine into a glass, there is a balance in the distribution of volatile molecules between those in a liquid phase and those in a gas phase. This balance depends on the substance's volatility coefficient, on the evaporative surface and its rate of renewal, and also on temperature. It is quite possible for there to be a thousand times less of a substance in the air immediately above a wine than in the liquid itself. In addition, the distribution of odor-bearing compounds is not the same above the wine as in the wine itself. Evaporation is fractional. A typical example takes place in a balloon glass of cognac, warmed in the hand and sipped gradually: The odors given off initially, with the evaporating alcohol, are the most volatile and lightest. Then, gradually, as the liquid decreases, the heavier, richer aromas are released, and, finally, when the glass is empty, it retains for a considerable time the least volatile fraction belonging to the large molecules of esters and oakwood *rancio*.

The odorous constituents of wine belong to various chemical groups: alcohols, aldehydes, ketones, acids, esters, terpenes, and many other compounds. For a given chemical series, the larger the molecule and the greater the number of carbon atoms, the higher the volatility coefficient will be. Alcohols with the largest molecules are the most aromatic of all. Paradoxically, it is the lightest substances that are the least volatile. This law holds good up to ten atoms of carbon beyond which substances are less volatile and less odorous. For the same carbon radical, esters are more volatile and more aromatic than aldehydes, which in turn are more volatile than alcohols. Acids are the least volatile and have the least smell of all.

The individual volatile substances which make up the smells of wine are beyond reckoning. They crowd at the outlet of a gas chromatograph column and their presence is revealed by hundreds of peaks appearing on a chromatogram. Researchers have counted over five hundred different peaks, fewer than half of which have been identified, and only sixty or so of which have been measured quantitatively.

Although gas chromatography is a highly sensitive technique, a chromatogram trace is very far from being an olfactory profile: Not all the odorous compounds are necessarily detected by the technique, nor are all the compounds identified necessarily odorous at the concentration indicated. Yet, even at a level below their perception threshold, many of these substances play a part in the wine's smell but, while it is possible to analyze the volatile constituents which make up the bouquet, there is nothing apart from actual smelling which can show their effect in combination.

In addition, many of these substances are not specific to wine; they occur throughout the plant world and in the products of fermentation. Virtually the same compounds are to be found in cider and beer and, among others, in foods such as cheese and sauerkraut. They are in a way the waste products of the reactions common to cellular metabolism, and their smells are individual and distinctive because the same compounds mixed in different proportions produce different smells. There certainly are odor groups specific to wine, but these are more difficult to identify.

The study of these odor-bearing substances reveals that only some of them have a direct influence, whether permanent or intermittent, on the olfactory characteristics of wine. These are the ones whose concentrations is above the threshold of detection within a complex milieu. The table on p. 59 (after Dubois, 1986) shows the role of some of the more commonly encountered substances.

OLFACTORY MEASUREMENT

The only means we have of measuring the odor of any substance is a physiological one using our own sense of smell as the apparatus. A number of gaseous dilutions of the substance being studied are made up to concentrations close to the minimum perceptible, the **olfac-**

The olfactory sensation thresholds for a number of odorous substances (Expressed in milligrams per liter)

Substance	Concentrations (mg/l)		Differentiation Threshold (mg/l)	Specific Smell	Role*
	Extreme	Average			
Phenyl ethanol	4–200	35	125	Rose	+
2 methylbutanol	8–150	300	65	Fusel oils	++
3 methylbutanol	6–490	300	70	Fusel oils	++
Hexanol	0.3–12		4	herbaceous	(++)
Acetic Acid†	200–700		175	Vinegar	++
Octanoic acid	0.4–20		13	"Rancio"	(+)
Ethyl lactate	6–500		150	Sour milk	++
Ethyl hexanoate	t–3.4	0.3	0.08	"Fruity"	+++
Acetates me2prop + me3but + me3but }		2	1.6	Banana	+
Ethyl acetate†	40–150	80	150	"Pricked"	+(++)
Acetoin	t–(140)		150		(+)
Ethyl phenol†	t–1 to 4		0.3	Horses	+(++)
Ethyl gaiacol	t–0.2 (white wine)		0.13	"Smoked"	+
Ethyl gaiacol	t–3 (red wine)		0.13	"Smoked"	(++)
Diethoxyethane	t–150		1	"Fruity"	(+++)
Sotolon	0.02–0.14		0.01	Curry	(+++)

* + to +++ indicates an increasingly significant role. ( ) indicates the role varies enormously according to the wine.
† Impact and character are very variable depending on the concentration in the wine.
t = traces

tory threshold, and a representative cross section of people then smells these with the help of machines called olfactometers. The olfactory threshold of the substance is defined as the concentration at which there is a 50 percent positive response. The unit used for measuring smell is called the **olfactory potential,** which represents the number of molecule-grams per liter of air at threshold concentration. Laffort has shown that the most strongly smelling compounds have an olfactory potential close to fourteen, while that for the least intense is around four.

In reality, the concentration values involved at the olfactory mucosa itself are not really concentrations in air, but concentrations in the watery outer layer of the sensitive mucous membrane. Thus it would be a combination of air inhaled and the solubility of odorous compounds in the watery phase of the mucus which actually regulated the sensation. According to this concept, a substance not soluble in the olfactory mucosa would have no smell. However, it has been recognized recently (conversations with Philip Ente, a Californian neurologist) that this is far from the case, and that certain olfactory neurons can detect aromas directly. This more precise understanding of the sensory mechanism is of little consequence for the winetaster, who perceives aromas both nasally and retronasally, in the presence of both water and alcohol.

To determine the effective role of an odorous substance in solution, its concentration is expressed in **olfactory units** reckoned as the ratio between its concentration in the given medium and its threshold value. Ethyl lactate, for example, has a threshold in water of 14 mg/l. A solution of 10 mg/l would therefore have an olfactory unit of $10/14 = 0.71$, and its odor would be imperceptible. A concentration of 35 mg/l would give $35/14 = 2.50$ olfactory units and the odor would be a pronounced one. I will come back to this concept when considering the phenomena of "addition" and "synergy" in blends of odors.

Studying the influence of an odorous substance in wine is more complex because the olfactory threshold is radically altered by the presence of alcohol, other aromatic substances, and even by the fixed constituents making up the dry extract. Any tests performed should be repeated with different wines and by doubling the concentration of any substance; if there is little perceptible difference, it can be concluded that the substance plays little part in the smell of wine. The point is that individual sensitivity varies, and that differences in ability to smell are much more marked than in the case with taste. Our sensitivity as children is much greater than as adults, and we all have memories of smells, agreeable or disturbing, that we have not smelled since childhood.

A taster's sensitivity is also affected by certain abnormalities: **anosmia**, the temporary or permanent, partial or total loss of ability to smell; **merosmia**, the inability to smell certain odors; **hyperosmia**, an excessive sensitivity to smells, usually associated with poor health; **cacosmia** where the perception of smells is constantly unpleasant; **parosmia** where the perception of smells is distorted; and **autosmia** where odors are perceived in the absence of any odor stimulus. The ability to smell is intimately linked to one's state of health.

AROMA AND BOUQUET

The terms "perfume" and "scent," but above all **aroma** and **bouquet**, refer to the pleasant smell given off by a wine, which varies in both intensity and complexity. "Fragrance" belongs more to the realm of poetic description. The smell of a wine will depend on its grape variety, where it comes from, on its age, and how it has been kept. It is one of the most appreciated of fine wine's distinctive aspects.

There is often confusion over the terms currently used to describe smell in wine, and the taster finds it useful to make a distinction between **aroma** and **bouquet**, using these otherwise synonymous terms to convey slightly different meanings. Some would say it is only white wines which have aroma, and red wines which have bouquet. This is so where the whites are drunk young and the reds old, but it does not hold true for all wines. A ten-year-old Montrachet is all bouquet, a Beaujolais Nouveau all aroma.

For others bouquet is the smell perceived when inhaling directly through one's nostrils, and aroma that perceived via the retronasal passage with the wine in the mouth at the moment of swallowing. In this case the definition of aroma would be limited to describing the aroma in the mouth, a definition which is at odds with current usage, that is, "the odorous elements released by various substances of animal or vegetable origin" and which can therefore be smelled by direct inhalation. Examples include meadow smells, the scent of flowers filling a room, and the all-pervading aroma of coffee beans roasting or of coffee being percolated.

To me it seems best to use aroma to designate the sum of odor elements in young wines, and to use bouquet for the smells acquired through aging, which develop gradually over the course of time. Defined in this way, young wines owe their charm more to their aroma than their bouquet, while the appeal of wines with several years of bottle age will be due entirely to their bouquet. However, I must admit the distinction is very subtle and hardly worth arguing over.

To pursue the analysis, there are two types of aroma to be distinguished. **Primary aroma** is the original aroma, intrinsic to the grape, extracted from the skin of black grapes, and already present in the must. It is the scent of the fruit itself, characteristic of the grape variety or even of an individual clone. It varies in intensity and finesse according to the vineyard, the maturity of the grapes, and the amount of fruit on the vine. We shall see that certain noble varieties, such as Cabernet, Pinot, Sauvignon, Riesling, and Muscat, are remarkable for both the character and penetration of their primary aroma.

The **secondary aroma**, which evolves during the course of fermentation, is the intensely vinous smell developed as a result of yeast activity, whose volatile character saturates the vat room at harvest time. The phenomenon has been called "aromatic fermentation." Subsequently, these fermentation odors are refined by benign microbial transformations which create subtle additional aromatic characteristics. In the end the smell of a young wine is a blend of aromas combining those of the grape variety itself and those produced during the course of fermentation. This corresponds pretty much to the hydrolysis of esters produced during alcoholic fermentation. The fermentation odors may be both intense and very attractive, but by themselves they neither account for nor guarantee the olfactory characteristics of more mature wine.

The aromatic character gradually dissipates so that after several years of keeping it practically disappears, giving way to bouquet. In fact, one result of improved vinification methods is that modern wines always retain some aromatic character even when mature— the art of graceful aging is that of prolonging the virtues of youth.

There is, above all, with age an intensification of smell and an increasing complexity brought about by transformation within the wine and by an accumulation of new compounds. That complex medley of sweet smells which a mature old wine yields in the glass is a wine's bouquet, doubtless so called by analogy with the elaborate perfume imparted by a bouquet of flowers. Its development during the aging process is very likely due, in part at least, to the elements of both primary and secondary aroma, and there are some who call it the **tertiary aroma**.

The ultimate harmony of a bouquet is only acquired with the

passage of time and can be recognized on the nose as particularly harmonious and mellow. Only fine wines have the potential to progress from aroma to bouquet; others are said not to age, not to "bouquet."

This is an appropriate place to contrast two types of bouquet in relation to the technology of storing wine. In one case the wines generally come from a warm region and are either naturally high in alcohol or have been fortified by the addition of brandy. Fortification is a method of preserving wine and protecting it from attack by bacteria which would ruin it. As alcohol of 16° to 18° will kill most bacteria, it is no longer necessary to take so much care to keep the wine from contact with oxygen and it can be exposed to air in partially full barrels. This method of storage promotes what is known as oxidative aging. The wine develops an **oxidative bouquet**, characterized by aldehydic compounds smelling of quince, apple, dried nuts, butter, *rancio*, and madeira. It is this type of aging that led Pasteur to say "oxygen makes the wine." And so it is with various Vins Doux Naturels such as Banyuls, the Picardan used as a base for vermouth, vins de liqueur, mistelles used as a base for aperitifs, port, *oloroso* and *amontillado* sherries, madeira, marsala, Italian Vin Santo, Mavrodaphne from Patras, and many others. Aged in contact with air, these wines become immune to it. Most do not improve in bottle, but neither do they deteriorate after several days in an opened bottle.

Much commoner is the **reductive bouquet** acquired by wines from temperate regions which are stored in conditions which avoid contact with air as far as possible. The barrels and vats are always kept filled to the brim and topped up frequently. Where it is not possible to prevent contact with air completely, for example, during racking or transfer between containers, the wine is immediately protected by an antioxidant such as sulfur dioxide. Wines of this type finish up in bottle hermetically stoppered with long corks which ensure an airtight seal for twenty years or more. Old red wines and fine dry or sweet wines have reductive bouquets. The wines are sensitive to the oxygen in air and an opened bottle will soon deteriorate. Berthelot's axiom "oxygen is the enemy of wine" refers to such wines as these.

For a long time it was thought that wine aged through a process of ester formation. This seems unlikely. The phenomenon known as "esterification," the slow formation of esters by the reaction between a wine's acids and alcohols, only produces compounds that have

Different types of aroma and bouquet (recommended terminology)

	Primary	Fruity in character, deriving from the grapes themselves
Aroma		
↓	*Secondary*	Vinous in character, deriving from fermentation
	Oxidative	Wines aged in contact with air
Bouquet		
(tertiary aroma)	*Reductive*	Wines aged in the absence of air
		(wines matured in sealed casks and wines aged in bottle)

very little smell. What is beyond doubt, on the other hand, is that certain elements of bouquet originate from substances that are without any odor of their own, for example, the hydrolysis of heterosides or the transformation of tannins. Another distinction must be made here between the bouquet resulting from maturation in cask or vat and that resulting from aging in bottle. It is known that in the first case the bouquet's intensity is always limited, whereas the most profound bouquets are those acquired after several years in bottle. When a wine becomes very old, the bouquet often recalls the smell of certain fungi; eventually, it coarsens and becomes very pronounced, a sign of advanced old age.

PRIMARY OR GRAPE VARIETY AROMAS

Climate, soil, and grape variety are natural elements of quality but human skill is necessary to make the most of them. "Air, soil, and the planting of vines are a vineyard's foundation," was how Olivier de Serres put it. The grape variety puts its mark on a wine and gives it an identity. If the taste of wine is infinitely variable, this is primarily because there are so many varieties of vine grown in an infinite number of locations and climates.

The grape variety gives a wine firstly its taste and secondly its aromatic properties. The first depends on the grape's richness in sugars, acids, and tannins; the second on the intensity and finesse of the fruit's aroma-yielding substances. There are noble varieties which are the only ones capable of producing wines of refinement and longevity, recognizable for their fine flavor and the power and individuality of their aromas. Some of these have become so well adapted to their original production zones that, transplanted elsewhere, they become virtually unrecognizable. Such is the case with Pinot and Merlot. Other noble varieties such as Riesling and Cabernet Sauvignon have a more stable character and their more general success has meant that they are planted worldwide.

There are also semi-noble varieties which can produce an excellent wine in a particular area, but which yield something very ordinary elsewhere. Examples of these are the Tempranillo in Rioja, the Palomino in Jerez, the Nebbiolo in Piedmont, the Sangiovese in Chianti, the Grenache in Châteauneuf-du-Pape, Navarre, or Sardinia, and many others.

Finally, there are the common grape varieties which produce neutral table wines of little quality. They are grown purely for their high yield which makes an indifferent product profitable; often, alas, all too profitable.

In addition to their aromatic characteristics, quality in black grapes depends on parameters such as color, acid balance, and tannin, without which there would be no long-maturing wines. Certain wines are made from just one variety: Red burgundy is made solely from the Pinot Noir, Beaujolais solely from the Gamay grape; but many others are produced from a blend of several grape varieties—Bordeaux, Côtes-du-Rhône, and Rioja wines are examples.

Vinification may be said to reveal the primary aroma concealed within the fruit, for wine smells more of fruit than the grape itself. There are various explanations for this phenomenon: First, during maceration the aromatic elements, contained mainly in the skin, pass into the wine (the skins of ripe grapes, steeped in a dilute alcoholic solution, yield an aromatic, colored infusion). Furthermore, fermentation serves to release the odor-bearing constituents and so to reveal the latent aromas.

These phenomena are still poorly understood. Sauvignon Blanc is a particularly instructive example in this respect. This grape variety originally came from Bordeaux, but it made its name in Paris as a wine from the Loire, from Pouilly and Sancerre especially. It has a very specific smell, floral, musky, smoky with a slightly raw herba-ceousness suggesting bruised leaves, in keeping with its derivation from the French *sauvage*. When you bite into the thick-skinned, golden Sauvignon grape, you can smell this particular odor, albeit rather weakly; similarly, the freshly squeezed juice of the grape has relatively little smell, and in the mouth, too, its aromatic quality is limited. It is only twenty or thirty seconds after swallowing the juice that you suddenly experience a powerful aromatic rush at the back of the mouth as the Sauvignon fragrance returns. Doubtless saliva reacts with and releases the Sauvignon essence which is present in the grape in a relatively odorless form. The winemaker may notice another fact which is explained by a similar phenomenon, that of hydrolysis: It sometimes happens that a Sauvignon wine, when it has just finished its fermentation, has little specific Sauvignon char-acter and is disappointing to taste; yet a month later it shows well and is remarkably aromatic.

Vine varieties are grouped into families, originally from the same regions. The Bordeaux region is home to the Carmenet family. The archetypes of this numerous family are the Sauvignon Blanc, just discussed, and the Cabernet Sauvignon, but it also includes the Semillon, Cabernet Franc, Bouchet, Verdot, and Merlot, all of which have a common morphological parentage and an obvious family affinity of aroma. The odor palette of the Cabernet Sauvignon is ex-ceptionally rich and becomes richer still as the wines age. These odors vary between the fine smell of crushed black currants, or bet-ter still, a refined black-currant liqueur, and impressions of smoke, spice, and resin reminiscent of cedar wood; sometimes a metallic-mineral character and a bouquet which becomes more truffle-like with age, qualities which one finds in the Grand Cru Médocs. In Cabernet Sauvignon wines from soils that are too fertile, or from grapes grown in climates that are too hot, the aromatic character tends to be rather crude and vegetal, evoking more the bruised leaf than the fruit.

Today's most fashionable grape variety is Cabernet Sauvignon. Wines made from it are now encountered worldwide. They smell of resin in Porto Carras, of cloves in the Guadeloupe Valley in southern California, of licorice in Rioja, of seaweed in wines from the Golfe du Lion sand flats, of grape stems in the Languedoc, of industrial fumes near Santiago in Chile, and of soot from Eger in Hungary. There are some which closely resemble the Médocain model (to be found, though rarely, in California, Australia, or Chile); but much more common are those which bear little resemblance to the Bordeaux benchmark. In the latter cases what would be considered a defect anywhere else is presented as a virtue: the smell of green peppers, green olives, of new mown hay, of creosote, or of suspect odors suggestive of indole. The herby-stemmy flavor of some Cabernet Sauvignons (and Merlots) from the Alto Adige is also presented as a sign of quality.

Northeastern France is planted with a different family of quality grapes called the *noiriens* (literally the "blacks"), comprising Pinot Noir, Meunier, Chardonnay, and Gamay. The first three are the grapes used to make champagne, while the Gamay gives the beaujolais its rustic scent of cherry and small red fruits and its smoothness. The aroma of Pinot Noir defies description as does that of Cabernet Sauvignon. It suggests a blend of fruits (black currant and raspberry), often softer and sweeter because its tannin is less obtrusive, but it is also more one-dimensional in character, and develops less than Cabernet Sauvignon. It attains an incomparable quality in the *premiers crus* wines of the Côte de Nuits and Côte de Beaune; no other site in the world suits this grape so well. It lasts well into extreme old age, and the wine remains good for as long as its fruit does.

Chardonnay is not, strictly speaking, a white form of Pinot Noir but its identity is sometimes confused; it is not the same as the Alsatian Pinot Blanc or the Klevner, and grapes that are called Pinot Blanc in northern Italy and South America are themselves not always Pinots. The Chardonnay grape has a powerful aroma and wide range of styles: It is light and lively in champagne from the Côte des Blancs; it is fuller, more vigorous, and harder in Chablis, requiring four or five years in bottle to mature. Like red burgundies, Chardonnays from Corton-Charlemagne, Montrachet, Meursault, and Pouilly-Fuissé are kept and develop in oak barrels after malolactic fermentation. White burgundy is one of the rare white wines, perhaps the only one, which can stand this fermentation. Chardonnay is also found in the Mâconnais where its character is more pronounced and sometimes earthy; in which case it is said, locally, to "chardonne." One other area where Chardonnay does well is in the "mountains" of the Napa Valley in California. Wines from some vineyards on the slopes here can acquire a bouquet as pure as that from Burgundy itself.

The Riesling grape reigns supreme in the terraced valleys of the Rhine and its tributaries. Here it grows on slopes whose exceptional exposition means it can survive the vagaries of the continental climate. The Rhine's right bank is said to produce the finer wines, but in good vintages Alsace also produces great Rieslings. It is one of the four noble varieties whose wines have had a worldwide reputation for many generations. From the eighteenth century white wines made from the Riesling grape were exported by river from Cologne in the same way that claret was shipped from Bordeaux via the Gironde. Their paths never crossed and wines from the Rhine are as little known in France as claret is in Baden or the Rhineland. The Riesling is also found in Austria, in Italy on the lower, south-facing slopes of the Alps, in the former Yugoslavia, and it followed the Anglo-Saxons to South Africa, Australia, and California.

Sweet and gentle or sharp and lively, but always light and delicate, Riesling makes wines of exquisite fragrance, perfect models for today's whites. (They have been described as "handkerchief wines," and their bottles likened to bottles of scent.) There is no other white grape variety whose bouquet varies so much according to the soil in which it is grown.

The smell of broom, green and sweet, is sometimes suggested as a touchstone for the Riesling aroma, but it can also smell of peach blossom or the vine in flower; grown on schist in the Mosel, it is somewhat smoky, even tarry. To say that it can remind one faintly of petroleum products would, by itself, convey a highly misleading impression even though the terpenes in the grape are hydrocarbons; an apter comparison would be the smell of white truffles. In the same region, the Riesling is surrounded by the Sylvaner, the Traminer, and the latter's most aromatic form, the Gewürztraminer. If the aroma of the first is quite straightforward, the other two might be called somewhat extrovert in olfactory terms. For the novice they have the advantage of being easy to recognize. This opulence of bouquet can certainly be very appealing even if it does lack finesse.

Muscat grapes provide the best illustration for the notion of primary aroma because their fruit is the most highly perfumed of all, and the Muscat aroma has a universal appeal. The Muscat aroma is also the one that has been most closely studied, and whose constituents are the best understood even though they cannot be reproduced exactly by artificial means. Its specific smell is due to terpenes, a family of chemical substances mainly found in the essential oils of many plants. Examples include geraniol and nerol, which smell of roses, linalool (rosewood), terpineol (camphor) and limonene, and citronella oil whose odor is citric. Grape juice and wine from the different Muscat varieties contain 0.5 to 3.0 mg/l of terpenes (see the following table), whereas the threshold for their perception starts at only 0.1 mg/l. The same terpenes are also found in other aromatic varieties such as Riesling, Silvaner, Müller-Thurgau, and Gewürztraminer, still above the identification threshold but in much lower concentrations.

There are many other grape varieties which give an individual aromatic character to numerous quality wines: Among the white grapes are Semillon and Muscadel from Bordeaux, the Melon of Muscadet, Chenin from Touraine and Saumur, Tokay's Furmint, Malvasia and Savatiano from Attica, Athiri from the Greek islands, and Ugni Blanc, called St-Emilion in the Charente, which is the cognac

Terpene content in the juice from Muscat and other aromatic grape varieties

Maximum concentrations expressed in micrograms per liter (based on Terrier)

	Linalool oxides	Terpineol	Linalool	Geraniol	Nerol	T
Muscat of Alexandria	578	117	815	1,059	263	2,720
Muscat of Frontignan	1,228	145	846	702	405	3,326
Muscat St-Vallier	552	140	1,506	441	46	2,655
Muscat Italia	217	53	638	285	47	1,127
Muscat Hamburg	713	114	489	618	447	2,381
Muscat Ottonel	449	35	596	209	47	1,331
Riesling	72	42	145	96	17	275
Müller-Thurgau	—	8	30	65	—	103
Gewürztraminer	80	19	134	150	37	420
Silvaner	—	29	32	38	—	99

grape. Among the red grapes are the Syrah of Hermitage, Malbec of Cahors, Grenache, Barbera from Piedmont, Xynomavro from Naoussa, Zinfandel from California, and so on. There are dozens of others, less widely known, but which yield attractive and individual wines. These are all varieties which the winetaster can distinguish on the nose but which cannot be identified by analysis of their aromatic constituents. Here one's nose is a more sensitive and reliable guide than modern gas chromatography. The latter can, however, identify certain odor-bearing molecules. Thus the particular aromatic character of Cabernet Sauvignon is based on n-octonal and 2-methoxy-3-isobutylpyrazine. The realm of smells is one of highly complicated chemistry and terminology.

SECONDARY OR FERMENTATION AROMAS

The billions of yeasts which break down the 200 or so grams of sugar per liter of grape juice into alcohol also synthesize a whole host of other different organisms at the same time. This "yeast" factory not only manufactures floods of alcohol and torrents of carbon dioxide gas, accounting respectively for 47 percent and 44 percent of the metabolized sugar, but it also produces minute quantities of several dozen other substances, so-called secondary products of fermentation. For this purpose the yeast cells have at their disposal an arsenal of enzymes, which are so many tools suited to the transformations they produce.

Thus fermentation is much more than the simple formation of ethyl alcohol; indeed, the secondary products are more important for the taste quality of a wine than the alcohol. Of these secondary products, some are sapid, such as succinic acid which is both bitter and salty, many others are volatile and odorous; it is these that constitute the secondary aroma and which are responsible for the tastes that different wines have in common. Alcohol is merely a medium, the vehicle for the aromatic elements, and it is the latter which give fermented drinks their flavor and personality. The same goes for spirits, whose quality depends essentially on the so-called nonalcohol substances.

Fermentation aromas belong to various chemical families: alcohols with heavy molecules, so-called higher alcohols, esters, aldehydes, and acids. More or less the same substances are to be found in all wines and other fermented products, but their respective proportions, and consequently the character and appeal of their bouquets, can vary a great deal. These variations are due to numerous factors, the three principal ones being the primary material being fermented, the types of yeast used, and the external conditions in which fermentation takes place.

Secondary aroma depends on the level of sugar in the grapes, and thus on how ripe they are. The greater the quantity of sugar involved, the more intense is the secondary aroma, hence chaptalization can improve the aroma. However, the fundamental make-up of the grape must also be taken into account. Odor-yielding products are directly related to the supply of nitrogenous matter available to the yeasts and therefore to the nitrogenous constitution of the grape must. If the level of ammoniacal nitrogen is higher the yeasts will use less organic nitrogen and produce less of the higher alcohols. According to the amino acids at their disposal, they will form more or less of a given constituent and the wine will have more or less isoamyl alcohol, phenylethyl alcohol, and so on. Vitamins in the grape oligoelements also play a part, for yeasts, like all living organisms, need vitamins. They help the yeast secrete enzymes which will catalyze aroma-producing reactions. The presence in the grapes of natural chemical inhibitors interferes with certain reactions and modifies the end product.

Another factor relates to the type of yeast. Some thirty species of this monocellular mold have been identified as capable of causing fermentation and thus of playing a part in vinification. There are predominant species such as *Saccharomyces ellipsoideus* (whose name literally means "the fungus which is elliptical in shape and converts sugar"), and at each vintage it is this species which converts three-quarters of the harvest's grape sugar into alcohol. It is the true wine yeast. However, numerous other species have been recorded which function in a very different manner. Among the *ellipsoideus* species there are several varieties which have become specially adapted to fermentation as a result of their prolonged use for this purpose. Each of these has its own way of converting sugar and creating secondary products, and in consequence it also produces its own individual aroma. Oenologists have observed that, in relation to elliptical yeast, the little lemon-shaped yeasts, *Saccharomyces apiculatus*, produce a high proportion of esters and amyl alcohol; that *Saccharomycodes*, large spoilage yeasts, produce a large amount of isobutyl alcohol; that the *Schizosaccharomyces*, able to ferment malic acid, yield few superior alcohols and few esters; finally, that the *oviformis* yeasts, a good "finishing" species, form a significant amount of acetaldehyde and ethyl propionate.

The distribution of yeast species in local microflora depends on the climate and on random agents of propagation such as dust, wind, and insects. Technically, it is possible to ferment with pure, selected yeast culture; the aromas obtained are more clear-cut but also simpler. For a number of years now musts have been "seeded" with selected dried yeasts. These tend to produce more intense fermentation aromas as well as enhancing the specific varietal aromas of the grape.

Yeasts are highly sensitive to the conditions in which they work, notably to those of temperature and aeration. In the case of white wine vinification, it has been shown that sulfiting, settling the must (a technique for removing suspended matter and so clarifying the grape juice prior to fermentation), and fermenting at a low temperature will all reduce the final level of superior alcohols, whereas maceration and aeration during fermentation will increase their level. In addition, there are more esters formed at a temperature of 18°C than at 25°C. These practices and the choice of low-temperature fermentation have developed in the making of white wine because the reduction of higher alcohols and the increase in esters result in a wine that is much more attractive to drink. The winemaker, therefore, has some room for maneuver in selecting the odor substances which will produce the best effect.

Some current thinking suggests that a renewed fermentation in a wine with residual sugar from a prior fermentation generates additional odor elements and a heightened aromatic character. Indeed, certain special fermenting techniques are based on a secondary or double fermentation. Such is the case with champagne and sparkling wines whose aromas are refined by a second fermentation which produces their *mousse* at the same time. The practice of **governo** in Chianti is another case in point. This method consists of retaining a certain proportion of grapes at harvest time, and laying the bunches on latticed frames in a well-aired location, so allowing the grapes to become overripe and concentrated. In March, selected grapes are lightly crushed and blended with the new wine. In this way a gentle second fermentation is initiated which gives the wine a slight prickle and an enhanced fruit before bottling.

There are certain short-lived aromas in wine some of which are quite pleasant, some not. These are fermentation odors, smells of fresh yeast, dried yeast (similar to thiamin or vitamin B1), sourdough, wheat bread, and bruised apples. These smells, which originate from aldehydes, diminish and finally disappear as a result of clarification and sulfuring during the months following fermentation. The ester-based fermentation odors remind one of bananas, solvents, nail varnish, acid drops; these partially evaporate, along with carbon dioxide gas, during the course of racking. Similarly, malolactic fermentation bacteria form compounds which influence taste and smell. Diacetyl, the substance responsible for the smell of fresh butter, may reach 2 mg/l, sometimes more; some wines are strongly marked by this "dairy" character (Australian reds, for example). Other substances produced during malolactic fermentation and which account, to a greater or lesser extent, for profound changes are propionate, ethyl butyrate, and ethyl lactate; the last is present in several dozen mg/l and has a fine and pleasing odor. Malolactic fermentation is not only a means of making fine wines more supple, but also a means of refining their aromas as it accentuates their vinosity. It is rightly considered to be the first stage in the flavor maturation of wines that need aging.

Lactic acid and lactic bacteria can cause obtrusive lactic smells in wines with very little primary aroma. The wines smell of sour milk, cheese, even dirty linen, all smells one does not normally expect to encounter in wine!

THE GENESIS OF BOUQUETS

The quality of wine's smell depends firstly on its primary aroma (that due to the grape variety) or, to be more precise, it depends on the relative proportions and respective appeal of this and the secondary aroma. The latter, the fermentation aroma, adds a new list of odor-bearing substances to that of the grape, but the primary aroma should always dominate in both quality and intensity. Wines in which the secondary aroma prevails may be attractive enough but they do not show any marked characteristics of their origin, nor do they display the qualities of a good soil. Such wines have little future and should be drunk young, for they rapidly lose any flavor interest as they age. Besides, part of the fermentation aroma is highly volatile and disappears along with the release of carbon dioxide during the course of fermentation and during the initial months of storage. Indeed, it is necessary that this should be so, as, in a way, the process of aging begins with the loss of the "new wine" odor.

The formation of bouquet is complex, and the transition from the aroma of a young wine to the bouquet of an old wine, whatever its character, is a function of several phenomena which may take place simultaneously or successively. I have just mentioned the evaporation which begins with the release of gas during fermentation (50 liters of gas per liter of wine) and which continues each time the wine is manipulated or exposed to air. Carbon dioxide is a substance foreign to and ill-suited to red wines, the more so the more tannic they are. The level of carbon dioxide, which is about 2 g/l after fermentation, needs to be reduced to 100 mg/l at the time of bottling. The gas which escapes is saturated with alcohol vapors and with some of the most highly volatile odor substances. Attempts have been made to recover these products in order either to make an unusual alcoholic drink or to reintroduce them into wines later on. With this aim in mind released carbon dioxide has been passed through small condensers maintained at a very low temperature (−20°C) in which the volatile constituents condensed. The results were disappointing in that the products recovered had a smell that was strong, unpleasant, piquant, and burning. The substances in question are in fact those which do not normally remain in such large quantities in wines and spirits, and which need to be removed from new wine. In the same way evaporation during the course of early rackings eliminates fermentation odors and brings out the primary aroma.

Another phenomenon which occurs during the maturation of a wine is the transformation of primary aroma into bouquet as a result of the chemical reactions of cyclization (modification of the form of the molecule) and oxidation (the influence of contact with air). These bring about a change in the wine's odor which tends to become somewhat heavier, less estery, and to lose some of its fruity character. At the same time the blend of smells appears more homogeneous, more mellow, and more harmonious. This change be-

74

gins to be noticeable during the course of the first summer. Wines that are rich in primary aroma develop the most bouquet, while those with little primary aroma do not improve; they are said not to "hold" and they are at their best within a year of the harvest. The progressive changes in the polyphenols of the tannin family are certainly a further source of bouquet, at least in wines made from grape varieties well endowed with good-quality tannin. We shall see that tannins constitute the evolutive fraction of a wine, that which matures and develops. For example, in old wines made from Cabernet Sauvignon, the tannins contribute to the bouquet, indicating that they do develop a smell.

Where wines are aged in wood, the odor element yielded by oak also forms part of the bouquet, and the effect is more pronounced the smaller the container and the less it has been used. Here, too, there is a balance to consider. The smell of oak should not mask the other aromas, nor should it replace them as the sole constituent of the bouquet which would then be artificial. Mature wine should not be an extract of oak. Wood should be used for wines in the same way that spices are used in cooking, simply to bring out the other flavors. For wines kept in barrel the contribution made by oak is beneficial in as far as it complements and enriches the existing flavors and aromas, but the oak character ought not to be immediately identifiable; it should remain discreetly in the background. However, on this point fashion and taste vary substantially from country to country. An oaky taste in red wines, and even in whites is sought after and much appreciated in certain regions of Spain, Italy, California, Australia, the Cape, and Chile. Every year the Bordeaux-classed growths lodge all or part of their wine in new oak barrels, and fine burgundy is also kept in new oak casks. On the other hand, consumers in countries such as Germany, Austria, and Switzerland, who are used to young wines, care much less for wines that have an oaky taste.

True, this taste shocks the palate in a wine intended for drinking within the year, yet it is looked for in wines for aging because the oakiness develops and slowly becomes part of the total effect. The oak component ages in the wine in the same way that a branch of vine or oak ages and develops a fragrance. Our understanding of the substances diffused into wine during the course of barrel maturation has improved recently as a result of research into oak origins (European or American) and techniques used for drying the wood, bending staves, and toasting the inside of barrels. Old wood and old tannin release vanilla odors because vanillin is an element in the make-up of their molecules. These perfumed odors are more easily detected in old cognacs and armagnacs where they are more concentrated. After thirty years and more old wines develop refined smells reminiscent of truffles, fungi, and mushrooms, precisely those cryptogams which are the parasites of wood.

The aging cycle of tannins in wine is the same as that of tannin in wood, and doubtless in cork, too. For the poetic winetaster the bouquet of old wines evokes undergrowth; for the more literally minded taster it also recalls the humidity of an old cellar.

During the initial years of aging, the less contact the wine has with air, the better sealed and more airtight the container, the better the bouquet. In barrel or in vat the bouquet acquires a certain intensity, but it is in bottle, under much more hermetic conditions, that it reaches its peak. Whereas the wine can breathe a little (to use the cellarmaster's terms) in contact with and through wood, in the bottle it is completely stifled under the cork. The joint made by a swollen cork in the neck of a bottle is so effective that the amount of oxygen which can get into the bottle cannot be measured. The bouquet thus formed is called a "reductive bouquet," reduction, for the chemist, being the reverse phenomenon of oxidation.

The presence of sulfurous acid (H_2SO_3) in a wine has a generally beneficial action because of its reducing properties. The use of this additive is sometimes decried, but it does, however, really improve a wine's flavor. Of course, it is all a question of dosage. To start with, it improves the primary aroma of a young wine by removing the aldehyde smells which mask it. Even the aroma from an infusion of ripe grape skins is heightened by the addition of a few milligrams per liter of sulfur dioxide.

A pronounced reductive bouquet can give certain wines an unpleasant smell. The odors in question are known as "reduced," "bottle stink," and "light-" or "sun-induced" smells, the last two being so called because the photochemical effect of light intensifies this fault. These are perceived on the nose as a lack of clarity, a faint stink, like garlic in character and sometimes suggesting sweat. Derivatives containing reduced sulfur (thiol groups) such as ethyl mercaptan are responsible for these smells. Furthermore, they are also present in any normal reductive bouquet but only in trace quantities. The unpleasant smell of reduction is perceptible once the level of volatile thiol derivatives is above several fractions of a milligram per liter.

The formation of oxidation-induced or oxidative bouquets follows the reverse process to that just described. With the wine not being protected from oxygen, the abundant formation of acetaldehyde dominates every other character right from the start. Its smell of apples, quince, then almond and nut entirely replaces the primary and secondary aromas. For this reason wines of this type are generally made from neutral grapes (Palomino, for example).

Muscat wines are a special case. In order to preserve their primary aroma, fermentation is avoided or curtailed and the juice is "muted" (fortified) with alcohol, after which they are protected from oxidation until bottling. A few Muscats from warm regions, exceptionally rich in terpenes, can stand a light maderization.

F i v e

Taste and Tasters

THE ANATOMY OF DRINKING

The organs of taste are located in the mouth. Drawing a liquid into the mouth when drinking is usually done by suction. The commonest method is to take liquid into the mouth from a spoon, cup, or glass, at the same time using one's lips to help draw it in more or less mixed with air. It is difficult to drink in a position other than vertical, and one can only taste standing or seated. Atmospheric pressure and gravity affect the way we drink, and one can imagine that tasting would be particularly difficult in conditions of weightlessness. We must ask an astronaut!

Swallowing is the series of movements which conveys chewed food, or in our case liquid, into the esophagus and then into the stomach. The operation is a delicate one as the swallowed liquid has to cross the path of the air passages. There is, however, a double security system: for the upper airway by the closing off of the nasal cavity from the mouth and for the lower airway by the closure of the inlet to the larynx. If these operations fail, the sensitive upper laryngeal nerve will trigger a cough: You might choke, but your windpipe would be protected.

When a mouthful of liquid has entered the esophagus, the respiratory circuit is reestablished. The air breathed out crosses the oral cavity and becomes impregnated with the aromatic vapors of the drink just consumed; it then comes into contact with the sense of smell via the nasal cavities and so stimulates the olfactory nerves. I have already stressed that the moment of swallowing is when the pleasant sensations of tasting and consumption are at their height. Even though this happens involuntarily, it is advisable to swallow a very small amount of wine once or twice during the ten seconds or so that it remains in the mouth.

THE TONGUE'S PAPILLAE AND THE SALIVARY GLANDS

The taste receptors are located in certain types of the tongue's papillae which are concentrated mainly at the tip and on its upper part. There are four types of papillae: **foliate, circumvallate, fungiform,** and **filiform.** Not all of these play a part in the perception of taste; the filiform papillae are above all tactile. Only the circumvallate papillae at the rear of the tongue and the fungiform papillae found at the tip have taste buds sensitive to specific tastes. (See table below.)

The Tongue and taste

Name	Papillae Number	Location	Number of Taste Buds	Associated Nerves	Particular Sensitivity
Fungiform	Several hundred	Front of tongue	3–5	Chorda tympani, facial nerve, lingual, and trigeminal nerves	Chemical, tactile, thermal
Circumvallate	Dozen	Rear of tongue	Several hundred	Glosso-pharyngian	Bitterness
Foliate	——	Sides of tongue	——	Glosso-pharyngian, chorda tympani, facial nerve	——
Filiform	——	Widely dispersed	——	——	Tactile

Information perceived by the papillae and taste buds is relayed by the associated nerves to the hypothalamus, thalamus, and cortex, where it is decoded and interpreted on the one hand as a reflex action, and on the other as a function of one's knowledge and cultural experience.

We all have more or less the same number of taste buds in similar proportions, though I have heard the expression "a taster well endowed with taste buds." The circumvallate papillae, larger and more numerous, form a V-shaped barrier at the back of the tongue. Each circumvallate papilla contains several hundred taste buds and each taste bud contains a dozen taste cells whose sensory hairs protrude from a small mucus-filled depression. We have several hundred thousand sensitive cells available to perceive "tastes" proper. Their turnover is rapid, all the taste cells being renewed within a few days.

It should not be thought that each taste bud is sensitive to only one type of taste. Some are simultaneously sensitive to sweetness, acidity, and bitterness; others perceive only two, some only one of these tastes. The circumvallate papillae are mainly sensitive to bitterness. One survey of 125 papillae revealed that 79 were sensitive to sweetness (3 exclusively so), 71 to bitterness, and 91 to acidity (12 exclusively so).

As yet there is no comprehensive explanation of the sensation of taste. In the case of sweetness there is thought to be a protein in the taste cells which has the particular property of reacting with sweet substances and which is called a sugar-sensitive protein. The relative sweetness of a substance depends precisely on its bonding strength with this protein. There are also thought to be several types of lingual receptors for sweet tastes, such that an individual's greater or lesser sensitivity to sweetness is genetically determined.

The network of nerve fibers transmitting impulses from taste cells to the brain follows three cranial nerves. The impulses reach the nerve center in the medulla brain. The taste receptor center in the brain is situated close to the motor centers for chewing and swallowing, and the perception of tastes is closely linked to these two functions.

The tongue is constantly moistened by secretions of saliva. A substance only has taste if it is soluble in the liquids of our food and in the saliva which is produced by a series of glands and lubricates the mucous membranes of the mouth. Because of the uneven distribution of taste receptor sites, muscular movements of the tongue during eating and drinking are required to bring the dissolved sapid substances into contact with the taste cells. For this reason the winetaster works the wine around his mouth with the tongue in order to get all its nuances of flavor.

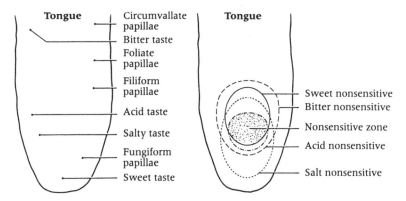

Principal distribution of the four types of papillae and the four basic tastes.

Areas of the tongue which are insensitive to particular tastes. The shaded area is insensitive to all tastes.

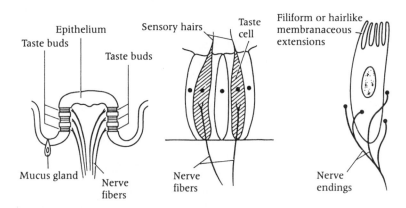

From left to right, diagrams show a circumvallate papilla on the tongue, a taste bud, and a taste-sensitive nerve cell.

The blend of salivas from the different glands is a colorless, opalescent, neutral liquid, somewhat ropy in texture due to the presence of 2 g/l of mucin, a glycoprotein with a high molecular weight of which there are several types known. This saliva mixture contains mineral and organic matter and, among numerous others, the alpha-amylase enzyme (ptyalin) which hydrolyzes starch and glycogen. Parotid saliva is fluid, watery, and powerfully hydrolytic. Saliva from the other glands, however, is thick and viscous.

Claude Bernard has described the roles of saliva during eating and drinking thus: (1) to facilitate chewing and swallowing by lubricating the mucous membranes and foods, also by moistening the latter when dry (insalivation); (2) to render food soluble in order to bring it into contact with the taste buds and so to awake taste sensations; (3) to lubricate the mucous membranes of the cheeks and tongue so as to ease speech; (4) to exercise a digestive action.

During winetasting salivation is considerable, the more so the longer the wine is kept in one's mouth. In the end a taster spits out a greater volume of liquid than the wine originally sipped, in spite of the small quantities swallowed.

Certain tastes make one salivate, acid ones in particular. The flavors of glutamic acid and succinic acid, at once salty and bitter, last long on the palate and give an attractive character to a blend of flavors. It seems that foods with the most flavor, those that are the most savory, make one salivate more.

There is a lack of scientific data on the role of saliva in tasting, but we know that it is important. In fact, saliva may chemically modify wine that is kept in the mouth for a long time. Saliva's pH is close to neutral and the presence of bicarbonates in saliva give it a "buffer potential" on the acidic substances that we consume. Saliva tends to diminish acid tastes in two ways, by dilution and by partial neutralization. Thus the nature of one's saliva and the amount secreted may influence the tasting of acid wines according to the relative proportions of wine and saliva and also according to a coefficient peculiar to the taster. This might perhaps explain people's varying sensitivity to acidity. During the course of any one tasting, taste and smell or, more precisely, aftertastes, the elements of aromatic persistence, may undergo some form of enzymatic transformation, but this is not certain. I have already mentioned the example of Sauvignon Blanc where the aromatic aftertaste appears after several dozen seconds.

The lubricating, viscous element of saliva, mucin, is coagulated by the tannin constituents in wine, and the rough-textured sensation which results is due in part to the tongue's contact with the lips and the rest of the mouth's surface without the protection of mucin. The way in which the properties of saliva are modified will be considered again under the definition of astringency.

Independently of salivation, other digestive secretions are certainly triggered during tasting. As soon as wine comes into contact with the mouth, gastric secretion starts, taste messages act on the stomach's motor nerves, and eventually the taster experiences hunger pangs. The professional taster is said to need a strong stomach. There are probably other reflex reactions which are also set in motion, pancreatic, for example; the diuretic effect of tasting is well known. I have seen it stated that the stomach's reactions are based on hunger and thirst, but in reality it is changes in blood composition which are the determining factors. However, hunger and thirst do stimulate the sensations of taste and smell, and the sight and smell of food do make one hungry.

ON THE PRIMARY TASTES

Brillat-Savarin wrote: "The number of flavors is infinite, for every soluble body has a special taste which is not quite the same as any other." It has taken a long time to sort out the complexity underlying this concept. Man has always sought to analyze his sensations in order to share them, so inventing a vocabulary with which to describe them. Aristotle had already contrasted sweetness and unctuosity to saltiness and intermediary tastes such as sour, harsh, astringent, acid. In 1751 the botanist Linnaeus distinguished ten taste qualities: moist, dry, acid, bitter, rich, astringent, sweet, sour, slimy, salty. In 1824 Chevreul made the distinction between tastes as such and tactile sensations. However, it was Fick in 1864 and then Cohn in 1914 who defined "the four primary tastes" as the standard basis for our description of flavor. This seemed to be a coherent theory and for a long time it was accepted that there were only four fundamental tastes: **sweet, acid, salty,** and **bitter.** All tastes, whether pure or mixed, were classified into these four categories. According to this theory, a given substance could, on its own, either have only a single taste or be a combination of several of the primary tastes. The oversimple and therefore inexact nature of this analysis was confirmed by Henning and it has since been the subject of further research by neurophysiologists. What then is our current understanding of the matter?

The four basic tastes and their benchmark products (sucrose, sodium chloride, tartaric or citric acid, and quinine) represent a sensory reality which is beyond question. The ability to perceive them even seems to be a prenatal acquisition, derived from the amniotic fluid. The Japanese have proposed a fifth primary flavor, *umami*, represented by sodium glutamate. This is present in Asian food (soy sauce is the obvious example) to a much greater extent than in Western diets. The existence of only four primary tastes is a notion that has been largely maintained by and based on Western culture and research, always using the same reference products.

Nerve fiber reactions to the four basic stimuli have indicated an apparent specialization of the taste buds. However, more thorough research over the past fifteen years has shown this specialization to be illusory, and that the nerve fibers react to a number of chemical stimuli, but to a varying degree. This "selective polyvalence" induces a "discharge profile" from the nerve, and each taste stimulus is subject to a very rich "activation image," much more efficient for the recognition of taste than the very simple analysis of an all-or-nothing response to four possibilities.

The current approach is less simple than the traditional one, but the two are not incompatible. Recent research improves on the traditional view with a much more comprehensive notion of a taste continuum. This is akin to the way we perceive color across a rainbow continuum of different wavelengths: There are no apparent breaks, yet we can still distinguish the primary colors (red, yellow . . .) alongside the secondary colors (orange. . .). Taste perception clearly distinguishes sweet and salty at the same time as perceiving "intermediate" tastes depending on the substances present and their concentration: Highly sweetened sodium saccharinate, for example, starts to taste bitter as well.

A more complex mechanism such as this would seem to be a possible approach to the well-known, but hitherto poorly explained, phenomena of synergy and antagonism in taste. On this basis, the fundamental balance equation for wine—sweetness $\leftrightarrows$ acidity + bitterness—would proceed from a superimposition of various "taste images" of differing intensity, leading to an overall sensation of balance or imbalance.

The existence of this partially selective specialization of the taste buds has been confirmed by both sensory and electrophysiological studies. Electrophysiology (Yamamoto and Kawamura, 1971) shows the characteristic "profiles" of the four primary tastes, more or less clearly according to concentration. Other substances with complex flavors do not tie in with these basic profiles. The systematic study (Faurion, 1981) of sensitivity to the sweetness of different substances (sucrose, saccharine, aspartame, dehydrocalcone) showed no correlation whatsoever between different individuals. One person could be sensitive to one sugar molecule and insensitive to another. The sweetening power of "sweeteners" is a statistical reality, but with pronounced differences between individuals. The inescapable conclusion is that there is no such thing as an absolutely specific characteristic for sweetness which can be perceived as such. It cannot be said there is a *unique* sweet taste, perceived by *one* category of receptors; instead, there is a "sweet profile" produced by one or more particular molecule(s)-receptor(s) combinations. The same is true for other tastes.

When you taste a liquid containing the four primary tastes in solution, the different tastes are not perceived at the same time. The reaction period differs according to the tastes. In addition, tastes evolve on the palate at different rates. The sweet taste of a crystallized-sugar solution at 10 g/l, for example, is perceptible from the moment it contacts the tongue. The intensity of sweetness reaches its maximum after about two seconds and then diminishes progressively to disappear after ten seconds or so. Salty and acid tastes are also rapidly perceived, but they persist longer. As for bitterness, it is slow to develop but its intensity increases and it lingers on the palate long after spitting out.

These facts are important to know because they explain the succession of tastes experienced during the course of tasting a wine; the final impressions are quite different from the first. The winetaster needs to note this temporal evolution carefully. The initial tastes may be sweet and pleasant, but gradually give way to a hard acidity or an excessive bitterness.

Differences in speed of perception are also partly due to the fact that the different tastes are not perceived by the same parts of the tongue. A large part of the tongue's surface is insensitive. If you carefully place a drop of flavored liquid on the insensitive part of the tongue, you will taste nothing, until, thanks to the tongue's movements and the diffusion of the liquid into one's saliva, the flavor substance comes into contact with an area of the tongue that does have taste buds. Sweetness is felt only at the tip of the tongue; it is enough just to touch the surface of a sweet liquid with the tongue's tip to perceive this. Acidity is perceived on the sides of and just underneath the tongue; saltiness is felt by the edges and not the central surface. Bitter tastes are detectable solely at the back of the tongue by the circumvallate papillae which are only encountered when one swallows.

It should also be noted that in the mouth tastes proper are perceived principally by the tongue. However, sometimes one has the impression that one's lips or the back of one's throat react to an intense sweetness or bitterness. In fact, taste is only perceived on the lips when the tongue passes over them, and it may be that at the moment of swallowing the abundant nerve endings of the pharynx localize sensations there that are actually felt by the tongue.

The four primary tastes are found in wine and they are dealt with in the sections which follow. The balance between the principal two, sweetness and acidity, determines the harmony of a wine's constitution.

The sweet taste in medium-dry and sweet wines is due to sugars, alcohol, and glycerol. The taste of acidity is due to the numerous acids in wine. The concentration of mineral salts in wine is not insignificant, and in a simple solution of similar concentration there is a distinct salty taste; in wine, however, it is masked by other flavors. However, mineral salts certainly highlight flavors and give freshness to the wine. On the other hand, a touch of bitterness, accompanied by a discreet astringency, is necessary in good red wines. Excessive bitterness in wines is the result either of accident or bacterial disease.

Evolution of tastes during the course of tasting

	Attack ⟶	*Evolution* ⟶	*Final impression*
Duration in seconds	2–3	5–12	5–125 and beyond
	Dominance of sweet tastes	Progressive diminution of sweet tastes and augmentation of acid then bitter tastes	Dominance of acid and, above all, bitter tastes

The preceding table shows the typical progression of flavors during the course of tasting a red wine, with the initial sweet and pleasant tastes being superseded by more or less acerbic flavors, dominated by acidity and bitterness. The initial mouth-filling impression from the moment the wine contacts the palate is called the **attack**. In it vinosity, sweet, quasi-sweet, and rich impressions predominate. Next the winetaster concentrates on what is called the **evolution**, the progressive modification of the initial flavors. In young, supple, easy-to-drink wines and in fine wines which have acquired the mellowness of age, the initial agreeable impression is prolonged. Such wines are said to be long, to hold up on the palate without unevenness, to develop well. However, quite often the initial sweetness diminishes, yielding to an increased acidity, a change which lessens the wine's appeal. If this sort of evolution is rapid the wines are said to be short, to develop briefly or poorly. Lastly, the bitter and astringent flavors of red wine appear and develop in conjunction with the acidity in the final seconds of tasting. When these characteristics are hard they dominate the **final impression** or **finish**. The analysis of a wine's evolution on the palate is a good guide to its flavor make-up and also to its overall tasting qualities.

Methods for Testing Taste Sensitivity

Our sensitivity to the four primary tastes appears to vary greatly. We all react differently. If the total loss of taste is rare, diminished taste sensitivity is less so. I have come across people who do not find a solution of 20 grams per liter of crystallized sugar sweet, and who habitually consider medium-sweet wine as dry.

To demonstrate the primary tastes in pure form, it is most practical to use simple solutions of saccharose, tartaric or citric acid, sodium chloride, and quinine sulfate or caffeine. And to individuals' thresholds of perceptive for the primary tastes, the following procedure may be adopted.

For each test, samples of water and dilute sapid solutions are presented separately and successively in an order of increasing concentration. Several identical samples may be included, all, of course, without the knowledge of the subjects. Each person should taste a quantity of about 15 ml of solution and then immediately record the absence of sensation or the sensation produced on the form provided. A minute should be left between the tasting of any two solutions.

For a long time I have used a procedure based on the triangular comparative test (pp. 160–161) which leaves little room for chance correct answers. In these tests three glasses are presented for each concentration, being either two glasses of water and one of the solution to be recognized or the reverse, and in any order, unknown to the tasters. The detailed procedure is shown on page 270. The following table records the average results for a large number of similar tests carried out over several years. The people tested were professional tasters or trainee tasters and thus represent a good cross section.

In order to be meaningful these tests need to be carefully and systematically organized. Performances are better if tasting begins with the lowest concentrations. Sensitivity to a given taste also varies considerably in the triangular test according to whether people are given one or two glasses of water among the three; it is always greater in the latter case.

Sensitivity of a group of people to the different primary tastes

(The threshold is the minimum concentration correctly perceived; distribution is according to sensitivity by percentage)

Sweetness Sucrose g/l		Acidity Tartaric acid g/l		Saltiness Sodium chloride g/l		Bitterness Quinine sulfate mg/l	
For 820 people		For 495 people		For 100 people		For 374 people	
Threshold	%	Threshold	%	Threshold	%	Threshold	%
4	4.5	0.2	11.8	1.00	6	2	23.8
4	12.3	0.2	38.8	0.50	33	2	27.4
2	34.6	0.1	21.2	0.25	40	1	24.5
1	30.6	0.05	28.2	0.10	21	0.5	24.3
0.5	18.0						

In extreme cases differences of the order of ten have been found between individuals' sensitivity to sweetness and acidity: There are some tasters who can detect 0.5 g/l of sucrose or 50 milligrams of tartaric acid, while others are insensitive to 5 g/l of sucrose or 0.5 g/l of tartaric acid. Differences of an order of double the concentration are normal among professional tasters. Results for sensitivity to salt are a bit more consistent, while the ability to taste bitterness is the most variable of all.

Tasting practice improves perception and the most experienced tasters are generally best at perceiving the lowest concentrations. A good taster should not have an obvious weakness with respect to any particular taste. It would be equally instructive to determine each taster's sensitivity to tastes in combination, just as important a concept as sensitivity to tastes in isolation.

The identification of taste thresholds might also explain certain eating and drinking habits. Those insensitive to bitterness (and who are not on a diet) drink their coffee without sugar, while those who cannot taste sweetness easily drink it with three lumps of sugar. Some people do not like lemon juice, vinegary dishes, acid wines; others, on the other hand, go out of their way to find them, depending on their sensitivity to acidity. And we use more or less salt on food according to our capacity to taste it.

Classically, there are three different thresholds distinguished for each sensation: those of perception, identification, and differentiation. While the study of these thresholds applied to a group of people means individuals can be divided into more or less able categories, it is clearly impossible to judge overall ability to taste just by taking account of sensitivity to all the constituents of wine. Tasting is more than the simple capacity to perceive; it includes, among others, the acquired skills of synthesis, memory, expression. . .

The **threshold of perception**, or threshold of detection, is expressed as the concentration at which one "starts to notice something"; indefinable, but which enables one to distinguish one solution from another "neutral" solution. For example "a little" salt in pure water.

The threshold is generally expressed as the concentration at which 50% of a relatively large group of people (20–30 or more) give a positive response. This threshold varies considerably according to the base solution (water, water + alcohol, wine. . .) and the general conditions such as temperature, lighting and so on. But with standardized conditions the established threshold can be compared to other constants of the substance under consideration such as its density, melting point etc.

The **threshold of identification** is the concentration at which one can say "that tastes sweet, salty. . ."

The **threshold of differentiation** (differential threshold) is the variation in concentration at which one can say "this solution is more concentrated than that one." Expressed as a percentage, it varies enormously according to the initial concentration, but it is generally a minimal percentage for "average" concentrations.

The notion of a threshold of saturation is sometimes used, and implies a concentration above which one can no longer perceive any differences in intensity. However, one can sometimes notice differences in the character of the taste, painful sensations, for example, such as the bite of acidity or alcoholic burn. Occasionally, this threshold is more than 100 times that of the threshold of perception.

The study of taste thresholds provides various information that is of practical use. The average thresholds for numerous substances are well known. They reveal marked individual differences for different tastes, notably for bitterness. A study of a group of 243 English students (Kalmus, 1971) showed that 30 percent were insensitive to the bitterness of phenyl-thio-carbamide at concentrations of 64 to 2028 times that of the other 70 percent of the group. This particularity is genetic. There are many others, recognized or not, less obvious and which can be changed by training. This is probably a typical case where one might describe a subject as "gifted" or otherwise. The talent is real but relative, and it can almost always be compensated for by training and practice. The percentage of people who have no sense of taste (*agustics*) is of the same order as those who are blind: too many, yet very small. It is interesting to note that the word blind is much better known than either *agustia* (inability to taste) or *anosmia* (inability to smell); because in our culture sight is much more important than either taste or smell.

Perception thresholds are very sensitive to the phenomenon of adaptation by tasting, to contrasting tastes, and, happily, to the learning process. Repeated tasting of sweet substances accustoms one to the taste so that one becomes less sensitive to it and the palate requires increasing concentrations to perceive it. Similarly, the threshold of detection for salt, for example, is reduced a hundred times if the mouth is rinsed immediately beforehand with distilled water, so eliminating the natural salinity of one's saliva.

Individual sensitivity may be genetic or cultural; the latter includes prenatal influence, and whether we prefer our food "soft and sweet" (e.g., the United States) or piquant and spicy (Africa, the Caribbean. . .) or it may also be physiological. The perception of acidity, for example, varies according to the buffer potential of our saliva, that in itself varying largely according to one's state of health, whether any medicine is being taken, and so on.

As for quantitative tasting, what is the relationship between the intensity of taste perceived and the concentration of the sapid substance? This question has occupied physiologists for a very long time. The first formulation (Fechner, 1860) held that the sensation (S) is proportional to the logarithm of excitation (= stimulus 1):

$$S = k \log 1 + b$$

If to move from a sensation of intensity 1 to intensity 2 requires the stimulus to be multiplied by X, then a further multiplication by X is required to increase the sensation intensity from 2 to 3. A century later, in 1957, Stevens extended this research by establishing the proportionality between the logarithm of the sensation and that of the stimulus:

$$S = k1^n \quad \text{or} \quad \log S = n \log 1 + k$$

THE SAPID SUBSTANCES IN WINE

Considered from a chemical point of view, wine is an aqueous ethanol solution containing 20 to 30 grams of substances in solution, which constitute the extract and give it flavor, and several hundred milligrams of volatile substances, which constitute its odor.

The substances which make a wine taste sweet are also the source of suppleness, weight and richness, and a soft, mellow character. Sweetness is not, however, solely the property of substances commonly called sugars: Saccharin, for example, five hundred times sweeter than ordinary sugar, cyclamates, dutane, and even chloro-

Sweet-tasting substances in wine

			Concentrations in grams per liter
Sugars from the grape	Glucose	Dry wines	0.2 to 0.8
		Sweet wines	up to 30
	Fructose	Dry wines	1 to 2
		Sweet wines	up to 60
	Arabinose		0.3 to 1
	Xylose		0.05
Alcohols from fermentation	Ethyl alcohol		72 to 120
	Glycerol		5 to 15
	Butylene glycol		0.3 to 1.5
	Inositol		0.2 to 0.7
	Sorbitol		0.1

form all have molecules which bear no chemical relationship at all to those of sugars. The sweet substances in wine belong to two groups: the sugars properly so-called from the grape, which remain, partly unfermented, in sweet white wines but which are also present in small quantities in dry white and red wines; and substances which have one or more alcoholic functions, formed during the course of alcoholic fermentation.

It is easy to demonstrate that alcohol has a sweet taste. Prepare two solutions of pure, neutral ethyl alcohol, one at 4 percent (4° or 32 g/l) and one at 10 percent (10° or 80 g/l). At 4° alcohol has a vaguely sweet, lightly sugary taste, clearly apparent by comparison with water, but without the particular taste of alcohol being recognizable as such. The taste is different from the sweet taste of sugar while belonging to the same family of tastes. At 10° of alcohol there is a strong sweet taste along with a warm, slightly burning sensation. This solution clearly shows the complex taste of alcohol, affecting both taste buds and the mucous membranes at the same time.

If solutions of 20 g/l of sugar are prepared with different degrees of alcohol, 0°, 4°, and 10°, for example, alcohol will be found to reinforce the sweet taste of sugar quite clearly. This tasting is even more convincing than the preceding one because the differences in sweetness are considerable. On the other hand, at this concentration, sugar does not lessen the warm impression of alcohol.

The acid taste of wine is due to a whole series of organic acids. These are found in two states in wine: The greater part is in a free state and constitutes the total acidity; it is this part which tastes acidic. The other part is in salt form, combined with bases in the wine. The mineral anions of wine are in a salt state and do not directly influence acidity.

Wine is known to contain 6 principal organic acids which play a part in the acid taste. Three come from the grape and have a pure acid taste; these are tartaric, malic, and citric acid. Tartaric acid is hard, malic acid green, and citric acid fresh in taste. The three others—succinic, lactic, and acetic acid—are formed by alcoholic fermentation and bacterial activity. Their taste is more complex. Lactic acid has a lightly acid taste, rather tart and sour; acetic acid has a vinegary taste; succinic acid has an intense taste, bitter and salty at once, which also makes one salivate. It is the acid in wine which has the most taste; it gives fermented drinks the "winy" savor they have in common. In wine, succinic acid gives sapidity, vinosity, and sometimes bitterness. In this connection it is worth remembering the common chemical origin of succinic acid, a sapid substance in fermented drinks, and of glutamic acid, a substance with a meaty flavor, used in cooking in the form of monosodium glutamate.

Acid-tasting substances in wine

		Grams per liter
Originating in the grapes	Tartaric acid	2 to 5
	Malic acid	0 to 5
	Citric acid	0 to 0.5
	Gluconic acid	Up to 2.0 in wines made from rotten grapes
Originating in fermentation	Succinic acid	0.5 to 1.5
	Lactic acid	1 to 3
	Acetic acid	0.5 to 1

Other acids which are present in very small quantities are galacturonic, glucuronic, citramalic, pyruvic, ketoglutaric, etc.

To gain a more profound understanding of the role of acids in wine, specialist tasters have tried to clarify whether the acid taste is due to hydrogen ions (H^+), as is sometimes claimed, or whether it is due to anions or even to undissociated molecules. The answer is not simple and the following discussion is addressed to the reader who has some understanding of physical chemistry.

If one tastes $N/50$ solutions of the principal acids in wine after they have been neutralized with a base to a pH of 7, sulfuric and acetic acid are found no longer to have any taste at all, while succinic acid keeps its pronounced bitter aftertaste and the other organic acids have just a light taste. Thus the taste of acetic acid is due to undissociated acid molecules, whereas the taste of succinic acid is due to the succinate anion; the sulfate anion has no taste, at least not at this concentration, and the other organic anions have but a feeble taste.

Other very simple observations have established that the undissociated organic acid molecules have an acid taste by themselves. An $N/1000$ (0.1 percent) solution of hydrochloric acid, entirely dissociated and having a pH of 3, seems barely acid on to the palate. On the other hand, a tartaric or acetic acid solution with the same concentration of hydrogen ions but obviously a higher solution concentration ($N/10$, 10 percent, for example), has a clearly acid taste. This taste strengthens if one increases the concentration of undissociated tartaric or acetic molecules. However, hydrogen ions (H^+) do play a part in a wine's acid taste and, at an equal concentration, solutions of tartaric or acetic acid taste more acid to the palate the lower their pH.

In fact, interpreting these observations is not as easy as it might seem because the buffer power of solutions must also be taken into account. Indeed, as we have already seen, the saliva which constantly bathes the mucous membranes and taste buds is an almost neutral buffer milieu. We know that the taste of a nonbuffered, dilute solution of hydrochloric acid is modified by dilution in saliva much more than the taste of heavily buffered solutions of tartaric or acetic acid with a pH of 3.

The conclusion of such studies on acidity is that the agents responsible for acid sensations are not purely chemical, and do not depend solely on molecular structure and the phenomena of dissociation. In experiments to compare the tastes of the principal wine acids, firstly in equal quantities and secondly at the same pH, the following results were obtained. In the first case, at an equal titrated acidity, the order of acid strength on the palate was as follows: malic was stronger than (>) tartaric > citric > lactic. In the second case, at an equivalent pH, malic > lactic > citric > tartaric. So malic acid would seem to taste the most "acid" of the acids in wine.

It has been proved that as far as the acid character of a wine is concerned, total acidity is more significant than pH. Wines which have either a particularly low or, alternatively, a particularly high pH in relation to their total acidity have generally been found to taste, in terms of richness, in accordance with their total acidity rather than their pH. The same result obtains whether the wine is red or white. Besides, experiments show that while adding water diminishes the acid taste it does not affect the pH.

Wine contains 2 to 4 g/l of substances with a salty taste. These are the salts of mineral acids and some organic acids. They are represented, approximately, by wine ash obtained by burning off its extract. They are part of a wine's savor, giving it freshness. Potassium bitartrate, for example, has a taste that is both salty and acid. However, the addition of chloride or sulfate salts generally decreases the wine's appeal. The old practice of adding salts, now forbidden, has little technical justification. Potassium salts also have a certain bitterness.

Constituents of the principal salty substances in wine
(Concentrations in grams per liter)

Anions		Cations	
Sulfate	<1	Potassium	0.5–1.5
Chloride	0.02–0.2	Sodium	0.02–0.05
Sulfite	0.1–0.4	Magnesium	0.05–0.15
Neutral tartrate		Calcium	0.05–0.15
Acid tartrate		Iron	5–20 (mg/l)
Neutral malate		Aluminum	10–20 (mg/l)
Acid malate			
Neutral succinate			
Acid succinate			
Lactate			

Mention should also be made of other minerals present in wine and referred to as trace elements: fluoride, silicon, bromide, boron, zinc manganese, copper, lead, cobalt, chrome, nickel, etc.

Bitter substances belong to the group of phenol compounds or polyphenols, formerly known as tannic substances or wine tannins. Their bitterness is generally accompanied by astringency and it is sometimes difficult to distinguish the two sensations. Bitterness is easier to perceive in a less acid milieu. These substances play an important role because they are responsible for a wine's color and a large part of its flavor. As they evolve during the course of aging, they also account for the transformation of wine during its maturation. The taste of red wines and, more specifically, the difference in taste between red and white, is due to these phenolic substances. Additionally, they possess the property of coagulating proteins, and play a part in clarification of wine by fining. Finally, some phenolic substances affect the nutritional quality of red wine particularly because they are bactericidal and contain P vitamins (which regulate the permeability of the blood capillaries).

The phenol compounds belong to several chemical groups not all of which taste bitter. Anthocyanins, the red pigments which are present in some 200 to 500 mg/l in young wines, do not seem to have any particular taste, at least while they are in a free state and not condensed with tannins.

Bitterness comes from certain phenol acids, but above all from the condensed tannins in the pips and skins of the grape, and found in equal abundance in the stalks. There are 1 to 3 g/l of tannins in red wines, several dozen milligrams per liter in whites. Their bitterness and astringency are linked to their degree of polymerization (condensation resulting from the association of numerous molecules). Another source of tannins, foreign to the grape though, lies in the addition of commercial tannin, or comes from the wood used for barrels. These tannins have a pronounced bitterness and pharmaceutical astringency. If, to follow Max Léglise's example, you dissolve a pinch of tannin in a glass of lightly acid water you will obtain an astringent sensation, one of roughness. The same amount dissolved in a glass of Vichy water or carbonated water will produce mainly bitterness.

Finally, there are many other constituents in wine which are said to be neutral and tasteless: nitrogenous substances, polysaccharides, pectins, gums, mucilages, etc. The colloidal phase in wines may generally be considered not to have any role in their taste. Among the amino acids, however, glutamic acid should be accorded a special mention. Its appetizing flavor is well known, salty and mellow at once. If some 200 mg/l were present in a wine, its effect on the taste would not be negligible. On the other hand, the polysaccharides do not contribute to the suppleness of wine, but if accidentally present in large quantities they may make the wine's texture rather thick.

ASTRINGENCY AND OTHER SENSATIONS

In the table of senses used in winetasting (page 21), we can see that the mouth also reacts to sensations of quite a different kind from those of taste proper which we have just been considering. These sensations are grouped under the term *haptic* (pertaining to touch). The mouth is very sensitive to chemicals, a sensitivity called the common chemical sense, which can perhaps be considered as having a warning function for the mucous lining of the mouth against the attack of certain molecules. Various parts of the mouth are also sensitive to touch and temperature; the two sensations are closely related and, in fact, it is difficult to distinguish precisely between a mucous and a tactile reaction in the mouth. For the taster, however, the distinction is of little use. What matters is not to confuse either of them with tastes proper. Acidity is felt at the back of the throat and is a similar sort of reaction. Certain chemical and thermal reactions, when particularly strong, may actually be painful. Acidity sets the teeth on edge and very acid wines can produce a persistent feeling of inflamed gums. Astringency is a sensation we can all recognize but which few of us can define easily as there are rarely any opportunities to experience it by itself. In natural products it generally mingles with and is intensified by sensations of acidity and bitterness.

Bate-Smith has described astringency very well and has also analyzed its causes. It produces a sensation of dryness and roughness. Instead of the moist, slippery feeling we are always aware of as we move our tongue around the palate, gums, teeth, and lips, we feel instead a resistance to this slipperiness as though the tongue had become raspy and the tissues of the mouth had tightened up. Indeed, the Latin root of astringent means precisely to draw tight. Astringents are defined as substances which provoke contraction, the drawing together of organic tissue. Astringents harden these tissues and prevent them secreting. Certain metal salts (alum and salts of iron, zinc, and copper) have the property of **stypticity**, a synonym for astringency.

The causes of astringency appear to belong to three types of phenomenon. First, there is the coagulation of the mucin in saliva whose glycoproteins are rendered insoluble by astringent substances. The mixture of red wine and saliva precipitates the colored filaments which can be seen in the winetaster's spittoon. Saliva's viscosity is reduced under the influence of astringents and it no longer fulfills its role of lubricating the mouth's surfaces. Second, the sensation of dryness may also be due to the salivary gland canals being constricted so that their saliva secretion is stopped, particularly in the case of the scattered glands which irrigate the mucous membranes. Finally, as a result of an additional reaction, astringents fix themselves to the mucous tissues and these are hardened in consequence by the loss of water and reduction in permeability. While making due allowance, the latter reaction is similar to that of tanning, where collagen, a water-attracting gel, is transformed into leather which is relatively water repellent. Similarly, after a tasting of tannic red wines, the upper surfaces of the tongue, and this part only of the mouth, remain deeply colored as though tanned for several hours in spite of repeated rinsing.

The astringents in vegetables belong to the polyphenol family. A long list of the foods we eat are astringent to some degree; generally, they are eaten cooked as this lessens their astringency. The astringency is primarily in the woody parts, in skins, shells, pips, seeds, hulls, husks, and skin of fruit. Some vegetables such as artichokes, cardoons, and green beans are astringent. Examples of fruits rich in astringent tannins are cider apples, perry pear, certain winter pears and late peach varieties, fruit hulls, Japanese persimmon, medlars, the skins of almonds, chestnuts, and walnuts. However, not all the phenolic components of wine are astringent. Chemical determination of tannin content is an imperfect measure of this sensation, for different wines with the same tannin content produce different degrees of astringency on the palate.

The astringency caused by tannin seems to be a function of molecule size, of the degree of molecular condensation, that is. Phenolic compounds with a low molecular weight have molecules which are too small, too weak in reactive power to be particularly astringent; highly condensed, extensively polymerized tannins have molecules which are too large to adjust to those of proteins. The maximum astringency comes from tannins with an intermediate molecular size, and their astringency is in direct proportion to their potential to coagulate proteins and to be fixed by skin. This is also the reason why fining wine with egg white or gelatin makes wines more supple as it reduces their astringency.

Another reaction which is one of chemical sensitivity is the sensation of causticity, the pseudo-warm, burning sensation produced by certain substances in modest concentration when accidentally brought into contact with the mouth; substances such as acids, bases, metals and metal salts, or solvent products which rapidly dry the mouth's mucus. However, our familiarity with these sensations comes mainly from the consumption of alcoholic drinks. Alcohol has abundant taste. Brillat-Savarin said "Alcohol carries the pleasures of the palate to their highest degree." Low-strength alcohol is simply sweet. Upwards of 10° or 12°, one begins to feel the sensation of warmth called vinosity. At 20° or 25°, the level of aperitifs and certain liqueurs, the fiery taste of alcohol is generally tempered by sugar. Brandies are always consumed in a special way, and spirits are not drunk like other drinks.

The sensation of effervescence is complex. Alongside the acid taste of carbon dioxide, the gas which is released on the mucous surfaces of the mouth is also felt as a tactile sensation, as a prickle from so many tiny pulses. The tongue's tactile sense can perceive 500 mg/l of carbon dioxide in a wine and the tongue is still the best means for a winemaker to detect the start of fermentation in a must.

Poupon draws a distinction between passive touch, that of the palate, cheeks and lips, and active touch, that of the tongue. The tongue is dextrous; it actively explores and thus gains impressions of texture, consistency, fluidity, viscosity, and smoothness during tasting. Also involved are kinesthetic sensations, those perceived as a result of muscle movement and which form part of the texture impression. The sum of tastes and textures produces an image of wine in relief, a sort of geometric profile that has form and volume. This assertion always surprises the nonspecialist, yet the graphic concept of a wine in terms of form and shape is something very real in the mind of an experienced taster.

Finally, the mouth is the site of thermal sensation and constitutes an efficient means of protection for the digestive tract against hot and cold. The sensitivity of the system is very precise, capable of distinguishing temperature variations of close to 1°C. Further on we shall see how temperature affects our sensitivity to different tastes. In the same way that there are pseudo-warm reactions so there are imaginary feelings of coolness. Certain volatile, aromatic products (menthol and eucalyptus, for example) produce an impression of cold when one breathes in without there being any change in the mouth's temperature in reality.

AFTERTASTE, THE PERSISTENCE OF TASTE AND AROMA

In the analysis he made of the sensations of taste, Brillat-Savarin described three stages: the "direct sensation," or the initial impressions on the front of the tongue, which we now call the attack; the "complete sensation," or the sum of taste impressions and perfume at the back of the mouth, which he called aftertaste or fragrance; and the "considered sensation," which is the judgment of all these impressions. Putting the theory into practice, he described tasting (*gutturation* is his expression) thus: "While the wine is in one's mouth one receives a pleasing but imperfect impression; it is only when you have finished swallowing that one can really appreciate the taste and discern the bouquet particular to each type of wine; and then a few more moments are required before the gourmet can say: that's good, passable, or bad. . . .

"Thus it is clearly in accordance with the principles I have described, and also with well-understood practice that the true amateur sips his wine, for as he pauses to reflect after each mouthful, he gets just as much pleasure as he would have experienced had he downed the glass at a single draft."

The experience of tasting, then, does not finish with the act of swallowing or spitting out the wine; there are many sensations which follow. Some wines are described as having "a fine return" when they leave one's mouth filled with their flavor, or as having a fine *fumet*, the aromatic aftertaste defined by Poupon as an after-bouquet. On the same subject Sabatier describes a group of wine-makers from Châteauneuf-du-Pape tasting in a vaulted cellar in Bédarrides: "We compared, defined, and measured the duration of the pleasure lingering on our taste buds."

The following table outlines the sequence of final sensations after swallowing through to their disappearance. It follows on from the table on page 86 which outlines what happens while the wine remains in the mouth. The sensations experienced from the moment one has swallowed or spat out the wine are called the **finish** or **aftertaste**. At this stage the mouth, pharynx, and nasal cavities remain impregnated with the wine just tasted and its vapors; the senses of taste and smell continue to be stimulated. Gradually, as though in successive waves, the sensations diminish until they disappear completely.

Evolution of tastes and aromas in the final phase of tasting

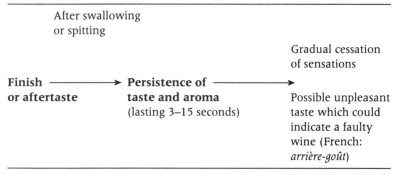

After swallowing or spitting		Gradual cessation of sensations
Finish or aftertaste ⟶	**Persistence of taste and aroma** (lasting 3–15 seconds) ⟶	Possible unpleasant taste which could indicate a faulty wine (French: *arrière-goût*)

This **persistence** of sensation varies in length and has two possible causes: first, the physical presence of a small quantity of increasingly dilute wine and of a small number of volatile, aromatic elements gradually driven out by breathing; and, second, a kind of delayed response, an echo, a memory of sensations now past, as though the senses remained stimulated after the stimulus has disappeared. The second of these explanations might be better termed *remanance*, sometimes used as a synonym for persistence.

The sensations involved in the finish are complex, combining taste, smell, and the common chemical sense. To try to separate the various aspects of these three factors is a difficult and perhaps futile exercise. To begin with, one should try to assess the quantity, strength, and duration of these impressions, and also their quality, that is to say, their appeal, for the finish is not always pleasant.

The French terms *arrière-goût* or *déboire* both describe an after-taste with a disagreeable aspect, generally defective in character and differing from the preceding impressions. To give two examples: the raw, styptic taste of copper salts, perceptible above a level of 4 to 5 mg/l, and the "mousy" taste (mouse urine to be more precise), a rare defect about which the only thing known is that yeast or bacteria are its cause. The sensations of the aftertaste are particularly important for defining a wine's class and quality. If harmony and balance are the hallmarks of good wine, what distinguishes great wine is the length and aromatic character of its aftertaste. In effect, a wine is judged by its "length on the palate." A good white wine leaves the mouth fragrant and gently stimulated by fresh acidity; a good red wine fills the mouth with its bouquet and the rich, sapid character of its tannin. Sometimes, however, an attractive flavor is more impor-tant than length as such. There are aromatic white wines fleeting in flavor and with little aftertaste, but which have much to offer in spite of their brevity.

The persistence of tastes proper is based on the sensations of acidity, bitterness, and astringency. In the case of white wines it is principally acidity which will dominate the aftertaste, so that the final impression will be either fresh and balanced or hard and green.

In the case of red wines it is principally the varied and complex flavors of tannin which determine their length. However, until more is known about them the taste of different tannins can only be dis-tinguished in a very subjective manner, according to their state of polymerization and how they affect other flavors.

Noble tannin, flavorsome and developed, comes from ripe fruit, good grape varieties, and fine, old bottles; **bitter** tannin is found in certain ordinary varieties or sometimes in wines with very low acid-ity; sharp, **acid** tannin is that of thin, aggressive wines; rough, **harsh** tannin, with a marked astringency, is found in young wines and press wine; **wood** or oak tannin comes from barrels made of good-quality oak; and **vegetal** tannin is the product of unripe grapes or wine regions with undistinguished soil.

A wine's aromatic persistence is very likely due to the least volatile and most durable of its constituents, but we would need a better understanding of the odorous substances in wine to be able to classify them, as perfumers do, into main fragrance themes and fleeting impressions. There are many similarities between the qualities that a perfumer demands from a good perfume and those expected from the bouquet of a fine wine: clarity, volume or intensity, vigor, diffusive power, finesse, individuality, personality, and lasting qualities.

Tasters consider the aromatic element of a wine's finish to be particularly important. The problem lies in how to isolate this aspect from the other sensations. Vedel gives the following definition of what he calls **intense aromatic persistence**: "When considering the sum total of sensations which constitute a wine's aftertaste, careful observation of olfactory sensations shows that after a period when the intensity is roughly uniform, it falls off sharply. The initial period has been called the intense aromatic persistence and its length can be measured by the taster in seconds. The French term *caudalie* is the standard unit of measure, corresponding to one second's persistence."

Some writers propose using this measure for the classification of very different types of wine, envisaging five classes corresponding to the following *caudalie* groups: up to 3 caudalies, 4–6, 7–9, 10–12, 12 and beyond. This method has the advantage of demanding a careful analysis when tasting, but it can be criticized for being too rigid and for implying a precision which does not exist. Besides, taste length and aromatic length are frequently confused. In much the same vein Léglise advises: "Concentrate on the persistence of flavors and the allied change in one's salivation. Record the number of seconds at which the sensation diminishes and salivation returns to normal." In reality, the sensations do not stop suddenly, but diminish almost imperceptibly following the rhythm of one's breathing.

My advice is to describe all the sensations of the finish in as much detail as possible: the intensity of flavors and aromas; refinement, appeal, and, of course, the length, or its absence, of all these impressions. In my opinion, the time when the taster will use metronome and stopwatch as standard equipment is still a long way off.

S i x

Tasting Problems and Errors of Perception

Tasting Is a Difficult Art

The winetaster encounters difficulties at every stage of tasting, above all when learning to taste. The first of these is the problem of considering taste sensations at a given moment, in particular conditions, and of being able to focus one's attention at will on a specific characteristic. There is also the problem of freeing oneself from the influence of external factors and the various forms of suggesion which might alter one's perceptions. No less significant are the difficulties encountered when trying to describe sensations which are always difficult to put into words. The requisite effort of memory is also demanding, as are interpreting and evaluating the sensations one perceives. And these in turn presuppose a quick, accessible memory for wines and a wide tasting experience to provide the necessary comparative yardsticks.

The primary difficulty arises from the subjective nature of winetasting, for it is based on personal impressions where the key factor is the taster's own personality. Unlike winetasting, an objective phenomenon lends itself to measurements which can be expressed in figures; it exists independently of the observer. When weighing or measuring, for example, the result is always the same, whoever is doing it and whatever the time, technique, or equipment. It is not possible, however, to measure a taste or a smell, and attempts to do so have not met with much success.

We have already seen how arbitrary measuring individual primary tastes can be, how much more so, then, when measuring a combination of flavors. And sweetness, acidity, saltiness, and bitterness counteract and modify each other; they are not simply cumulative. Numerous olfactometers have also been tried, but none of them can dispense with the human nose. In one method, a given concentration of an odorous substance is placed at one end of a long tube, and at the other end the nose notes when the smell is first detected, measurement is made of the time it takes to become deodorized. Here again, the length of time for which the air retains aromatic elements is a measure of volatility rather than intensity. In another method, a measured amount of an odorous substance is released into a room with a controlled, odorless atmosphere; the apparatus serves to determine precisely the olfactory thresholds of the substance being tested per liter of air, but it is useless for measuring the odor intensity of a complex solution. In other experiments, air impregnated with wine odors is passed through a column of substances such as charcoal, silica, and alumina, and a measurement is made of the time it takes to become deodorized. Here again, the length of time for which the air retains aromatic elements is a measure of their nature and concentration, not necessarily of their odor intensity.

It is only possible to define the intensity of a taste or an odor by comparing it to an equivalent or alternative stimulus, an exercise which only makes any sense when the taste or smell involved is the same. And while we can state with certainty that one is stronger than the other, it is impossible to say by how much.

In other words, there is no simple proportional relationship between the concentration of any sapid or odorous substance and the sensation it provokes. It has been found that the relationship between the variation in concentration of stimulus required to produce a perceptible change in sensation and the total concentration is a constant. Put more plainly, this means that there is a perceptible change when a given amount of stimulus is added to a small initial quantity, but when the same amount is added to a large initial quantity the difference is no longer perceptible. Sensations are proportional to the logarithms of the concentrations of the stimuli. Without being an absolutely precise description, what this law expresses is that sensations increase in an arithmetic progression as the substance concentration increases in a geometric progression, which is also why they are difficult to evaluate. To double the intensity of a sensation requires four times the dose.

Tasting results depend on the overall competence of the professional taster; on his tasting ability, vocabulary, and the exact meaning he attributes to individual words, as well as on the importance he attaches to various qualities and faults. From the outset of this book I have been at pains to emphasize the importance of the taster's personality, for the value of any tasting judgment will depend on the quality of the taster. Every time he takes a glass in hand, the taster calls on all his expertise and professional experience. As the training of tasters varies, one can appreciate why judgments can vary, especially where borderline or unusual wines are concerned.

If one compares the notes and marks given to a series of wines by a group of tasters, one generally finds there is broad agreement for, say, eight out of ten wines. The two on which opinions differ are often enough either very fine wines or those that are technically faulty in some way. Some tasters disagree categorically and no amount of discussion will alter their opinion. Such disagreements used to irritate me until I realized that the aim of group tasting was precisely to highlight such differences in opinion. Tasters generally disagree less about what they perceive than how they interpret these perceptions, for each individual will have a personal image of the quality norms for a particular type of wine, and will consider this or that fault as more or less serious depending on his or her training. If winetasters were unanimous in their judgments, then tasting as a group would be pointless; one opinion would suffice. By appealing to several people one gains a wide range of views, a sort of protective umbrella against error.

SOME TASTING PITFALLS

Tasting and tasters are not infallible, and it must be said that the opinion of the same taster can vary with the conditions in which he is working.

When a taster has become accustomed to certain conditions, a regular tasting room, a particular shape of glass or *tastevin*, for example, then he may well be put off in different circumstances. For this reason tasting conditions should be as systematically organized as possible. In later chapters we will be looking at the numerous external factors which influence one's perceptions. Professional tasters try to avoid such errors by always tasting in the same environment, and by a consistent use of the same terms of reference for their comparisons.

The worst type of tasting takes place when visiting wine cellars, where the proprietor or cellarmaster wants to show his wine. Poupon and many others share this view: "There is such an abundance of vinous odors in a cellar and such an optimistic atmosphere that you find yourself in an olfactory context where impressions are easily distorted. In spite of habit, and whatever one thinks, the cellar is the place where one tastes least well."

The cellarmaster fills your glass from a vat, using a spigot or a pipette. He wipes the foot of the glass with his thumb and passes it to you. Even assuming the wine has been cleanly and correctly drawn, your tasting is very likely to be valueless. In the vinous atmosphere of the cellar it is impossible to judge the wine's own nose; all wines appear good because one cannot perceive their defects, and because there are no independent points of reference. It comes as a surprise when retasting the wine in a tasting room the following morning, to find oneself judging it much more severely.

Our daily physiological rhythm has a considerable influence on the sensitivity of our senses, and one should not be surprised if notes on the same wine vary, expecially if they have been made at different times before, during, or after a meal, for example. One's appetite for wine varies according to the time of day, as does the sharpness of one's senses, which are at their keenest on an empty stomach. Thus the best time for tasting is at the end of the morning, before lunch, between say 11 A.M. and 1 P.M. Tastings very early in the morning are an unattractive proposition, but those which take place in the early afternoon, coinciding with digestion, are the most arduous and least effective of all. If need be, another possible time is around 6 P.M., even though one's tasting performance will not be so good.

When interpreting what one tastes there are other factors which need to be taken into account: palate fatigue and the phenomena of saturation with and habituation to certain characteristics, or what the specialists call the effects of convergence, when one's response to differences in stimulation is diminished. And the nature of the sensations themselves may change. The sense of smell especially is rapidly dulled; it cannot continue to perceive the same odor, even a strong one, for a prolonged period. Indeed, the stronger the odor and the longer one continues to smell it, the longer one's sense of smell will be inhibited. One gets accustomed to the smell of the apartment where one lives, the locality or laboratory where one works, precisely because one can no longer smell it. Similarly, people become so used to the smell of their own perfumes or the lingering smell of tobacco smoke that they no longer notice it themselves; but it can offend the people around them.

A similar mechanism accounts for the way in which the consumer gets used to the taste of a certain wine and then will not accept, or at any rate will be less appreciative of, other wines even if they are a better quality. How many people, having regularly drunk a faulty wine, find they can no longer recognize its defects!

It is sometimes said that certain characteristics change rapidly during the course of tasting and that bouquets fade; but having disappeared they may also return. This is said to be the case with the moldy, vegetal smell called *rambergue* (garden mercury) in Bordeaux. On tasting a wine with this character, the first impression is very unpleasant, but it gradually becomes less obtrusive, and at the third or fourth sip the fault becomes acceptable; finally, by dint of continued tasting, one no longer notices the fault. It is not that the characteristic increases or diminishes, as is said to be the case, but that one is more or less sensitive to it according to the mood of the moment and, above all, because habituation has blunted perception. After a few minutes' rest the same unpleasant smell will be found again in the same glass.

For me the following incident is the best illustration of the temporary inhibition of the sense of smell. A Médoc vineyard owner heard from his clients that his wine had an unpleasant and unacceptable taste, one which he could not detect himself. He asked for my advice as an independent judge. The wine was lodged in barrels in a new cellar which had been treated against woodworm. Immediately upon opening the door, the moldy smell of the product used was suffocating, but after a few minutes in the building it became imperceptible, as though it had disappeared. Tasting the wine on the spot, I found it attractively fruity and showing its class—not a trace of the nasty odor. However, half an hour later, in the car on the way back, I suddenly found I could smell the insecticide again very strongly. In the tasting room the next day, I found the wine overwhelmed by this chemical stink. The wine had acquired the defect in the cellar atmosphere, saturated with the vapors of the insecticide, but one could not notice it in the building itself. This example demonstrates how background smells can influence one's judgment. Inside the cellar my sense of smell, selectively saturated by the odor of the product in the air, had become insensitive to the same smell in the wine while remaining capable of detecting all the other odors. When the inhibitory effect had passed, the incriminating smell became quite clear again and then obliterated the rest.

In a different category, certain unpleasant tastes such as acidity, bitterness, and astringency are said to tire the palate rapidly. During the course of repeated tasting, they reinfore each other so that, when comparing two tannic wines, for example, the impression of hardness becomes more pronounced at each successive taste and the wines appear increasingly harsh. In the case of acid wines they become sharper and sharper. Long tastings can also irritate the mucous membranes and make them unduly sensitive to acidity and astringency.

The passage of alcohol across the mucous membranes of the mouth and nose also results in a certain fatigue during extended tasting; even spitting all the wine out will not avoid this effect. The taster should not wait until he is tired before breaking off.

Finally, the effects of contrast can also alter one's judgment: A dry white tastes more acid after a sweet one; a tannic red seems harder when tasted after a supple red. To avoid these misleading results, the wines should be grouped in a logical order before being tasted. Where professional tastings are concerned in Bordeaux, red wines are generally tasted first, starting with the lightest, followed by dry whites, and finishing with medium-dry and sweet whites in order of increasing sweetness. Rosés can be tasted before the reds or the whites. In regions making predominantly dry white wines, these are usually tasted before red wines.

The aim of this chapter has been to point out some of the many pitfalls which the taster should know how to avoid. What singles out a taster as a professional is precisely the fact that he is well aware of these problems and takes them into account when tasting.

THE WINETASTER IS EASILY INFLUENCED

Suggestion is the insinuated thought, the idea planted in someone's mind. When a winetaster has a tasting problem to solve, he is wide open to suggestion, very susceptible to the impressions of other people. He is easily influenced and easily led astray, at least when the perceptual differences involved are small. He may be pointed in one direction or another quite discreetly, simply by the way a question is framed, by the wording of a label, or by the way samples are presented. Thus he may be put on the right path or deliberately misled.

The taster is subject to autosuggestion as well. When short of information he tends to imagine, extrapolating from the slenderest of details glimpsed and interpreted. Suggestion and autosuggestion can both induce tasting errors and the taster must be able to resist them. He needs to be wary; a taste imagined or anticipated is already half perceived.

Some cases of suggestion have already been mentioned, in particular, the effect that color and appearance have on the perceived tasting qualities of rosé wines, and there are numerous other examples.

Let us look first at the evidence presented by Pasteur, and quoted by Got. He describes a revealing episode which he observed during a series of tastings by a group of expert tasters, where wines which had been subjected to heat treatment were compared with the identical wines which had not.

"The group had just got used to telling the differences, large and small, between the two samples that I gave simultaneously to each member. From then on it was easy to predict that if, without their knowing it, I were to ask them to compare two identical samples, which they still thought were different and in which they had hitherto found differences, their imaginations would lead them to find further real differences.

"So, without having said or done anything which might arouse suspicion, I gave each person two glasses containing the same wine from the same bottle. Each of them, convinced that one glass contained a wine which had been heat treated and the other glass an untreated wine, noticed differences between the two samples."

In the same way, if a taster is asked to compare a filtered wine with the same wine unfiltered, and he already has the preconceived idea that filtering tires and thins a wine, he will indeed find that the clearer wine is leaner and less rich than the other.

What passes through the mind of a taster when, confronted with two glasses of wine to compare, he is asked to describe the differences? He tastes the first glass attentively and methodically, carefully noting its appearance and nose, and then, on the palate, its attack, evolution, finish, and length. Moving on to the second glass, he compares the same sequence of impressions to his memory of those in the first wine. Having been told there is a difference to be found, he will always find one; or, more precisely, he will perceive one, real or imaginary. Suppose the taster has judged the second glass to be more supple and thus more attractive than the first, he does not stop there. He will go back to the first wine and make the same comparison in reverse. If he finds it less supple than the second, his initial conclusion is confirmed and he has good ground for saying that there is a real difference. If, on the other hand, his first impression is not confirmed, or if he judges the wine differently on this occasion, he has to say that he can find no perceptible difference between the two glasses. However he will not say "it's the same wine," rather "there is no appreciable difference." It is difficult for a taster to admit that he can find no difference between two wines and few are capable of such a frank admission.

The following incident which I experienced made me think about the powerful influence of autosuggestion. In a grand restaurant in the Etoile quarter of Paris, we were having oysters, and to go with them we ordered a bottle of 1970 Château Carbonnieux, a classed growth Graves from Léognan. The wine waiter, his official *tastevin* hanging around his neck, questioned our choice: "But that's a Bordeaux, and you don't drink a sweet wine with oysters. . . ." But Carbonnieux is a dry wine. . ." (I knew it was dry, I have analyzed it, it has but a trace of fermentable sugar in it: 1.5 grams). "Gentlemen, everybody knows that all white Bordeaux are sweet." We insisted on our choice of course and enjoyed the vigor and aromatic concentration in this fine wine. Afterwards we suggested to the wine waiter that he might like to try the wine to confirm that it was actually quite dry. He tasted it and declared triumphantly: "Just as I said, it isn't dry, it's sweet!" He had the deep-seated and erroneous conviction that all white Bordeaux are sweet, and thus, in good faith, he found the Carbonnieux to be sweet.

Just for the pleasure of it I will round off the discussion of this subject with an extract from Rabelais. The content is perhaps a bit exaggerated but it is, after all, allegorical and must be one of the clearest ever descriptions of autosuggestion. His point is that where worship of the divine bottle is concerned, even fountain water will taste like wine if the drinker's imagination so wishes.

> Bacbuc said to us: "A long time ago a wise and chivalrous Jewish captain, leading his people through the desert in a state of famine, obtained manna from heaven which their hunger led them to imagine tasted like the meat they used to eat. The same applies here. As you sip this wonderful water you will taste whatever wine you care to call to mind. Now, use your imaginations and drink!" Which we did. Then Panurge exclaimed:
>
> "By Jove, this is Beaune, and better than any I ever drank before."
>
> "Well, I'll be. . . ," cried brother Jean, "this is a fine and lively Graves. . . ."
>
> "To me it's a Minervois," said Pantagruel, "because that's what I thought of before drinking."
>
> "Drink, drink," urged Bacbuc, "once, twice, thrice; and by changing your minds you will taste whichever flavor or liquor you have thought of."

THE DIVERSITY OF WINE TYPES AND HIERARCHIES

Wine is the product of a series of complex interrelationships, between man and nature, between an area and its community, between ecology and society. No two wines are ever identical, wherever they are made, whatever their vintage.

In truth, these drinks are called wine simply because they are all made from grapes, for their tastes may bear little relationship to each other. The influences of different climates, numerous grape varieties, and new vinification methods have all led to the creation of a large number of different types of wine, which offer a whole range of colors, odors, and flavors. There is little in common in terms of taste and aroma between champagne, Banyuls, Médoc, table wine, Anjou Rosé, Sauternes, or Alsace, to name but a few French wines at random. Their qualities cannot all be judged by the same norms, and for each type there is a hierarchy based on different criteria.

One problem for the winetaster, in addition to those mentioned in the previous section, is to know the various wine styles and the quality standards by which to judge them. Wines can only be judged within their category, that is, taking into account their origin, their name or brand, and their price. This assumes that the taster is fully conversant with all classifications, but no one can have studied all the world's wines and there is no such thing as a truly universal taster. Most winetasters specialize in one wine region or a particular category of wine. To encounter expertise which covers several regions is rare, and several countries even rarer. The problem is also compounded when judging the wines from different countries together, for one ought to take into account the particular tastes of their peoples as well as their eating and drinking habits. Outside their own wine regions tasters should make a special effort to judge from a local viewpoint.

Let us take a look at the rules and regulations in order to see the extreme complexity of the French classification system. French wines are subject to the European Community rules which in turn are the basis for the organization of the wine market. These rules divide wine into two categories: **Table Wine** [Vins de Table (VDT), formerly in France vins ordinaires, vins communs, vins de consommation courante] and **Quality Wines Produced in Specific Regions** or **QWPSR**. In France country wines (Vins de Pays or VDP) belong to the first category and Vins délimités de Qualité Supérieure (VDQS) and Appellation d'Origine Controlée (AOC) wines to the second.

Each of the numerous controlled appellations in France has rules codified according to the characteristics of local production: permitted grape varieties, styles of viticulture, maximum yields, methods of vinification and conservation, and so on. There is a complex heirarchy among the appellations themselves which regulates their commercial value. This depends on various more or less subjective elements such as taste quality, aging potential in some cases, or simply reputation and market demand. A taster is helped in judging if he knows the prices being quoted for the various appellations.

The "club" of AC wines brings together the elite of French wine production. The appellations correspond to a sort of pedigree of bouquets, an anthology of vinous nobility, as it were. Initially, it consisted only of wines that had been acknowledged as elite for generations, noble by birth, but recently appellations have proliferated: The AC system is becoming more democratic; new talent is being discovered. The numerical growth and geographical scattering of appellations are making the professional's task difficult and the consumer's comprehension impossible.

Hierarchy between appellations, hierarchy within appellations, everything here is organized in hierarchies. The *crus* of the Haut Médoc, Graves, and St-Emilion are officially classified, as are the *crus* of the Côte de Nuits and the Côte de Beaune. In the first case *cru* is synonymous with a property or château, in the second with a commune or part of a commune.

In Bordeaux the primacy of Châteaux Haut-Brion, Latour, Lafite, and Margaux dates from the end of the seventeenth century. Since then there have been several classifications leading up to the historic 1855 classification into classed growths (five categories), superior bourgeois growths, bourgeois growths, and peasant growths. With the exception of Mouton Rothschild, belatedly elevated to First Growth in 1973, this classification still holds good today, at least broadly speaking. The quality of a growth depends primarily on the vineyard site and on its soil. What is not remarked on often enough is the fact that this classification has withstood a whole series of revolutions, social, technical, and economic. There are no comparable examples for other processed agricultural products. It is not quite correct to say that this classification "was a proud affirmation that the human palate could distinguish sufficient nuances in quality to justify six or seven different price levels"; its heirarchy was above all a reflection of reputation. Quality is a significant element in reputation but it is not the only one and the changing differences in price between the categories certainly do not indicate equivalent differences in quality.

Bordeaux has some 178 classed growths divided up as follows: 60 Médocs since 1855, 28 Sauternes also since 1855, 75 St-Emilion since 1954, a dozen Graves since 1959. Classed growth production, however, represents barely 3 percent of the total AC yield in the Gironde. Even if one adds to this an equal number of Crus Bourgeois this would still only represent a total, at most, a 5 percent elite. These figures show the enormous number of châteaux and the relatively small percentage of classed growths. A common error today is to identify a region's production with that of its top wines. The whole appellation benefits from their renown but clearly the elite are only a tiny minority.

Pierre Coste's Attempt at a Universal Classification

As a personal guide to the exceptional variety of French vineyards, and deliberately ignoring any official classifications, Pierre Coste was led to define not only the wines but also the people who drink them, or more precisely to classify their attitudes according to what and how they drink. In his book *Les Revolutions du Palais* (1987) he considers recent history in the vineyard, winery, and laboratory. He starts with the idea that each category of wine has a corresponding category of drinker, and he has devised four categories.

The first is that of the "French national drink," wine generally drunk as a matter of habit, without being tasted, arousing no particular feelings one way or another, the sort of wines described by professionals as "having neither vice nor virtue." This is the simplest and certainly the most common combination of wine and drinker. The point of the wine is simply to moisten food and quench thirst at the same time as producing the agreeable side effects of alcohol consumption. The wine passes from glass to stomach without arousing any reaction from the drinker. There are those who down the worst and the best in exactly the same manner, epitomizing the glutton. It is only this sort of indifference to the pleasures of taste and smell, or travesties of them, that can explain the sale of such vast quantities of table wine, wines whose price is calculated solely on the basis of their alcoholic content. And it is the annual forty million hectoliters of such wines, which have neither appeal nor pretension to any, that account for the French per capita consumption, one of the highest in the world. The consumer himself often criticizes the quality of these wines, but if the bottler makes the slightest change to his blend, even to improve it, the complaints increase and the sales decrease. Fortunately, the consumption of these wines, which do the image of French winemaking no good at all, is decreasing slowly in favor of something of better quality.

The second category is that of "false fine wine," wine that may be illustrious in origin and which may have been made by the book, but whose quality is illusory. Its defects are usually of a technical nature: in the case of reds, the wine may be hard, astringent, thin, overoaked, too high in fixed acidity, volatile acidity, or ethyl acetate, etc.; in the case of whites, oxidized, green, oversulfured, and so on. The drinkers of such wines are categorized by Coste as "label drinkers," often people who have picked up a limited and hazy knowledge of wine. In league with the so-called "traditional" producer and susceptible to advertising, they have a blind faith in bogus "tradition" even if a grand label conceals a suspect or a faulty wine. Coste observes that it is human nature to put one's trust in something that guarantees to have followed time-honored customs to the letter, but he adds: "Tradition is almost always the primary commercial justification for an elevated price," and this type of customer is prepared to pay for reputation. With a well-known label in front of him, our spurious connoisseur decides that the associated taste and bouquet are what he likes. It is a typical case of autosuggestion; he knows the wine is good because it is so by definition. He mistakes oxidized for age, ethyl acetate for bouquet, and acid for full body. Were it not for his ignorance, he would be an appreciative gourmet. And it is thanks to these second-rate but very useful drinkers that second-rate wines and poor vintages sell for a reasonable price.

Coste's third category comprises what he calls "good wines," well balanced, straightforward, but attractive and easy to drink. They are wines which are generally drunk young, tasting of ripe fruit in the reds and having a floral aroma in the case of the whites. Their style is relatively recent in concept and owes its existence to modern vinification techniques. They are wines whose emphasis is very much on fruit flavor and whose urban customers are busy, active, and often young. These drinkers like wines from a moderate price bracket, wines which are fresh and lively, without any pretension to class and whose youthful, grapy character recalls holidays in the country, even if unconsciously: "countryside peace, beautiful vineyards and the carefree conviviality associated with wine and its traditions." They are gourmands, in the best sense, because they regard wine as a real but uncomplicated pleasure. They do not spend any time swirling it in the glass in order to analyze its characteristics; they just drink it with pleasure, and they know why they like it. A large number of wines from both France and its neighbors cater to their requirements.

Finally, the fourth category is that of "fine wines," wines as unique and flawless as a work of art. They are complex, individual, rich in flavor and odor, difficult to describe, even more intriguing and attractive to taste. These are wines for the informed amateur, privileged gourmet, erudite epicure; drinking them involves an almost religious ritual. It is not enough just to know where to buy them or to have the means to do so; the rituals of the *sommelier* are needed to show them to the best advantage. They should only partner dishes worthy of them, prepared and presented with an equal care and attention; they lose their point unless served in a manner that matches their own level of refinement. The way to appreciate them is by repeated sipping and contemplation, for they have as much to offer the mind as the senses. Wines in Coste's third category inspire one to dream; the really fine wines provoke reflection. This art of good drinking is part of the art of good eating, and no one knows better than Pierre Coste how to describe the wonderment experienced on tasting a great wine. We can but hope, as he does, that his last two categories will eventually eclipse the first two.

The Bordeaux writer James de Coquet achieved the remarkable feat of writing for gourmets, gourmands, gastronomes, and gluttons without mentioning wine and barely mentioning drinking. However, just to fill in the gaps, I feel fairly sure that the gourmet considers what he chooses to eat as an intellectual pleasure, and the gourmand, tasting everything and tasting all the time, enjoys everything that is good; these two groups would only drink wine from categories three and four. The gastronome/epicure, whose eating and drinking habits develop on a strictly scientific basis, would only be interested in the greatest of fine wines—monuments, museum pieces, classic masterpieces from the last group. And finally, the glutton, staunch consumer of quantity, unable to control his tastes and inclinations, will simply soak up the mediocre products of the first two categories.

S e v e n

Tasting Techniques

ON HOW TO SMELL WINE

We can use our senses to taste wine in many different ways. The act of tasting is easy to describe in broad terms, but its detailed practice may vary a great deal. Wine is poured into a glass of a certain shape and size at a certain temperature; it is examined visually, then smelt after being swirled—which may be done in various ways—and then drawn into the mouth, at which point it may be kept in contact with different parts of the palate as briefly or as long as desired. Tongue and cheek movements may or may not be made, air may or may not be drawn in to aerate the wine, a little wine may be swallowed once or more, or not at all; finally, the wine is spat out and its impressions disappear gradually. Throughout these actions attention is paid to various sensations, how they evolve and how long they last. Afterwards all these impressions need to be described, interpreted, and a judgment made. Obviously, there are several possible procedures and everybody will have his or her own technique.

It is often stressed that the senses of taste and smell are delicate, and that they need to be used carefully and methodically, that is, following a well-adapted technique, if a particular end is to be achieved. In effect, winetasting is an activity comprising a series of actions, muscular movements, and the successive or simultaneous exercise of several senses: The sense of smell functions by itself to

118

start with and is subsequently combined with taste. A conscious effort of attention needs to be applied at the appropriate juncture during each of these sequences; otherwise no perception will take place.

We have already considered how to examine the visual aspect of wine, and we also know that smelling is one of the most important phases of tasting. There are different ways of releasing a wine's odor. The intensity of smell will depend on how the wine is swirled in the glass, and on how close one's nose is to the wine's surface when sampling the odor-laden air. It will also depend on the shape of the glass and how much air there is inside it.

Imagine the vapor given off as floating just above the wine, filling the empty part of the glass with a fine, invisible mist. These vapors are denser when the wine is swirled and when the glass shape narrows at the rim, but they are diluted in a glass with a flared opening. The composition of these odorous vapors is first of all a function of the vapor tension, of the volatility of the substances therein. The vapors are hydroalcoholic but the alcohol is at a higher concentration than in the wine itself. Alcohol certainly facilitates the liberation and diffusion of odor-bearing constituents. Additionally, a strong agitation of the wine's surface creates an emulsion of liquid particles in the air, a sort of aerosol effect whose features are quite different from those of volatility.

When a wine is still, very few volatile constituents rise from its surface, and their diffusion in the air is slow. For this reason it is useless to put one's nose to the neck of a bottle whose cork has been drawn in order to smell the wine, something one occasionally sees people doing. The wine is several centimeters down the neck and cannot be smelt in such circumstances. What one does smell instead is the rim of the bottle or odor traces left by the cork.

It is easy to understand that, for any given wine, the strength and make-up of the odor yielded will vary according to the surface area available for evaporation and the relative volumes of liquid and air. If just a little wine is poured into the bottom of a glass, its smell will have neither the same composition nor the same intensity as when the glass is nearly full. A revealing tasting exercise is to smell the same wine in four identical glasses filled to different levels; with 20, 50, 100, and 200 milliliters, for example. Both the odor and its finesse increase as the volume of wine increases up to 100 milliliters; beyond this level you cannot swirl the wine in the glass without spilling it, and if the wine is still you inhale air from outside the glass. When nosing a wine, therefore, you should follow a systematic technique which prescribes the shape and size of the glass, the amount of wine, and the way it is swirled.

There are three ways of smelling wine in the glass, sometimes called the three *coups de nez*, or "three nosings."

The first consists of smelling the wine before agitation, in a glass that is one-third or two-fifths full. After emptying your lungs, you smell the air above the wine by inhaling slowly. You can put your nose to the mouth of the glass while it is standing on the table; alternatively, you can lift the glass, tilt it as necessary but without swirling the liquid, and bring your nose close to the wine's surface. If the first case, where the glasses are not touched, rapid but careful comparisons can be made of wines lined up side by side, showing closely related odors. The odors perceived will be light because only the most diffusible elements can be smelt in this way and the taster cannot rely solely on this method.

The second method is more common and is always to be recommended. The wine is smelt immediately after having been swirled, an action aimed at increasing the surface area in contact with air and so increasing the evaporation of odorous substances. The rotating motion imparted to a glass held by its foot hollows the wine's surface, making it rise up the inner walls, leaving them wet, and at the same time filling the empty part of the glass with odorous vapor. If swirling is difficult to begin with, it is simpler to put the glass on the table and rotate it gently in circles without lifting it from the flat surface. Kressmann notes that "an anticlockwise movement seems to be the easiest for right handed people." This motion considerably increases evaporation and the wine's smell is intensified in a most agreeable way. Then tilt the glass and bring it nearer to your nose so as to sniff the wine from close up. This action can be repeated several times, but each time the impression will be the same.

The third method is best suited to bringing out olfactory faults and is used when the two preceding techniques leave room for doubt as to how clean the nose is. In this case the glass is agitated in a brisk or even violent manner so as to break up the wine and emulsify it. Wine may be spilt while doing this, so in extreme cases the glass can be vigorously shaken up and down after the top has been covered with the palm of one's hand. Smell the surface of the wine immediately afterwards. This method emphasizes less agreeable smells, such as those of ethyl acetate, oxidation, rotten wood, mold, and styrene, and also sulfur-related stinks.

Experimentally, the intensity of vinous odors can be heightened by vigorously whisking wine in a beaker or by aerating it with air or inert gas. Extraction by gas stream has also been used as a technique for studying volatile and odorous substances.

Another recommended procedure (a fourth *coup* in effect) is to sniff the odors left in a glass which has just been emptied, as is generally done with fine spirits. In the case of many wines there is nothing left to smell, but wines aged in good-quality wood leave dense odors dominated by the tannins from wine and wood, both modified by aging.

During the course of smelling wines in this way, your breathing rhythm ought to be carefully controlled. You should smell by slow inhalation, breathing in more or less deeply according to the intensity of the wine's aroma. Sniffing rapidly achieves nothing.

A series of two or three inhalations, each lasting two to four seconds, is normal, during each of which a range of odors emerges in succession. As our sense of smell is rapidly dulled, every impression should be noted as it appears and each series of inhalations should be followed by a period of rest.

Olfactory comparisons require a very precise technique; you should breathe in the same amount of air each time at the same rate, and likewise breathe out in the same way between inhalations. Becoming used to a smell means that it soon disappears, for our olfactory memory rapidly loses its precision and we can only compare smells effectively if the period between respective nosings is very brief. During this interval you should breathe deeply and calmly while concentrating on the memory of the sensations just experienced. The least distraction means starting all over again. Roudnitska gives similar advice to perfumers who must exercise the same discipline in smelling as winetasters.

The study of an aroma or a bouquet requires considerable application and many repeated attempts. As a rule as much time should be devoted to this phase of tasting as to the analysis of taste sensations proper. Even though the nose of a wine is so revealing, some tasters have an unfortunate tendency to curtail or even omit this olfactory phase altogether, and to make a somewhat hasty, ill-considered judgment based on taste alone. Yet nothing so clearly reveals a wine's class, finesse, and age as does its nose. Certain quality wines, such as port in Vila Nova de Gaia, for example, are checked almost entirely by smell.

Without even being aware of it, the taster is affected by the phenomenon of olfactory familiarization, otherwise known as sensory adaptation. It is not possible to taste or smell accurately unless your mouth has first been rinsed with wine and your nose impregnated with wine odors. The first wine one tastes is always badly judged. At the start of a tasting the first two or three wines should not require too much attention, besides which it is desirable to prepare one's palate by beginning with familiar wines which will serve as reference points. In this way one gets used to the intense vinous odor, the factor common to all the wines to be tasted. While your palate becomes overall less sensitive as a result, you end up better able to discern subtle differences in taste or smell. When repeatedly sniffed a wine gradually reveals nuances previously unnoticed.

WINE ON THE PALATE

Nothing would seem easier than drawing wine into one's mouth, yet apprentice tasters have often asked me: "But what exactly do you do when you taste? What goes on inside your mouth? How do you move your tongue; which are the best movements to make, and how often?" There is no easy answer because the facial movements and expressions of the taster are unconscious. He has become used to making certain mechanical and muscular movements and repeats them automatically; indeed, if his tastings are to be properly comparative they ought to be repeated exactly without the taster having to think about it.

Let us take a close look at a taster at work and see what goes on in the reaction between wine and palate. The taster lifts and tilts the glass toward his lips, with his head inclined slightly back in the typical drinking attitude. However, the wine is not allowed to flow freely down his throat as is normal when drinking; instead, the taster controls its progress, gently sucking it in, mouth open, lips forward, and with the rim of the glass resting on his lower lip. The tip of the tongue comes into contact with the liquid between open jaws and the wine then flows over the tongue which is held flat to keep it at the front of the mouth. The cheek and lip muscles work quite unconsciously, using the air breathed in to raise or lower pressure inside the mouth, and in this way all the wine's movements during tasting result from a carefully controlled drawing in or expelling of air. Taking wine into the mouth is accompanied by a first inhalation of odorous vapors which thus form part of the impressions of the wine's attack.

Although everybody has an individual preference for how much wine to take in per mouthful, a relatively small volume of 6 to 10 milliliters is recommended. This is also Puisais' recommendation. However, some writers, gluttons no doubt, suggest 20, even 25 milliliters, which seems a lot to me. Too much wine takes longer to warm up and is difficult to hold in your mouth, forcing you to swallow the excess. Besides, it is just not possible to taste a large range of wines in this manner without suffering from the effects of too much alcohol. On the other hand, too small a mouthful means the wine will not reach all parts of the palate, and, diluted by saliva as well, it will have an insufficient concentration of flavors. The professional taster's ring of lip muscles can measure the requisite amount of wine with the precision of an automatic dispenser. The quantity should remain constant from one wine to another; otherwise accurate comparison is impossible. One of the first exercises for the beginner is to establish this quantity. It is sufficient to weigh the wine glass before and after taking a sample mouthful, and then, if necessary, to correct and practice taking this amount.

Having taken a mouthful, the lips are closed and the head tilted slightly forward so as to keep the wine in the front of the mouth. Part of the tasting process takes place here, but wine flows back into the mouth proper, in a to-and-fro movement provoked by the tongue, and an initial swallow is soon made. Jaws remain slightly apart but moving nonetheless, and it is this that conveys the impression of chewing a wine; hence tasting is sometimes compared to chewing. During this phase of tasting the wine is gently moved around the mouth, coming into repeated contact with different parts of the palate. The tongue, whose muscles can move in any direction, constantly changes shape, gently working the mouthful of wine and pressing it against the roof of the mouth. The tongue normally remains within the jaws' confines; only after spitting out does it move to the very front of the mouth, sliding between the teeth, gums, cheeks, and lips to savor the aftertaste. The cheek muscles contract, reducing the space for liquid inside the mouth, and these movements increase salivation. After four or five seconds a further small amount is swallowed and, if the original mouthful was the right amount, this will be the last swallow.

Both the aroma in the mouth and a volatile defect can be enhanced by hollowing one's cheeks, pursing one's lips, and drawing in a little air through the wine two or three times. The air emulsifies the warmed up wine and the aromatic vapors released by this aerating effect are drawn up into the rear nasal passage.

A taster will vary the time he keeps the wine in his mouth according to the particular aspect of it that he is interested in: the initial impressions of the attack, tannin-related impressions and flavors, or the aftertaste. Thus the wine may be kept in the mouth for just two to five seconds, or extended for some ten to fifteen seconds. In the first case the tannic flavors of red wine will not be sensed. You can taste rapidly and superficially for reference, just dipping your lips in as it were, or, alternatively, in a profound and thorough manner, using the taste buds at the back of the tongue, rear of the mouth, and in the pharynx.

When at work professionally, tasters generally spit out as much wine as possible. Not because this improves the act of tasting, the reverse if anything; but during the course of tasting anything from ten to thirty wines at one session, something a professional does regularly, it would clearly be impossible to swallow several mouthfuls of each wine without some ill effects. Obviously, the amateur, tasting a limited number of wines, need not be so prudent, and it is quite normal for him to swallow wines he tastes, at least if he likes them. Some people are convinced that until they have swallowed they will experience no taste sensations; they are quite prepared to locate their tasting apparatus in their throats. In effect, they are simply swallowing directly, not tasting at all.

To spit out the wine, gather it in the front of the mouth, tighten and slightly purse the lips, and increase the pressure inside the mouth until the wine is more or less completely forced out, using the tongue as a piston. Just how adroitly you can do this will depend on how skillfully your lips can shape the wine's trajectory. Understandably, the art of spitting is treated with a certain amount of circumspection, yet it is a hallmark of the professional taster who can spit in an almost clinical fashion from the edge of his lips, and control the force of the jet according to the distance of the spittoon, all without dribbling.

With the exception of rapid tasting exercises, where one is only looking for an overall impression, you should wait a while before tasting the next wine, in order to appreciate the finish of the previous one and also to allow all its sensations to disappear. Tasting the same samples many times in succession is useless; such repeated attempts simply result in a total loss of sensitivity. So long as they have been carefully registered, first impressions are the best, and in any case you should have formed a definite opinion about the wine by the second time you taste it.

Normally, rinsing the mouth with water between tastings is not recommended; on the contrary, we have already seen that the mouth should remain accustomed to wine. After a rinse with water, sensitivity is altered and comparisons with preceding wines are made more difficult. Only when his palate is tired will the taster rinse his mouth with water, swallow several mouthfuls, and take a rest before continuing. He could at the same time eat a morsel of bread or a dry biscuit without harm; but in a professional tasting foods such as cheese or nuts should be avoided, as they weaken or mask tannic impressions. The amateur, on the other hand, has every reason to eat while tasting, but what he is practicing then is no longer the art of tasting so much as the art of drinking.

THE TASTING GLASS

What a beautiful object the wineglass is! It holds the wine and also offers it, a trap and a display case at the same time. It seems to me that the essential qualities of wine can only be revealed within glass. Can you imagine wine being properly tasted before the advent of clear glass? Ancient drinking vessels such as the chalice, hanap, pot, and Roman patera concealed their contents and served only as containers from which to swallow. Similarly, the pitcher needed replacing by the glass decanter. Perhaps the truth of the matter is that fine wine could only start to make its appearance at the turn of the eighteenth century as a result of glasses being made that were better suited to tasting.

There is said to be a sort of relationship between cellarmasters and master glassblowers; indeed, wine has always needed glass both for its conservation and for its consumption. Drinking glasses date from the seventeenth century, the bottle, as we know it, from the mid-eighteenth century. Around 1750 the rich drank from Bohemian and Venetian crystal; in the homes of the middle classes and in good-quality inns, one used cups or goblets in earthenware, stoneware, or pewter; and in the taverns the mugs were made of wood.

Crystal was discovered in England toward the end of the eighteenth century, and from 1820 onward it was manufactured in France by Baccarat. Nothing sets off the splendor of a claret, burgundy, or cognac so beautifully as the limpidity and purity of fine crystal. Toward the mid-nineteenth century balloon glasses began to appear, forerunners of the tasting glass. The glass is the tool which serves to bring wine and our sensory organs together. It should allow our senses to work under the very best conditions, meeting all the requirements demanded by eyes, nose, and mouth. The type of glass, its shape, and size, all influence our sensations, as does the manner in which we use it.

In my youth I knew an old wine broker whose shiny old frock coat hid a wealth of experience. "Look," he said to me one day, showing me his tasting glass, "look at this crystal bowl. In it I can see the wine, its past, its present, and its future." His intuition and imagination indeed made him a kind of seer.

A functional glass corresponds to precise standards and there is a particular technique to handling it. To start with, a distinction must be made between the tasting glass used by professional tasters and the everyday drinking glass.

The distinction is necessary because their functions are not quite the same. Both should show the wine in a way that flatters its color and brilliance, but the drinking glass need not be quite so well adapted for smelling because at table this activity is limited and perhaps the tasting glass need not be quite so convenient for drinking from since it is only used for sipping.

Drink ordinary table wine in any glass you like. However, a wine of some distinction cannot show at its best in just any old goblet; it needs a stemmed glass made of fine crystal, smooth, transparent, colorless, and without ornament or engraving. The glass should remain in the background, leaving the wine as the center of attention.

Poupon puts it like this: "I like glasses which seem invisible, in which the wine appears to be hovering several inches above the table-cloth." Heavy cut glassware, elaborate stems, audacious modern design, and colored glass all belong in the shop window. Once I was served a splendid Lafite in a glass whose bowl was supported by an unseemly little naked lady in frosted glass! How many fine wines there must be which are ruined by poor glasses, and there are whole sets of such glassware which serve the wine ill. I constantly fear that a glassmaker's bad taste may adversely affect the taste of the wine.

If well designed, the simplest stemmed glass is the best. Do not put fine wines in tiny wineglasses. When this happens I sometimes prefer to be served my wine in a tumbler. "A great wine needs a glass to match" runs a wine bibber's proverb, implying not how much wine should be drunk, but how best to drink it in order to derive the maximum pleasure. A good glass holds a quarter of a liter. However, avoid the other extreme as well, using giant glasses the size of a small fruit bowl. These are more decorative than functional, making an impressive display on the table in the same way that very large dinner plates do. A glass of this kind may be an impressive goblet in ringing crystal, but a straightforward wine is simply lost at the bottom of a half-liter-sized container. I have, however, come across great burgundies which emerged triumphant and enhanced from such an encounter; that said, such glasses are best regarded as curiosities.

The rim of a glass (the edge in contact with one's lips) should be thin, something only possible with crystal. The feeling of thickness does actually influence our impression of what we drink, and we have developed certain preferences in this respect. We prefer beer in a heavy tankard, and while an earthenware mug is all right for a long morning coffee, fine porcelain is preferred for a mocha or an espresso. Ask a taster to try the same wine in two different glasses , one light and fine, the other thick and heavy, and there is a fair chance he will prefer the wine in the first glass. This is a good example of our conditioning where presentation is concerned.

Wineglasses need to be furnished with a slender stem of sufficient height and a foot, both of which are used to hold and manipulate the glass between thumb and index finger. Some glasses have a very small foot which cannot be grasped and, like goblets, their only use is for drinks which are neither looked at nor tasted with any care.

Never hold the body of a glass, its cup or bowl, in the hand; it is cumbersome and also crude to behold; the only exception to this perhaps is when the wine is too cold and the glass is warmed in the palm of one's hand. Offer someone a wineglass and you can tell immediately by the way they hold it whether or not they are connoisseurs. Avoid glasses with thick, square, or fancy stems.

Every wine is said to have its own particular glass shape. Glasses certainly vary in form from one region to another, and the originality of glassware is part of the attraction of a table setting. Before 1914 it would seem that a complete glass service comprised a dozen each of six different glasses: water, burgundy, claret, champagne, port, and liqueur; plus water carafes and decanters, decanting being popular at the time. Nowadays, glasses for water, burgundy, and claret, and flutes for champagne are all that are normally used. A water glass usually holds 24 to 27 cl, and one for burgundy 19 to 22 cl. Older Bordeaux glasses used to be quite small, holding only 12 to 15 cl, but they are preferred somewhat larger today, the admirably constructed glass of the Académie des Vins de Bordeaux (Bordeaux Wine Academy) holding 27 cl, for example.

You can also choose a glass whose shape and size are equally suited to all types of wine: a pure oval, for example, or an egg-shaped cut so that the glass curves in slightly at the rim; alternatively, a tulip shape, a tulip still in bud or barely open, broader at the base and more pinched in at the top. A tulip glass is also suitable for champagne, much more suitable than the flat, wide champagne *coupe*, which wastes both bubbles and bouquet, and which should be consigned to the service of chilled fruit. The flute shape both prolongs the release of champagne bubbles and shows them off to much better effect.

A wine's odor cannot be analyzed in exactly the same way if it is examined in differently shaped glasses. Indeed, this is one of the exercises carried out as part of a taster's training. The relationship of surface area to volume of wine varies according to the shape of the glass and so, consequently, do the phenomena of evaporation, surface tension, and capillarity. If the glass is too wide open at the top, and if it is also too tall, the surface of the wine remains a long way from the nose. In the shorter type of balloon-shaped goblet, the odor is more easily perceived because the nostrils can get closer to the wine; however, the opening is usually a large one so that external air is breathed in along with the wine odor. The most suitable type of glass is one with an opening just larger than the nose; as the nose almost blocks the opening, the odor within can be experienced at its most intense, and it is this configuration that allows the best study of the complexity and subtleties of aroma and bouquet in fine wines. The glass on page 130 was developed around 1970, especially for tasting wine. It was designed by a group of French experts, based on the work of INAO, and the aim was to come up with a standardized glass. It consists of a bowl in a so-called elongated ovoid shape, supported by a stem resting on a foot. The opening of the bowl is narrower than the convex part so as to concentrate the odors. It is made of totally colorless, transparent glass to "crystalline" specifications, that is, with a lead content of about 9 percent. The rim is smooth, regular, and rounded; it is cut cold initially, abraded to ensure its horizontality, and then refired. The glass holds 210 to 225 milliliters, allowing one to work with 70 or 80 milliliters of wine; for the comparison of sparkling wines the bottom may have a small, coarse-ground circle, 5 mm in diameter, in its center to promote the formation of bubbles. This type of glass is highly recommended for the olfactory study of wines, and it is generally acknowledged that its use considerably improves the consistency of winetasters' opinions.

Finally, it should be remembered that, for the purposes of tasting, a glass should not be more than one-third or at most two-fifths full. This allows the wine to be swirled in a brisk, circular motion without being spilt, and it also means that the part of the glass above the wine contains a fine, aromatic mist. For these reasons, too, to fill someone's glass to the brim is just as wrong (though for a different reason) as overfilling a plate, as it actually prevents the wine from being appreciated. Wine cannot be tasted properly from a glass that is too full.

On the subject of cleaning glasses, it is generally recommended to wash them until they are quite odor free and then to rinse them with distilled water. Attention is often drawn to the fact that most commercial detergents are scented and that towels used to dry may well transfer the smell of the powder they are washed in to the glasses. How often have I heard tasters with the most critical senses of smell complain bitterly at the unpleasant smell of an empty glass.

I myself find the following method very effective. The glasses are washed and rinsed with warm water immediately after use. No de-

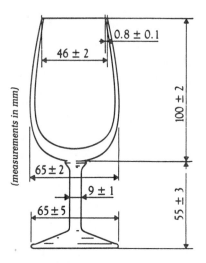

The standard tasting glass, known as the ISO glass
(International Standards Organization).

tergent is employed, and soapy water from an odor-free soap is used if there are grease marks to remove. In order to dry them the glasses are never wiped with a cloth, but are hung upside down, suspended by the foot, before being put away in an odorless glass cupboard. Glassmakers recommend that glasses should never be stood upside down on their rims, but always upright on their feet. When they are to be use they should be rinsed again under the tap and the excess water shaken off before the inside is wet with a little of the wine to be tasted. The French call this *enviner* (to give the smell of wine to a bottle or glass) opposed to *aviner* which means to saturate with wine, and refers to the wood of the casks.

THE TASTEVIN

The first object used to drink from was probably a ladle, a hollow, cup-shaped, earthenware vessel. Terracotta and ceramic examples have been found as well as ones made of wood and of metal. It was a simple matter to plunge one of these into a container such as an amphora, crater, pitcher, or urn, to stir the liquid's surface, and to scoop up or ladle out a drink. The cup would have been furnished with an elongated handle or an index finger ring to avoid wetting the fingers, and the same vessel would have been used quite naturally for drawing, tasting, and drinking on the spot as well. During the fifteenth century, and no doubt before, a small, flat cup with sides that were either smooth or covered in small bosses was known as a *taste vin*. The Burgundians ensured the word's fame by writing it *tastevin*. It is derived from the French *taster, tâter,* or *tester,* meaning to taste or to try. Many languages have only one word for these two. The word *tastevin* was not a Burgundian monopoly, and the erudite Mazenot details the same object as being called a *tassou, tassot, tassette,* and *tasse à vin* in the Pays d'Oc region.

Curiously, the name *tastevin* is also given to the pipette used to draw wine up through the bunghole of a barrel. This instrument is made of glass or plated metal and has a ring-shaped handle at its upper end. As the pipette is lowered into the wine, so the liquid rises up inside and fills the tube. The hole at the top, whose rim is wide and flat, is then blocked with the thumb, the instrument is withdrawn, and the requisite amount of wine is allowed to run into a glass or *tastevin* by lifting the thumb as necessary. The *tastevin*-pipette became the indispensable partner to the *tastevin*-cup when wine began to be stored in wooden barrels with small openings. The *tastevin*-cup's handle and thumb rest were no longer necessary. The Bordeaux *tastevin* has never had either.

Mazenot has studied the *tastevin* down the centuries. He has examined more than a thousand examples, ranging from those belonging to the prehistoric Cretan, Mycenean, and Anatolian civilizations, down to those that were polished, embossed, and chased by eighteenth-century goldsmiths in the golden age of the *tastevin*.

A typical example of a silver, Burgundian *tastevin* would be about 85 millimeters in diameter and 29 millimeters deep, holding 9 centiliters. The sides are punctuated all around the rim and on the base by a series of intermittent pearl-shaped indentations. The asymmetry of the relief decoration inside is customary. One side has twenty or so parallel grooves; they may in some cases be rather short, spiral shaped, and slanting; and on the opposite side are eight evenly spaced, dimple-shaped depressions.

Listen to Poupon describing a *tastevin* being manipulated, used to examine the brilliance and sheen of a burgundy, for it was invented with red wine in mind and the gleam of a white wine is lost in it. We could equally well have chosen Engel as our expert, for the Burgundians reign supreme where *tastevin* matters are concerned. They have turned the word into a verb, *tasteviner*, and created the *tastevinage*, an annual contest for wines from their appellations. However, back to Poupon: "When the *tastevin* has received its measure of wine, each of its reliefs and its hollows, each of its bosses or grooves is brought into play. The wine should first be examined close to a light source, with the wine quite still, its surface horizontal and motionless. The central boss limits the quantity of wine available and also reduces its depth. . . . Next, the *tastevin* should be tilted alternately away from and then toward you, so as to move the wine from the grooved side to the indented side: the interior of the wine will then either be lit with flashes and pinpoints of brilliance, or else appear opaque and clouded by shadows. The color either intensifies or becomes lighter."

Viewed from one side, the wine appears lighter, weaker, and more transparent; this is known as the buyer's side because it judges the wine more harshly. From the other side the wine seems denser and darker; this is known as the seller's side because it flatters the wine to some extent.

Mazenot considers that the unembellished simplicity of the Bordeaux *tastevin* is the direct descendant of the ancient Greek or Roman cupel, whose shape and size were the same. Smooth, unadorned, and resting on a pedestal several millimeters thick, its classical beauty lies in the harmony of simple forms. Alain Querre's silver *tastevin* is 112 millimeters in diameter, 48 millimeters deep, and holds 7 centiliters. The pronounced swell of the central dome and the 30° angle of its sides create in the wine a depth ranging from 1 to 20 millimeters, where the effects of light and the wine's brilliance can be observed through the liquid against either a convex or a straight, sloping background. Having neither handle nor any other appendage, the Bordeaux *tastevin* or tasting cup has no scoop or ladle function, but is simply a means of displaying the wine.

Each French wine region has its own version of the *tastevin* derived from one of the two preceding types. The wealth of decoration on the cups, the originality of handle design (vertical, horizontal, plaited, serpentine, or shell-shaped), their age, the silversmith's hallmarks—all give value and interest to these neglected but beautiful implements.

I barely knew the time when the tasting cup was still a cellar implement in Bordeaux, before it became a shop window ornament. At that time the itinerant wine broker, tasting from cellar to cellar, would keep his *tastevin* in a pocket or small clasp bag, wrapped in a soft cloth which he would use to wipe and polish the cup after use. It was used in an attractively ritual manner, in movements that were precise and economical. In this way purchases were made "by the cup," that is, on the basis of tasting alone, and prices were not related to alcoholic degree, nor always to the wine's origin. However, the tasting glass has so many advantages over the *tastevin* that it has replaced it everywhere. Whether it is a question of observing the limpidity of a wine, its depth, and hue, or examining the clarity, intensity, finesse of a bouquet, in all respects the *tastevin* is shown up as a tool of limited utility. Assessing the appearance of a wine on the basis of a shallow cross section is bound to be imprecise.

The *tastevin* is quite useless for smelling wine; odors are lost due to the extensive surface area of liquid and they are also diluted in the surrounding air. Nor is it much better for sampling wine. The metal is thick, and, being a good conductor of heat and cold, it is variable in temperature, both factors which make it less than pleasant in contact with the lips. And, whereas comparing several wines one after another using a single wine glass is straightforward, the trouble and continuous refilling involved when trying to do the same with a *tastevin* make it quite unsuitable for such precise comparative tasting.

However, I know a professional taster who still uses a *tastevin* in the way that some people still use a quill pen, as much from a natural sense of refinement as from nostalgia. He first observes and noses the wine in a glass, and then pours a little into his *tastevin* which he actually tastes from. I could not taste as he does, but I envy him a bit. I myself have never owned a *tastevin*.

Tasting Rooms and the Tasting Environment

Inaccurate tasting and the fact that results cannot always be duplicated (which means they cannot be verified) can most often be explained by inadequate working conditions. Obviously, it is not always possible to follow Verdier's advice to taste only on fine mornings, "rain and fog being prejudicial to wine."

The fact that the taster is aware of external influences and consciously isolates himself from them is not enough; he requires the best available environment furnished with appropriate and practical equipment. There are two sorts of circumstance which influence sensory acuity: the conditions and surroundings of the tasting room or office, and the taster's own tasting fitness (in the sense of being able to perform).

Puisais has made detailed experimental studies of tasting conditions and the following paragraphs are based on his work. The effect of a wine's temperature, according to its type, is well known and will be tackled in detail later (see pp. 143–150). For example, in the case of red wines with a fairly high polyphenol content, a variation in temperature of just 2°C is enough to account for disagreements as to how tannic they are. Consequently, samples should be selected sufficiently in advance to enable them all to be tasted at a uniform temperature. During the course of their regular tastings, professionals do not usually chill white wines or warm reds, both of which flatter the taste of the respective types; nevertheless, they avoid tasting them below 15°C or above 20°C.

The taster is also sensitive to room temperature. If it is so cold or warm as to be uncomfortable, then his judgment may be affected adversely. The ideal working conditions for tasting seem to be a temperature of about 18°C and a humidity of around 60 percent. Odors are less easily perceived in dry conditions, but as one's nose is anyway practically touching the wine's surface inside a glass, atmospheric humidity is not a significant factor.

The sense of hearing can interfere with the other senses during tasting and quiet has always been considered necessary for a taster's concentration. Without insisting on absolute silence, difficult to obtain within a group in any case, one should avoid too high a level of background noise as well as occasional noises which can divert the taster's attention. During exercises demanding very precise tasting, participants should not be allowed to talk to each other. Indeed, anything which might distract the taster or make him uncomfortable is undesirable.

The decoration and lighting of the room also need to be taken into account. Bright colors are not suitable; pale, uniform, and fairly neutral colors are. Puisais thinks that green has a tendency to reinforce impressions of acidity, and blue those of bitterness, whereas red tends to make wines taste better in general. Harsh lighting and shiny surfaces are just as unsatisfactory as poor light. An adequate level of light is between 200 and 400 lux, though whenever possible daylight is always preferable. As an alternative, artificial lighting can be installed which approximates the uniform and well-diffused character of daylight; in this context filament light bulbs are preferable to fluorescent lighting which generally dulls and falsifies colors.

The tasting room is often right next to a laboratory, office, or cellar; moreover, tasting itself, cleaning materials, and wine being handled or spilt all leave persistent smells. The room should have windows opening to the outside; or the air should be renewed mechanically about ten times an hour. Some tasting rooms have such a strong smell of sawdust that I can only taste after opening a door or window; indeed, it is sometimes better to actually taste outside in the fresh air.

Should the taster work standing up or sitting down? This depends on the circumstances and also on what one is used to, though problems best tackled standing up differ from those best approached sitting down. On a property one tastes standing up, either in the cellars or sometimes in a separate area specifically set up for tasting. Tasting is also done standing up at the premises of merchants or wine brokers where office and tasting room are often combined. However, more and more professional bodies are installing rooms specifically designed for seated tasting, because, after all, when the wine is finally drunk the consumer will be sitting down. Each method has advantages and disadvantages. The standing taster has more freedom to move around; he helps himself to wine and moves away; he can range freely up and down the series of wines on the table, examine wine by daylight at a window or by artificial light, step up to the spittoon, and step back to record his impressions. However, all this movement can also be distracting, especially if several people are trying to do the same thing at the same time, and notes made when standing are made after a few seconds' delay. The taster sitting down in front of a row of glasses can concentrate better on the problem in hand. His comparisons are more accurate because they are quicker and he can make his notes progressively, as and when he likes. However, he can only taste a limited number of samples at a time, and he will not be able to maintain the same rhythm and concentration for as long as the standing taster, for I have noticed that sensory fatigue sets in sooner when one is sitting. Finally, for any group work, seated tasting requires both more room and more equipment.

A taster's working environment will have the greatest influence on his tasting efficiency. He gets used to a particular tasting room and his best results are obtained in his everyday surroundings. He feels more at ease there, he knows where things are, his tasting routine can be automatically followed. In these circumstances his sensitivity is also at its most acute and in some cases, before giving a formal opinion on a wine tasted elsewhere, he may want to confirm his judgment in his own tasting room. It is sometimes said, lightly, that a winetaster carries his tasting equipment with him wherever he goes, but it is at home that it is most finely tuned.

Tasting room equipment has recently been the subject of study and rationalization, and it has inspired the installation of many new tasting centers. For regular tastings with a few people who normally taste standing up, the arrangements can be very simple. The only requisites are a table that is easy to clean, covered in Formica, glass, or tiling on which to place glasses and sample bottles of wine, a fairly deep sink for spitting into, and a cupboard with glass doors and shelves for storing clean glasses.

For work that needs to be more precise (involving experimental research, testing, wine and winetasting competitions), it is better to have a more specifically functional installation. Every wine region now has a tasting center of this type, some of which are extremely well designed and equipped.

Vedel has given a good description of such a tasting room. Each taster works in a booth isolating him from his neighbor. The booths have partitions at the sides and front, made of a light material and which come up to the head height of a seated taster. For certain uses, teaching in particular, it is useful if these can be removed. Each booth is 80 to 90 cm wide and has a working surface 40 cm in depth and 75 cm above the floor. The floor should be smooth and easy to clean—Formica is a suitable material. On the left of the table there is a spittoon about 30 cm in diameter, preferably in black. Water for the spittoon and for rinsing glasses is supplied from a swansneck tap, high enough to allow the glasses to be passed underneath it.

Some spittoons have an integral circulating water supply similar to a dentist's rinsing bowl. It is also useful to provide a shelf in front of the taster on which equipment can be placed and from which glasses can be suspended. Each booth has a seat, adjustable for height if possible. The colors of any equipment should be neutral in tone; pale fawn, beige, or off-white. Apart from the room's general lighting it is worth installing a mobile spotlight with a narrow beam for checking limpidity.

THE WINETASTER SHOULD ALWAYS BE FIT

The taster's palate is a kind of receptor of extraordinary complexity and sensitivity; however, it is so subject to influence that it only functions well in very particular circumstances. We have seen that a taster will only taste well to the extent that he can ensure he does so in favorable working conditions, and that is largely a question of organization. However, the sensitivity and accuracy of his personal tasting equipment depends fundamentally on the individual's physiology which changes constantly according to health and mood. Thus a good taster will also be someone who keeps fit and who knows himself, his potential, and his limits. He will taste only when his tasting apparatus is in good order.

To taste effectively, one must be relaxed, alert, unpreoccupied, and in good health. Fatigue, worry, and pain, muscular or otherwise, do not actually affect one's perception thresholds but they hinder concentration and reduce one's appetite for wine. One must relish the prospect of wine and want to taste it in order to do so well; thus one tastes better when hungry than when replete. Any chronic or temporary disorders of the air passages or digestive system, even minor ones, preclude tasting: coughs, colds, sore throats, asthma attacks, stomach ache or an upset stomach, breathing problems are all obvious examples. Moreover, some illnesses actually distort tastes and smells; liver complaints, for example, may cause the sufferer to detect nonexistent or "phantom" odors, a condition known as hyperosmia.

The taster also needs to have a particular reason for tasting if he is to do so effectively. Even if the wine samples are anonymous he should be quite clear in his own mind as to the precise purpose of the tasting as well as being fully aware of any information which has been given relating to a particular problem posed. The attention with which he tastes will then depend on how much he wants to solve the problem.

Any taster should observe certain basic rules of hygiene, firstly by regular care of his teeth so as to keep them clean and healthy—remembering, however, that it is difficult to taste properly for an hour after brushing one's teeth or rinsing with a mouthwash. Tasting a large number of wines can irritate the mucous lining, in particular, the most sensitive part of the tongue, its upper surface, which can become quite painful. If this happens an antiseptic mouthwash should be used and a rest taken from tasting for several days. Acid wines can also irritate the teeth and leave one's gums feeling inflamed which is unpleasant when chewing. In such cases one should rinse several times with an alkaline water such as Vichy or soda water. False teeth can be a hindrance to tasting and they also diminish one's sensory acuity.

The French view on drinking wine is that it is made to accompany food. However, depending on what they are, different foods react in different ways on the sensitivity of our senses, probably by modifying the pH and buffer effect of the saliva. For example, eating meat prior to drinking raises the sensation threshold for sweetness and acidity while lowering that for saltiness and bitterness. Green salad has the opposite effect. Cheese and lemon also alter sensitivity to the four basic tastes. This explains the different impressions we have of the same wine according to what dish it accompanies, and depending on whether it is drunk before or during the course of the meal. Matters are further complicated by the fact that individual reactions are not necessarily the same. Personally, I would not go as far as to recommend, as some do, a special sort of menu for the day preceding a tasting; a taster will know from experience that he does not taste well after an overindulgent, indigestible meal. Any excess affects one's ability to taste. A winetaster cannot also be a hard drinker. Involving daily contact with alcoholic drinks as it does, his profession is only for those who are sensible and self-disciplined where drink is concerned. Wine tasting is in education in sobriety, and knowing how to taste implies knowing how to drink. On the other hand, tasting makes one very choosy, and the taster, having lost sight of wine as a pleasure, can often only rediscover the simple enjoyment of drinking by setting aside his critical stance to some extent. Obliged to drink in moderation, he prefers only to drink well.

The taster cannot afford to neglect training either, meaning that regular and frequent exercise is necessary to maintain his tasting form; without it, his palate will become as out of practice as any neglected skill. While training may not improve one's taste thresholds, it keeps the memory fresh and gives one stamina.

Careful tests have shown that moderate smoking does not affect one's sensitivity, but it is advisable not to smoke for an hour before a tasting. I know people who light up a cigarette just at the thought of tasting, and who then hold a glass in one hand and cigarette in the other; wretched smokers and mediocre tasters, these are the sort of people who smoke between courses at table. The smell of tobacco smoke in a room, on clothes, or on a taster's hand prevents any serious tasting; cigarettes and wine do not make good partners. Cigars and fine spirits, on the other hand, apparently enhance each other. I only assert this from hearsay as, for reasons of prudence and preserving my palate's sensitivity, I have always denied myself such experiences.

In group tastings there are other annoying smells, those of perfume, cosmetics, lipsticks, and aftershave. One becomes impervious to such smells worn by oneself, but sensitive to those worn by others, and the same goes for certain clothing, velvet and leather, for example.

It is not surprising that there is a progressive decrease in sensitivity of taste and smell with age since our other senses also deteriorate, sometimes to the extent of actual infirmity. Loss of taste, for example, is explained by the reduction in the number of taste buds from the age of fifty, and above all the age of sixty onward. If young people have an average of 245 taste buds per papilla, the average for those aged between seventy and eighty-five is only eighty-eight. Nevertheless, there are people in retirement who remain good tasters. Toward the end of his career a taster compensates for his sensory deficiencies by a more deft perception in difficult cases, the result of greater experience and hence access to a more extensive range of wines as the basis for comparison.

The way in which sensitivity varies during the course of a working day has already been described. The variations depend on one's way of life and eating habits, and for this reason they can vary from one region to another. We are well aware of the cyclic nature of our reactions, dependent on habits and routine.

A chapter on the taster's physiological reactions would be incomplete without mentioning the effect of alcohol absorption via the mucous lining of the mouth. During the course of a large tasting, even without drinking any wine, the body may absorb sufficient alcohol to raise the blood alcohol level to several tenths of a gram per liter. It is quite possible that this amount is one of the causes of the fatigue experienced by some professional tasters at the end of a heavy day's tasting. The need to remain sober demands that the taster should swallow the minimum possible quantity of wine and that he should not taste for an excessive length of time.

A REMINDER OF SOME OF THE RULES OF SAMPLING AND TASTING

Sometimes when you retaste a wine that you have already tried a few days previously you find your impressions of it are not the same. You conclude that it must be a poorly prepared sample. This sort of uncertainty often occurs in practice and the disconcerted taster consoles himself with the assumption that the samples must be unrepresentative.

One day I was doing a test on sampling methods in thirty Bordeaux châteaux. In each case I let the cellarmaster prepare a half-bottle sample of the current year's wine as he would normally do with his own equipment. I then prepared my own sample from the same vat or barrel taking all the necessary precautions. In ten of the thirty cases the cellarmaster's sample showed less well, the faults noted being as follows: unclean, odors of dust or bad wood, an excessive taste of new wood, or wine that was slightly oxidized and flat. Thus one-third of the wines had been spoiled by the method of sampling. This observation bears thinking about; sample preparation is not as easy an operation as it may seem.

In general, three cases are met with in cellar practice: In the first case, the wine is all in one vat and the sample is homogeneous; in the second case, the wine is stored in barrels of about 200 liters, in which case two samples taken from neighboring barrels may be slightly different, for each cask of wine develops in its own way;

third, the batch of wine is in bottle, and each bottle may be considered an individual sample because, after several years of storage, one can never be sure that all the bottles will taste exactly the same.

In the first case, preparing a sample would appear quite simple: One just has to take a small amount from the vat. However, the homogeneity of a large mass of wine is only relative. The limpidity may vary from top to bottom and wine from the surface, exposed to the air to some extent, generally tastes less good. When possible the best solution is to sample from the depths of the wine, using a bottle fixed to a rod which one plunges into the middle of the wine through the trap in the top of the vat. If the tasting spigot halfway down the vat is used, several liters should be run off first so that the sample is clean and clear.

When wine is in barrels, the sample is drawn from several different casks with standard precautions being taken to avoid drawing what is directly in contact with the wood. A small amount of wine is first drawn from the barrel and the pipette is then lowered through the bunghole into the heart of the barrel; alternatively, one can siphon the wine out. When the cask is in the "bung $\frac{3}{4}$" position, a curved, stainless steel tube is introduced into a taphole, and the initial flow of wine is thrown away.

In general, the wine should be tasted immediately after the sample has been taken in order to avoid any spoilage from the effects of oxidation. If tasting has to be delayed, the sample should be rested for several days, well corked. The practice of decanting from sample size bottles into smaller ones as the wine brokers do is always detrimental to the wine's quality, especially in the case of wines still charged with yeasts, and yet more so because these very small bottles are generally inadequately stoppered. Many wines are misjudged because the samples tasted are saturated with oxygen; this seems to be the case for a number of wines shown to merchants, on the basis of which they will select stock.

As far as bottled wines are concerned, it is essential not to aerate the wine, nor to disturb and so mix in any deposit. The cork is drawn and the wine poured straight into the tasting glass. If decanting is preferred, it should be done at the last possible moment. Alternatively, the wine can be decanted avoiding contact with air by using a siphon placed directly into the receiving vessel. Even a light aeration is enough to modify old wines.

A number of rules should be observed when organizing tastings. First, remember the general law that any one sensation tasted after another can only be accurately judge if the subsequent one is due to a different or stronger stimulus. Wines should therefore be grouped in a tasting order of increasing intensity: from the lowest to the highest in alcohol, from the driest to the sweetest, and from the lightest to the strongest in flavor. In other words, there is a logical tasting sequence to follow; certain tastings produce more reliable results simply because they are better organized. It is useless to compare wines that are very different in character or origin, or, alternatively, newly made wines with older wines; tasting should deal with wines of the same type. An effective tasting rule is: Only compare what is strictly comparable.

Planning before a tasting is therefore essential, especially as, in the case of professionals, many samples may be offered. Within the limits of a given appellation, one might have to judge wines from the same vintage but different vineyards, or wines from one vineyard but different vintages; in the latter case one would start with the youngest wines. There might be different grape varieties from a single vineyard to compare, or wines from a single variety but coming from different properties or regions.

When tasting a series of wines from the same region, they should be presented in order of rising value or appellation hierarchy. Thus in the case of Bordeaux one would begin with Bordeaux rouge, Bordeaux supérieur, and wines from the Côtes before those of Fronsac and the satellites of St-Emilion (Parsac, Puisseguin, Lussac, Montagne, and St-Georges); then one would move on to wines from St-Emilion, Graves, Pomerol, Médoc, and Haut Médoc with the classed growths being tasted last of all. Similarly, a Burgundy merchant would start with Beaujolais and Beaujolais Villages, continue with Mâcon reds, and then taste Côte de Beaune and Côte de Nuits wines in two separate groups. In each wine-growing region the local hierarchy should be followed.

If one had to choose the best wines from a group of dry whites, the samples should be presented from left to right in order of increasing alcoholic strength. If the wines have any degree of sweetness, they should be ranged according to their densities or ascending order of sugar content. Red wines are also frequently put in order of alcoholic strength, but a more rational order can be made if their polyphenol indices, indicating their level of astringency, are known. Red wines can be divided into several groups on this basis, for example, wines with an index of less than 30, those between 30 and 40, 40 and 50, 50 and 60, and, finally, those wines whose index is more than 60. Press wines are tasted last of all.

Tasting fine wines is obviously both the most interesting and the most arduous of tastings because of the diversity of types and range of quality. Comparing wines which are fairly similar is difficult and requires much retasting, as, for example, when trying to rank a group of wines which are clearly on the same quality level.

It is always more interesting to taste and compare "straight" wines than those which have been blended, whose individuality has been diluted, and which then resemble the commercial styles that are uniform and without fault, but often without identity either. In everyday wines one is content with a certain neutrality or uniformity and absence of defects; but such wines are so lacking in personality that it is impossible to describe them.

Before judging a wine, tasters should also take into account any excess carbon dioxide which makes the wine thinner and gives it a prickle, as well as any excess sulfur dioxide which spoils a wine's aroma and makes red wines dry. However, too little carbon dioxide is equally harmful because it releases aldehyde odors associated with flat and overoxidized wines. These are passing faults which are easily remedied by racking and other routine cellar procedures. To get rid of excess carbon dioxide in a recently fermented wine before tasting, pour it from one glass to another, letting it fall from a certain height so as to create an emulsion, and repeat the process a dozen times or so. The improvement in young wines so treated is both considerable and surprising.

THE INFLUENCE OF TEMPERATURE ON OUR SENSES

The sensation of cold in one's mouth and throat is part of the pleasure of drinking, quenching one's thirst, and feeling refreshed. "Drink cool where possible" was Rabelais' advice. The warming effect of a hot drink is similarly appreciated at other times.

Our experience of cold or hot when drinking liquids is due to thermal sensitivity, part of our tactile sense, which is found above all in the thicker part of the lips and tip of the tongue, the surfaces which first come into contact with whatever we eat or drink. The lips play an advance warning role which prevents any painful contact with the more sensitive mucous lining of the mouth, the walls of the pharynx, and the esophagus. Our lips have a quite astonishing sensitivity: Without much practice it is possible to distinguish the difference between two wines with a temperature variation of only a degree or so, at least between 10°C and 20°C, the range that concerns us in winetasting.

The areas sensitive to hot and cold are not the same. In the mouth and on the tongue there are some nerve fibers which are sensitive to heat, others to cold. The temperature impression also depends on the conductive properties of the object in contact with the mouth's tissues, and there are many examples to illustrate this: the unpleasant feel to the lips of a cold *tastevin*, the strip of wood used to eat ice cream from a tub, and or the little wooden fork one is given in St-Sébastien with which to eat elvers fried in hot oil. The cooling effect of menthol is due to the fact that it heightens the sensitivity of the cold receptors and inhibits those for warmth.

Tasters know that a wine's temperature also has a considerable influence on the way that it smells and tastes, and they take this into account when preparing tastings. Wines can only be compared if they are at the same temperature, whence the need to leave all the samples in the tasting room for an hour or two before actually tasting, as I have already emphasized. Two glasses of the same wine presented at different temperatures can, in effect, be considered as two different wines. Wines that are too warm or too cold are difficult to judge.

Temperature is also an essential consideration in serving wines properly. According to its temperature, a wine's taste and smell may be heightened or neutralized and modified both in terms of quality and intensity. It is as harmful for a red wine to be offered too warm as too cold. There is an optimum temperature for every wine, at which its taste qualities show at their best, and a deviation of just a few degrees is enough to make the difference between its being attractive to drink or not. Mistakes concerning temperature can have serious consequences; the bottle which has taken so much time, care, trouble, and money to arrive ready to drink at the consumer's table can all of a sudden be ruined by being served a few degrees too warm.

What are the appropriate adjectives to define temperature? The following table attempts to relate, as far as possible, a value in figures to a subjective impression in words.

Terms used to describe the temperature of wine

frozen	temperatures around 0°C
ice cold	
well chilled	4°–6°C
cold	6°–12°C
cool	12°–16°C
cool to moderate	16°–18°C
room temperature	
tepid	temperatures above 20°C
warm	
hot	

The effect of a wine's temperature on its smell is related above all to physical causes. Volatile odor substances evaporate more easily at a higher temperature than at a lower one. In a glass, therefore, the air space above a wine, which is in a state of equilibrium with the volatile constituents of the liquid, fills to a greater or lesser extent with odorous vapors whose concentration in aromas is higher if the wine is warm, lower if it is cold. Thus aroma and bouquet appear enhanced at 18°C, reduced at 12°C, and practically neutralized below 8°C. The evaporation of alcohol, and its particular smell which supports all the others, follows the same laws; over 20°C it reduces a bouquet's appeal and destroys its finesse. Faults also emerge more clearly when a wine is warm; the acescent character and the lack of cleanness and clarity due to ethyl acetate stand out, and unpleasant tastes show up. At higher temperatures the chemical smell of sulfurous acid is accentuated, causing a prickling sensation at the top of one's nose and even sneezing in sensitive subjects; it disappears below 12°C. The best means of minimizing the olfactory faults of certain wines is to serve them colder.

One of the differences between aroma in the mouth and the aroma perceived via the nostrils, between interior and exterior aroma one might say, is due in part to the differences in temperature between the two sensations, both of which are made up of roughly the same volatile elements. Keeping a wine in one's mouth long enough for the aromatic elements to be released and perceived by the sense of smell is, therefore, recommended. A white wine at 10°C rises to 25°C if kept in the mouth for ten seconds.

The ways in which temperature affects taste follow physiological laws that have not been clearly established, but it can be said that there is an optimum temperature for drinking every wine. In fact, it is the respective levels of sugar, acid, tannin, carbon dioxide, and alcohol which determine the best temperature at which to taste a wine. Nevertheless, there are some wines which, even when served at the same temperature as others, seem to have an extra degree of freshness. On this basis, choosing the right temperature would be very complicated, but from a practical point of view it is possible to offer some simple rules which should be remembered in order to get the most out of a wine.

Temperatures of less than 6°C or 8°C literally anesthetize the taste buds. Between 10°C and 20°C, the various tastes develop in different ways. A higher temperature increases the sensation of sweetness so that a sugar solution seems sweeter at 20°C than at 10°C. This effect applies to all the sweet-tasting substances: the various sugars, glycerol, and alcohol. A sweet dessert wine or liqueur will taste less sickly sweet drunk at a low temperature; in a wine which is called dry, but which in fact has 5 g/l of sugar, the sugar will not be perceptible if the wine is served very cold.

Sensitivity to acidity as a function of temperature has given rise to contradictory observations. The perception threshold for acidity does not change, but acid is sensed most keenly at high temperatures, between 35°C and 50°C. Léglise finds a wine more acid when cold, and it has also been said that a flabby wine has a better acid balance if served cold. However, if one tastes potassium bitartrate solutions at 10°C and 20°C, the lower temperature seems to make the acidity more acceptable, especially in a 10 percent alcohol solution. The burning character of acid and alcohol together is heightened if the liquid is warm. There still seems to be room for research here.

A dry white wine with a total acidity of 5 g/l, for example, seems very acid at 18°C; its green acidity dominates its taste after 3 or 4 seconds of development. At 14°C its acidity is less aggressive to the palate, needing 8 seconds to become apparent, and at 10°C the same acidity is merely an agreeable freshness. The results are the same for a wine with 4 g/l total acidity. It is a question perhaps of an indirect effect; or it may be that there is a strong personal factor in the notion of acid balance dependent on temperature, or simply a more or less marked preference for a cold wine or a cool to moderate one.

There is general agreement, however, on the fact that sensitivity to saltiness, bitterness, and astringency is greater the lower the temperature, exactly the reverse of what happens in the case of sweetness. For example, sodium chloride, or table salt, has a perception threshold in water of 20 mg/l at 17°C and of 50 mg/l at 42°C. The bitterness of caffeine or quinine is also three times stronger at 17°C than at 42°C. The same red wine will seem hot and thin at 22°C, supple and fluid at 18°C, full and astringent at 10°C. This is the rationale behind the practice of bringing a red wine to room temperature, and the basic rule for serving red wines could be rendered thus: **The more tannic a wine is, the warmer it should be served.** The only red wines that can be drunk cool with any pleasure are those with very little tannin. To generalize for all wines, then, one might say that it is above all the amount of tannin which governs the temperature at which a wine should be served: White wines, which are by nature practically devoid of tannin, are drunk cold; rosé wines, which contain little, are drunk fairly cold; red wines made with limited maceration, such as *primeur* or *nouveau* types, taste better when cool; on the other hand, wines made for keeping and tannic in structure are drunk at a moderate to warm room temperature.

The same law could be rephrased as follows: Wines which are rich in aroma, and which therefore still have the fruity character of youth, benefit from being drunk on the cooler side precisely in order to enhance their fresh, aromatic character. Wines which have acquired a bouquet thanks to bottle age are served at a somewhat warmer temperature which brings out their bouquet and enhances their supple texture. This is logical enough since there is generally an inverse relationship between fruitiness and tannin.

Vinosity, the warm impression made by alcohol on the palate, is lessened by cool temperatures. Alcoholic wines are better drunk cool. The alcoholic strength of a fruit brandy or liqueur is more acceptable when drunk very cold. At high temperatures, on the other hand, vinosity is accentuated to the point of being a burning sensation in the throat. When drinking mulled wine or grog, for example, you can actually feel the suffocating effect of alcoholic vapor.

Temperature also affects the solubility of carbon dioxide contained to some extent by all wines. Carbon dioxide tends to be released as the temperature rises. The prickling sensation typical of a white wine containing 700 mg/l of carbon dioxide is clearly perceptible at 20°C, barely so at 12°C to 14°C, and not at all at 8°C. Much the same goes for a red wine containing 400 mg/l; drunk cold, the carbon dioxide is imperceptible, while at a room temperature of 18°C to 20°C it is disagreeably prickly on the tongue. Champagne and sparkling wine are poured cold into their flutes so as to limit the liberation of gas, for it is only thus that they are pleasant to drink.

So, to those people who suggest that white wines are drunk cold and red wines drunk at room temperature simply out of habit, one can offer a number of physiological reasons in justification of the practice.

Suitable Temperatures for Tasting

Now that we know to what extent temperature affects organoleptic sensations we have the wherewithal to answer the questions: "At what temperature should one taste, and at what temperature should one drink?"

The two temperatures are not the same. The winetaster tastes from a critical standpoint and he should not do so in ideal conditions which would minimize any defects. Professional tasting is best undertaken with all wines between 15°C and 20°C, irrespective of type. In effect, no special measures need be taken except to avoid tasting wines too cold in winter (those coming straight from the cellar, for example) or too warm in summer, as with samples which have been left in a warm room or office.

On the other hand, for purely pleasurable exploration, amateur or informed drinker alike should serve the wines as near as possible to the temperature judged best to flatter their good points and minimize their faults. However, this temperature is not easy to define. It is subjective and if it depends on the wine, it also depends on the circumstances in which it is served and on the tastes and habits of the drinker. The right answer would be covered by the axiom that "there is a temperature for each wine and a temperature for every taste," which leaves room for a wide diversity of opinion and which would be an adroit way of dodging the issue.

If you want to be sensible and offend as few as possible, the suggestions in the table below should be carefully followed. They are the opinions of an informed majority, carefully collated and based on wide experience.

Standard temperatures for serving wine

Red Bordeaux	18°C
Red Burgundy	16°C
Tannic red wines (with a tannin index above 36) and Vintage Port	16°–18°C
Red wine with little tannin (tannin index less than 36), Beaujolais, Côtes-du-Rhone	14°–16°C
Full-bodied and aromatic white wines, sweet wines, rosés, Banyuls, sherry, and white port	10°–20°C
Light, acid, and sparkling white wines	8°–10°C

According to these guidelines, it can be seen that the general tendency is to drink red wines too warm (few wines can withstand a temperature of more than 18°C) and white wines too cold. However, if one wants to deviate from these norms, then it is better to serve a degree too cold than a degree too warm. Wine that is too cold will warm up in the glass quite naturally following the curve shown below; it just requires a little patience.

Between 4°C and 10°C wine warms up by roughly one degree every three or four minutes; between 10°C and 15°C a one-degree rise takes six to eight minutes. Thus white wines served too cold, between 6°C and 8°C, would reach 10°C to 12°C in twelve to fifteen minutes, and it is always possible to accelerate the process by cupping the bowl of the glass in the palm of one's hand.

However, the suitable temperature need not always be the one dictated by the thermometer: A red wine at 20°C may well suit a hot dish, but feel too warm drunk with the cheese. In cold weather the temperature range in the table above might be better raised a little, while in summer we prefer our drinks a bit cooler because they are more thirst quenching that way.

Different customs and opinions must be taken into account, too. There are some people in the Médoc who serve very old wines almost lukewarm, whereas there is a recent nonconformist vogue to drink red wines very cold. In the realm of taste, where there is always room for debate, it is easy to be original by simply rejecting accepted views. However, there is often a very thin line between exception and anomaly, between originality and a lack of common sense.

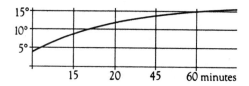

A standard tasting glass was filled with 10 centiliters of white wine at a temperature of 4°C and was placed in a room at 21°C. The curve shows the rate of warming against time in minutes.

Eight

The Interpretation of Tasting Tests

TASTING THEMES

Each tasting exercise relates to a particular problem, and how it should be carried out depends on the question to be answered. It is important, therefore, to define the question carefully in advance and formulate it precisely. As I have already said, some tastings do not produce the results one might expect simply because the aims of the tasting and what is expected of the tasters have not been adequately defined.

The tasting themes most commonly encountered can be split into three groups:

First, **differentiation between, and the identification of samples:** daily fare for professional tasters. These tastings allow for comparisons between wines in order to decide preferences, to check the results of experiments in winemaking and storage, to follow the evolution and to observe the effects of a particular treatment or additive, to finalize the make-up of blends, and so on. This group also includes blind tasting exercises where the aim is to identify the origin of an anonymous wine, at best to recognize its precise identity.

Second, **appraisal and quality ranking:** These tastings consist of comparing and classifying according to their qualities and defects wines which are preferably of the same origin or price. Such, for example, is the object of official quality-control tastings where the aim is to eliminate substandard examples from a given group of wines; or of tasting competitions to choose the best wines of a batch, or again of tastings which set out to grade a range of wines in order of quality. More often today this kind of tasting consists of assessing a wine's commercial quality for sale or purchase according to its type or brand.

Third, **analytical tasting,** which could also be called descriptive analysis according to taste. This consists of studying and listing all the sensory reactions to a wine, and of describing and explaining them as far as possible in terms of the wine's analytical make-up. The exercises use a precise and detailed vocabulary which requires codifying in order to be intelligible to everybody. Description is followed by a judgment which can take the form of a numerical score or a verbal assessment. This is also the theme of tastings which are being put on with increasing frequency by clubs, societies, and commercial bodies for audiences of professionals or interested amateurs.

Whatever the aim, all tastings must lead to a comparative judgment, for tasting is only of use if it makes comparisons. These are made by relating wines to control samples presented and tasted at the same time, or by comparison with models which each taster has in mind. In the first case the results are more objective as the reference points are there at the same time. In the second case precision depends on how good the taster is and how well he is tasting at the time, because obviously each individual is drawing on his or her own particular professional experience.

All tastings pose questions, implicitly; and if the questions themselves are not clear the answers are likely to be wrong. The countless different types of tasting can be divided into two broad categories:

Tasting for pleasure: where one tastes and drinks purely for pleasure—be it sensual, intellectual, or cultural—in the company of friends. In the final analysis this the whole point of wine, to give pleasure to the consumer.

Professional tasting: where one is tasting for the purposes of assessment, classification, purchase, sale, improvement. This is the daily fare of wine professionals whose eventual goal is to provide the consumer with a product that can be enjoyed. This work is extremely varied: It may be to judge the influence of two different root stocks on the tannins in a wine or to supervise the final blend of a quality brand; to grant or refuse the right to use an appellation of origin on the label or to award a competition medal; to organize the maturation of a wine in oak barrels; and so on.

In the same way as an understanding of the rudiments of music or composition can increase the pleasure one gets from listening to music, equally an understanding of professional tasting practice can but enhance the amateur's pleasure in wine.

Whatever the tasting context, it is essential to have clearly in mind both the problem under consideration and the type of answer required: a simple yes/no response or a detailed description, for example. It is also important to remember that one always tends to judge (consciously or not) from the point of view either of a salesman—finding and promoting all the positive qualities—or of a buyer—looking for and describing all the shortcomings. The second attitude is easier to adopt and far too frequent, even in the absence of any commercial transaction. The sound commercial ability to buy cheap and sell dear, the latter argued on the basis of quality, is more easily acquired if one has a clear and objective understanding of one's own motives.

Any sample presented for tasting should correspond exactly to the total volume available of the wine it claims to be. The question is quite straightforward when one is simply enjoying the only bottle available from one's own cellar, opened for a special occasion at home. The matter is much more complicated when the question is whether to grant someone else the right to an appellation of origin (in effect, the right to make a living) or to a place in a particular quality hierarchy which will be visible worldwide. Let us ponder these last two questions for a moment.

The wine presented to a judging panel for an official certificate of approval a few weeks after the harvest will be granted or refused such approval according to how good an example of its category it is likely to be after a few months or years. Preparation of such samples should be done with particular care in order to be representative of the whole harvest as declared, and without any problems such as oxidation, lees aromas, copper taint from stopcocks, and so on. The problem is even more ticklish where competition wines are concerned; whether regional, national or international, or indeed wines for the innumerable "private" tastings the results of which are nonetheless "public." Simple rules which guarantee honesty and a serious approach seem often to leave room for question. The sample of wine to be tasted should be drawn by somebody both competent and neutral. A bottle brought by the owner or chosen by the organizer himself leaves too much room for human weakness.

Such competitions should only compare wines of the same category and characteristics. For does it really make any serious sense to pit "special reserve" selections amounting to only two or three hundred bottles, against lots of several thousand bottles representing an entire harvest?

Tasters should be competent for the particular task in question. It is quite possible to be an expert at identifying the four Médoc First Growths, on the one hand, and yet find it difficult to grade the five hundred barrels in a Sauternes *chai*, or to blend a vat of Beaujolais Primeur, on the other. Modesty is a prerequisite in this business! If a certain verbal facility can conceal professional limitations, it cannot prevent the troublesome consequences. Anyone can become a "good" taster given practice, and yet more practice; for there is no such thing as a born universal taster.

Tasting conditions are a potent influence on any conclusions. One avoids coughing in a concert hall; the Louvre galleries have very carefully considered lighting. Equally, wine requires appropriate conditions in which to be clinically assessed or, alternatively, simply enjoyed. And these general observations apply as much to the austerity of a research laboratory as to the dining room of a first-class restaurant. In each case the objectives are very different, and the ideal conditions not interchangeable. How many wines which are appreciated as light yet delightful in the cool, damp vaults of a *petit vigneron* seem weak and disappointing during the course of a sumptuous meal; and how many harsh judgments of "barrel samples" need to be enthusiastically revised "from bottle" several years later . . . and vice versa.

With the ideal combination of wine, judge, and ambiance, efficient tasting and notation is possible. In practice, one tends to make either a description of the wine, a "portrait," or to give a score, locating it in a hierarchy. A "simple" distinction (is wine A identical to wine B or not?) may be arrived at by either means. In all cases as many opinions as there are tasters are collected for each wine. And how then are final decisions to be made from the varied opinions? By one expert or by majority decision? The former is both simpler and more common; it is the norm, for example, in the case of the cellarmaster in a winery and in most wine books and journals. A majority decision is more difficult to manage; democratic but, as a consensus, sometimes too neutral. There are different techniques which may assist in making a final choice, but they cannot reconcile differences of perception. To put the question in a rather extreme form: Is it simpler to rely on a single really "good" taster to solve a given problem, or to try and solve it with ten or twenty palates? And is an average of those ten or twenty less certain assessments any more satisfactory an answer?

The method of tasting will vary as much in the way that samples are presented as in one's personal tasting technique. Various tasting exercises have been described in detail in several books and repeated in recent French works. To me it seems that tasting exercises could be categorized in a simpler way, according to the number of glasses being used.

First let us look at the case where there is only one glass and only one wine to taste. This is a difficult test because the taster has to judge the wine solely on the basis of information given, and with no other reference points save those in his memory. An example of this is where an expert or technician is asked to give his opinion on an isolated sample. Unless the wine has marked positive or negative characteristics, one should not expect detailed and positive information from this type of tasting. In such cases the taster would be well advised to be prudent.

Another fairly common tasting exercise is where a series of wines are tasted one after the other, only one glass being used because there are not as many glasses per taster as there are wines. But however carefully one tastes in this way, it is only suitable for a rough sorting. This method can be used for a fairly rapid preliminary look at wines that have marked differences and whose details are known (origin, alcoholic strength, quantity available, and price). The verdict is of an all-or-nothing kind; the wine is declared good or bad, suitable or not for a particular use. With a bit of practice one can manage to grade wines in such tastings on a 1 to 5 basis, but reproducing the results is likely to be chancy as any scoring will depend on the average quality of all the wines tasted. In effect, the taster relies on a double comparison in this sort of tasting; one is with his own mental image of the type of wine being tasted, the other is with the fresh and immediate memory of the preceding wines. However, one's impression of any given sample is modified by the memory of those already tasted, and the memory of any individual wine fades after trying a further three or four.

BLIND TASTING

In blind tasting nothing is known about the wine being tasted. It leads to a more objective assessment because the wine itself is the only source of information for the taster. And it is an exercise much to be recommended to anyone, at any age; for it prevents one's judgment from being affected by other factors, cultural or intellectual, which may have nothing whatsoever to do with the real characteristics of the wine. Every taster, whether amateur or professional, should set aside vanity and subject himself to blind tasting. In order for such tastings to be effective and to avoid needless psychological influences or "traps," it is essential to make the context of the tasting clear (research into different winemaking techniques, sorting out a hierarchy within a comparable group, for example) and to ensure that any questions to be answered are equally unambiguous. Whatever the case, it remains an unpredictable activity. Here is Broadbent on the subject: "It is my firm opinion . . . that to assess the qualities of a wine by tasting it completely blind, without any hint of what it might be, is the most useful and salutary discipline that any self-respecting taster can be given. It is not infrequently the most humiliating." In fact, it is so difficult because the taster has no point of comparison, and the extent of his expertise is no help; on the contrary, its very breadth may well be a hindrance. "The more one has tasted, the less clear-cut may be one's reactions and the less dogmatic one's pronouncements. This is because the experienced taster (almost always a professional) has been exposed to such a wide range of closely related smells and tastes, and has met with so many exceptions to the rules that he has learned to qualify and temper his judgments."

The amateur whose skill is limited to the contents of friends' cellars has a better chance of shining at this game than the professional. The latter also has far fewer opportunities to taste wines ready to drink than young wines which he is grooming to become the good bottles of the future.

In reality, guesswork tasting is not a professional activity, but an amusement for the dinner table, and it is as much a game of chance as is betting on horses. The names and vintages of several wines need to be identified from dozens and dozens of possibilities. Of course, one is helped to some extent by what the wine tastes like, but above all by knowing the resources of your host's cellar.

The winetaster is frequently asked whether it is really possible to recognize where a wine comes from, to identify its vintage and individual vineyard. First, one cannot identify a region unless the wine really displays regional characteristics; what would be easier to identify is the grape variety. However, when the wine is made from a blend of grape varieties, as is the case for a Médoc or St-Emilion, the distinction is less clear. Wines from these two regions might be thought of as making up two groups; most of the individuals can be identified, but there is a fairly large fringe of atypical individuals whom it is impossible to recognize. It sometimes happens that wines will even taste like those from another region, in which case the taster making a mistake is actually tasting well. As for trying to distinguish the Médoc communes from each other, Pauillac wines from those of St-Estèphe, or a Margaux from a St-Julien, it is a chancy enterprise. Margaux is said to be fine and supple, Pauillac full-bodied and tannic, St-Estèphe rounder in style, St-Julien elegant and well balanced, but these are really just the commercial styles which were followed when blending in merchant's cellars years ago; the reality is quite different. For my own part, I would not claim to be able to identify the communes of a series of Médocs tasted blind. The problem is just as difficult in Burgundy where the distinction between wines from the Côte de Beaune and the Côte de Nuits is a matter for endless debate.

For anyone who has followed the winemaking of the past thirty or so harvests, identifying a vintage may seem somewhat easier; the process is one of reasoning, elimination, and deduction. Knowing the annual weather cycles and consequent state of the grapes at vintage time will enable one to rule out certain vintages leaving just a few from which to choose. The success rate is fairly high when limited to identifying vintages of the last decade, but the older the wines the less pronounced are their differences of character and vintage.

As to identifying an individual vineyard or property, the wine needs to be one with a very distinctive personality. There are a number of recognizable properties from the Graves in particular. I have had a certain amount of success in identifying La Mission-Haut-Brion 1957 and Pape-Clément 1961. Among the Médocs it would seem possible to pick out Lafite and Latour, if present, from among a group of wines, and, for different reasons, Lynch-Bages and Calon-Ségur of a certain period. However, the number of conceivable choices is vast and in reality the chances of successful identification are minimal.

Bernard Ginestet, a specialist where "a storm in a wineglass" debates are concerned, writes as follows on the subject: "In matters of winetasting there is no such thing as infallibility . . . there are excellent tasters whose reliability index is above average. More significantly, all of us go through some periods that are better than others, during which we can be remarkably successful at identifying wines blind. I know of tasters who live by a reputation forged on the basis of two or three inspired guesses. I myself have experienced moments of glory where everything seemed obvious to me, and I have also drunk the cup of humility to the dregs when, unable to interpret any clue at all, I have ended up making enormous blunders." And Bernard Ginestet joins Michael Broadbent when he says: "Winetasting is one of the finest schools for teaching modesty."

TWO WINES IN TWO, THREE, OR FOUR GLASSES

Tasting two wines in two glasses, known as **paired tasting**, is the most common tasting exercise. The two wines, A and B, are presented together.

In the **unilateral test**, glass A is identified and presented as the reference sample; sample B must then be assessed with reference to sample A. In the **bilateral test**, the reference sample is not identified and the glasses can be presented in either order. According to the AFNOR code, paired sample tests should be used in three cases:

1. To distinguish differences in taste between two wines, where the question to be answered is: "Is there a difference between the two glasses?"
2. To differentiate between varying degrees of intensity of a characteristic under study, where the question asked is: "Which is the sample with the greater intensity of such and such a characteristic?"—more precisely, "Which is the sweetest, the most acid, the most aromatic, the most tannic?"
3. To establish a preference by asking: "Which do you prefer, A or B?"

Generally speaking, the taster should avoid discussing the identity of wines in his answer, and also avoid saying that they are the same, as this would imply that the wines were identical, a risky conclusion to draw. It would be better to say they are indistinguishable; that is, the taster cannot distinguish between them on the basis of their taste. There are in fact wines from different sources which are similar enough to be confused, notably blended wines.

I recommend tasting the two samples both ways around, first comparing glass A with glass B, and then B with A. Start by smelling A, followed by B, then A again, and so on alternatively with a glass in each hand. Look for any possible differences in smell, and in taste as well, by moving from A to B and back again. It is no use actually tasting repeatedly; any difference should be perceived at the first attempt and confirmed, in reverse, by the second. If no difference can be detected, a final attempt should be made a few minutes later. It is worth remembering, though, that the first impression is often the best. Variations of the paired sample test can also be devised: For example, taste the first time around knowing what the difference is, then try to identify the two wines blind at a second attempt. This method is also used for an extended series of samples being compared to one another, but which one has to taste in pairs.

Paired tasting is at once the most simple, the most accurate, and the most sensitive of tasting exercises, and by comparison with exercises using more than two glasses it is also less tiring. However, one should be aware of its disadvantages, too: For example, one is inclined to detect differences which are in fact nonexistent, and if the difference to be detected is at the limits of what is effectively perceptible, then there is a 50 percent chance of getting the answer right by chance. The validity of results can be judged by repeating the tests and assessments, either using a sufficient number of participants or by increasing the number of tests for a smaller group.

The various tasting exercises using three glasses can be summarized thus:

a. Two different wines are presented at the same time as a third glass containing one of them; the taster is asked to match the third to the first two.

b. One of the three glasses is designated the reference sample, and the taster is asked to say which of the other two is identical to this reference sample. Two of the three glasses are unidentified and this interesting but little-used exercise is known as the **duo-trio test**.

c. Three glasses are presented, two of which are identical and the taster must identify the odd sample. This exercise is called the **triangular test**.

d. In another version of the preceding test, the taster is given the choice of three answers: "There is no detectable difference between the three glasses"; "there is no detectable difference between two of the glasses"; "the three glasses are all different."

Suppose one wanted to test the effect on a wine's taste of adding a small amount of citric acid (an authorized acidification treatment). Tasters are presented with three glasses blind; two unaltered and one containing an acidified sample, or alternatively, two acidified and one reference sample. If, in these circumstances, the majority of tasters can identify the glasses with added citric acid, then there is almost certainly a difference in taste and it can be concluded that the treatment has affected the taste. The probability of getting the answers right by chance is only one in ten. In this way the triangular test results are made more objective, especially if the test is repeated six times with the samples being presented in a different variation of the six possible combinations each time.

The triangular test is particularly recommended for technical tastings, for a small group of tasters, or for the selection of tasters. These types of test generally show up any individuals with an inferior sensitivity. I have observed many times with qualified tasters that in a triangular test they cannot always detect a difference which they can perceive when presented with only two glasses.

160

Table of different tasting exercises

Type of tasting exercise	Presentation of the glass	Other permutations of presentation	Probability
Unilateral pair test	⚲ ⚲ A B ?*		
Bilateral pair test	⚲ ⚲ A B ? ?	AB or BA	1 in 2
Duo-trio test	⚲ ⚲ ⚲ A A B ⚲ ⚲	AAB or ABA	1 in 2
Triangular test (which glass is different?)	⚲ ⚲ ⚲ A A B ? ? ?	AAB, ABA, or BAA	1 in 3
Triangular test (which is the sweetest, the most acid . . . ?)	⚲ ⚲ ⚲ A A B ? ? ?	AAB, ABA, BAA, ABB, BAB, BBA	1 in 6
Triangular test (with the possibility of three identical glasses)	⚲ ⚲ ⚲ A A A ? ? ?	As preceding test +AAA or BBB	1 in 8
Four-glass test (find the odd one out)	⚲ ⚲ ⚲ ⚲ A B B B ? ? ? ?	ABBB, BABB, BBAB, BBBA	1 in 4
Multiple-pair test	⚲ ⚲ ⚲ ⚲ A B A B ? ? ? ?	ABAB, AABB, ABBA, BABA, BBAA, BAAB	1 in 6

Number of comparisons required: with 2 glasses 1
with 3 glasses 3
with 4 glasses 6

*Question marks indicate the unidentified glasses.

161

Minimum number of correct answers needed to give a significant variance in the different tasting tests

For a significant variance of 5 percent (P = 0.05)

Number of answers	Pair test	Triangular test	Duo-trio test	Two-out-of-five test
6	6	5	6	3
8	7	6	8	3
10	9	7	9	4
12	10	8	10	4
14	11	9	11	4
16	12	10	12	5
18	13	10	13	5
20	15	11	15	5
22	16	12	16	6
24	17	13	17	6
26	19	14	18	6
28	20	15	19	7
30	21	16	20	7

The price of trying to make this test more rigorous would seem to be a loss in sensitivity, for the taster's state of mind plays a crucial role in his conclusions. And there are several reasons which explain this loss of sensitivity. Tasting with three glasses involves a greater number of comparisons so that the sense of taste is dulled sooner. Besides, it is always easier to perceive and confirm a difference than an identity between two samples. When tasting the first two glasses one always perceives some difference, real or imaginary; the source of error lies in the difficulty of distinguishing the third glass from the first two, and in deciding with which of these it is identical. At least three comparisons must be made. One finds that the taster can distinguish and identify two of the samples in most cases; confusion arises when trying to assess the third. One also finds a tendency to choose the sample in the middle as the odd one. Frequently, tasters will find variations of intensity between the two identical glasses.

Two tasting exercises for comparing two wines in four glasses have also been devised. In one case the glass which is different from the other three has to be found; in the second, two pairs of two different wines are presented in any order and the pairs must be identified. Both these tests involve six successive pair comparisons which makes the exercise long, tiring, and difficult.

TASTING TO GRADE WINES

Tasting a large number of wines using numerous glasses allows for a very wide variety of tasting procedures. Two wines might be presented in several glasses and tasters asked to differentiate between them in the ways described in the previous section, or as many wines can be shown as there are glasses, with all, none, or just some of the wines being identified with a view to ranking them. And between these two extremes there are all sorts of tests which could be devised.

The taster is constantly grading wines, whether it be unfinished "brut" samples, the basis of future blends, or finished wines already in bottle. From any group he has to sort out the best and eliminate the inferior wines. His choice will be made on the basis of general quality impressions, at the same time taking into account the use envisaged for the wine. Thus after vinification is complete he may be asked to grade vats of new wine at a property or in a merchant's cellars so as to divide them into lots of varying quality, or to grade a series of wines from the same appellation which are destined for blending. He may also be required to rank a series of numbered bottles tasted blind so as to see how individual products match up to their competition. One of the most popular forms of this sort of tasting is that of comparing and ranking a number of well-known properties of the same vintage, given that they are indeed of comparable style and quality.

Ranking by preference is often difficult for wines may merit the same score for different characteristics. Should one score a wine which is fuller but has less aromatic finesse higher than one which is lighter but which has a finer bouquet? In such cases taster's opinions may differ and it may be worth classifying the wines on the basis of smell first, and then by taste.

Ranking may also be based on a constituent of the wine. For example, one might classify white wines on the basis of their acidity or sweetness, and red wines according to their tannic characteristics, without, of course, knowing the analyses of the wines beforehand. Ranking is also useful when comparing wines from vines of varying ages, from different parcels of the same grape variety, or wines that have been made, treated, and aged in a variety of ways.

Successful tasting depends on the equipment used and on rigorous organization. Ideally, the samples should be presented in uniform bottles with standard labels. Bottles should be ranged in line on the table and a glass placed in front of each one. In this way up to fifteen samples can be considered at a time. Beyond fifteen the wines should be divided into groups, so that twenty wines, for example, would be tasted in two groups of ten, sixty in four groups of fifteen. The best wines are selected from each group and, as in any contest, these are then compared to decide the winners. Ranking a large number of wines requires a lot of time-consuming, methodical work. The order in which the wines are lined up initially should be maintained throughout the tasting; bottles should not be moved forward or backward, taken out of line or have their places changed, and, above all, they should not be switched around. Grading can be facilitated, however, by moving the sample glasses instead, advancing them to a greater or lesser extent so as to produce three rows: The good wines are brought forward, the poorer wines left back, and those of average quality are left in a central row. In this way a visual classification is shown by the positions of the glasses and subsequent comparisons are made easier.

A recommended method for ranking a series of wines precisely consists of tasting them in succession from left to right, in glasses marked with the sample number on the base. The comparisons are made in pairs with the better wine being replaced on the left in each case. After the whole series has been tasted, the wines will have been sorted into an approximate order of quality. The exercise is then repeated, and the third time around should confirm that in every case the wine on the left is better than its neighbor on the right, and that the wines are effectively aligned in decreasing order of quality.

Another method of grading is to give each wine a mark as one tastes, the wines being automatically ranked according to their scores. The technique is simpler and quicker than the one of multiple comparison just described, but it is much less precise if the differences between the wines are small. In fact, it is easier and more accurate to award marks after an initial ranking. Depending on the circumstances, equal scores may be admissible; otherwise the taster will be asked to ensure a different score for each wine. The advantage of marking systems (which will be examined later) is that they relate the wines to each other more precisely. Simple numerical order in a series does not indicate the extent of the difference between adjacent wines; they may be only a fraction of a point apart, in which case the wines will be very similar in quality, or several points apart, in which case there is a marked difference in quality.

A common method of judging wines is by competitions where medals, gold cups, the Asti Fair's Douja d'Or, and so on are awarded. The awards are so numerous in France and elsewhere that, going back to the turn of the century if necessary, it would be remarkable if any property that had made the effort had not managed to win some kind of medal. Classification tastings are an annual event and exist at all competitive levels; they are a major activity for official tasters—regional competitions, organized by *départements* and run by the local viticultural associations, competitions at commercial shows and fairs, the prestigious General Agricultural Fair held in Paris, and international competitions. At one time the Eastern Bloc countries made a specialty of competitions where the participants paid to enter and gained their diplomas by purchase, as it were.

Jacques Luxey sought to compensate for the variations in scores which are always present in group tastings, and where a few widely divergent figures distort the group average and therefore the result. He applied his method throughout his numerous fine winetastings, and the guidelines were very clear. The team should be relatively large, competent, and homogeneous in ability. (Luxey himself normally worked with a group of fifteen to twenty, eight being the minimum, his tasters being recruited from the best Parisian professionals: *sommeliers*, chefs, and wine journalists.) The group needs to be fairly large because of the wide range within which different tasters mark. Luxey grouped tasting judges for this type of work into four categories, according to their broad marking band. Suppose the 100-point marking system is used: Some judges will use a wide range of marks, say 25 for the worst and 90 for the best, and others, less confident perhaps, will mark over a narrower band, from 60 to

72, for example. There will be those who are generous—"everything is very good" they say—and those who are more mean with a span of perhaps 38 to 57—"everything is rather ordinary!" Results are normally calculated by adding up the marks given to each wine and dividing the total by the number of tasters.

Of course, it must be said that this "arithmetic" conclusion is itself only an approximation. In effect, it amounts to measuring length using different scales and, as the proverb has it, "the measurement is only as good as the yardstick." Luxey also suggested taking into account each taster's reliability by comparing the discrepancy between individual scores and the group result, and he also proposed eliminating both marks and opinions which were clearly aberrant within the group context. Computers can easily resolve such complicated problems, and no doubt they will soon be an integral part of our tasting rooms.

How the Winetaster Prepares Blends

The importance of blends in winemaking needs to be stressed. Edouard Kressmann has said in their praise: "Everyone knows that the best tobaccos, the best teas or coffees, and many other products of the soil are blends. Blends of elements with differing characteristics, possibly from different sources, all harmoniously combined for the greater satisfaction of man." The same holds true of spirits. Fine cognacs, like the most luxurious perfumes, are born of a complex interplay of blends. One particular brand of cognac bases the advertising of its Fine Champagne on the subtlety of a blend in which some eighty different brandies intermingle. Another cognac boasts of drawing on the four great vineyard regions of the Charente. "It derives its power and structure from the Grande and Petite Champagnes, its roundness from the Fins Bois and it owes the finesse which lingers on the palate to the Borderies." The glories of whisky are also due to skillful blending.

However, is not all wine a blend? The producer mixes his grapes, sometimes of different varieties, in the fermentation vat, and he blends the different lots of new wine and the free-run wine with the press wine. It is these blends that are responsible for the balance and complexity of a great wine. On this subject I remember a tasting put on in 1966 of the 1953 wines of a St-Emilion property. Several wines had been made, vinified separately according to grape variety and soil; and these were then aged in bottles separately. The great majority of experts rejected these in favor of a wine made from the combined blend of all the vats and grape varieties.

The wholesale merchant needs to blend his wines in order to have uniform blends in sufficient volume to be commercially viable. In fact, very few wines can be sold in the original state in which they leave the vineyard. Even if they are of the requisite quality, they may not always be in the required style. A good example of integral blending is the Spanish solera system as practiced in Jerez: Several times a year wines of all ages selected from the total stocks in barrel are blended together in order to make a product that is absolutely consistent in style and quality from year to year.

A distinction must be drawn between several blending operations. *Égalisage* is the blending of the various vats of a single vintage from one property or wine cooperative in order to achieve a uniform whole; this is also known as assembling the wine. *Assemblage* is the making of a certain type of wine by mixing wines from the same source and appellation. A *cuvée* is the blending of wines from various communes within a generic appellation: A champagne cuvée, for example, can be a mixture of wines from both white and red grapes, and from several vintages (for a vintage cuvée the Champenois are authorized to use up to a 20 percent proportion of other vintages). In the context of an individual property *the cuvée* is also used to mean the *unification* of the various harvest lots. Finally, there is *coupage*, a term generally reserved for the blends of wines from different years and different regions, and, in the case of the EEC, even from different countries.

Before these various blending operations are carried out, they are always tried in small quantities; this trial is entrusted to the taster. To take a precise example: A wholesale merchant decides to make up a new AC Médoc blend before the previous one is exhausted. For this purpose he has at his disposal a dozen different lots of Médoc in varying quantities, recently bought from a number of properties. The taster begins by carefully establishing the taste characteristics of the twelve wines he has available, comparing them at the same time with the previous blend whose style the new cuvée must imitate. While tasting he tries to define the contribution that each lot will make to the final blend. He notes the positive elements: For example, this particular wine is useful because of its low acidity which will have a softening influence, that one's advantage is its good-quality tannic flavor which will strengthen the blend, and this other one is of interest for its concentrated Cabernet Sauvignon vigor. He will note the negative characteristics, too: Some wines may be low in alcohol, lack color, or have an obtrusive acidity. He takes all these observations into account when calculating the respective volumes of wine to go into the blend. As he tastes each wine he is able to estimate the approximate percentage of it that should be used. He may feel that one wine, not quite true to type, must be limited to 10 percent of the mix, while another, which would be quite acceptable on its own, can be used for half the total volume. His experience in this sort of work will mean he can already imagine fairly well what the planned blend will be like. He knows the rules of blending, especially the first one: Always choose the formula which utilizes the greatest possible number of wines.

The sign of a successful blend is when the resultant wine is better than the elements of which it is composed. The winetaster comes across many exceptions but he knows that, in general, a wine which is a little worse or a little better than average, and which is used for no more than 5 percent of the volume will simply drown in the blend. If he wants to improve a blend with a better quality wine, however, then at least 10 to 15 percent will be required, maybe more. A lot of good wine is needed to improve a faulty wine, whereas a very small amount of poor wine is enough to mar a blend, so that blending can never be a means of using up defective wine. There are so-called complementary wines, to which the addition of the opposite characteristics, of an opposing sign as it were, produces a balanced wine. There are also wines which, even when used in small quantities, will have an ameliorating, strengthening, or softening effect; these are called *vins médecins*, remedial wines. Similarly, there are wines with a strongly dominant character which mark a blend so palpably that they need to be used with great care. Finally, there are wines whose defects of dryness and thinness, for example, are difficult to mask, and these reappear in the long run; these are said to have a destructively drying, caustic character. When a particular degree of alcohol is required or, for sweet white wines, a certain level of sugar, then the taster uses rules to calculate the proportions of the blends. However, the final formula is not solely mathematical; taste is the final arbiter and will help decide between the different means of obtaining the desired degree of alcohol or level of sugar.

To return to our example: The taster will look at several trial blends, each slightly different, made up in test tubes and tasted in direct comparison with the Médoc blend currently on sale. Sometimes these first attempts do not correspond sufficiently to the desired style and a correction is required. As a result the taster will adjust the proportions of wines used, perhaps rejecting one altogether, and start all over again.

Thus the composition of the new blend is established by a process of trial and error and after several attempts. In some cases the desired result is only achieved after five or six attempts. A company's reputation and commercial future rely on the quality of the blend which must satisfy the present requirements of continuity and also be easy to reproduce in the future if necessary. One taster rarely makes all the decisions by himself; usually a group of colleagues will decide together after exchanging views and coming to an agreement among themselves. Besides which, the final decision is not reached until the trial sample has had a few days to settle and the tasters a few days to retaste and reconsider. Tasting a trial sample immediately after preparation allows one to judge the basic style and structure of the wine, but after the necessary period of rest the balance and aromatic elements of the wine can be better judged. Sometimes one can be quite surprised by how a blend evolves, in one direction or another. The cellarmaster would say that such are the surprises brought about by marriage.

TASTING AS A GROUP ACTIVITY

Several opinions are worth more than one alone, and one means of obtaining better results consists of working with a sufficiently large group of tasters. The method whereby wine is judged by only one taster is liable to error precisely because it is tasted by just one person. Obviously, the concurring opinions of several tasters make for a greater feeling of certainty, and they will carry more weight providing one is happy with the homogeneity of the group and the tasting ability of the individual members. For winetasting is not a simple opinion survey; quality of discrimination is more important than numbers of tasters.

The greatest care needs to be devoted to the selection of tasters and the composition of tasting panels. According to experts in methods of tasting, judges should be selected on the basis of repeated testing in order to ensure the reliability of their answers. Unfortunately, this sort of testing is rarely undertaken in the wine profession where people without any particular training can be seen improvising as tasters. Why should not there be a classification of tasters into categories, just as there are ranking systems in sports?

One possibility might be a hierarchy with four grades of ability, and with the levels carefully defined as follows. An **expert taster** would be someone who, as a result of his job, his profession, his knowledge, and his well-proved competence, has acquired a reputation as a taster in or beyond his own region. Tasting is not his only activity but it is something he does on an almost daily basis. He is called upon to give commercial, technical, and legal advice, and he arbitrates in disputes. He uses a precise and varied vocabulary, can analyze the taste characteristics of a wine, and rationalize his conclusions. The opinions of such expert tasters are authoritative references. In Great Britain, once they have passed the particularly demanding examination, they are called Masters of Wine (M.W.).

Similarly, the **qualified taster** would be someone working in one of the many jobs within the wine trade and who therefore tastes regularly. He should have received a specialized training in how to taste. His professional work should demonstrate his profound knowledge of wine, a good descriptive vocabulary, the ability to explain his judgments, and he would have a thorough knowledge of the typical taste characteristics of the different appellations. He would be on quality control panels and work with private tasting groups on the production side of wine or in the commercial sector. I would like to see all the diploma-level oenologists in this category. There are some amateurs capable of rising to this level. Qualified tasters usually work in groups of three or six.

The **occasional taster** belongs to the wine milieu, but has few opportunities to taste and lacks formal training. As a regular wine drinker he has a good sense of taste in that he can distinguish what is good from what is not. He can identify certain faults but he does not perceive subtleties and his vocabulary is limited; perhaps he lacks words rather than a sense of taste, and his judgments are based more on personal taste than on the criteria used to define a particular appellation or type of wine. For example, as a producer of red wine he does not like white and vice versa, and he prefers his own wine to any other, however prestigious, because he is used to it. In all good faith he would class his wine above the best of properties and then be genuinely astonished that the latter sells for five times as much as his own. Interpreting the results of a panel made up of such people is a hazardous affair.

Finally, following the example of other sectors of the food industry, **consumer teams** could be used to judge the acceptability of individual wines, though this is not commonly done. Following modern marketing practice, the reactions of consumers are usually registered in terms of prices and purchasing habits or through surveys too various to generalize about.

In consumer tasting surveys wine should be served in the same conditions as those in which it is normally drunk; this poses a considerable limitation on the number of comparisons possible. The questions asked should be very simple and limited to notions of preference. However, even with a group of fifty people, panels of such a disparate composition tell us nothing that we do not know already, and in any case some selection must be made when assembling such panels. It has been shown that any group of individuals can be split into two according to their tasting ability with respect to certain substances, bitterness in particular: those who are **natural tasters**, who have a fairly high level of sensory acuity, and **nontasters** whose sensory acuity is low. All in all the same goes for taste and smell as for sight and hearing; some have little ability in this respect and one cannot entrust tasting matters to them.

For these reasons there are good grounds for being wary of concepts which treat tasting as a simple psychophysiological test applied to a group of nonspecialists. The part played by chance in the replies of inexperienced judges is corrected by the use of statistical formulas. This concept of tasting is very far removed from that entrusted to skilled experts, of recognized ability, in the traditional wine regions. The quality of the tasters involved is the only means of guaranteeing the value of any tasting.

However, let us return to the training of professional groups. In business houses tastings are generally conducted by those responsible for buying, helped by the cellarmaster in charge of preparing blends, and sometimes by technical staff, and in many cases the firm's directors may take part, too. On the principle that those who sell should not also be those who buy, sales personnel do not normally take part in these tastings. Some firms have adopted a quality control system, occasionally led by an outsider to the business who can be a completely impartial judge. This panel regularly checks the quality and follows the development of wines in stock and on sale, and from time to time it organizes blind comparative tastings of the firm's wines with those of its competitors. To play fair in these tastings, all the wines, including those of the organizing company, should be purchased from retail outlets.

Control tastings organized by the viticultural syndicates, by INAO, by professional advisory bodies, or by the Fraud Prevention Service are always carried out by a group of qualified tasters drawn from wine producers, wine brokers, and those in commerce, with oenologists attending increasingly often. This is the beginning of a body of qualified tasters whose numbers are increasing with the development of specialized training in winetasting.

All group tastings follow a precise set of rules. Generally speaking, once the theme of the tasting has been announced, each taster should work independently as though just for himself, and as though his colleagues were not there. There should be no communication between tasters nor should they note each other's reactions or hear their observations, both of which might distract and influence them, and so falsify their assessments.

There are some tasters who love to talk as they taste and who treat those near them as an audience. Modern tasting installations guarantee a better privacy. According to Pierre Poupon, tasting also has its own expressive sign language: As is the case with card players, tasters should also avoid facial expressions and vocal undertones which might influence their neighbors and interfere with their freedom of assessment. You only disclose your game when the hand has been played. A discussion is always useful after everyone has had the chance to give his or her opinion, and where there is disagreement this may lead to a retasting of the wines in question. In the interests of honesty, however, only one's first impressions should be considered when forming one's own conclusions.

I have taken part in many tasting groups and have known many personalities. Mr. B was a taster of the old school, and although he remained silent it was impossible to get him to keep his opinions to himself, to prevent him revealing them as he tasted. From the moment the wine came into contact with his palate, his eyes showed his feelings: question, uncertainty, astonishment. Then, if he liked the wine, he could not contain his delight and, mouth closed, his eyes would light up and his whole face became wreathed in smiles. If he did not like it, he would shake his head, his face indicated disapproval and more subtle feelings: "This is just not possible! Awful! What a pity!" And he would punctuate all his gestures with meaningful grunts. One had understood all he wanted to say before he had actually spoken at all; and then, when he did finally speak, it was but a word: "Splendid!" or "Foul!" or some such exclamation. Mr. C, on the other hand, was a wonderful actor who could mime to perfection the reactions to tastes that he, poor man, could no longer perceive. He only continued tasting in order to drink. With the wine in his mouth he would cast a searching glance over those around him waiting for the sign that would enable him to enthuse or show his displeasure as appropriate. We helped him along with a good-natured wink.

Group-discussion tastings, which may produce good results through a process of mutual correction and clarification, are only really possible with three or four people who know each other well and who work together regularly. They will have the same concept of quality and similar tastes, though they may have different reactions, for, as I have already said, if there were always total agreement group tasting would be pointless. In these tastings everyone's viewpoint is taken into account in a compromise conclusion.

TASTING SHEETS

It is not enough just to taste; impressions from the work in hand need to be carefully described and conclusions drawn. Nor is tasting simply for pleasure, which is anyway often marginal, but rather for making judgments and decisions. Interpreting one's sensations is the most demanding aspect of tasting.

In the first place it is essential to insist on written opinions and comments both from oneself and from others. The taster should make notes on every wine, immediately, while the impressions are fresh in his memory. Verbal comment is not enough unless the work involved is that of rapid, superficial selection or the periodic checking of wines one knows well. The need to describe the characteristics of a wine clearly, to draw conclusions, or to make a written report on a tasting, all demand an analytic effort that will produce precise notes and a considered judgment. I know of firms where all the wines tasted used to be recorded in a register; sadly these good habits have not always been kept up.

The format of tasting notes varies according to the circumstances. One can describe color, aroma, and the balance of flavors in a brief, telegraphic style, concluding with one or two well-chosen words, or, when the wine justifies it, the analysis can be detailed, in language that is more explanatory and more qualified. To describe is already to interpret and a sound conclusion will follow naturally from a precise description.

To help the taster record the results of his observations, he is often asked to fill in a form which is both a description of the wine and its identity. He has to write down the details of his tasting analysis in the form of comments, marks, or in certain cases, just by ticking boxes that correspond to various quality levels, circling appropriate adjectives, or, alternatively, by crossing out inappropriate assessments. The benefit of such forms is that they give the beginner a fairly complete plan from which to work, and they encourage inexperienced tasters to express themselves more fully and to collate the results of a group tasting. Moreover, they are easy to store and they serve as documentary records of a wine at a given moment. They make it easier to get the best out of tasting results and most of them are designed to facilitate making notes on wines.

Many different forms of tasting sheet have been suggested. Indeed, every interested organization [regional offices of INAO, Institut technique du Vin (Technical Institute of Wine), Office international du Vin (International Bureau of Wine)] seems to have its own model which takes no account of other designs. Even the smallest school of viticulture devises its own tasting sheets, and the same goes for other winemaking countries as well.

These tasting sheets come in several types among which can be distinguished:

- Those designed solely for a descriptive record of taste characteristics and which do not make use of any detailed numerical marking scale. In these cases the wine can simply be given an overall score if desired.
- Those which award points for each of the principal taste characteristics, the final score being obtained by adding up the subsidiary points which are sometimes modified by a coefficient.

The design of tasting sheets is quite varied. Some, which are too simple, allow insufficient room for description and analysis of the wine's characteristics, while others, sometimes comprising several pages, are far too complicated.

The latter require several retastings and sometimes one finds oneself spending more time filling in the forms than actually tasting. The more precise they try to be, the more complicated they become so that one occasionally encounters unexpected categories or ambiguous phrases. For example, one can understand a possible hesitation over what marks to award to "the mobility of taste sensations" or "the link between sensations."

If filling in forms is a sign of our bureaucratic times, it should not become an end in itself. It seems to be forgotten that a tasting sheet should also be easy to read and interpret. In the final analysis one might conclude that if the use of tasting sheets has not become part of daily professional tasting, then either one can do without them, or in their present form they are poorly adapted to their purpose.

The subject of number-based tasting sheets will be reexamined in the next section, devoted to different methods of assessing and scoring wines.

The Bordeaux Institute's tasting sheet (illustrated on page 176) follows the logical sequence outlined in the table of the senses used in winetasting as shown on page 21. Here the taster can express himself as freely as his own vocabulary allows, in a manner more subtle than permitted by the limits of preestablished lists, without which he is also forced to make a more effective effort of analysis and synthesis. This sheet has been used in the teaching of tasting

Descriptive Tasting Sheet

Date _____

Taster's name _____

Wine _____

_____

Appearance	Color (intensity, hue) _____ Limpidity _____ Other observations _____

Nose	Cleanness _____ Intensity _____ Description_____ Quality _____ Defects, if any _____

Taste	Description	Attack _____ Evolution _____ Finish _____
	Balance and overall structure _____ _____ Aroma in the mouth (intensity and quality) _____ Aromatic persistence _____ Other observations _____	

Judgment	Conclusions _____ _____ _____ Assessment_____ Corresponding score (out of 5—out of 10—out of 20)[1]

[1]Delete acordingly

Translation of the tasting sheet used by the Bordeaux Institute of Oenology
(Institut d'oenologie de Bordeaux).

vocabulary for several years, and it is equally well suited to the expressive needs of experienced tasters.

METHODS OF SCORING WINES

The question of giving marks which indicate qualitative and quantitative levels for smells and flavors, or which represent a wine's overall value, is a tricky one. It is not easy to express the appeal of an aroma or, alternatively, a defect in a wine's structure in figures, that is, to express them as the percentage of a notional ideal. For example, if one were to mark a wine 12 out of 20, this amounts to giving it 60 percent of the marks for the maximum possible quality. The first difficulty in scoring is that of establishing scales of measurement appropriate to the numerous characteristics of wine, the more so as in most cases these criteria are not tangible and objective but internal and subjective. Vedel considers that "this multiplicity of criteria demands mental gymnastics from the taster that are difficult when all his faculties are engaged in examining the wine." Finally, one has to realize that quality is linked, above all, to balance and a harmony of flavors, both of which are even more difficult to evaluate.

It would be completely impossible to give an objective mark to characteristics which are essentially subjective if the taster were not also used to assessing the wines as a whole. Indeed, he should practice this, for it is not so much the detailed analysis which enables him to grade, as the ability to synthesize that analysis as well. Vedel and his colleagues have made a very thorough study of the questions raised by marking, and they explain that the conventional scales of measurement are characterized by a variety of symbols. The word-symbol scales consist of simple expressions or words in an increasing or decreasing order of the quality that they represent. The figure scales are characterized by the location of respective levels in relation to a median which represents the average situation or one at the limits of acceptability. **Cardinal scales**, mathematical values represented by scores of 0–5, 0–10, or 0–20, are distinguished from **ordinal scales**, whose divisions are graded from superior to inferior. If you like, a student's mark in an examination is expressed by a cardinal scale, his place in a competition by an ordinal scale. Normally, ordinal scales consist of an odd number of grades: 3, 5, 7, 9, grouped symmetrically around the median figures 2, 3, 4, and 5, respectively. Here are three examples of ordinal scales, the one with five terms being the most commonly used:

1 Weak	1 Very weak	1 Very weak
2 Average	2 Quite weak	2 Weak
3 Strong	3 Average	3 Quite weak
	4 Quite strong	4 Average
	5 Strong	5 Quite strong
		6 Strong
		7 Very strong

An intensity scale is used to describe subtle gradations of strength in taste and smell sensations. For example, aroma or acidity are noted in this way. The value scale here involves an assessment of the degree of pleasure experienced; it is an expression of hedonistic value, that is, related to the pleasure or otherwise yielded by tasting a wine. In this case the adjectives **weak** or **strong** would be replaced by **good** or **bad**. Alternatively, one could use phrases, as the ampelographer Max Rives has done in a notable incursion into the territory of the oenologist: **like** or **strongly dislike, like** or **do not much like**, etc.

We have already seen that several basic methods of scoring wines are used: an overall mark for the wine's impressions taken as a whole, or the sum of individual marks given for different aspects, marks which may be weighted by various coefficients. In the latter method, appearance, smell, taste, length, and overall quality are marked independently. Each of these marks may itself be the sum of subsidiary characteristics, so that on a tasting sheet the mark for appearance will encompass the individual marks for fluidity, limpidity, color, and brilliance. In another case, the mark awarded to bouquet would be the sum of those given to its intensity, finesse and harmony, and cleanness. The same goes for taste, so that some tasting sheets group together a dozen or so subscores for one wine.

The objection to this system is that the quality of a wine is not just the sum of its characteristics, positive or negative; it is not a mathematical sum of color, smell, and taste. The different characteristics are not all equal in value, nor can a defect in one category be compensated for by quality in another. To give an example: A wine which has too much acidity or bitterness cannot be considered any better because it is also limpid in appearance or even because it has a fine bouquet. Jacqmain is very much of this opinion: "A mistake that is frequently made is to assess the overall quality of a product by adding up the different marks awarded for various characteristics (appearance, smell, taste, texture, among others). In reality, if one is bad, then no matter how good it is in other respects it won't be any the more acceptable."

Some tasting sheets confront the winetaster with plenty of obstacles. Who can really mark apart, as is sometimes required, individual aspects such as structure, typicity, harmony, and overall impression? In some forms one sees the mark for fluidity worth as much as that given to bouquet, finesse, or the body of a wine. To try and avoid these absurdities, other tasting sheet compilers have modified the marks for each section by coefficients. Yet how can these be anything but arbitrary? Can it be argued that taste is worth two or three times the value of appearance, or as much as, or twice as much as smell? The notion of harmony is not always given a mark but in the case of one detailed tasting sheet it is worth two-thirds of the total score.

In my view a tasting sheet should be purely descriptive. Certainly each characteristic can be given a mark if this is felt to be helpful, but the overall score given to the wine should not be the sum of these; it should be fixed independently of the subsidiary marks.

In winetasting, then, giving a mark can in no way measure a quality or a quantity. Scores are not mathematical units of value so one cannot add, multiply, and divide the figures as objective units of measure. Furthermore, it is illogical to deal very precisely with figures which one knows to be essentially arbitrary, and to calculate averages to a second decimal point from figures provided by the taster which are themselves imprecise.

In any case, a given system of marking is only valid for one particular category of wines, and it should take into account their type, class, and appellation. Wines can only be judged by norms appropriate to their category. The comparison and marking together of very different wines is not only impossible but also pointless.

One often sees that the overall marks given by tasters to a range of wines tend to be close to the average. It seems that for fear of making a clear-cut decision the taster tends to narrow the range of his top and bottom marks, so minimizing both faults and virtues. Thus on a scale of 0 to 20 the marks most frequently awarded by certain groups of tasters range from 10 to 15, so that without meaning to they have effectively marked from 1 to 5. The latter scale is very useful in day-to-day work but, in general, tasters feel that it is too restricting and they tend to use half marks—which, in the end, amounts to marking out of 10. When the scale is too large the marks they give reduce it, when it is too small they enlarge it instinctively.

As is the case with all examiners some tasters mark more severely, others more leniently, for everyone has a personal notion of what represents quality. A given defect may be judged differently by different tasters and so affect the final mark to a greater or lesser extent. An oenologist will mark a technical fault very harshly, bacteriological spoilage, for example, whereas he will be more indulgent than a nontechnician over a fault that he knows to be temporary, excess carbon dioxide or a light and reversible state of oxidation. Obviously, more coordination is desirable. This can be achieved to a fair extent by prior consultation and discussion, but the method I have found the most successful is to ask the taster to assess the wine with a verbal rating before giving it a mark. The latter will then follow naturally, though most people do it the other way around.

In order to improve the use of a marking scale from 0 to 10, for example, so that all the tasters use the same basis for awarding points, one might agree that 10 would be for a **perfect** wine (and there are some which deserve it); 9 for **excellent**; 8, **very good**; 7, **good**; 6, **quite good**; 5, average or **just acceptable**; 4, **inadequate**; 3, **mediocre**; 2, **poor**; and 1, **very poor**. A zero score would be given in the extreme case of an undrinkable wine.

The more flexible scale of 0 to 20 allows for an ordinal classification of wines which are slightly different but which merit the same overall verbal rating: 20 would be given for **perfect** wines; 18 and 19 to those that are **excellent**; 16 and 17 to wines of very high quality, described as **very good**; wines scoring 14 and 15 are good with slight imperfections. . . **good**; **quite good** is worth 12 or 13; ordinary or **acceptable**, 10 and 11; below an acceptable level or **inadequate** would score 7, 8, and 9; **mediocre** and **bad**, 4, 5, and 6; and **very bad**, 1, 2, and 3. Marks below the average are more difficult to give because it is easier to discriminate between qualities than between defects.

To reiterate my advice: In order to award a wine an overall mark, do not think directly of a numerical value but give it a verbal assessment first; the numerical score will follow automatically within the chosen scale.

The attempts to design score cards are so many experiments in codifying sensation. Research along a very different path, that of representing a wine in a numerical profile, seems to me a particularly interesting area of progress. The system was used for a long time by the tasting team of the Paris firm Nicolas; and it applies to all types of wine. Louis Plessis, who taught me the method, was worth seeing at work, encoding a wine with a few strokes of the pen or decoding a profile at a glance.

The taste characteristics of a wine are represented by a series of ten figures, read individually one after another and not making up a number. The first five figures represent the following aspects in the order given: **color**, **bouquet**, **balance**, **cleanness**, and **finesse**, all marked from 1–10. The five subsequent figures represent, respectively: **body**, **personality**, **acidity**, **hardness**, and, finally, the state of **maturity**. These characteristics are also marked from 1–10, but optimal quality is indicated by a score of 5 or 6. From 5 down to 1 indicates an increasing degree of weakness or inadequacy; from 6–10 indicates an increasing degree of excess. Here is an example of the profile for a good young red wine:

$$6 \quad 7 \quad 7 \quad 9 \quad 8 \quad 6 \quad 7 \quad 5 \quad 6 \quad 4$$

The wine has good **color** (6), and attractive **bouquet** (7), it is well **balanced** (7), very clean in **flavor** (9), and very **fine** (8); it is moderately **full** (6), **characterful** (7), with good **acidity** (5), just the right amount of **firmness** (6), and its state of **maturity**, while well developed (4), is not yet at its peak and it can be kept before drinking.

I would say of its inventor that here at last was someone who, wanting to describe the taste of a wine with a view to drinking it, avoided trying to summarize the various tastes of alcohol, acids, and tannins along with a description of color and the smells of various aromatic substances!

STATISTICAL INTERPRETATION OF GROUP TASTING

The following examples illustrate the disagreement which can exist within a group of tasters. The interpretation of a group tasting is based on the opinions of a majority. Now, because tasting sensitivity is unequally distributed, there are cases where an individual or a minority can be right.

The threshold of perception for a substance is defined as the minimum concentration identifiable by 50 percent of those tested. However, gifted tasters can identify substances at levels well below the threshold established in this way, at doses which are called infraliminary in the jargon of sensory analysis

Another example: At the end of a lecture on the use of sorbic acid (an additive which is authorized, though little used, for the conservation of sweet wines) in which I had stated that the perception of this substance in wine was possible at a lower level than that generally indicated, a member of the audience asked me if I could specify the number of judges making up the panel which had authorized this conclusion. I surprised him greatly by replying that there was only one judge and that it was myself, and that if I were sensitive to sorbic acid at low doses, then other people could be as well.

The following situation is not uncommon. Out of five tasters independently tasting the same wine, only one feels that it is not absolutely clean and identifies a slightly acetic odor. Analysis reveals 150 mg/l of ethyl acetate, confirming the fault indicated, which is then perceived by all on retasting. It is for precisely this reason that one works in groups, so as to increase the chances of identifying a fault or anomaly. The quality of a wine is not necessarily guaranteed by the opinion of a majority of tasters. It should not be forgotten that in this field it has often been competent minorities who have made or marred reputations. This is what distinguishes winetasting from sensory analysis applied to other manufactured food products, and it also means that wine is not the best case in which to apply statistical interpretation to group work. The notion of esthetic preference does not belong to the realm of scientific exactitude, and that which cannot be measured is often of greater significance than that which can.

I have examined a wide range of literature in great detail in an attempt to discover just what statistical calculation could contribute to the work of a winetaster. I would be the first to be interested if it improved my work or made my task any easier. However, this method has few possible applications in daily winetasting because the problems posed by comparisons between wines are simple and can generally be resolved by common sense. A professional may consider one wine to be better than another in absolute terms, but if he judges the difference between them to be insignificant in terms of relative value he will put them on the same level commercially. The notion of how much significance to attach to a difference in taste is part of the interpretative quality of a taster.

I have read Boggs, Bengtsson, Bradley, Dawson, Harrison, Roessler, and many others, also those French agronomists who have applied the statistical laws of experiment to winetasting, something which is not their specialty. From among this literature I have chosen a good popular account by Jacqmain, and I have borrowed several elements from this in order to write the following paragraphs.

Statistical analysis in the interpretation of group tasting results seeks to answer the following questions: (1) What would be the conclusions if chance alone determined the tasters' answers? (2) Given a defined probability, are the tasters' actual results significantly different or not from those that would have been obtained by chance alone?

In any particular case, different statistical calculations permit one to decide whether the difference between actual tasting results and those that chance alone would have provided are significant or not. The most common statistical method is variance analysis, that is, of the variability of results between the wines and according to the individual tasters. One determines if the variance between two samples is significantly greater for a given probability than the variance due to chance (the residual variance). Tables such as Krum's give the minimum number of correct answers needed in relation to the total number of samples, as a function of the number of tasters. Other tables such as Kramer's deal with the qualitative ratings of various products and show which differences between place-result totals are significant. The Fisher-Yates tables allow one to exploit the different methods of scoring to the best advantage.

Take the case of six samples, designated I, II, III, IV, V, and VI, tasted and ranked by five tasters called A, B, C, D, and E. The following table shows the ranking given by each taster. By adding up the place results for each wine, a figure is obtained whose value is the inverse of the wine's quality ranking. The decreasing order of quality is VI, V, III, I, IV, II. The differences between the totals for each wine are variable, being respectively 6, 5, 2, 7, 5. By just looking at the results one can ascertain that the ranking which is the most dubious is the one where the difference between neighboring results is the narrowest, between III and I in this case. Statistical analysis does not reveal anything more. And Kramer's tables show indeed that, for the case in point, the significant results, given a probability of 5 percent, are those place-result totals falling outside the 11–24 bracket. Consequently, the rankings are significant for samples VI, V, IV, and II; they are not for III and I whose positions are too close together.

A study of six wines tasted and ranked by five tasters

| Tasters | Wine samples | | | | | |
	I	II	III	IV	V	VI
A	4	6	2	5	3	1
B	4	6	3	5	2	1
C	3	6	4	5	2	1
D	4	6	3	5	2	1
E	3	6	4	5	2	1
Totals	18	30	16	25	11	5

The values are the wine placings in a ranking from 1 to 6.

THE VALUE OF TASTING EXPERTISE

To start with, it should be made clear that tasting alone cannot be considered an adequate means of identifying wines. Identifying a wine proceeds along similar lines to identifying a person. This involves recognition and naming; or at least a partial recognition, that is to say, being able to define its qualities, type, class, age, and geographical origin, and possibly to identify the grape varieties from which it is made and what its hierarchical status is.

It is only possible to identify wines with distinctive characteristics, and characteristics which are also typical of their kind, having what is called typicity. A wine without any personality gives one no reference point by which to remember it, and if it has no family traits, no indications as to its origin, it has little chance of being recognized or identified.

On this point, there are numerous myths about tasting ability which need debunking. It is an absolute fiction that a taster, even a prodigiously gifted one, can identify without fail, and from the thousands of possible cases, the name and vintage of a wine put before him.

The role of tasting expertise is not the identification of anonymous wines, but the exercise of quality control. Its function is to judge whether a wine is free of faults which might lessen its value or render it unfit for consumption, and to see whether it has the qualities required by its denomination. In these roles tasting is becoming increasingly important, as much for checking Quality Wines Produced in Specific Regions (QWPSR) or Vins de Pays, as for providing additional proof in legal cases.

Approval by tasting is part of the discipline which a region's producers and merchants freely impose on themselves with the common aim of improving production across the board. Decrees concerning AOC wines state that these wines "may not be put into commerce without a certificate issued by an INAO approved tasting committee." Details for the running of these tasting committees are laid down in rules specific to each viticultural association which organizes the committee's composition and activities.

In addition to these production controls, certificates are required for the export of wines from certain appellations.

The new European Union rules further specify that producers must submit all QWPSR wines for tasting. Other activities also require the service of expert tasters approved by the Minister of Agriculture, for example, declassification where a denomination of origin may be withdrawn after requests by merchants, or following checks at the property or at a wholesaler's.

In the case of judicial inquiries, the importance attached to tasting in France should be clearly stressed. Several successive decrees specify that "wines stored by retailers which, in spite of normal appearance and no obvious change in their constituent parts, are clearly pricked when tasted, cannot be considered fit for consumption and must be taken to a vinegar factory or distillery." It must also be said that in the absence of a legal limit for the level of ethyl acetate, the substance responsible for the character of acetic wines, wines have been condemned purely on the basis of tasting. Other wines considered unfit for consumption are those with "a phenyl, moldy, or rotten taste, or any other manifestly unpleasant flavor." These recent provisions constitute a new legal position, a contrast to the former rules whereby the subjective nature of tasting and the fundamental impossibility of communicating its judgments always excluded it from having any significance in legal matters. This was expressed in various ways: "jurisprudence has never admitted tasting tests alone as a basis for conviction" or "the art of wielding the ancestral cup will never be of anything but secondary and auxiliary significance in legal matters." Today it is clear that in addition to chemical analysis, the information provided by careful tasting carried out by experts is increasingly taken into account and can influence court decisions one way or the other.

Expert tasters are not only involved in legal proceedings instituted by various administrative control bodies, but also in litigation between professionals, and the matters they have to rule on are many and complex.

Sometimes it is a question of disputes over quality between buyer and seller, sometimes a question of valuing wines held in stock at properties which are up for sale. Alternatively, it might be assessing the damage caused to wines during transport, or as a result of their being lodged in defective barrels which have given them a nasty taste. Suppliers can be held responsible for unpleasant tastes due to new storage containers, for styrene flavors, those due to solvents used in plastic linings, or even for corky tastes due to poor-quality corks. In all these disputes properly conducted tastings by qualified experts provide sufficient proof.

To end with, let us quote the conclusions of a study by Charles

Quittanson, an expert in the field. "From the analysis of these three areas (penal, administrative, and qualitative) it seems that tasting is considered to be a decisive factor in determining the quality of a wine, spirit, or other food product, whether the product carries an appellation of origin or not. This tendency is becoming even more pronounced in the latest European and national regulations."

Nine

Balance in Wine

THE RELATIONSHIP BETWEEN THE COMPOSITION OF WINES AND THEIR TASTES

The characteristics of a wine, its qualities or defects, are obviously linked to its chemical composition—to the substances that it contains by virtue of its being a drink made from fermented grapes.

On the one hand, wine contains fixed acids, sugars, salts, and phenolic substances, all of which have their own particular tastes. These different tastes add to, highlight, or, alternatively, oppose and neutralize each other. The taste of wine might thus be visualized as a kind of algebraic sum of these diverse flavors. They blend into a **form**, a more or less harmonious **volume** which makes up a **structure**. These essential flavor constituents, perhaps some twenty in number, are fairly well known and are present in quantities which are measured in grams or fractions of a gram per liter. They constitute the bricks and mortar of a wine, its **framework**, also sometimes described as its bone structure.

On the other hand, wine contains volatile substances, that is, those able to separate from the wine with varying degrees of facility by evaporation in the glass or in the mouth. These belong to the chemical families of alcohols, volatile acids, esters, aldehydes, acetals, hydrocarbons, sulfur compounds, terpenes, and so on, which have smells that vary both in intensity and in appeal. Similarly, these various smells add to, reinforce, or, alternatively, mask each other; and together they form a new smell. They are linked to an impressive array of substances, present in very small concentrations and which are expressed in milligrams or fractions of a milligram. Because of their number and because they exist only as traces, they are difficult to identify analytically, and, apart from a few, it has not yet proved possible to establish precise relationships between this subtle composition and the aromatic characteristics of wine. Yet these are the substances which play the most crucial role in determining a wine's style and quality; it is they above all which give a wine its personality. And, for the moment, recent, more refined analytical techniques pose yet more questions rather than providing more answers. Such is the progress of understanding.

The taste and haptic characteristics (the latter being those sensations which are perceived by the palate as a whole, not the tastes strictly speaking) may be seen as the supporting elements, support, that is, for the olfactory characteristics. Schematically then, wine is made up of two parts: the elements which stimulate the taste buds and so give wine its flavor; and those which stimulate the sense of smell, so providing the wine's aroma and bouquet. However, these sensations are not all separate; they are concomitant, blended together, inextricably intermingled. Taste underlines smell and smell reinforces taste.

This is the first type of balance that we encounter in detailed analytical tasting. The word balance here is used in the sense of "the balancing of diverse or opposing elements so as to produce harmony" or, better still, "a balancing of parts which are mutually enhancing." For a wine to be successful, there needs to be a correct relationship between the main taste and odor groups, a favorable combination of constituent parts. From this balance is born a harmony defined as a coherence between the parts of a whole. A wine is said to be harmonious when its elements form a pleasing and well-proportioned whole. This concept of balance seems very abstract but we will encounter it wherever quality is analyzed. It can be made more concrete by giving examples of its opposite, by describing cases of imbalance between taste and smell: Inadequate acidity in a white wine destroys the freshness of its aroma; too much sugar without actual fruit flavor makes for a sweet but lifeless wine; excess tannin in a red wine masks its fruit. There are highly aromatic wines whose overlight structure renders them thin and lacking in harmony, while, at the other extreme, there are very full-bodied wines with little smell, whose poverty in aromatic elements may derive from neutral grape varieties, from an excessive yield, or from grapes ripened in a very hot climate.

Jean Ribéreau-Gayon has described the taste-smell relationship very well: "To use a metaphor, one might think of wine as having a **consistency** or **texture** which makes it attractive right from the start, offering its odors to the senses in a pleasing manner, similar to the way in which a fruit's physical consistency plays a crucial role in its quality; not only in itself, but by the manner in which it yields the fruit's tastes and smells to the tongue, palate, and nose."

This concept is also fundamental to the art of preparing food: The aromatic harmony of a dish and its harmony of taste are one and the same; if it wants a little salt the flavor of the whole dish seems to need it.

The same author also defines the harmony that should exist between the wine's support elements and its volatile phase: "Great wine is characterized by a plenitude, a power, and finesse of taste and odor, a flavor that is both intense and attractive."

In the second half of the last century, when only a few of the constituents of wine were known, one could, as Fauré did, attribute its quality to a hypothetical element which he named oenanthine, and which he considered essential "not because it gives fine wines their perfume but because it gives them a softness and velvety character which brings out their bouquet." Later on many people thought that glycerol was the fundamental quality element which gave wine those highly sought-after qualities of richness and roundness.

The following sections will show that the majority of wine's qualities are not the result of a unique constituent present at a particular level, but of a harmony of all its constituents and of certain relative concentrations. It might also be thought that this harmony is entirely natural, inherent in the grape, whereas, in reality, it is a thorough understanding of the art of vinification which makes for a judicious balance of constituents, and which produces a wine that is harmonious in smell and savor.

Are the balances responsible for a wine's appeal or lack of harmony measurable? Doubtless, if it were possible to make an absolutely complete analysis of a wine, one could relate all its characteristics to chemical concentrations and so define the wine by a sheet showing its chemical compositions. Reading such an analysis would then suffice to indicate its quality. If this has actually been achieved to a more or less satisfactory extent for certain characteristics, for certain faults in particular, it is not yet possible for a wine in totality. The reason is that not all the constituents of wine are known. Some complex yet essential elements have an effect in infinitesimal doses, and they are more easily perceived by taste than by analysis, or else they are only accessible to chemical analysis with difficulty, and this is particularly so with certain elements which influence the richness of wine and its specifically vinous bouquet. Furthermore, it is likely that the physiochemical structure of a substance, its degree of molecular condensation, and the form of its molecules also influence its taste or odor.

Paradoxically, the more progress we make in learning about wine, the further we are from a really profound understanding. It just becomes more and more complicated. In 1956 Jaulmes estimated the number of known constituents at 150, and in 1965 he recorded the concentration limits for 125 of these. According to Pascal Ribéreau-Gayon, "during the last few years the list of constituents has become longer still, and today there would be no difficulty in identifying 250 or 300 chemical substances which are present in wine." In the mid-1970s, according to Drawert, the list had reached "many hundreds," and now, in the mid-1990s, the estimate would be in the thousands. Indeed, an Australian research team has identified some 180 volatile substances in Chardonnay alone. All in all, explanation and interpretation seem to recede further and further the more our knowledge advances.

In our present state of knowledge then, it is better and simpler to determine the qualities of a wine by tasting it than by trying to analyze it. These comments in no way diminish the role of chemical analysis which remains important for anticipating a wine's evolution and for deciding how best to treat it in order that its potential qualities may be developed to their maximum, something which tasting is hardly capable of doing as it can only perceive qualities at a given moment.

The advantage of a taster who has a knowledge of oenology derives from the fact that he always attempts to link his sensory impressions to a wine's chemical composition, to discern within the overall complex of sensations the elements of which the wine is made up, and to link basic qualities and faults to specific chemical substances. He has memorized the sensation associated with a large number of analytic characteristics.

If, as we shall see, the analysis of wine's supporting elements requires relatively simple determinations of groups of sapid substances, the analysis of wine's odor aspect is highly complex. The techniques of gas chromatography, mentioned earlier, are required for this. On the basis of analysis it is possible to gauge the intensity and harmony of taste to some extent but, with the exception of a few directly measurable faults, this is not the case with smell.

It used to be thought that the colloids in wine did not affect its organoleptic characteristics, but recent research has demonstrated the essential role of both the structure and molecular weight of the phenolic compounds, either alone or in association with polysaccharides. The mucilaginous substances in young, sweet white wines seem to make them more unctuous and possibly richer.

INTERFERENCE AND BALANCE BETWEEN FLAVORS

"The taste of wine is for the most part the result of a balance between sweet and sugary tastes and those of acidity and bitterness. Quality is always related to a certain harmony of tastes, where no one taste dominates another. This is true for medium-sweet white wines which contain residual (unfermented) sugars, but it is equally true for dry white wines and red wines which contain no sugar. Indeed, experiments show that of the substances in wine which have a sweet taste, alcohol is paramount."

During the course of thirty years' teaching and with the help of a series of appropriate practical exercises, I have continued to demonstrate these points tirelessly and so effectively that what were initially just interesting as original ideas have become scientific postulates on the basis of their evident truth. It is no longer realized that this simple statement, written in 1949, was the beginning of a different concept of the make-up of wines, and of a new philosophy of quality. It

contained the germ of the new doctrines which were to revolution-
ize vinification techniques over the last few decades. The era of solid
fixed acidity, the prime requisite for long aging, has given way to the
era of low total acidity, the essential factor for a supple texture.

The most difficult thing to accept, perhaps, was the reality of alcohol having a sweet taste, and there is still a reluctance to accept this
today. For example, Berg states clearly that alcohol heightens the
sweetness of sugar, but he will not go as far as to say that alcohol itself is sweet. Its sweet taste is not exactly the same as that of crystallized sugar; it is less pure and less obviously sweet. This is because
there are subtle differences of taste between the various sweet substances, just as there are between different acids, different salts, and
even the different bitter substances. Ethyl alcohol is sweet even at
low concentrations, but at the level at which it is found in wine its
sweet taste is significant. It is easy to demonstrate that at 4° (32 g/l)
a solution of alcohol in water already has a clearly sweet taste, without its being particularly recognizable as the taste of alcohol. One
would describe it rather as sweetish, having a certain insipidity, that
is. At a higher concentration the gentle warmth of alcohol on the
mucous surfaces slightly modifies the pure impression of sweetness.
This is best demonstrated by comparing the taste of three solutions
containing 20 g/l of saccharose; one without alcohol, one with 4°,
and one with 10° of alcohol (80 g/l). It will be quite clear to everyone
that sweetness is considerably increased in the presence of alcohol; in
the first case the solution will seem almost twice as sweet. On the
other hand, 20 g/l of sugar do not diminish the impression of warmth
given by 10° of alcohol. Anyone who has done this exercise cannot
deny the considerable sweet influence of alcohol. The first impression
of wine on the palate, the softness of the attack, is due to alcohol.

We know that the tastes of bitterness and acidity mask each
other. The same goes for sweetness and bitterness or sweetness and
saltiness, due to the phenomena of interference, competition, and
compensation. These tastes diminish each other reciprocally, but
not, however, to the extent of canceling each other out and being
able to produce a tasteless solution from a combination of two sapid
substances. They will remain perceptible side by side, simply weakened to some extent.

If one acidifies a sweet solution its sweet sensation is diminished, and, conversely, if one sweetens an acid solution its acid impression is diminished. However, both the acidity and the sweetness can be distinguished at the same time, and one can concentrate at will alternately on either taste. These ideas are common enough and there is no need to dwell on them. We normally sweeten strawberries, fruit salads, or lemon juice to make their acidity more tolerable. At certain relative levels of concentration it is possible to say that the taste of sweetness balances that of acidity; as in a solution with 20 g/l of saccharose and 0.8 g/l of tartaric acid, for example. If you increase the quantity of acid the acid taste becomes dominant, and the reverse is the case if the quantity of sugar is increased. A commercial drink based on fruit juice sometimes needs to be acidified with citric acid in order to appear balanced.

The point of balance varies according to the individual's sensitivity to the two tastes, and personal criteria for deciding what this point is also depend on habits and acquired tastes. Léglise noted that, "in the German and Scandinavian countries [and he could have added the Americas, too], what is adjudged a satisfactory balance calls for a strong preponderance of sugar over acid. The same goes for female palates everywhere, and for urban consumers as well. In the French countryside, however, where there are still some hardy palates, the reverse is preferred." To return to wine, and as a matter of interest, most "dry" (*brut*) champagnes contain up to 15 g/l of sugar to temper the acidity of these northerly wines.

The sweetness of 20 to 40 g/l of saccharose masks the unpleasant bitterness given by 10 mg/l of quinine sulfate. We sweeten tea or coffee for the same reason, but in this case to compensate for the bitter tastes of caffeine and tannins. To take another example from the world of aperitif drinks: The abundance of sugar in Campari or in the Italian vermouths is there in order to compensate for the bitterness of quinquina and other bitter elements. Bitterness continues to be perceived in the presence of sugar but the overall impression is no longer disagreeable. Similarly, 32 g/l of alcohol mask the bitterness of 10 mg/l of quinine salts. Bitterness also adds savor to a sweet solution.

Sugar has the same effect on the astringency of tannin. Its presence delays the moment when the bitter and astringent sensations begin to appear, and the greater its concentration the longer is the delay. When tasting a one-gram-per-liter solution of tannin, the tannin is perceived immediately; with 20 g/l of sugar its perception is delayed for two or three seconds but the final impression is not diminished. With 40 g/l of sugar, its action masks the tannin for five or six seconds and the astringency is also tempered. Alcohol, on the other hand, far from attenuating the astringency, tends to accentuate its unpleasantness on the finish.

Small quantities of sugar weaken the taste of salt; a little salt, on the other hand, brings out sweet tastes, a fact well known and put to good use in baking. The salt taste in wine is far from negligible. The strongest saline element is certainly represented by potassium bitartrate: When first tasted, a bitartrate solution seems to taste simply of acid, but when compared with the hard, aggressive taste of a solution of unsalified tartaric acid, one can clearly notice the taste of salt which increases the savor and freshness of the bitartrate solution.

When tasting individual solutions of the four primary tastes, one quickly realizes that sweetness is the only one which is a pleasant sensation and which we actually want. In reality, we only like things which are sweet and sugared, often without realizing it. Sugar has been called the "soft drug." We accept other tastes only to the extent that they are weak or weakened by the presence of sugar. They are, however, indispensable for giving breadth of flavor to a blend, which is appreciated all the more for combining the tastes of salt, acid, and bitterness balanced by a judicious level of sweetness. By comparison, a simple sugar solution appears insipid and unappealing. We like the complexity of flavors where sweetness protects us from excess acidity and bitterness. As for salt, it is a means of giving relief to the rather sickly sweetness of pure sugar.

Another important concept is the effect of the sum total of unpleasant tastes. Bitterness and astringency reinforce acidity and make it excessive; acidity masks bitterness to begin with, but this only makes its appearance on the aftertaste even more pronounced. And salt simply accentuates any excess of acidity, astringency, and bitterness.

This cumulative effect also shows up in another form. During the course of repeated tasting, the more one tastes the same solutions which are acid or bitter or both, the shorter is the period of latency before these tastes are perceived and the more aggressive they appear.

These concepts of the balance of flavors, fundamental to explaining the taste of wines (or more precisely for defining their **support structure**) and which apply equally to all our food and drink, can be represented in the following way ($\leftrightarrows$ = balances):

Sweetness	⇆	Acidity
Sweetness	⇆	Bitterness
Sweetness	⇆	Bitterness + Acidity

This formulation will be useful in the following sections.

For the sake of simplicity the incidence of salt may be omitted from these equations, bearing in mind that the levels of salt in wine are small and somewhat more constant than those of other flavor constituents. Salt does not improve wine even though its addition was both practiced and authorized in the past. Experiments show that any addition of salt beyond the level which modifies the wine's flavor, always accentuates any hardness and harshness.

THE BALANCE OF FLAVORS IN WHITE WINES

Because they possess little or no tannin, white wines have a simple balance of flavors by comparison with red wines. Their **support structure** is conditioned solely by substances that are sweet and by those that are acid. The formula "sweetness ⇆ acidity" represents their basic taste structure. In the case of dry wines, alcohol alone, and in the case of sweet wines, alcohol and fermentable sugars, are the elements of sweetness which counterbalance the acidity. We have already seen that, in spite of its reputation, glycerol plays an insignificant role. Because of this simplicity of constitution, tasting white wines seems simpler to the beginner who easily gets lost amid the tangle of complex sensations in red wines. Hence it is recommended to begin learning to taste with white wines and thus to move from the simplest to the most difficult.

White wines, particularly when they are dry, generally have simpler "shapes" or "images" on the palate than those suggested by red wines; they lack the dimensions of bitterness and astringency. Furthermore, the relationships between support structure and aromas are easier to grasp in white wines because their aromatic aftertaste is not masked by lasting impressions of tannin.

Some rosé wines made with very short maceration have more in common with white than red wines and so present a similarly uncomplicated taste image.

A distinction should be made between dry white wines containing no residual sugars, and white wines whose fermentation is incomplete, which still contain grape sugars to a greater or lesser extent, or which have been sweetened with must. In France, these are known commercially under the names *demi-sec, moelleux* (both medium-dry and/or medium-sweet), *liquoreux* (sweet), and *vins doux naturels.* The fermentation of the last is interrupted by the addition of alcohol.

For dry white wines the balance is simply bipartite and can be written: "alcoholic degree ⇆ acidity." Alcohol represents the principal element of sweetness balancing the acidity. However, do not expect me or anybody else to translate this balance into precise figures indicating what levels of acidity correspond to which degrees of alcohol. This is not possible because the equivalence is not linear, and many other chemical factors intervene, quite apart from any questions of personal taste.

Alcohol does not have a chemically neutralizing effect on acidity. Its flavor is complex; it gives both strength and softness, two antagonistic sensations, and at higher alcoholic levels its caustic effect, the impression of warmth which it conveys, counters the effect of sweetness, reinforcing vigor and firmness rather than sweetness. Furthermore, for a given level of titrated acidity an acid's taste may vary according to its salified fraction (its pH in the final analysis) and what type of acid it is. A wine's acidity is acceptable or not according to whether it is mainly malic or mainly tartaric. A white wine which has undergone its malolactic fermentation always seems less acid than another wine of the same acidity which has kept its malic acid.

The acid balance in dry white Bordeaux has been the subject of considerable variation over the last forty years. In the 1950s Semillon wines from Bordeaux had an average acidity of 3.5 g/l; they seemed heavy, lacking freshness, and were often described as "sweetish," even though they had no residual sugar. By the early 1970s the wines had an acidity of 5 to 5.5 g/l as a result of different viticultural techniques (the "rediscovery" of Sauvignon, better management of vine fertilization) and differing methods of vinification (earlier harvesting, more carefully controlled sulfuring, settling, and clarifying the must). More recently, around the mid-1980s, the trend was once again toward less acid wines of around 3.5 to 4 g/l; more supple yet still dry. This sort of evolution is the consequence of both consumer preference and a number of technical changes such as picking at greater maturity, prefermentation skin contact, and so on. Such changes in overall balance—by no means limited to dry whites from Bordeaux—may seem surprising. In effect, they are simply a reflection of the wide range of tastes that exist for differently structured styles of white wine, a diversity of tastes that is far greater than that for reds. Consumer tastes and producer styles do not always evolve in step, but sooner or later they synchronize . . . only to set off yet again in a new direction.

Using the ideas of Max Léglise, the specialist in those sublime white burgundies, the various balances which govern the supporting structure of dry white wines can be graphically represented by the following diagram. The rising acidity axis intersects that of increasing alcoholic degree, thus defining four categories corresponding to various types of dry white wine:

Ac^+Al^+	hot, alcoholic, vigorous, firm, hard
Ac^+Al^-	light, weak, thin, acidic, green
Ac^-Al^+	alcoholic, supple to mellow, rich to heavy
Ac^-Al^-	little, flat, thin, insipid

Medium-sweet and sweet white wines, rosé wines with some sweetness, and *vins doux naturels* pose more complex problems of balance between sweetness and acidity. For these wines the formula "sweetness $\leftrightarrows$ acidity" can be written "alcoholic degree + sugar $\leftrightarrows$ acidity." Three factors are involved and the relationships are tripartite. To the balance between sweetness and acidity is added another balance linking sugar and alcohol: "alcoholic degree $\leftrightarrows$ sugar," meaning that the richer a wine is in sugar, the higher it needs to be in alcohol, too, in order to appear harmonious. The sickly sweet taste of sugar needs to be compensated by more warmth and vinosity. The imbalance of minor white wines which seem too sweet can be explained by saying that their sweet taste dominates everything else.

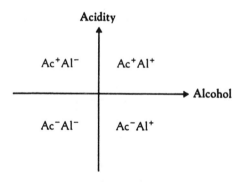

The bipartite balances of dry white wines.

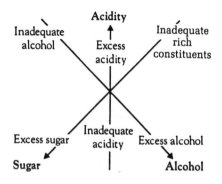

The tripartite balance of medium-sweet and sweet white wines.

Other consequences of these balances are: Dry white wines, being devoid of tannin, can support much higher levels of acidity than red wines; in certain dry white wines which are called *tendre* (gentle, delicate), small quantities of sugar, 3 to 5 g/l, are enough to mask an acidity which would be too strong in a totally dry wine; sweet wines can take more acidity than wines without sugar. Thus Sauternes usually have a total acidity of 4.5 to 5.0 g/l. Inadequate acidity or excess sweetness make these wines seem flabby, syrupy, and lacking in backbone.

The impression left by a sweet wine should be similar to that left by eating fresh, firm grapes. The sweetness tones down the acidity and turns it into freshness, while the light tingle of acidity corrects the thick, heavy impressions of sweetness. The aromatic aspect of the wine is thus brought out by a favorable relationship of flavors, for I must emphasize once again that olfactory sensations are involved in this balance. The harmony of the support structure is complemented by a harmony of aroma and bouquet. An intense aroma or a very fine bouquet can mask possible faults in the support, whereas they are more apparent in wines which are poor in aroma and bouquet.

Some rare, great white wines are so rich in aromatic elements that their flavor is harmonious even if their acidity is marked or even if it is weak. An intense aroma can thus conceal defects in structure. Aromatic wines gain personality from what would be a lack of balance in other wines. And, conversely, whatever the balance of their support structure, it is not possible to give neutral and odorless white wines an acceptable and attractive balance on the palate precisely because they lack odor constituents.

THE BALANCE OF FLAVORS IN RED WINES

Red wines are wines made by the maceration of red grape skins and grape pips. The more or less bitter and astringent flavors extracted from these solid tissues are specific to red wines. As a result, their balance of tastes is not that of fermented juice from the pulp of the grape alone. And in their case the sum of sweet flavors must balance the sum of acid flavors plus those that are bitter and astringent, a balance which can be briefly expressed as "sweetness $\leftrightarrows$ acidity + bitterness."

The following exercise is recommended to illustrate the balance between these contrasting flavors in a particularly instructive manner, and it also demonstrates the significant role played by alcohol as a sweet taste. It is one of the exercises used in teaching tasting.

A certain volume of well-balanced red wine is distilled in the laboratory. To do this, it is brought to the boiling point in a balloon flask, or better still a steam current is passed through the wine in an appropriate piece of apparatus. The volatile part thus drawn off is condensed via a cooler and contains, along with the distilled water, all the wine's alcohol and its volatile odorous substances. The *residue* remaining in the balloon flask represents the concentrated wine deprived of its alcohol. After cooling, these two liquors (to use the chemist's term) are brought back to their initial volume with pure water. Finally, one is confronted by two liquids: one, the *residue*, the residuary liquor, containing the fixed acids and the tannins at the same level as in the wine and containing no alcohol; the other, the *distillate*, effectively consisting of water and alcohol in the same proportions as in the base wine. When tasting them, their violently contrasting tastes and their difference from the flavor of the wine itself come as real surprise. The distillate gives a sweetish sensation along with the warmth, the vinosity of alcohol allied to a certain blandness. The residue, on the other hand, has an acidity, a greenness, and a hardness that are quite unexpected, which render it frankly unbearable and undrinkable. A simple distillation suffices to separate the wine's acid, bitter, and astringent substances from those that are sweet, and to illustrate the notion of balance in a most tangible fashion. From the moment one has done this it is clear that the base wine was only agreeable because its acidity and bitterness were balanced by its alcohol content. The same experiment performed with a dry white wine would equally enable one to appreciate the aggressiveness of its raw acidity when not counterbalanced by alcohol. And a similar impression is to be had from "dealcoholized wine," wine that is thus deprived of its sweetness.

When tasting a red wine, we can say that if its alcoholic degree is insufficient then the acidity and bitterness dominate; the impression one has is of the *residue taste* to a greater or lesser extent and the wine is described as hard, harsh, astringent. If, on the other hand, the tannins and acidity are weak, the *distillate taste* stand out and the wine will be judged too soft, over heavy, and flabby.

Whenever one tastes a red wine then, in order clearly to define the balance of its support structure one would try and determine which are the really dominant tastes in the light of these observations. Are they those of the *residue*? In which case the wine will seem thin, acerbic, and astringent. Or are they those of the distillate? In which case the overwhelming impressions will be of alcohol, fluidity, possibly flabbiness. Or, finally, is the overall impression one of harmony? I recommend this distillation exercise to anyone who wants to understand clearly how the taste of wine is made up. It reveals something new and sets one thinking each time. I myself do the experiment several times a year, and each time I am astonished at the renewed evidence for these concepts of balance. Anyone who has experienced the aggressive acidity and astringency of a red wine relieved of its alcohol will certainly not forget it.

On this subject it should be said that wines are among the most acid, the most tannic, and the most alcoholic of our drinks. And, given the preceding experiment, one can understand that they are only drinkable and attractive to drink because their level of alcohol is high in relation to other fermented drinks.

Ciders are generally lighter than wines; a little sugar is appreciated in them in order to neutralize the acidity of certain apples, or, alternatively, a little carbon dioxide to give them a refreshing tingle. Beers are much less acid than wines as well as being much weaker in alcohol; here it is the acidity of carbon dioxide and the bitterness of hops which counterbalance the alcohol sweetness. In actual fact there is an infinite variety of beers, and all kinds of balance, from the full-bodied English beers to the pale, acid, and practically gas-free beers from Berlin. Still considering the balance of our drinks: Grape juice, with its high concentration of sugar, is only pleasant to drink if it has sufficient acidity. Its relative failure as a refreshing drink is perhaps due to a lack of understanding of the balance principles which hold good for all types of drink.

As has been done for white wines, various diagrams have been devised to represent the tripartite balance of red wines. In the first diagram below (which could also have been designed in triangular form) the area above the broken line, which represents the point of balance, is that of supple wines whose dominant characteristic is softness. The lower half corresponds to wines which give an overall impression of hardness, which may be due variously to excess acidity (left-hand side of the diagram), to excess tannin (right-hand side), or maybe even to an excess of both which is by no means impossible.

The second diagram illustrates how a good balance may be obtained for a whole series of differently constituted wines. For a given alcoholic degree, a balanced taste is as well achieved in the case of a relatively high acidity accompanied by little tannin, as in that of considerable tannin counterbalanced by a very moderate acidity. Between these two extremes, there are numerous intermediate positions, all of which represent a satisfactory balance.

The interpretation of this diagram has a considerable practical

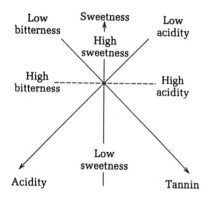

Low
bitterness

Sweetness

Low
acidity

High
sweetness

High
bitterness

High
acidity

Low
sweetness

Acidity

Tannin

A graphic representation of the triparitite balances which govern the tastes of red wines.

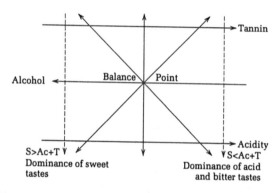

Tannin

Alcohol

Balance Point

Acidity

S>Ac+T
Dominance of sweet
tastes

S<Ac+T
Dominance of acid
and bitter tastes

A graphic representation of the various balances between alcohol, acidity, and tannin in red wines. The arrows with continuous lines represent balanced states; those with broken lines represent states of imbalance.

importance, for it provides the winemaker with the key to making balanced wines according to their type. When seeking to make red wines whose dominant characteristics are fruit and freshness, and which will be drunk very young (*en primeur*) or during the course of their first year, a limited maceration will produce wines with a low tannin index and retaining sufficient acidity. In contrast to this, when aiming to make wines which will mature over a long period in wood and in bottle, techniques will be followed which emphasize maceration and abundant tannin. Tannin from good-quality grape varieties is the guarantee to long life for such wines, whereas their acidity should be low to satisfy the requirements of balance.

There are three corollaries to this fundamental law: **The less tannic a red wine is, the more acidity it can support (necessary for its freshness); the richer a red wine is in tannins (necessary for its development and for its longevity), the lower should be its acidity; a high tannin content allied to a pronounced acidity produces the hardest and most astringent wines.**

Various attempts have been made to establish a relationship, which can be expressed in figures, between the elements which influence a wine's **suppleness** and **richness**, and so determine a sort of **suppleness index**. Jean Ribéreau-Gayon and I have defined this index for red wines of average quality and standard style by the following formula: alcoholic degree – (total acidity + tannin level). The acidity is expressed in grams of sulfuric acid and the tannins in grams per liter. The latter are measured by determining the index of total polyphenols and calculated approximately in the following way: 1 gram of tannins per liter corresponds to an index of 20. The following is an example of a suppleness index calculation: A red wine of 12°, having 3.6 grams of acidity and 1.8 grams of tannin (an index of 36) will have a suppleness index as follows:

$$12 - (3.6 + 1.8) = 6.6$$

Another wine of 10.5°, which has 4.2 grams of acidity and 2.4 grams of tannin (an index of 48), will have a much lower suppleness index:

$$10.5 - (4.2 + 2.4) = 3.9$$

However, it should not be forgotten that other factors also influence qualities of suppleness, notably volatile acidity, ethyl acetate, other elements contributing to hardness, and probably also volatile substances which make up the aroma in the mouth. The tannin index also includes elements which are devoid of bitterness. In addition, during the course of aging, certain polyphenols lose their astringency; as a result, the indices of suppleness only apply to relatively young red wines.

Although there is no absolute limit, it would seem that a wine does not really deserve to be called supple unless its index is clearly above 5. And it needs to be even higher if the wine is to be described as rich; this is the case for the first wine mentioned above whose index is 6.6. The second wine, with an index of 3.9, is inevitably hard, without suppleness, and probably fairly unpleasant.

The validity of this index also confirms the preceding remarks on balance, and, because of their fundamental importance, I have no hesitation in repeating them. The taster will make no progress in his profession if he is ignorant of these basic laws of the balance of flavors: **A wine tolerates acidity better when its alcoholic degree is higher; acid, bitter, and astringent tastes reinforce each other; the hardest wines are those which are at the same time acid and also rich in tannins; a considerable amount of tannin is more acceptable if acidity is low and alcohol is high.**

Another consequence is implicit in these notions of balance: the role of a sufficiently high strength of alcohol. Alcoholic degree is a quality element, not because of the taste of alcohol itself, but by virtue of the better balance which it makes possible. A high degree also implies grapes that are richer and riper. The traditional addition of sugar to the must, an ancient method of improvement, has made a considerable contribution to the wine lover's taste for supple wines with plenty of vinosity. Where wines which require aging are concerned, chaptalization should be considered more as a means of tempering the character of tannic grapes than as a means of improving an acid crop. This is a point of view which has not always been understood.

AROMA AND BOUQUET DEPEND ON A BALANCE OF ODORS

The aroma of a fine wine when young, or its bouquet when it has aged, has a considerable complexity which is not easy to describe. On careful examination an experienced taster would recognize a succession of perfumes recalling a particular flower or fruit, and he would also distinguish various smells of, for example, a fatty, acid, esterish, or spicy character. As in all perfumes there is often a dominant note in a wine's bouquet; but a blend of balanced odors may react on one's sense of smell in very different ways. The laws which govern the intermixing of smells and the way in which they interact have not been completely defined. In an experimental blend of smells some remain detectable, as though they dominated the others, but most of them simply get lost in the crowd and become anonymous; either they mask each other in a way which makes them unidentifiable or else their effect remains below the threshold of perception.

The total blend constitutes a complex which cannot be analyzed, where only a few of the elements are recognizable but where they all contribute to creating the particular smell. In fact, a harmonious blend of several smells forms an ensemble of its own, a new and unexpected perfume whose constituents are difficult to identify.

However, it is possible to outline some empirical rules concerning mixtures of smells. The first concerns their cumulative effect. The intensities of individual odors often combine so that a blend of smells may be stronger than those which make it up. The best demonstration of this consists of putting several odorous substances in solution at concentrations below their sensation thresholds—that is to say, at levels where, individually, they have no smell at all; the blended solution, however, has a very clear smell. In this case it can be said that the odor intensities add up. However, there are synergetic effects which can be noticed as well, a mutual intensification of odors. In this case the terpenes of aromatic grape varieties can be taken as examples. In a sugar and acid solution similar to that of grape juice, the floral odor of linalool can be perceived from 100 micrograms upwards per liter, that of geraniol from 130, those of nerol and terpineol from 400; and 5 milligrams per liter are needed to smell linalool oxides. Now the mixture of these five substances has an olfactory threshold lower than the average of the five together, as it is in the order of 200 to 250 micrograms per liter depending on the percentage of linalool. Thus odors of the same family are apt not only to add up but also to reinforce each other. The other laws concern the identification of odors in combination. Here two contrary reactions may be observed. When odors which are dissimilar in character but comparable in intensity are combined, they can be detected individually and in turn within the mixture, according to which one is the focus of attention. In this case the odors concerned are not capable of mixing. Conversely, there are other odors which mask and neutralize each other. The question is also one of proportions. A greater concentration of one odorous substance or, at the same concentration, one which has a stronger smell, will blot out another smell. Experiments have shown that, when combined with other odorous products, the identification threshold of a substance is significantly shifted and its smell affected in consequence.

The following observations about ethyl acetate, the ester which gives wines affected by acescence their specific faulty smell, are good examples of olfactory interaction. In a water solution the smell of ethyl acetate is easy to detect at concentrations of 30 milligrams per liter. In a 10° solution of alcohol the threshold of sensation is modified, and its smell can only be detected at 40 milligrams; thus the smell of alcohol masks other smells, and one can see from this example how too high a degree of alcohol can diminish the intensity of a wine's odor. If one adds another ester with a strong smell to the ethyl acetate solution (ethyl oenanthate, for example), then 150 mg/l of ethyl acetate are necessary to be able to identify it. Finally, in wines its smell only begins to appear at 160 to 180 mg/l. The more complex and intense the mixture of smells, the more the particular odor of ethyl acetate is masked. Similar quantitative observations could be made for ethyl lactate which has a fine, fruity smell, or with a terpene such as linalool.

The harmonious fusion of perfumes normal to wine explains the impossibility of increasing the natural bouquet with artificial products. Such practices are, of course, illegal and reprehensible, but, in addition, they are futile. If a small amount of such artificial concentrates is added, the additional odor will be drowned in the overall smell with no result. If its threshold is passed, the smell is so dominant and foreign in character that it is instantly recognizable to an experienced taster. This is the case, for example, with the muscat-like odor given to white wines by infusion with elder flowers or sclacate sage; or with the addition of cassis or iris root to red wines. These practices might fool an inexperienced consumer, but a knowledgeable taster would suspect them and chromatograph tests in a laboratory would reveal them with ease.

We have seen that when a wine is tasted the sense of smell plays a part in the taste impressions; these sensations have been called "gusto-olfactory." There is no doubt that odor substances also form part of one's impressions of savor, body, and richness. If, by treating it with a solvent, you remove all the odor constituents from a wine, it is at the same time made much thinner, even though its basic analytical balance has been modified very little.

Another surprising observation is that the fixed substances which constitute a wine's extract also affect the intensity of its smell. Boidron demonstrates this to his students by having them smell 300 milligrams of isoamyl alcohol, first in water and then, for comparison, in a wine which has had all its volatile elements removed by distillation in a vacuum. The smell of the isoamyl alcohol is weaker in the second case. This effect is also known to take place with sugar which, in high concentrations, generally reduces the intensity of a wine's smell. (There are exceptions to this in the case of certain terpenes where, on the contrary, a high level of sugar enhances their odor.)

I would like to refer again to the opposition that exists in wines between their fruit-like aromas and their tannic constitution; this concept should serve as a guideline for all winemakers. By applying different vinification methods to the same red grape harvest, one can make a white wine, a rosé, a light or a strong and full-bodied red wine, depending on the extent of maceration and, as it were, on one's inclination. The white wine is the most aromatic, and the lively aroma of fruit decreases progressively until one has a red wine that needs long aging and whose aroma is heavier and less esterish. Recent research has confirmed the existence of these interactions between aromatic substances and odorless macromolecules. Both phenomena of masking and synergy are already exploited by winemakers during vinification.

There is also a kind of balance between the fruit aromas derived from the grapes, and the woody and tannic aromas due to phenol compounds. A wine's primary aroma is all the more pronounced and attractive the less full-bodied and the less tannic it is. Tannin masks the fruit. According to the level of tannin, and thus depending on its method of vinification, a red wine will be fruity or, on the contrary, it will smell and taste of skins, stems, and pips; what I call a woody taste. On this basis there are three categories of red wine: wines tasting of a particular grape variety, not too full-bodied, intended for drinking young; in contrast, there are wines with an excess of phenol compounds, which are very long lived, but which will always be bitter and astringent and which represent an old-fashioned style of wine; and, finally, well-balanced wines, which are more difficult to achieve and which, while having the tannic support necessary for savor and longevity, should at the same time retain the freshness of their primary aroma.

The taste of wood deriving from oak barrels and the vanilla aroma which is produced later are intimately linked to the bouquet of some fine wines to such a point that some wine lovers are misled into thinking that these are the true criteria of an old wine. The feeling today is that oak should remain discreet, and should increase aromatic complexity without dominating it. Thus the effect of wood is beneficial, but if it is allowed to predominate the wine becomes a caricature.

To sum up: "In a good wine, everything should be harmonious; quality is always linked to a subtle play of balances between tastes and smells."

Ten

Winetasting Vocabulary

The Inadequacy of Words

We have already seen that there are considerable differences between ordinary drinking and winetasting. The act of drinking is usually silent whereas that of tasting involves speaking. It is rare for those who are just having a drink to make comments on their sensations; they do not always analyze them, or at most they say that something is good or bad. The winetaster, however, is obliged to describe his sensations and to make a judgment. He tastes in order to increase his knowledge of wine and to talk about it. In addition, a taster's worth does not depend solely on his sensory sensitivity, or on his ability to recognize smells and tastes, and to assess their harmony; it also depends on his ability to describe his impressions. It is not enough to have an experienced palate, keen and accurate senses, a quick and agile memory, and to know how to organize the best conditions in which to judge wines; the taster must also be able to convey his sensory reactions clearly. He needs to have a tasting vocabulary that is sufficiently wide and precise to describe his perceptions and to rationalize his judgments. What makes a taster's reputation, for the most part, is his ability to talk about wine and the clarity, accuracy, and subtlety of his comments. Beware, however, of the eloquent taster; he may hold forth better than he tastes!

Talking about wine in a precise manner is not easy. In this subjective area the relationship between sensation and expression, between the word and the quality it describes, is not as clear as it is elsewhere. We suffer from a lack of vocabulary; the difficulty of description encourages unwarranted expressions and one can understand the temptation to conceal one's inability beneath verbiage.

When faced with a wine of ideal proportions which we cannot describe, or with a subtlety of aroma which defies analysis, which of us has not echoed Orizet's cry of: "I need to invent the words"? And who has not felt impotent trying to define the varied and fleeting components in the bouquet of a great wine? When trying to talk about wine in depth, one rapidly comes up against the limitations of our means of expression, against the barrier of the inexpressible. We need to be able to describe the indescribable. We tasters feel to some extent betrayed by language. It is impossible to describe a wine without simplifying and distorting its image. For the skillful there is but one resort: to exploit the evocative value of words.

We know that underlying the words we use in speaking or writing there is more than the literal meaning. Some words are charged with ideas and images; that is the magic of a style of speech or writing which makes words say more than they actually mean. There are some words which suggest and evoke more than they say, and others which one uses to say nothing at all. My career as a teacher has taught me that words and phrases only convey thoughts if these are expressed immediately they are conceived. Words spoken off the cuff, even if they are clumsy, are the most meaningful.

However, lines of communication are not always so direct. The listener may form a different image of the same word; more or less precise, stronger or weaker, depending on the meaning and value he attaches to it and depending on how closely he is listening. Not all words are faithful messengers; I have, however, come across many examples where the right word revealed and triggered the sensation. Such is the force of the well-expressed idea.

But the taster's language is not all poetry. Habit and training eventually forge a link between impressions and the vocabulary one uses. Obviously, it matters that the terms used signify the same for everybody, and they acquire precision as the taster acquires experience alongside other professionals. Nevertheless, it must be said that the language of tasting is often imprecise and ambiguous, for the words may have a different meaning from that in everyday use. The wine grower, for example, cherishes local expressions which are unknown elsewhere, or which mean something different when used in a different region or by a different profession. It is also true that one cannot always use the same terms in speaking of different kinds of wine. It is important, however, for tasters to have the same language and, in order to understand each other and to make themselves understood, to use the same words for the same perceptions. For these reasons the profession's vocabulary must be rationalized; a start has been made and I will be returning to the subject later. In addition, the vocabulary should be sufficiently rich and subtle to offer adequate means of expression.

Terminology signifies all the words used in a special sense in a branch of art, science, or technology. Because of its specialist nature all terminology appears somewhat hermetic and esoteric, that is to say, addressed only to the initiated. The winetaster's language is surprising to the layman, perhaps because as a simple accompaniment to our meals wine is too familiar to be taken seriously. What taster, talking about wine, has not detected mocking and uncomprehending smiles in his audience? A student once said to me: "I drink wine every day and your phraseology makes me laugh."

The same goes for descriptions of taste as for criticism of literature or art. The beginner, unable to see and understand by himself, is surprised at the abundance of commentary. However, he needs to be told why a wine is good in the same way as one would explain why a work of art is beautiful.

We must accept that all science and technology need to have their own terminology. Words must be found to express new things, new entities. A precise and expressive vocabulary is indispensable to communication; after all, things need to be given a name.

To know is to be able to name. Now, describing a smell or a taste is extremely difficult. It is not an activity which comes naturally because, as children, we are not taught many words to describe what we eat and drink.

I find the jargons of medicine, business, computers, and sports, to name but a few examples, made up as they are of foreign words and neologisms, all in all much more esoteric and obscure than that of tasting. The latter is certainly metaphorical but it uses only an everyday vocabulary. (Here I am deliberately not taking into account the vocabulary of sensory analysis which winetasters have not adopted anyway, for fear of appearing pedantic.)

The taster has managed with the words that he already knows and he has not felt the need to create new ones in order to talk about wine. He has simply used them rather more in their figurative senses; so much so, and so effectively, that a glossary has now become essential.

The inadequacy and clumsiness of the taster's language has been well described by Poupon: "All that the layman retains of these approximate descriptions, with their occasional poetic brilliance and imagery, is the memory of elegant verbal juggling over a glass. In fact it is a question of an honest and step-by-step attempt to get closer to the elusive truth."

WINETASTERS' LANGUAGE

It seems simple to assemble several hundred words used in winetasting. I would obviously only include those terms which are sensible and in common use in tasting rooms, discarding the host of vinous expressions dreamt up in wine literature in general. For some time now there has been no lack of dictionaries, glossaries, and reference lists; indeed, wise and eminent bodies are busy in their production. Among those confined to definitions alone one could mention: Norbert Got's 250 words in 1955, Le Magnen's 150 in 1962, and the 450 words in the *Dictionnaire du Vin* edited by Féret in 1962. In 1972 Vedel and his team mentioned more than 900: After discarding general terms and the names of chemical substances, there are about 470 left which refer to taste characteristics. French and foreign wine magazines publish regular series of tasting notes. And, while I have not counted exactly, the book you are reading must contain a good thousand or so wine terms; nearly 200 have been listed for describing the appearance of wine alone.

However, these terms are not all of equal merit and they cannot all be recommended in the same way. In effect, they belong to several different levels of vocabulary. The terms used in a tasting session depend on the subject of the tasting, and they also depend on the quality of the winetaster. This has already been emphasized when dealing with terms used to describe color. In an oversimplification, I myself distinguish three types of vocabulary. The professional taster's vocabulary is not the same as that of the amateur in charge of presenting a wine to guests at a dinner tasting, or of a wine journalist writing for the readers of a wine magazine.

There are several ways of talking about the taste of wine depending on circumstances, training, and the taster's state of mind.

The expert, with the benefit of wide tasting experience and a good professional and oenological training, seeks clarity and precision above all in his expression. His style is strict and economical but his comments are reasoned; his conciseness is not due to a lack of imagination but to a choice of the most precise words, and in his reports he only uses terms with an accepted and agreed-upon meaning. In spite of his skill his language should be simple and intelligible to all. Where technical terms are concerned he will only use those which are commonly understood and, although he understands the relationships, he will, for example, refrain from defining smells by analogy with little known chemical substances. As Léglise has put it, on being shown a wine he would not say: "It smells of isoamyl acetate, alpha-ionone, glycerhysine and benzaldehydecyanhydrine, but more simply that it smells of acid drops, violets, licorice, and cherries."

The more occasional taster and the informed amateur do not always express themselves precisely. Their vocabulary is more limited, their style more full of imagery but less precise.

They speak in metaphors and allusions, and not always in the best of taste. The inventiveness of their vocabulary conceals its vagueness. However, there are eloquent amateurs whom it is a pleasure to listen to when they have a glass in their hand. Certain wines lend themselves well to such effusions, but not all: I have often admired the oratorical skill of presenters who can ease themselves out of a tight spot by distancing themselves sufficiently from their subject.

Great wine has that marvelous quality of immediately establishing communication between those who are drinking it. Tasting it at table should not be a solitary activity and fine wine should not be drunk without comment. This would be a serious omission and practically an insult, as much to the guests as to the wine itself. An effort should be made to describe the sensations it awakens which follow each other until after the wine has been swallowed. It should also be compared with other wines which one remembers and with other vintages. Each guest expresses an opinion, offers a point of view, and displays his or her knowledge. There are few pleasures which loosen the tongue as much as that of sharing wine, glass in hand. In essence, it is easy to describe what one senses provided one has made a sufficient effort to notice it. What is clearly perceived can be clearly expressed.

Wine has always had a significant place in literature, and the greatest of writers have devoted some fine pages to it. However, I would condemn the empty, showy style of a certain type of modern wine-writing. Some are really informative and abound in judicious expressions; but any writer who talks of wines as "funny, amusing, jokey, coquettish, naughty" (and the list could easily be lengthened) plumbs the depths of the insignificant and gratuitous.

Orizet has given examples of how vocabularies can vary according to the aims of the tastings and of the taster's perception of what he is trying to convey. In effect, the tenor of commentaries will differ and the terms used vary according to whether the tasting is analytical, comparative, aimed at identification, classification, or simply description. And vocabulary will range from telegraphic to lyrical, via the technical and scientific. "The chemist will look primarily for analytical faults; the repressive official for legal faults; the oenologist for technical defects; the wine maker for character; and the merchant for commercial virtues. . . . Each will appraise according to his training, that is according to conditioning in his job, and his prejudices."

BIRTH OF A VOCABULARY

In order to speak about wine there must evidently be something to say, and there can be no vocabulary of tasting unless there are wines with numerous and complex qualities which are worthy of comment. It seems that in earlier times wine was not always discussed beyond a few words describing its excellence and strength; this was doubtless because at that time there was nothing else to say. Even today there are still millions of hectoliters of neutral, shapeless, and impersonal wines about which the taster can say nothing once he has spat them out. In fact, the birth of a taster's vocabulary dates from the advent of quality wine, and the merit of these wines can be inferred from the style and profusion of expressions used by professionals and wine lovers of the period.

The creation of quality wines in Europe and their slow development dates back two and a half centuries at most. Professor Enjalbert tells how at the beginning of the eighteenth century, above all as a result of the influence of the English merchants and following the invention of the new drinks (chocolate, coffee, liqueurs), the great wines that we know today were born or were discovered and started to circulate: port, Graves, and Médocs for laying down; champagne, burgundy, *oloroso* sherry, and cognac. These fine wines arrived just at the right time at a period of economic and cultural expansion, when a more refined way of life was being sought. And immediately, as usually happens when quality is recognized, demand rises, and a reputation is established, a hierarchy of wines came into being. According to historians, in the Middle Ages there was no trace of a quality premium being accorded to wines with the best reputations, no doubt because they just did not exist. At the beginning of the eighteenth century, on the other hand, a cask of Haut-Brion or Latour was already selling at twice the price of a simple Médoc and four to five times that of everyday table wine; fifty years later the price differential between the first growths and the *palus* wines had advanced to twenty! Thenceforth there was clearly a need for some form of critical tasting, precise and descriptive, with a vocabulary which would enable the various classes of wine to be distinguished. There was also a need to convey the pleasure to be had from drinking these wines.

There has certainly always been a winetaster's language. A hundred or so descriptive terms are said to have been detailed in Greek literature. If, as René Dage has done, one reads through the old documents regulating the profession of *courtier-gourmet* down the ages, one comes across far fewer such terms, although some of them are still in use today: In 1415 wines were already being described as "good, clean, honest, and commercial." What were lauded as the virtues of wine were more the effects that it produced than the merits of its taste. Thus Rabelais, who never ceased to praise wine and recommended that it be drunk at every opportunity, never once actually described it; he does not introduce us to the wines of his period. His knowledge and passion for the subject were considerable and his semantic imagination inventive, and yet he stuck to a poetically vague list of adjectives: delicious, precious, nectar-like, heavenly, joyous, god-like, tasty, laughing, praying, gallant, healthy, good for the stomach; and once he uses the attractive expression "taffeta wine."

Montaigne, who could speak well about anything and who also owned a vineyard, doubtless arrived on the scene too early to tell us about wine. He passed, as he says, "from white to red and then from red to white" and tells us no more about them. Without doubt there was no more to say about these wines at the end of the sixteenth century, wines which he held responsible for "man's worst state, drunkenness." Epicure that he was, a century later Montaigne would certainly have written a chapter on the excellent taste of his wine.

In 1600 the agronomist Olivier de Serres gives us some fascinating details about "making and managing" wines. He was a veritable expert; his knowledge was extensive, strongly influenced by ancient texts, but his vocabulary was succinct. He made a distinction between delicate and coarse wines, and used several adjectives to express the notion of strength above all: vigorous, powerful, harsh. He also described wines which were spoilt by oxidation or by sourness by refermenting or turning to vinegar.

It was in the eighteenth century that wine vocabulary became more varied. The agronomist Maupin had vines at Triel, a few leagues from Versailles (he was manservant to Marie Leczinska at court), and he wrote copiously on his methods for "improving all wines, both good and bad, during the course of vinification, methods suitable for use in all vineyards." Toward 1780 he was using some forty tasting words. In the list reproduced below there are many words still in use today, though they relate more to flavor than to smell: "By improving our wines and henceforth making them more graceful, more approachable, healthier, and better able to travel, we can be sure that the foreigner will take to them much more than at present when he complains at times of their poor quality."

In *L'Art de Faire le Vin* (The Art of Winemaking, 1807), Count Jean Antoine Chaptal uses about sixty terms. Oenological knowledge (we can begin to use the term because Chaptal defines both oenology and oenologist) advanced significantly with the development of chemistry. At the same time the wine vocabulary gained many new adjectives, listed in the table on page 218.

Words used by Maupin (1779)

acid	thick	biting
acrid, acridity	lively, spirited	small
sour, sourness	feeble	weighty
watery	fermentation	drinkable
burning	flavors	tasting of rot
heady	fire	refermenting or
hot, heat	fine, finesse	containing too
consistency	strong, strength	much carbon dioxide
full-bodied,	bouquet*	harsh
having body	heady, alcoholic	clean
flowing, fluid	gracious, great,	healthy
raw, rawness	fine	spirituous
hard, hardness	coarse, vulgar	green, greenness
empyreumatic	meager	vinous
easy, accessible	heady, intoxicating	

*Particularly of a very old wine in the sense of a "high," "gamey" smell.

In his studies on the history of the wine of the Médoc, Pijassou records the terms found in the notes of the Bordeaux wine brokers and the managers of the great estates during the period from 1798 to 1820. Tasting already had its own language. Lamothe, the administrator at Chateau Latour, wrote to the owner about a visit by some Parisian clients: "These gentlemen swallowed every mouthful of wine which does not say much for their ability as tasters." Among the quotations in Pijassou's work there are forty or so wine terms, a dozen of which had not been used by previous authors.

The celebrated *Topographie de tous les vignobles connus* by A. Jullien (1832) begins with an innovation: a vocabulary of about seventy technical terms "used to indicate the qualities, defects, and diseases of wine." The word "tannin" appears. The role that this substance plays in clarification by fining is noted, but its particular flavor is not described.

A few more supplementary expressions are to be found in Fauré

Other words used at the beginning of the nineteenth century

Chaptal (1807)		According to Pijassou (1798–1820)	Jullien (1832)
acéteux (acetic)	franc	arrière goût	acerbe
acescence	fût (goût de)	étoffé	astringence
amer	amertume	ferme	balsamique
amertume	gras	fermeté	droit
âpre, âpreté	insipide	lâche	évent, éventé
arôme	liquoreux	plat	froid
astriction	léger	plein	grain (qui a du)
austere	moelleux	plénitude	herbage (goût d')
bois (goût de)	moisi (goût de)	robuste	lourd
bouquet	parfum	rond	mâche
délicat	pâteux	ton (qui a du)	(qui a de la)
délayé	piquant	velouté	mou
douceâtre	rude	vigoureux	moustille*
doux	rudesse		nerf (qui a du)
fade	sève		sec
filant	tourné		solide
fluide	vif		soyeux

*Usually referring to the gentle working of a young wine undergoing its malolactic fermentation.

(1844), a Bordeaux pharmacist who carried out the first detailed analyses of wine: He speaks of a wine having energy, having had tannin added (*tannifiés, tannisés*), and being flabby, unctuous, styptic, and tile-colored. And, on looking through these lists, one can follow the slow birth over half a century of the notion of tannicity. Maupin only mentions acridity, Chaptal speaks of bitterness, harshness, and astriction, Jullien of tannins, and Fauré of their astringent flavor.

Tasting vocabulary increased by a large number of phrases during the course of the nineteenth century, along with the advance of knowledge about the composition of wine and its transformations.

One moves, in a single century, from the forty words used by Maupin to the 180 defined by the *Dictionnaire-Manuel du négociant en vins et spiritueux et du maître du chai* by Féret (1896), and in two centuries down to the thousand or so words in current use.

The advent of quality gave birth to the need for a wine language and the advance in oenological knowledge has meant the vocabulary can be filled out.

THE VOCABULARY OF STRUCTURE

However lacking in imagination he might be, when a taster works the wine in his mouth and feels it with his tongue, he absorbs not only sensations of taste but also impressions of **volume**, **form**, and **consistency**. He forms a physical image of the wine. This is part of the curious "optical effect" of taste, a phenomenon which it would not be inappropriate to call *stéréogustation*. The simultaneity of different sensations creates a taste profile in the same way that a blend of sounds from different sources creates a sense of aural profile. The wine does not appear to be what it really is, namely an elusive fluid film just wetting the palate's surface; instead, it feels like a substance with three dimensions. Tasters agree that it conveys an impression of thickness, of structure. They talk of a wine's profile, of its contours and its architecture as though the liquid had a design, a particular surface texture, an internal structure. A wine's ideal form is the sphere, which represents a space in perfect equilibrium.

However, matters are more complicated: This form that the wine assumes as soon as it is in one's mouth is not static and definitive; it changes as the taste sensations of the wine evolve. Sometimes the initial shape, that of the attack, diminishes and thins out. A wine is judged by this evolution in its form, and when it starts in one way and finishes in another it is said not to taste homogeneous, to lack unity, and to taste disjointed. If the initial roundness remains for a long period the wine is said to be **long**; if it changes rapidly the wine is **short**, it lacks length. Anyone who has tasted Jurançon, the sweet wine from the Pyrenees foothills, will understand Orizet when he writes: "It is the contradictory nature of Jurançon to be rounded at one end and pointed at the other." The initial taste is of the sweetness of sugar with its round or oval physical impression; but after a few seconds this impression wears off, giving way to the sharpness of acidity.

A whole vocabulary has been created to describe these notions, imagined and yet real enough because everyone perceives them. In his effort to describe, the taster tries to distinguish and to note in succession the various impressions of size, form, consistency, and balance.

One could begin by saying that there are wines of different sizes, dwarfs and giants as it were. Some wines are small in build; they have the prettiness and delicacy of miniatures, of small-scale models. There are others which, when well balanced, have a natural grandeur. These are very rare, grand-scale wines which remind one of photographic enlargements. The adjectives of size, **small** and **big**, are in common use. A wine is also said to have or not to have **volume**; to be slight, or, on the contrary ample, imposing, having breadth and stature.

The idea of shape has led to many more adjectives and a complete list would be difficult to establish. I have searched through numerous texts and have encountered all the expressions that I mention here at least once, but can I be sure of having picked them all up? A wine is **formless** if its image on the palate is unclear. The following words immediately evoke simple forms: spherical, **round**, rounded, oblong, **flat**, **threadlike**, rectilinear, lanky or long limbed, square, **angular, sharp, pointed**, twisted, crooked, concave, convex.

The image of a wine with an inadequate constitution, which lacks body, may be evoked by a large number of terms: **thin**, svelte, slender, tenuous, slight, graceful, **narrow, lean**, skimpy, puny, gangling, flat, stretched, **empty, hollow, dry**, stunted, **meager**, insubstantial. Wines are described as being airy in the sense of being light. Full-bodied wines are described as **complete**, stout, **well structured**, compact, **full, thick, heavy**, dense, **fat**, pudgy, enveloping, massive, large or ample, concentrated.

A wine which is full-bodied (*corsé*) has consistency. A wine's body is linked to its content of polyphenols, alcohol, and dry extract, in other words, to its general constitution; but certain aspects of taste, which are difficult to define, also play a part. The taste of wine is a rather vague concept which involves body and strength at the same time as breed (*race*), and the flavor derived from the soil (*terroir*).

221

What is meant by body can be understood to some extent by comparing a good wine with another sample of the same diluted with 5 to 10 percent water, for example. A full-bodied wine is said to have substance, plenty in reserve, and to have "center" and length. A full wine fills the mouth.

Impressions of balance are expressed in many ways: A well-constituted wine is said to be well shaped, well built, **harmonious.** **Unbalanced** or **inharmonious** wines are described as fleshless, spare or lean, dried out, breaking up, even boneless. A general remark about structure: When a wine is mediocre one tends to fault almost all its aspects: it lacks richness, softness, backbone, and finesse; conversely, a good wine seems to have all the qualities. Thus many qualities go hand in hand and one says of a well-constituted wine that it all fits.

When a wine comes into contact with the tongue, it produces a variety of impressions on its surface. Thus there are wines which seem smooth, slick, **flowing.** Others, aggressive in varying degrees to the mucous surfaces, are described as **harsh, rough,** cutting, pinched, piquant; they are sharp edged, rough textured.

A wine's consistency is its degree of solidity, a texture perceived by the mouth's tactile sense. It distinguishes wines which are **hard, firm,** unyielding, and severe from those which are gentle, **supple,** melting, **soft,** suave, **mellowed.** Wines with a solid consistency are those answering the descriptions pulpy, **rich,** gummy, mucilaginous, **sticky, unctuous,** pasty, or **cloying.** Ropy, oily, viscous wines are perceived as such on appearance (see page 34).

The terminology is vast, but more important than its size is to know how to use it. I do not much care for alphabetical lists which I find tiresome to read. The definitions they give are dryly abstract and require as much effort to read as they took to write. For this reason I have several times tried to work out a logical representation of taste vocabulary applied to the taste of red wines, one which would render the terms comprehensible at a glance. It is based on the notion of balance developed in the previous chapter: sweet tastes $\leftrightarrows$ acid tastes + bitter and astringent tastes. To recapitulate: The sweetness of certain substances (alcohol, glycerol, fermentable sugars) should balance the sum of acid tastes (each acid influencing the balance according to its own particular flavor and its greater or lesser acid character) and those of tannic substances (the latter are part of

222

Increasing sweetness		Increasing acidity
cloying, unctuous, thick, honeyed, flabby, hearty, rich in glycerin, sweet, soft, alkaline (high pH), flat, sweetish, mawkish, pleasing, feminine...	harmonious balanced	meagre, hollow, short, fleshless, empty, lacking in body, dry, dried out, arid, bone dry, biting, sharp, raw, hard, acerbic, austere, severe, angular, stiff, aggressive, piquant, acid, acidulous, green...
	light (in body) thin fluid flowing elegant velvety silky delicate gentle, easy mellow, mellowed soft, supple round	
	ripe full fleshy rich, lush	complete, long, rich, full-bodied, ample, well structured, concentrated, compact, masculine, solid, powerful...
		dense, hard, tannic, firm, rough, stemmy, bitter, harsh, coarse, astringent...
		Increasing bitterness and astringency

(left vertical axis label: Increasing richness)

An attempt at a rational representation of tasting vocabulary.

a wine's richness, but at high levels they make the wine seem hard and astringent). The diagram above summarizes this approach.

The central column groups together the words which define the harmony of tastes. The basis of their distribution is the wine's "richness" in flavor elements, or what one might call volume on the palate. The right-hand arrows represent situations of imbalance in which either acidity (upper arrow) or bitterness and astringency (lower arrow) become increasingly dominant. The apparently anomalous placing of certain terms indicates that they involve more complex balances. The left-hand arrow groups the terms describing an unbalanced sweetness. Thus there is a breakdown of some eighty terms whose diagrammatic distribution should facilitate their comprehension and use.

Something similar has been attempted by Vedel and his colleagues. They explain the presentation of their diagram as follows: "As a large number of balance adjectives relate closely to the three components: acidity, astringency, and sweetness, it seemed sensible to try and arrange them according to the intensity of these characteristics. Clearly there is no question of trying to give precise measurements here, it is an attempt to situate the adjectives in relation

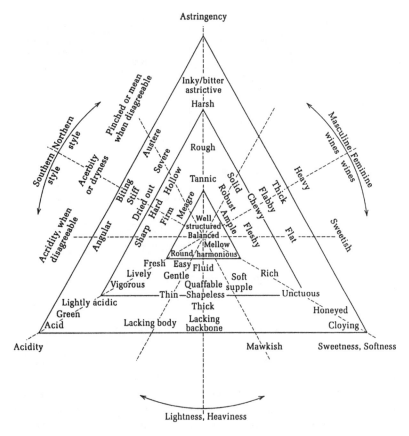

A graphic representation of terms relating to balance
(after Vedel).

to each other within a system which represents the relative concentrations of their basic components. A part of the available red wine vocabulary can thus be represented in a triangular arrangement."

THE VOCABULARY OF VINOSITY OR ALCOHOLIC STRENGTH

To say that a wine is **vinous** is not tautological. Vinous does not mean simply "having the characteristics of wine," in the sense of fruit with a winy taste or roses with a winy odor. The **vinosity** of a wine is a taste property relating to the amount of alcohol it contains, to its alcoholic strength. It is fermentation which confers the vinous character. Vinosity is defined thus: the warm and agreeably caustic flavor yielded by the presence of alcohol, which adds to the actual taste of the wine and which blends in with the wine's other qualities. It is only perceptible beyond a certain concentration of alcohol. Everything is relative, to be sure, but it seems that below 11° a wine cannot be described as vinous. In general, it is only above 12° that there is a clear impression of vinosity. This level of alcohol is required before the mucous surfaces, bathed in saliva, can feel the softening, penetrating, solvent effect of alcohol.

It has already been shown how a low temperature neutralizes the taste of alcohol. On the other hand, vinosity is heightened when the temperature is higher. In addition, other constituents may play a part in the impression of vinosity. This would be the case with 300 or so milligrams per liter of higher alcohols and with 1 gram per liter of succinic acid, both of which are present to some extent in wine; one could also add several esters here.

Vinosity is often confused with **body**, yet these are two different concepts. A 13° wine may lack body and a 10° press wine may be extremely full-bodied. Alcoholic strength by itself then does not account for the body of a wine. It may reinforce a full-bodied impression in the same way that it reinforces and amplifies certain flavors, but an imbalance of too much alcohol diminishes the body and renders the wine thinner. Vinosity is due to the excipient, the solvent; whereas the impression of body, which involves a certain notion of shape and volume, is due to dissolved substances, that is, to the extract and more particularly to the sapid complex of acids and tannins. The tannin index may serve as a good guide to the body of a wine; the alcoholic strength will not serve at all.

In some definitions vinosity is confused with **suppleness**. Obviously, as one is talking about balance here, alcoholic strength is involved. However, wines low in alcohol can be supple, whereas alcoholic wines may be dry and lean. A wine is not soft or fluid simply because it is vinous.

Vinosity has, however, always been synonymous with **strength**. It is alcohol which gives wine its strength and vigor; indeed, the phrase "alcoholic strength" is in common use. A strong wine is one which is high in alcohol. The concept of a wine's strength is very old; it was one of its appealing virtues, as Olivier de Serres recounts: "It was the strength of the wine which lured the Gallic forces to Italy when Arrion Clusien called on them to go to war in Tuscany." Numerous tasting terms express the impression of a wine's strength: vigorous, robust, **powerful**, even hefty or beefy; and, in a negative sense, **weak**, puny. A wine is described as **fortified** when its strength has been increased by the addition of alcohol.

There are a number of words appropriate to describing wines that are low in alcohol. They are said to be **little** or **small, poor, weak,** or **thin**. A **light** wine "weighs" little (in alcohol), though it may be refreshing and easy to drink. If, in addition, it has an attractive acidity it would be **fresh**. If it lacks acidity then it is **flat**. Wines which have none of the agreeable warmth that so appeals to the drinker are described as **cold**. Insufficient alcohol is perceived as **watery**, and makes the wine appear **wishy-washy** or **watered**.

Many expressions are used for wines that are high in alcohol. **Generous** wines belong above all to the dessert wine group, wines enriched either by alcohol or by the use of partially dried grapes; but this term, with its implications of appeal to the palate and a tonic effect, is also used for mature, well-made, and well-structured wines that have been vinified entirely naturally. Wines high in alcohol are those rich in "wine spirit," the alcohol fraction separable by distillation. If the taste of alcohol is clearly noticeable when tasting a wine, it is called **alcoholic**, as though it had been **fortified**.

When alcohol dominates the other elements to excess, the wine is alcoholic. The following expressions refer to the impression of pseudo-warmth caused by alcohol: **hot**, glowing, cordial, ardent, **burning**, fiery (but not to be confused with the fiery, "alembic" taste of a freshly distilled spirit). Finally, some other terms which refer to the uplifting and inebriating properties of alcohol: As the etymology suggests, **heady** wines go to the head; these are wines with abundant alcohol. The combination of **vigor** and **firmness** (*nervosité*) is due to more complex taste relationships. A wine with **sinew** (which has *nerf*, which is *nerveux*) is impressive on the palate, for it has an abundance of both alcohol and acidity; all the same it tastes neither too alcoholic nor too acidic. Generally, it has both body and strength, characteristics which are heightened by aromatic elements.

The winetaster instinctively detects the aroma of alcohol and is wary of high levels of alcohol. Vinosity is only perceived as a quality when it is in balance with all the other elements.

THE VOCABULARY OF RICHNESS AND SWEETNESS

There are two vocabularies juxtaposed here and they must not be confused. One defines the type of wine according to its sugar content; the other expresses the sweet flavors of wine, which are not necessarily due to its sugars, but rather to alcohol, to glycerol, or to a relatively low acidity. This latter group of words expresses overall impressions of appeal and harmony, and it is with this group that I shall start, commenting on the terms synonymous with *moelleux* which describe one of the most sought-after qualities today. Whatever some people may think, sweetness is the only taste that we really like, and other tastes are only pleasant when they are softened. *Moelleux* in the sense under discussion does not refer to a wine that is in between dry and sweet in style. Although it only contains fractions of a gram of glucose and fructose, a red wine may be called *moelleux* if the sweet flavors of its other constituents balance or dominate those of acidity and tannin. The following words have a similar meaning: **supple, fluid, soft, mellow,** rich, **gentle, velvety,** suave, quaffable (in the sense of easy to drink).

Supple means flexible, malleable, easy to shape, and it refers to texture. A supple wine is not harsh to the palate and yields easily to the tongue's movements; it is always attractive to drink, whether it be light or full in body.

This particular quality is linked to low acidity and to a modest level of phenol components (having a tannin index of less than 30 or 40, for example, depending on the grape variety and the type of wine). Wines become more supple as they lose acidity and astringency. A quaffable wine (one thinks immediately of Beaujolais) is one that is easy to swallow and drink at a gulp. A wine without will power, says Michel Fouchaux—an expression I find delightful.

Whether red or white, wines of low acidity seem sweet (*moelleux*) in effect, as though they contained several grams of sugar, even when they contain none at all. For this reason it is difficult for a winemaker to notice, just by tasting, the presence of several grams of residual sugar in a young wine of low acidity. Tasters sometimes say of a wine with little acidity and sufficient alcohol that it has "some sugar"; this does not mean analysis would show that it actually had residual sugar. They also say of such a wine that it has "glycerin," without being able to link this to a high level of glycerol.

Gras indicates a richly fleshy character. A wine described as *gras* fills the mouth; it has weight and breadth, it is both full-bodied and supple at once, and is also described as **fleshy**. It is a rare quality, a prerequisite for great wine. In essence, it is the result of very ripe grapes, a quality which is reflected in the wine. A **ripe** wine is *gras*; a supple wine is not necessarily so, whereas a wine which is *gras* is in principle supple.

Richness is linked to a sufficiently high degree of alcohol. More precisely, there is an optimum strength which depends on the constitution of the wine, but a wine of 10°, for example, cannot really be rich.

Alcohol is a factor in quality, and small variations are easily perceived, perhaps more easily, relatively, than for other constituents. However, its effects are complex and they sometimes appear contradictory. Adding alcohol to a thin, dry wine makes it even thinner and drier, whereas a rich wine seems that much softer and richer the higher its strength. Put another way, alcohol should be masked, covered by the elements of richness. To make a good wine, sufficient alcohol is necessary, but the other elements must match the level of alcohol. In fact, when wines of the same origin are compared, those with the most alcohol are generally rated the highest, not because of the effect of alcohol alone, but because a naturally high degree is the result of grapes which are very ripe. It is this which really affects everything else, for it also produces other favorable elements; notably a low acidity, a quality of tannin with plenty of savor but little bitterness or astringency, as well as an abundance of aromatic elements which by giving a wine more flavor also make it richer. For this reason enrichment of the must with sugar (chaptalization) can never completely disguise the consequences of grapes that are insufficiently ripe.

Wines may have an excess of sweetness which renders them unbalanced. These are called **flabby**, lacking in backbone, **flaccid**, **heavy**, mawkish, **sickly sweet**. A wine is flabby when it lacks body, vinosity, and taste, but above all the word indicates inadequate acidity. A flabby wine might be described as a wine in which nothing stands out. A sweet white wine with low acidity and inadequate alcohol, less than 12°, for example, is easily flabby as its sweetness dominates all. The term *douciné* used to be used in Burgundy to indicate the cloying insipidity of a wine starting to contract the disease known as *amertume* (bitterness, a problem that is very rare these days). Very rich, sweet white wines are judge **unctuous** or honeyed, and if their sweetness is excessive they are soft to the point of being oily (*pommadé*), **syrupy, cloying**.

For the sake of completeness here are the terms relating to abnormal sweet tastes: **sour-sweet** and mannitic. They concern wines affected by lactic acid bacterial spoilage. Any sweetness is more often due to residual sugar after an incomplete vinification than it is due to the sweet taste of mannitol which is difficult to detect; the sourness is due to acetic acid. This disease is gradually disappearing thanks to improvements in conditions of vinification.

To indicate wines which contain sugar as part of their style or type, it is more correct in French to call them *vins doux* (sweet wines) than *vins sucrés* (literally sugared or sugary wines).

"Is this white wine dry, medium dry, medium sweet, or sweet?" This question was posed independently to twenty-two German and seven French tasters who were given white wines from their own countries to taste. The wines had been sweetened by gradually increasing amounts from 1.5 to 48 g/l. The replies, tabulated below, were calculated as percentages.

The results show a great diversity of response within each group, demonstrating the variability there is in the interpretation of what constitutes sweetness in wine. The same wine may be described as dry, medium dry, or medium sweet depending on the taster. I witnessed the same sort of thing a few years ago when there were futile discussions between experts trying to define these terms in relation to precise sugar levels; the authorities finally gave up trying to regulate them.

It is nonetheless instructive to study these very different reactions from the two sides of the Rhine. There is a national taste, even a regional taste, and each has its own vocabulary. It may also be that the equivalent adjectives in the two languages do not have quite the

Descriptive terms applied to white wines according to their sugar levels

(The opinions shown in percentages are those of the tasters: French in the upper register; German in the lower one)

Sugar levels in grams per liter

	1.5	4	8	12	16	24	32	48
Sec	74	56	7	4	3	0	0	0
Demi-sec	26	41	74	64	49	11	11	8
Moelleux	0	3	19	32	48	62	61	60
Liquoreux	0	0	0	0	0	27	28	32
Trocken		100	92	53	10	0	0	0
Halbtrocken		0	8	47	85	39	1	0
Mild		0	0	0	5	61	70	10
Lieblich		0	0	0	0	0	29	90

same meaning. The French tasters are more sensitive to low levels of sugar: Whereas 92 percent of the Germans felt that wines with 8 grams of sugar were dry, only 7 percent of the French did. A quarter of the French even considered that wines with no residual sugar at all were medium dry, no doubt because their acidity was low and their alcohol high. At the other extreme, the French tasters only used the term *liquoreux* (sweet) for wines that were very rich in sugar: Wines with 48 grams of sugar were described as *lieblich* (sweet) by 90 percent of the Germans but *liquoreux* by only 32 percent of the French. The opinions of the French were generally more widely dispersed and less homogeneous than those of the Germans, and their judgments less consistent in relation to each other.

The border between "dry" and "medium dry" lies between 8 and 12 grams in Germany, and from 4 grams upwards in France. A wine is medium dry up to 24 grams in Germany and up to considerably more in France, doubtless because of a certain synonymity between *demi-sec* and *moelleux*. A Germany wine is *moelleux* (*milde*, medium sweet) if it contains 24 to 32 grams of sugar, whereas a French wine can be described as such anywhere between 12 and 48 grams.

These carefully conducted tasting experiments illustrate the different meanings attributed to tasting terms and the common disagreement there is as to the level of a substance in a wine and the intensity of sensation it produces. There would be the same problems trying to equate specific levels of total acidity with the expressions "very acid," "acid," "moderately acidic," or "lacking acidity," or similarly trying to define the levels of tannin corresponding to the terms "supple," "moderately tannic," "very tannic," and "astringent." It is examples such as these, where one is faced with the imprecision of tasting vocabulary, that make me think there can be no unanimous agreement as to the real meaning of these terms, even less so if the agreement is to be international.

To return to the vocabulary of sweetness: *Brut* champagne has from 5 to 15 g/l of sugar, *demi-sec* from 35 to 45 g/l. A sparkling wine is said to be too heavily **dosed** (*dosé*) when its sweetness is judged excessive.

For still wines the term *demi-doux* is sometimes used as an alternative to *demi-sec* or *moelleux*. A wine is described as *tendre* (slightly sweet) if it still has a few grams per liter of residual sugar. A wine is described as *bourru* when it is not fully fermented, still sweet, and cloudy with yeast lees.

A wine that has been sweetened (*édulcoré*) has been blended with unfermented or semifermented grape must, or even with must that has been concentrated by evaporation. Some wines which are very rich in sugar are called nectars (Samos Muscat), as much by analogy with the syrupy exudations of flowers as with a drink so delicious it is "worthy of the Gods." *Mistelles* are unfermented grape juice blended with alcohol; they serve as base wines for liqueurs and aperitifs.

Some special sweet wines take their names from the state of the grapes from which they are made; this is the case with *vins surmuris* (from overripe grapes), *vins de paille*, *vins passerillés* (from air-dried grapes), *vins figués* (from partly dried grapes), and *vins de pourriture noble* (from nobly rotten grapes). These are all wines from grapes that have been overripened by various methods in order to increase their concentration of sugar. They are said to represent the ultimate in extravagant quality.

THE VOCABULARY OF ACIDITY AND ITS SECONDARY EFFECTS

Any opportunity is good for stressing the role of fixed acidity in the quality of a wine's structure, defining it in the way that Jean Ribéreau-Gayon did in his teaching. This role is both more complex and more important than is generally realized, and it is still not always understood. The empirical facts, however, are that great red wines are always low in acidity, and successful white vinification depends on how one has managed to adjust the acid balance. In fact, when explaining the concept of quality, an understanding of fixed acidity and volatile acidity is just as important as an understanding of alcoholic strength; and it has been found that variations of quality in wine, depending on the hazards of storage, are closely related to variations in its acidities.

The range of adjectives describing fixed acidity is one of the widest there is, especially if one includes all the terms indirectly related to the taste of acidity.

Expressions relating to acidity in wine can be grouped into three categories: those which define acidity effectively perceived as acid, and thus considered to be to a greater or lesser extent excessive; those describing the opposite fault, a lack of acidity; and, finally, those which apply to an unrecognized and unidentified acidity which nonetheless plays a fundamental part in poor balance on the palate. This is the hidden aspect of acidity which I call secret acidity; it is underhand and destroys a wine's harmony while remaining anonymous.

There is a series of words describing acid flavor. The acidity of **freshness** and **liveliness** (generally due to malic acid) may make a dry white wine and a *primeur* style red wine attractive. The acidity of **hardness**, on the other hand, perceived as an aftertaste at the back of the throat (and due above all to tartaric acid), is less acceptable. I have also come across the following expressions describing acidity: irritating, stimulating, setting one's teeth on edge, awkward, the acidity of greenness, and obtrusive acidity.

The following words describe frankly acidic flavors and their variations: **acerbic**, stinging, **acidified, acidulous, aggressive**, sharp, tart, angular, citric, lemony, suggesting added tartaric acid, greenish, unripe, **green**. Acidulated drinks are those made with the addition of acids or acid juices; acidity is said to be thirst quenching. In the eighteenth century wines were sometimes described as green (*verds* and *verdagons*). Acid and vinegary wines (or fruit) were called tart (*surs* and *surets* from the German *sauer*), and sour (*suris*) when they had actually turned to vinegar. Verdot and Verdet are, appropriately, the names of acid grape varieties. Verjuice is the term for grapes picked before they are completely ripe, at the moment when they are just starting to color (*veraison*). Their acid juice is used in the preparation of certain foods and condiments such as mustard. Wine made from small, underripe grapes (*grapillons*), what the Médocains call *reverdons*, tastes of verjuice. In a fine wine, however, any such greenness, the taste of unripe fruit, would be a serious fault. An acid wine is also said to be **raw** (*crud*); the term is an old one, Maupin often spoke of the *crud* wines of poor years. The absence of malolactic fermentation may also be the source of this characteristic. Chemical correction of the fault produces wines termed **deacidified**, deacidulated.

A few other terms such as cutting, grating, mordant or biting, pinched, piquant, pointed, sharp, etc., are variations which vividly express the unpleasant character of excess acid.

Inadequate acidity is described as **flabby**, **flat**, flaccid, alkaline. A flat wine is similar to a flabby one except that it is more watery; it is a little wine lacking acidity and generally poor in aroma, too. The taste of wines with a high pH (around 4, for example), which are always in an advanced state of salification, is called salty or "alkaline"; not, of course, that the wines react as alkalis but they remind one of the soapy taste of a wine diluted with Vichy water. Their color is dull, an effect also produced by excess deacidification. The acid balance of these wines is close to that of beer, whence the expression "beer-like" used to describe some very flabby white wines. The taste of succinic acid, both salty and bitter, must also play a part in this impression.

Unidentifiable acidity produces wines which are: thin, **emaciated**, acid, austere, **short**, **hollow**, **fleshless**, dried out, **firm**, meager, nervous, **stiff**, harsh, **hard**, **dry**, severe. An impressive list of defects. A red wine which has dried out, which has become dry, is a wine which has lost its volume, which lacks softness, and which has too little sweetness or too much acidity, at least in relation to its alcohol. These terms evoking a dried-out character are also used for wines with a high level of volatile acidity but which are not necessarily completely spoiled, and for tired wines whose acidity is showing through.

Acescence, or acetic spoilage due to the action of acetic bacteria, is characterized analytically by the formation of excess acetic acid and ethyl acetate, and on the palate by the taste and smell of pricked, vinegary wine. From the moment of its birth wine contains a little of both these substances: 200 to 300 mg/l of one and 60 to 80 mg/l of the other. At these levels their influence on taste is completely masked and the wine is said to have "no volatile acidity," meaning that it cannot be tasted. However, from upward of 700 to 800 milligrams of the acid, and 150 to 180 milligrams of the ester, the wine appears at least suspect if not actually judged spoiled. It is then said to have "volatile acidity," meaning the fault is clearly perceptible. At the levels specified acetic acid has little smell, but it does have the sour taste of bacteria-produced acidity. As for the ethyl acetate, it has the aggressive smell of a pricked wine, added to a burning, acrid taste; it is ethyl acetate which spoils the freshness and clarity of a wine much more so than acetic acid.

Volatile acidity, the unpleasant kind of acidity, reinforces the disagreeable tastes of fixed acidity and excess tannin; but it is more or less masked by a high degree of alcohol, by the presence of sugars, or by a low fixed acidity. This explains why it can be identified from around 0.5 g/l in some wines with a puny constitution, yet not even suspected at 0.9 g/l in very well structured wines.

Some people would have it that a slightly high level of volatile acidity is necessary, that it accentuates the bouquet of some wines or even takes its place. Such people are bad tasters who are talking nonsense. Either they lack sensitivity or else they do not know how to tell good from bad.

I will save the list of wine diseases for further on and simply note here the specific terms used for wines of varying degrees of acescence: **acetic**, **acrid**, **sour**, sourish, soured, **spoiled**, fiery, hot, strong, **pricked**, tart, vinegary.

Acetic derivatives are acrid. Acridity (*âcreté*), which defines a strong, irritating smell or taste which is felt in one's nose or throat, should not be confused with asperity (*âpreté*), a sensation close to astringency, and which produces a feeling of roughness in the mouth. "Sour" is synonymous with acid, and one can rightly say of insufficiently ripe fruits that they are "sour." However, in tasting terms the word sour specifically describes an acid taste of an unpleasant kind, with a hint of spoilage or disease, and its use should be limited to this impression. It is also commonly said of a wine that it has a "point" of volatile acidity, which is a good metaphor for the sharp impression it leaves on the palate. All acids are sharp, but acetic is the most stinging. A pricked wine is also described as fiery or "hot," "feverish," and "strong."

It may come as a surprise to realize that in certain drinking circles pricked wine is not considered unhealthy and remains fit to drink. One might see in this a vestige of ancestral habits, but are they in fact that old? Vinegar and pricked wine watered down were for a long time the daily drink of peasants and manual workers. They grimaced and drank them, albeit with a shudder.

THE VOCABULARY OF BITTERNESS AND ASTRINGENCY

The flavors of tannin are the most diverse. On page 102 I tried to classify them empirically, for want of a better way, distinguishing the tannins as **savory**, **bitter**, **acidulous**, **astringent**, **woody**, and **vegetal**. With our present level of understanding it is not possible to link these characteristics to the chemical nature of tannins, to their degree of condensation, or to the presence of other substances, possibly aromatic, which accompany them. I should emphasize that the types of flavor we are dealing with here are even more complex than acid tastes because of the intensity of their sensations, their numerous styles, the fundamental influence they have on taste balance, and because of the way they themselves are affected by other flavors. The effect of acidity, for example, is to change the taste of tannin and to increase its hardness.

To make them easier to understand, I will divide the terms I have collected in the course of my reading and research into three groups. The first deals with the sensation of bitterness; it contains rather few adjectives because once bitterness is perceived there is nothing else to say. The second group deals with astringency, and the third with words relating to tannic balance or imbalance. In the third list do not be surprised to see expressions already mentioned in relation to the structure of wine or the secondary effects of acidity;

acid and bitter tastes are known to be cumulative and difficult to distinguish in their effects.

Bitterness is an elementary taste which may be caused by various substances, for example, quinine, cinchonine, certain other alkaloids, caffeine, and some heterosides. A number of drinks, notably vermouths and bitters, owe their tonic and aperitif bitterness to infusions of various plants: sage, chicory, quinquina, gentian, centaury, peel of bitter orange, hops, bitter aloes, artichokes, etc.

For a long time the adjective **bitter** was used exclusively for wines affected by the bacterial disease known as *amertume* (bitterness) which, in Pasteur's time, attacked the wines of Burgundy especially. However, tannins themselves have a bitter flavor which is all the more apparent in a slightly alkaline milieu, or at least in one that is neutral or that has little acidity. At the acidity level encountered in wine, the bitter taste of tannins is not pure; it is mingled with, and often dominated and masked by, astringency. Bitterness has many other causes whose origin is unknown and all tasters have encountered white, red, or rosé wines with a surprisingly bitter finish.

Length of finish in a wine is always based on bitterness to some extent, but when this is unpleasant it is a fault (known as *arrière goût*). Sometimes the fault is only temporary; certain young white wines, still cloudy with yeast lees, have a poor taste and are said to be "in a bitter phase" (*sur l'amer*); but this bitterness disappears after a few months. And, for reasons that are not understood, Muscat wines which are fermented dry become bitter and remain so. On the other hand, where red wines are concerned, a healthy bitterness is often considered to promise good quality and a favorable development.

Acridity and stypticity can be regarded as unpleasant variations of bitterness. The strong tannic character of certain wines sometimes seems to taste metallic although metals are in no way involved. In some soils one comes across Cabernet Sauvignon wines whose taste reminds one of the protective capsule on the bottle, made of tin-plated lead; these wines are said to have a "capsule" or "tinfoil" taste. (If you have ever inadvertently chewed a bit of silver paper in a piece of chocolate, it tastes similar to that.) Coarse wines, strongly marked by tannin, are described as having an "inky taste."

Wines rich in tannin are called **tannic**; they are to a greater or lesser extent **astringent** or astrictive. Astringency was defined as an impression of dryness and roughness on the tongue. Several adjectives describe this sensation and they are applied to tannic wines: The wine tastes of "vatting," it has been "overvatted," macerated for too long. It then tastes of grape skins, of stalks, or it tastes woody, it tastes of press wine. Storage may also be responsible for excess tannin, in which case it is described as wood, oak, or cask tannin. The term tannic is also used to describe white wines kept in barrel for a long time, and which have taken on a wood tannin taste even though the amount of dissolved tannin is less than 200 mg/l.

Jullien used the word *grain* (grainy) to mean "a type of asperity which, without being at all disagreeable, makes its presence felt in most dry or sweet wines when they are not very old." Today the term *grain* is ambiguous as Vedel points out, because it can refer either to high quality as in *avoir du grain* (to have a palpable but attractive texture), or to a fault known as *goût du grain* (a coarsely grainy taste) resulting from excessive pressing.

Pijassou has drawn our attention to the fact that when Labory, a Bordeaux wine broker, was tasting the 1820 Médocs shortly after the harvest, he found that they produced "the same effect as cachou" on the palate. Cachou is an extract from the acacia catechu tree, known best for the refreshing pastilles made from it. The comparison is still used for wines which give the combined impression of bitterness, astringency, and a certain freshness, too.

Tannin is an element in the **body** of a wine and a sufficiently high level makes the wines **full-bodied**, **ample** and **rich**, vigorous, **well structured, long on the palate**, sustained; it also assures longevity, as the saying goes: "long on the palate, long life." A wine that is well endowed with tannin has consistency and a thick, mouth-filling texture, it has follow-through (*de la suite*). Too much tannin, however, makes the wines **hard, firm**, rough, stiff, austere, severe, **coarse**. A wine described as **big** or **charged** (with extract) is tannic and deep in color.

In great red wines the quality of tannin is linked to aromatic quality. Finesse of flavor always goes hand in hand with aromatic finesse. The tannin of fine grape varieties and fine wines is called noble. As the bouquet develops during the course of aging so the tannic tastes mellow and become more supple. This almost leads one to believe that the tannins themselves are aromatic or that they become so. In contrast, a **harsh** wine, lacking character, is described as **common** and vulgar, the very antithesis of **fine**. Such wines are generally the product of mediocre vines or bad soils.

THE METAPHORICAL LANGUAGE OF TASTE

Tasters' language is made up of precise terms for concrete sensations: sweetness, acidity, bitterness, the smell of ethyl acetate, for example; for more subtle sensations it consists of imprecise, but conventional, terms which attempt to define a balance of flavors, to describe tastes or smells in detail, or to make judgments. In the first case the word fits the perception well and is intelligible. In the second case, by trying to clarify the blurred image of their sensations, tasters are led to juggle with words. To do this, they have taken everyday vocabulary, as we have seen, and somewhat stretched and altered its meaning. Above all they have applied words to wine in a metaphorical sense, as though discussing an object or a person, as though wine had shape and being.

What fundamentally shocks and surprises the layman is the idealization and personification of wines. He finds it difficult to understand their being described as geometrical structures, as materials, or as living beings. For in his comments a taster will attribute a shape and a texture to a wine; he will talk of its youth, its aging, its defects and diseases, and he will bestow on it the rarest of human virtues: Wine is honest, noble, lovable, generous, and so on.

Adjectives applied to the goodness of wine and to its pleasurable qualities surprise nobody: **good** or **bad**, **agreeable** or **disagreeable**, succulent, "tasty" (used for a wine which has abundant taste), or insipid; these are not out of place and cannot be objected to. However, those relating to the "beauty" of wine already involve a certain shift in the use of language. This is a convention one has to accept. A beautiful wine has cachet, style, verve, it is even sometimes called "chic"; and, depending on the taster's enthusiasm and creative imagination, it will also be described as smart, elegant, charming, brilliant, distinguished, gracious, and even, with a little exaggeration, sumptuous, enticing, opulent, seductive.

In much the same vein are expressions used to define a wine's place in an elite and hierarchical vinous "society." A great wine is presented as a nobleman. Classified wines (that is, wines which have

238

class), described as **noble**, **rich**, and with **breed**, are distinguished from banal wines which are uncouth, **common,** vulgar, plebeian, **poor, everyday, ordinary**, standard, unpretentious. There are also *curs bourgeois* and *crus paysans*. A wine is rich and opulent when its taste and odor constituents are present at high levels, and these words also express the notion of complexity well. In contrast, a poor, modest wine has little flavor, a taste which is simple and lacking in subtlety. A distinctive wine (*de précision*) is one which stands out, a wine in a superior class.

Allusions to human physique are even more conventional. Wine is given a certain shape by being depicted as corpulent, well fleshed (or, alternatively, fleshless, skeletal), muscular, athletic (or, on the contrary, puny, weak), masculine, virile, or feminine.

Further examples of this sort are to say of a thin wine that "it is all bones," "you can see its bones showing," or to say of a rich wine that "it is well nourished." And imaginative tasters, whose example I would not follow, would not hesitate to give a wine build, broad shoulders, backbone (or lack of it in the case of a flabby wine), a fine pair of hams, and many other muscular attributes! When tasting, old Casauvielh always talked of wines as characters. The light, young wine was a little page; the next, supple and buxom, a beautiful blond; and the third one, highly colored, full-bodied, and nervous, a mysterious brunette. There were only good wines to be had at his house, but his constant embroidering of this theme irritated me somewhat.

Adjectives referring to age, on the other hand, have a certain logic in their observation. Wines that need keeping pass more or less rapidly over the years through all the stages from youth to decrepitude. From being *nouveau*, **young,** then youngish to begin with, wine reaches the age where it can be drunk; it is then said to be **ready** (*fait*), in the right condition. A settled wine (*rassis*) is no longer young. When older, having lost the qualities of mellow maturity, it is said to have **grown old**, to be elderly, hoary or ancient, decrepit, senile, **worn out**, **past it**, finished, etc.

I agree that to attribute moral virtues to a wine is both inappropriate and ridiculous; but why can one not say of a wine without defects that it is **sound**, **straightforward**, clean, loyal, genuine, **authentic**, honest, pure, **commercial**? In any case, such vocabulary dates from the earliest commercial dealings.

The strength or generosity of a wine, one of its cardinal virtues, can be expressed by the words: energetic, **vigorous**, spirited, **powerful**, combative, **aggressive**, or in terms of "having character, energy, vigor," and so on. It comes as no surprise then to see a **feeble** wine noted as weak, puny, or anemic.

Friendliness attributed to wine is pure eighteenth century, and the following list is very much in the style of the period: gentle, pleasant, pleasing, toothsome, flattering, kindly, inviting, attractive, enticing, winning, caressing, blandishing, amusing.

If you add to these a few faults which could be human: proud, haughty, affected, capricious, malign, frivolous, or even mean, crusty, ill tempered, grim, brutal, and vicious, then you have an extensive list which is practically inexhaustible because it is fed by the imagination. A temperamental, changeable wine is one that is not stable, which is sensitive to external conditions, and which readily varies in taste depending on the conditions in which it is tasted.

There are other expressions which do not fit into any of the preceding categories. Among these are wines described as treacherous, sly, or roguish because of the way they go to one's head and because one is easily taken in by them. And a wild wine tastes of wild fruits, of undomesticated vines. However, without becoming totally irrational, how can one justify adjectives such as sad, intelligent, spiritual, exuberant, sharp witted, and alert?

A strange comparison is the likening of the textures of wine to those of various materials. The word *robe* is already used to define a wine's color, and if it lacks clarity it is described as creased or crumpled (*fripé*). A full-bodied wine is said to be well clothed, tightly woven, whereas it is loose knit if the wine is flabby. A meager, dry wine is "threadbare," "its weave is visible."

Wines which are both rich and ripe or sweet are satiny, silky, **velvety**; what Rabelais called "taffeta wines." Lacy wines are refined and impalpable. And then there are wines that are heavy, common, and like cotton.

In correspondence dated 1821 between the manager Lamothe and one of Château Latour's coproprietors, Pijassou has picked up the following expressions used by a wine broker in comparing samples of 1819 Margaux and Latour: "Having tried the wines, he held the cup of Ch. Margaux out to me, saying: 'My friend, this is cashmere and', holding out the other cup, 'this one is fine Louviers wool cloth.' " (At that time cashmere was used for fancy waistcoats, and was certainly considered too outré for a suit.)

There are hundreds of other possible images, depending on the poetic ability of the taster: Wines from exceptionally ripe grapes are termed sunny or sunshine wines; roasted, southern, or fiery; those that have a simple freshness of character are rustic or pastoral. Images of gaiety are implied in wines which are laughing, joyful, mischievous, alert, and merry; or suggestions of an explosion of flavors on the palate in such expressions as "Catherine wheel," "peacock's tail," and "with thousands of tastes."

There are circumstances where a little fantasy is appropriate, and a certain amount of success can be assured if one chooses from the 160 or so words listed in this chapter. However, a word of advice: Do not overdo it. Not all wines can stand exaggerated descriptions and not all audiences can put up with the absurd.

THE INFLUENCE OF CARBON DIOXIDE ON TASTE

Any discussion of carbon dioxide immediately evokes the image of bubbles in a flute of sparkling wine; but I would like to begin with the important role, relatively little understood even by professionals, of the invisible carbon dioxide in **still** wines.

Produced by fermentation, carbon dioxide practically saturates young wines, and it can be considered as a normal constituent of all wine. Old wines still contain some, and storage and normal handling never eliminate it completely. Carbon dioxide is soluble in wine but it is also volatile, so that its level continues to diminish little by little by evaporation, and, in particular, during cellar operations carried out in extensive contact with air. The means of storage itself influences the carbon dioxide level. For example, large, hermetically sealed vats conserve the gas in wine more than small wooden barrels, and the loss of gas in bottle is nil. The level of gas in wines at the time of consumption is very variable and, in most cases, uncontrolled. There are certainly ways of adjusting the level of carbon dioxide, but they are still too little used for wines made in these northern latitudes. And yet, carbon dioxide has a considerable influence on taste.

It acts on our senses in two ways. It has a simple, lightly acidulous flavor which is perceptible in water at 200 mg/l, and, at higher concentrations, it causes a prickling sensation of the mucous surfaces of the mouth as it escapes. We have already seen that this chemically sensitive reaction is called a haptic one (page 97), and it is by the prickling sensation that carbon dioxide is recognized. Now in a wine it is only perceptible above 500 mg/l (approximately 250 cubic centimeters). Levels below this are thus unidentifiable and unperceived; nevertheless, they exert a very clear influence on the impression of balance.

Nothing illustrates the complex flavor of carbon dioxide better than tasting a carbonated water. Depending on the quantity of carbon dioxide, the water appears either fresh and sapid or hard and acidulous, even somewhat suffocating because of the sudden release of the dissolved gas in the mouth.

Below the prickle threshold, carbon dioxide acts as an acidulant in wine. It adds to and accentuates acidity, it reinforces tannic flavors and diminishes sweet tastes, that of alcohol in dry wines as much as those of sugars in sweet and medium-sweet wines. Thus the presence of carbon dioxide has a direct influence on the fundamental balance of flavors, just as acidification does. It highlights the imbalance of hard and acid wines, or renders thinner those which would be balanced without it; on the other hand, it adds a freshness and liveliness to wines which are soft or flat. Its effect may be favorable or not according to its concentration, the type of wine, and the wine's balance.

Pascal Ribéreau-Gayon has noticed that tasters are more sensitive to normal variations of carbon dioxide and therefore carbonic acid than they are to those of a wine's own acids. The level of carbon dioxide in a red wine was modified so as to present fifty tasters with three samples, in random order, containing 20 mg/l, 360 mg/l, and 620 mg/l. In the event, 73 percent of the participants recognized the third sample in which the characteristic prickle was apparent on the tip of the tongue; in addition, 53 percent could distinguish between the first two samples in which the gas was not perceptible.

In another exercise the same tasters were asked to identify three samples whose acidity has been altered to a fairly marked extent (3.3 to 3.8 and 4.5 g/l). The result was that 38 percent of the tasters (as opposed to 27 percent in the previous exercise) got none of the answers right, and only 32 percent (as opposed to 53 percent) managed to identify all three correctly.

Another aspect of carbon dioxide is that its evaporation in a glass which is swirled draws out and highlights a wine's smells; the escape of the gas draws the odors with it as it were, thus the fruitiness of young wines is clearly reinforced and enlivened. On the other hand, if the bouquet of an old wine is slightly gassy it seems distorted by suggestions of acidity.

Some dry or barely sweetened white wines which are young and insufficiently acid are improved by the presence of 500 to 700 mg/l of carbon dioxide. Swiss wines are a striking example of this. Malolactic fermentation lowers their acidity to such an extent that saturation with carbon dioxide becomes indispensable in order to eliminate their dull flavor and restore their freshness. It is a mistake, however, to carbonate a wine possessing 5 grams of acidity as is sometimes done; it is quite acidic enough as it is. *Primeur* styles of red wine with very little tannin may profitably contain 400 to 500 milligrams of carbon dioxide. However, a red wine which is to be aged in bottle should have less than 200, even less than 100, mg/l, a level which is not always easy to obtain with some methods of storage. Carbon dioxide diminishes the suppleness and reinforces the hardness of such wines. Similarly, sweet wines are always richer with a minimal carbon dioxide content.

The effect of carbon dioxide in wine also depends very much on temperature: A given level will suit a wine drunk cold but make a wine drunk at room temperature almost spritzy (lightly sparkling). Furthermore, carbon dioxide considerably falsifies the taste of newly fermented or still-fermenting wines. The intrusive excess gas is easily eliminated by pouring the wine from one glass to another five or six times, and doing it from a sufficient height to emulsify the liquid. Many young red wines which appear thin and short are made more supple by this simple manipulation.

A specific vocabulary is used for wines which are rich in carbon dioxide. A wine is said to be **gassy** when it contains an abnormally high level of gas and needs to be degasified, decarbonated. Wines which are saturated with carbon dioxide and stored without pressure in corked bottles are described as *perlants* or *perlés*, slightly sparkling or having a light prickle. The cork is not forced out as the bottle is opened, and very little *mousse* is evident when the wine is poured into the glass; at most a ring of bubbles forms at the rim. Just a light pinch of gas is felt on the lips and the tip of the tongue with such a wine. When wines are oversaturated the pressure inside the bottle is fairly strong; the wines are then called effervescent or sparkling, they froth in the glass and give one's palate the "carbon dioxide shock."

To judge by the number of bottles of carbonated drinks which are consumed, the public very much likes the aggressive flavor of carbon dioxide. However, I wonder if this has always been so, and I would love to know how man could have acquired this curious taste. Very few spa waters are naturally sparkling and fermented drinks normally lose their gas after a few weeks or months. This taste for carbon dioxide must be recent and artificial. Sparkling wine itself is after all a relatively recent discovery, some three hundred years old or so, and to start with it had a limited following; witness the merchant quoted by Raymond Dumay, who was writing in 1713: "Sparkle eliminates what is best in good wines even if it does add some merit to little wines." The gas has had its revenge since. Never before has there been so much wine made by the champagne method, nor so many drinks carbonated. Carbon dioxide sells well. I would have nothing against all this "gas guzzling" if I did not fear that masses of carbon dioxide are used to make the rest of the wine more palatable.

THE VOCABULARY OF OLFACTORY QUALITIES

At first sight, the odor of wine appears to be in the realm of the indescribable. How can you use words to bring alive a smell? Using a Cartesian approach to the problem, the taster disciplines himself first of all to distinguish between the intensity or volume of odor and its subtlety or quality. Then, in an exercise that is more difficult, he tries to recognize a succession of perfumes which recall the smells of particular flowers, fruits, wood essences, etc. He does this by an attentive nosing of the wine, by short, repeated, insistent sniffing and smelling. He lets his imagination roam and plays a word game of evocation and analogy.

As long as it is simply a question of judging general qualities such as an indication of intensity or quantity of smell, or the olfactory appeal, then the words come practically by themselves; if the assessment is straightforward, there are no real difficulties in finding the right adjectives. However, as soon as it is a question of describing an aroma or a bouquet, when it is no longer a question of judging but of conveying and suggesting them, then one is even more aware of the poverty and inadequacy of words than when describing tastes. This is not because there is a lack of them, indeed, they are more numerous than those for taste, but because the sensations are finer and more complex. They are also less well codified and it is therefore more difficult to choose the most appropriate word, or the one which will least misrepresent the sensations perceived.

The appeal of a wine's smell is fundamental to its quality. A wine with an attractive smell is said to be harmonious, to be **fine**, refined. Finesse is the sum total of qualities which go to make up a fine wine; it "is distinguished by the delicacy of its aromatic savor [*sève*, see later], the appeal of its bouquet, its clarity of taste and color, and its overall perfection." The finesse of a young wine is based on **fruity** and **floral** aromas.

A good wine is one which, in addition to its balance of flavors, has a pleasant odor even if it is **simple** and not very intense. A great wine has an odor which is not only **agreeable**, but which combines qualities of intensity, complexity, rarity, and personality; it is then said to have character, typicity, **breed**, and be full of aromatic savor (*séveux*). A distinction should be made between finesse and breed. A wine may have finesse but not breed if it does not also have the characteristics typical of its origin. An unobtrusive wine lacks personality; it is ordinary and insignificant.

Sève (literally "sap") is an ancient expression. Initially, when little was known about the nature of wine, it was as imprecise as many other terms. A connection was made between *sève* and fire. For Chaptal it was synonymous with strength and vigor. According to another definition: "*Sève* flatters the palate and implies a good quality, generous wine; it is encountered in fine old wines of unquestionable class." I have noticed expressions such as *sève perçante*, meaning a wine beginning to develop, and *une sève plus nourrie*, corresponding to an aromatic wine. However, the question of whether *sève* referred to taste or smell was never asked. Jullien made matters clearer in 1832: "*Sève* is the name given to the aromatic perfume and spirituous aspect of wines which develop on the palate during the course of being tasted; they fill the mouth with their aromas and continue to be tasted after the liquid itself has been swallowed. This quality is also described as spirituous aroma (*arôme spiritueux*). The aromatic part of *sève* is the same as that of the bouquet, but it is usually sensed with greater intensity. . . . This quality is the prerogative of fine wines." It is clear from this admirably precise definition that *sève* is the equivalent of what today is called the palate aroma and its persistence. Any other interpretation is confused. The Burgundians have lost the meaning of the word *sève* which they consider, wrongly, to be exclusively Bordelais: "A term from the Bordeaux region whose meaning is unclear." It is amusing to note that, having coined the phrase "intense aromatic persistence," they do not seem to know that the word *sève* preceded it by a hundred and fifty years.

In contrast to these qualities, the term "common" describes wines without distinction, smelling barely agreeable or actually unpleasant. This characteristic is linked to the grape variety, to the type of soil, the geographical region, and the grapes' state of maturity. There are fine, semi-fine, and common grape varieties. The common type often has a vegetal, coarsely herbaceous smell. It is also said to bear the mark of its poor grape variety (*marqué*) and its poor soil (*terroité*).

Some wines, made from the hybrid vines *Vitis labrusca*, have a smell which is called "foxy." Once consumers become accustomed to it, the wines are appreciated by some drinkers.

The intensity of a wine's odor should always be noted on a tasting sheet. If the smell is **strong, intense, developed**, ample, then the wine is described as odorous, **aromatic,** or as having plenty of **bouquet**; it has an aroma, a bouquet, or in a more familiar phrase, it has "a good nose." If the terms perfumed or aromatized are used, it means one can sense something artificial. A wine which has started to produce a nose is **developing**.

If, on the other hand, the wine's smell is **feeble**, if it has no nose, then the wine is judged **neutral**, weak, poor. If its odor has disappeared it is odorless; if it is short lived it may be described as evanescent. A **closed** wine, also said to be closed up, dumb, discreet, distant, muted, secretive, is a wine which is "not expressing itself," which for the moment "says nothing." It is temporarily in a state where its smell is diminished, as when, for example, it has been in bottle for some months or years and one is waiting for its bouquet to open out. At the time of writing (1995) many fine 1985 Bordeaux are still closed up. As one of my friends says, we need to call on them again.

The clarity of a wine's nose indicates its openness, the absence of any foreign smells, a perfect state of health. The wine is described as **clean**, **healthy**, **sound**, genuine, pure, appetizing.

There are many ways of expressing lack of clarity and cleanness; the list of possible spoilage problems is a long one. Besides, there are always more words to describe faults than qualities. Here I am only going to consider terms which deal with the unpleasant smells developed by bacterial diseases, in particular, those which may be sufficiently serious to render the wine undrinkable. The other cases of distasteful smells (*dégoûts*) and unpleasant aftertastes (*déboires*) will be dealt with further on.

The opposite of clean is **dubious**, **defective**, dirty. The opposite of healthy is **sick**, sickly, **spoiled**, decomposed. Leaving aside the acetic-related defects already dealt with, let me mention other smells: rancid, yeasty, those of lactic spoilage, mousy or acetamide smells, the unripe and/or cooked character from grapes affected by heat, and the smell of undrinkably acid wine. Disease (bacterial spoilage) spoils, alters, and decomposes wine.

Identifying bacterial spoilage is more the function of the microscope and analysis than that of tasting. If the wine is spoilt on the palate, then it is too late to do anything about it. However, the taster can serve a very useful purpose by the early detection of a problem that is just beginning: dulling of color, traces of gas, a smell that is flat or lacking in clarity are the warning signs of bacterial infection, when volatile acidity and the microscope cannot always provide positive indicators.

AN ATTEMPT TO DESCRIBE ODORS

How does one describe a smell? One can only proceed by analogy with a smell one already knows, with which it can be identified, or which it resembles or reminds one of. The world of odors is so vast that identification is not always possible, but a resemblance is enough to evoke it. We have already seen on page 55 that odors can be classed into ten groups: animal, balsamic, woody, chemical, spicy, empyreumatic, estery, floral, fruity, and vegetal. A smell can be given either the name of its natural original (for example, the smell of rose, peach, rubbed black-currant leaf) or that of a pure chemical substance (for example, the smell of coumarin, diacetyl, benzaldehyde). Exceptional cases apart, the former is the preferable method. From the eighteen excellent pages on aromas written by Max Léglise, I have taken the liberty of quoting the paragraphs dealing with the reasons for this choice:

"Chemical terminology has two disadvantages which rule it out: a taster's memory has enough to cope with, without the burden of hundreds of dull terms which most people cannot understand anyway; but above all these unknown terms are incompatible with the associations of pleasure and satisfaction which are the essence of tasting. . . ."

"So we have kept to the oldest option which is to describe a wine's aromas by analogy with such and such a flower, fruit, spice, food product and so on. . . ."

"In any case it is better not to be rigid in one's terminology but to be evocative and to be able to recognize alternatives. . . ."

In reality, analogous comparisons are made to abstract and stylized smells. When the smell of roses is mentioned, for example, everybody understands that what is meant is a smell reminiscent of roses in general; but which rose in particular? 1978 Malartic Lagravière white, drawn young and straight from cask, smelt very much of red roses. However, each rose variety has its own fragrance and I have read that some twenty different roses have been distinguished by the approximate smell they evoke: tarragon, pepper, hay, Russian leather, French marigold, melon, apricot, alcohol (these are called vinous), strawberry, raspberry, cloves, musk, lily of the valley, carnations, mignonette, violets, elderflower, tea, peach, hyacinth, apple and plum jam, and one variety even smells of woodlice! The same comments could be made for the generic smells of peaches, pears, or apples. This lack of precision is the basic reason for the abstract and approximate character of olfactory description.

A simple smell, presented above the threshold of perception, is relatively easy to recognize and name. When it is a question of a perfume, that is, a blend of odors, then the description is more difficult. Smells mask each other, and the lightest of nuances only appear when the principal odor diminishes or disappears as a result of adaptation. One's nose becomes so saturated with the main fragrance that it can no longer perceive it, and it can then smell those scents initially hidden by the principal one. This is also the case with wines. The vinous odor that they have in common conceals an infinite number of secondary odors which give quality and personality. Some of these can only be perceived, and even then only fleetingly, after a sustained effort.

This is the reason why the inattentive taster and the drinker who smells little and analyzes nothing remain unaware of the hidden riches in a vinous bouquet, and why they smile skeptically at an observation like Orizet's: "Beaujolais' odor spectrum runs, depending on its soil, from faded rose to peony, from violets to mignonette, from peach to cherry," or when Coste finds in an old Cheval Blanc various tones of "glacé cherries, mint, orange, vanilla, and angelica."

Of course, not all professional tastings are detailed and exhaustive analyses of a wine's odor palette. Often the winetaster is only interested in the cleanness of the wine's nose and in its dominant aromatic quality. His daily work mostly involves tasting young wines, not yet properly "knit," and which are being looked after during the period prior to bottling. Nor does he taste great wines every day. Detailed descriptions of wine bouquets apply above all to wines of the finest quality, rich in aromatic nuance and at the peak of their development.

This game of odors, the practice of which develops as a function of one's tasting knowledge, these "inroads into the inexpressible" are a quite recent invention. The ability to speak about the flavors of wine preceded any attempt to name its odors. The smells of violets and raspberries were recognized long ago, but it was undoubtedly the Burgundian Rodier (1937) who enlarged our vocabulary of smells and who initiated the developments that were to be pursued by Chauvet and his school. And, speaking as a technician, probably prerequisite to these developments were advances in vinification which placed greater emphasis on the aromatic elements of the grape, and advances in storing and bottling which allowed them to show to better effect in the finished wine.

The way to learn about odors is with perfumers at a perfumery. If as a child one had neither the interest in, nor the opportunity to find out about smells, then one's accumulated reference bank of smells is likely to be very small, and all the hard work is still to be done. In this case, you should organize your own odor memory bank: Each season investigate the garden, meadows, and surrounding countryside; rub a leaf between your fingers, smell a flower, sniff crushed fruit; dip your nose into a cook's collection of herbs, spices, and condiments, the herbalist's selection of medicinal herbs, a wine merchant's liqueurs; smell soap and toilet water with care, learn to recognize a woman's perfume.

There is nothing more instructive than to spend several weeks with the perfumers at Grasse, and to be present during their "nosings." They have more than two hundred reference perfumes in small glass-stoppered bottles, ranged in groups on their display unit. To smell them, they moisten the end of a strip of paper and wave it under their nostrils in a gentle to-and-fro movement so as to perfume the air they are breathing. They smell carefully to begin with, inhaling very gently. Odor blends are studied by grouping paper strips of different perfumes, holding them in a fan shape between thumb and index finger, and waving them as before so as to mingle their scents. Through practice one learns to recognize the essences of different flowers and fruits, perfume and confectionery base products.

The following list groups together over 200 smells, or rather touchstones or odor nuances encountered in wine. I cannot pretend that all these terms are frequently encountered in people's tasting notes, but I have heard them, read them, and used at least some of them myself. And if you look further you will probably come across others. Do not be surprised as this olfactory profusion, for all these smells really can be found in wine. Indeed, it is inevitable that they will be found, though not all at once, of course; every wine possesses some molecules of several of these smells but they can only be detected by the skilled nose of a tasting sleuth.

The origin of these odors is written into the very nature of wine, that of a juice or maceration of grapes transformed by alcoholic and possibly also malolactic fermentations. The odorous substances come from the tissues of grapes in varying states of ripeness, or they are the product of yeast or bacteria.

Smells which recall fruit come from the pulp or the skin of the grapes. All fruits which contain pips or stones have a common chromatograph profile for aromatic substances. Cells in the skin contain aromatic essences which are specific to the grape variety; alcohol in which the skins of noble varieties have been macerated smells of cherries and cherry derivatives, or of cherry stones or maybe black currant. Among scented plants there is clearly a connection between the finer essences of flowers and the heavier, richer ones of fruit. It is not surprising therefore that certain white wines smell of vine flowers and, by extension, of other floral aromas. Indeed, we know of constituents which smell of roses and all their related scents. Unripe grapes, on the other hand, smell of greenery, of leaves. When wine made from barely ripe grapes matures, its green odor fades; it then smells of herb teas, newly mown hay, or of the herbalist's shop.

But what about woody odors you ask? The grape's pips are made up of a woody shell, itself enveloped in a thin tannic cuticle, all of which protect the fatty kernel. Now red wine is an infusion of pips; in a fermentation vat there is at least one pip per cubic centimeter of juice. The wood from the pips, at least what the wine has dissolved, ages and becomes aromatic as do all woods. Wood and, over the years, its vanilla and mushroomy derivatives are also encountered in the contribution made to wine by oak.

The aromas of fermented fruit are heightened by yeast; people even talk of aromatic fermentation. The yeast liberates aromas, enriching them at the same time with alcohol, aldehyde, and etherish nuances. It is well known that grape must itself has little smell, whereas its fermentation fills the vat houses and cellars with its reek. The action of malolactic bacteria results in all sorts of lactic compounds. In some wines one does not want too many of these, but those wines which already have a sound aromatic base are complemented by new smells which add to their complexity.

In fact, all kinds of smell are gathered together in wine in minute doses, making it a microcosm of aromas. An inspired taster is not lying when, with his eyes closed, he speaks of a whole world of scents rising from his glass.

A List of the Odor Nuances Encountered in Tasters' Remarks and Writings

Animal Group

Amber, game, game stew, venison stew, fur, wet dog, musk, musky, civet, sweat, wool fat, mouse urine, cat urine, meaty, indole, skatole, gamey, fresh sea fish.

Balsamic Group

Cade oil, juniper, pine, pitch pine, resin, resinous, turpentine, incense, vanilla.

Woody Group

Green wood, old wood, *rancio* wood, acacia, oak, cedar, sandalwood, lead pencil, cigar box, barrel stave, bark, woody.

Chemical Group

Acetic, alcohol, carbonic, hydrocarbons, naphthol, phenol, carbolic, sulfured, sulfurated, sulfurized, sulfurous, celluloid, ebonite, medicinal, pharmaceutical, disinfectant, iodine, chlorine, graphite.

Spicy Group (including Aromatic Spices)

Aniseed, dill, Chinese anise, fennel, mushroom, agaric, chanterelle mushroom, boletus mushroom, truffle, cinnamon, ginger, clove, nutmeg, pepper, green pepper, basil, spearmint, thyme, angelica, licorice, garlic, onion, oregano, marjoram, lavender, camphor, vermouth.

Empyreumatic Group

Smoke, tobacco, incense, burnt, grilled, caramel, grilled almonds, toast, rubbed flints, gunflint, silex, gunpowder, burnt wood, fire, rubber, leather, Russian leather, roasted coffee, cocoa, chocolate.

Estery Group (including Fermentation Odors)

Isoamyl acetate, acetone, amyl alcohol, banana, acid drops, pear drops, nail varnish, higher fatty acid esters (caprates, caproates, caprylates), soap, candle, candle wax, stearin, yeast, ferments, dough, wheat, beer, cider, lactic, sour milk, milk products, cheese, butter, diacetyl, yogurt, sauerkraut, sackcloth, cow shed, stable.

Floral Group
Flowery, floral, the blossom of acacia, almond, orange, apple, peach, elder, grapevine, hawthorn, sweet briar, honeysuckle, lemon, hyacinth, narcissus, jasmine, geranium, pelargonium, heather, broom, marsh mallow, magnolia, honey, peony, mignonette, rose, camomile, lime, verbena, iris, violet, clove, carnation.

Fruity Group
Raisins, crystallized fruit, grapes, raisiny, muscat-like, black cherry, wild cherry, morello cherry, whiteheart cherry, kirsch, cherry brandy, plum, prune, sloe, mirabelle, fruit stones, bitter almond, pistachio, wild berries, small red fruits, bilberry, black currant, strawberry, wild strawberry, raspberry, red currant, mulberry, apricot, quince, peach, pear, apple, melon, citrus fruits, bergamot, lemon, lime, orange, grapefruit, pineapple, banana, dried fig, fig-like, pomegranate, walnut, hazelnut, green olive, black olive.

Vegetal Group
Grass, herbaceous, pasture, hay, meadow smells, green leaves, bindweed smell, rubbed black currant leaf, drying vegetation, dried leaves, bay leaf, herb tea, dead leaves, artemisia, cabbage, cress, ivy, garden mercury, French marigold, horseradish, radish, French fern, green coffee beans, tea, tobacco, leaf mold, dust, undergrowth, earth, earthy, marsh, tree moss.

OLFACTORY ANALYSIS TAKEN TO EXCESS

The evocative search for smells is akin to the sensual delights of the imagination; but here, as in poetry, where are the limits of sincerity? And beyond these limits how big a part is played by autosuggestion and bluff? Irrelevance and exaggeration are the beginner's standard mistakes.

I remember a student, fresh from the benefits of a training period in Burgundy, who would count off on his fingers the benchmark aromas for a Meursault. He knew there were five, but on this occasion, in spite of all his efforts, he could only remember four, though he assured me the forgotten one would come back to him. All the while he paid little attention to what was in his glass. However, he reeled off the characteristic nuances of a Pouilly Fuissé to me without any hesitation, even before he had smelt them. He did not look for the odors on his own account and believed that the results of olfactory analysis were already known, wine by wine, once and for all.

Another commentator had an astonishing knowledge of smells and could make the most unexpected comparisons. He had no difficulty even in transposing tasting to the realm of art or music. However, he never discussed body, form, or structure, only aromas and their persistence. To listen to him, you would not think wine was matter, but pure essence, disembodied odor. I tried to dismantle the mechanism of his technique. He did not really experience the odor impressions he spoke about at the time he was discussing them, nor did he actually perceive them one by one as he recited them.

One sniff was enough for him to determine the dominant character of a wine. If he was talking about a fine Médoc, in which there were inevitably the aromas of Cabernet Sauvignon aged in oak, he would list all in one breath: black currant, resin, cedar, vanilla, cinnamon, nutmeg. And he described the nuances of a very ripe Merlot wine as prune, raisin, licorice, bark, truffle, leather, game. I heard him define a mature Vouvray, which I myself found floral, fruity, and spicy, with the following list: acacia, lime, jasmine, plum, quince, clove, and nutmeg. As for Sauternes, which come from grapes left to become overripe and raisin-like on the vine, they evoked the following for him: honey, wax, dried figs, currants, almonds, and hazelnuts. It only remained for him to add, for example, a trace of raspberry and mint for a St-Julien (spearmint if the grapes lacked a little ripeness, peppermint if the influence of wood was noticeable), a little strawberry and smoke (or even incense) for a red Graves, violets and cedar (or better bergamot) for a Pomerol, a hint of lemon in the case of a dry white, and that was it!

Not, however, that he cheated completely. He simply gave that impression because he did not take the trouble to convince his listeners. He invited no one else into his imaginary garden of smells and his virtuosity convinced nobody.

Happily, there are tutors at tastings who know how to involve the whole group. They perceive a succession of subtle odors and at the same time help others to do the same. The smells in wine never appear all at once grouped together and clearly identifiable; one's glass needs to be swirled to force them out and one needs to sniff with perseverance.

In effect, wine should be smelled in two ways, absorbing its odors first by inhaling through one's nose and then by breathing in through the mouth after swallowing. In this way the bouquet's subtleties are revealed one after another in a manner nicely described by a friend of mine: "The bouquet should evaporate from the glass rather like a wraith of smoke in which, with each breath, one discerns different folds." This is the vaporous impression which leads people to speak of odors that are fluctuating, unstable, lively, melting, alive.

Memory's inertia sometimes prevents one from naming smells immediately as they are perceived. One needs to keep going back in order to identify them, to release what they evoke. To begin with, the identity of the smell one is trying to name remains unclear, then all of a sudden it becomes obvious; definition and sensation are super-imposed exactly. And the moment one identifies it to the audience they will perceive it, too; they just needed to be shown the way.

One day I was dining at Thoissey with Chauvet, our mentor in olfactory analysis, and several other friends. This was one of those memorable evenings where the food set off the wines and where the wines in turn enhanced the food. Analyzing the tastes and smells only increased the pleasure. Chauvet was the last person to want to hold the stage; quite the reverse, his skill was one of moderation and sincerity. He put forward ideas, he would not proceed without your collaboration, and he needed your agreement. In his company that evening, we witnessed through our senses the birth of the astonish-ing odor profile of these marvelous wines. I was not a little proud of having pointed out several additional nuances myself.

OLFACTORY DEFECTS DUE TO OXIDATION AND REDUCTION

Wine is capable of astonishing resistance: Well looked after it will keep for years and age slowly. However, it is also disconcertingly fragile; it dislikes air and heat, neglect, and bad handling. A trifle is sufficient to make it lose, in a short space of time, an appeal to the palate that has taken a very long time to acquire. A thousand dan-gers lie in wait so that it is a miracle to see wine arrive at the consumer's glass in the peak of condition. Today, in spite of the progress that has been made, wine disorders are not rare and the vocabulary relating to olfactory defects is abundant. I will deal first with terms relating to the characteristics due to oxidation and then with those due to its opposite, reduction.

A blunt definition has it that oxygen is the enemy of wine. At all events, it is prejudicial in excess. Oxidation involves two stages: the dissolving of oxygen which accompanies any handling of wine or its exposure to air, and a slow combining of this oxygen with certain so-called oxidative constituents of the wine. As long as wine contains oxygen and as long as the process of oxidation is under way, its aromatic characteristics are disturbed. However, the wine will settle when it is once again protected from contact with air. In the presence of sulfurous acid, in particular, oxygen and its consequences disappear, a phenomenon which is reversible.

There is a series of adjectives to describe these temporary states of oxidation. After racking, filtering, or transport wine appears **fatigued** (*fatigué*); it loses intensity, finesse, and fruit on the nose and is also called faded or flat. After resting it generally regains its former freshness.

A wine with **severe fatigue** (*mâché*) is one which has been enriched in free aldehydes as a result of a strong aeration during, for example, transfer of the wine using pumps or through poor bottling. It has a taste reminiscent of bruised or crushed fruit. Sometimes it also smells of paper. I have come across a Negrette wine which, when exposed to the air, took on a surprising smell of bitter almonds from freed aldehydes. A wine which is *mâché* is more distressed than one which is *fatigué*, and less so than one which is *éventé*, meaning tired and flat though not irreversibly oxidized. A wine in this state has also suffered a certain amount of evaporation. These characteristics do not appear immediately after aeration, but become more pronounced after a few days.

Young wines from vintages with a certain amount of rot are extremely sensitive to contact with air and they easily acquire the smells associated with *casse*. Enzymatic oxidation of their polyphenols makes them cloudy and creates benzoquinone smells, somewhat reminiscent of flat beer. Wine which has become chilled or frozen by being transported in bulk in wintry weather takes on the smell of "frozen" wine (*gelé*), also due to an oxidative phenomenon.

A wine is said to be oxidized when its state of oxidation has been prolonged and the damage caused cannot be entirely rectified. The sickness has become chronic, so to speak. The oxidized character takes several forms according to its intensity and the quality of the wine. It sometimes smells cooked (in wines of low acidity) or burnt (in acid wines) or it may have the aldehyde-related smell of stale oil or butter (*rance*). A wine exposed to the air for a long period will have a high aldehyde content, but free aldehyde is not always a sign of oxidation. Thus the incomparable aroma of *fino* sherry, rich in aldehyde, is produced in a medium practically devoid of oxygen, under the film of flor yeast.

The term **maderized** is applied above all to wines that are too old, or to wines that have aged in accidental contact with air in barrels or in ullaged bottles. Their smell is reminiscent of madeira, though obviously without the latter's qualities; at the same time the wines turn deep yellow or even brown in color, and are dried out on the palate.

Rancio, on the other hand, is not necessarily pejorative, unless applied to a wine which ought to be fresh. *Rancio* wines are generally fortified with alcohol and deliberately aged in contact with air. Sometimes this takes place in barrels, but it may also be in glass carboys left outside in the contrasting conditions of day and night and the changing seasons. The use of wood contributes a great deal to this character. When applied to cognac and armagnac, rancio describes the attractive bouquet of spirits which have aged for a long time in oak.

In chemist's terms, the opposite phenomenon of oxidation is reduction, asphyxia, in effect. The "oxidation-reduction potential" measures the presence or absence of oxygen in a wine. The best and most intense bouquets develop in conditions where the oxidation potential is lowest. This type of bouquet is called a "bottle-age" or "glass" bouquet because it can only develop in the almost totally airtight conditions ensured by cork.

However, if reduction is excessive, it results in smells, almost stenches, that are little appreciated. Wines deprived of air too soon or subjected to a reductive influence smell **reduced**, stale.

White wines in white bottles which are exposed to sunlight, fluorescent, ultra-violet, or filament light, or even just to daylight acquire a taste known as *goût de lumière* or *goût de soleil*, that is, affected by light or sunshine. This variation has also been observed in beers. Bubbling hydrogen through a wine, or the formation of this gas as a result of metal contamination, by iron, for example, engenders a similar unpleasant odor. Reduction smells originate from sulfur derivatives and their character is that of hydrogen sulfide. They are based on traces of hydrogen sulfide or mercaptans (ethylmercaptan or ethyl sulfide, etc.). It is now known that white wines aged in bottle contain an average of 0.7 mg/l of hydrogen sulfide derivatives (mercaptans, thiols, SH); the wines are considered better with a level that is below 0.5 mg/l; above 0.7 mg/l they are too reduced in character and lose value.

The descriptions applied to these repellent smells are numerous: sulfur odors, sulfurous, rotten eggs, water from sulfur springs. They are also known generically as "lees odors" because they are mainly found in young wines that have been left too long on their fermentation less. There is often only a difference of storage conditions between a wine that is aromatic and fruity, and one which has an unpleasant sulfur-related smell. Racking or sufficient aeration will eliminate these faults in most cases.

There are worse and more intractable forms of reduction which render the wines undrinkable; smells that are fetid or putrid, reminiscent of garlic, decomposition, or stagnant water.

General competence, continual following of the wine's development by tasting, and constant cellar care are all required for good wine storage. In other words, an attitude quite the reverse of the laissez faire of so-called natural procedures. Whether due to oxidation or reduction, faults are always the result of negligence and a lack of care.

ACCIDENTAL ODORS AND THE RECOLLECTIONS OF AN EXPERT

Everybody knows the anecdote of the two tasters, one of whom found a slight taste of leather and the other a slight taste of iron in the same wine. They were both right: After racking the wine a small key in a leather pouch was found at the bottom of the vat. The story is an homage to tasters, and one so old that we would have to go right back to Shem, Ham, and Japheth to find the earliest version.

The way in which the vine, grape, and wine so easily absorb the odors of their surroundings and then liberate them again in the glass is astonishing. Molds are certainly the source of the majority of "off tastes" that one encounters. "Off odors" is what one ought to say, but for certain defects the substances responsible are not very volatile and they are better perceived via the palate aroma than by the sense of smell, strictly speaking.

Molds may form on the grapes as well as on many of the materials in contact with the wine during storage and handling. Their smells are varied as are the species of mold and their hosts. For the sake of convenience I divide them into five categories:

- smells of mold, rot, and fungi.
- smells reminiscent of phenol and iodine, and which for that reason are called chemical or pharmaceutical smells. These first two categories are the result of particularly rotten grapes.
- the smells of rotten wood or faulty corks, odors which are sometimes confused; in these cases the wines are described as woody, casky, corked; they have a "tart-dry" taste (*goût de "sec"*).
- the most unpleasant smells of rancid mold.
- the tenacious moldy smells of a vegetal character, recalling artemisia or garden mercury (*rambergue*).

It would be tedious to list all the possible off odors and their causes, and I have no desire to reveal to the layman a range quite unknown to him. The cordon of wine professionals is sufficiently effective to spare him the noxious and offensive odors which chance or negligence has allowed to appear in certain wines abandoned on their lees.

All experts have had to resolve problems of weird smells during the course of their careers. Paul Montagne was particularly proud of the delicately resinous aroma of his Graves, an aroma which distinguished it from its peers. He attributed it to the balsamic scents given off by the thick pine forests which cover the sandy area between the Garonne and the ocean, and carried on the prevailing west winds; alternatively, to the pollen which yellows the puddles of water after an April shower. The expert remained perplexed by these explanations. Put in charge of the vinification, he noticed every year that this particular taste started to appear after a few days in vat.

After several hypotheses, his suspicions fell on the wood of the fermenting vessels. Before the harvest he got inside the vats and cut a few chips of wood off with a penknife. As a result he discovered that the joists supporting the vat tops were made of old pitch pine. They never came into contact with the grapes or the wine; nevertheless, the turpentine odor that they gave off was enough. They were changed for oak beams and the resinous smell disappeared. Any reputation based on chance or contrivance is suspect. This fine wine had no need of a defective flavor in order to be unique and appreciated.

Monsieur Lenne had owned a respectable property in St-Emilion for a short time. Originally a cereal farmer in Morocco, he had turned to quality winemaking, successfully adapting his intelligence and methodical approach to the new enterprise. One year, at the end of the vinification, he needed the advice of an expert: He was unhappy with the wine from one of his eight vats. Every now and again he could detect an indefinable smell, not particularly unpleasant but strange in the sense of unusual and foreign to wine.

In a blind comparison the expert confirmed that vat 3 was indeed different. He spent some time identifying the fleeting smell: burnt? smoky? rubber? tar? benzol? phenol? naphthalene? coal tar? bitumen? Trying to find the cause of an abnormal smell is rather like a police inquiry. Everything was looked at, the harvesting implements, any material in contact with the wine, the vinification vats. Why was it that only one vat had this particular problem? The answer had to lie elsewhere, in the vineyard. And suddenly, in the middle of the investigation, Lenne remembered that in June, at a time when the vine flowers had barely ripened into hard little grapelets, the lower road, bordering on a parcel of land called the Barrail, had been tarred. He looked through his harvest book and found that the grapes from the Barrail had indeed been put into vat 3. Evidently, the smell from the resurfacing of the road had been absorbed by the leaves and distributed through the tissues of the vine by circulation, in the same way that a systemic product is absorbed. It was there in the grape tissues at harvest time three months later, and after that in the wine.

Such examples of the vine's absorption of off odors are not rare. Cases one might mention include one in Pomerol where the smell of creosote from the new railway sleepers pervaded the next vintage; that at Frontignan where the smell of smoke from a cement factory reappeared in a Muscat; or the case of acrid fumes from the public rubbish dump in an old gravel pit, which resulted in a complete section of the vineyards at St-Lambert being contaminated, the grapes ruined, and whole vats lost.

Sometimes the expert's work is easy. A producer rounds on his cork supplier because his clients are complaining about the corky taste in his wine. The expert takes ten bottles at random from the pile, uncorks them, examines and smells the corks, and then tastes each wine. The corks are healthy but all the bottles have the same smell and the same taste, that of moldy wood. Thus it was not the corks which were the problem but the fact that the wines had been faultily stored in casks in bad condition. This happens time and time again. If, out of the ten bottles, only one or two had been faulty, then the suspicion might have fallen on the questionable quality of the corks.

Champagne itself is not exempt from serious taste faults. For some time the bottles of a *grande marque* were deteriorating in quality. The wine was criticized as being oxidized, dried out, and with unpleasant flavors. The response of the company's cellarmaster in Reims was: "It's the corks."

He changed his suppliers, moved from Portuguese to Spanish corks or vice versa, adopted a stricter selection, and sterilized with sulfur dioxide. Nothing helped; the complaints persisted even from as far away as Japan.

The expert discovered the roots of the problem in poor vinification techniques: inadequate sulfiting, far too long a malolactic incubation, and at too high a temperature. These by themselves were sufficient to cause a loss of freshness and aromatic quality, as well as to develop lactic and acetic odors. The solution meant replacing the equipment for vinification and storage and also required the acquisition of a certain amount of oenological knowledge. The cellarmaster ("The corks, I tell you") continued to try and sort matters out, but all was resolved as soon as a set of new, temperature-controlled stainless steel vats had been installed and were used under the supervision of an oenologist.

Experts have sorted out many other problems and detected many other smells, those of styrene or solvents, for example, leached by plastic-lined metal vats. In these cases the tank makers and painters have not been able to acquire the barrel makers' experience of what is suitable for wine. These smells are difficult to identify when they are light, and the way to "get at" them is to seal the top of the glass with the palm of your hand, agitate the wine violently, and then immediately smell the surface of the emulsified wine. Any chemical odors will appear more readily as a result.

VARIOUS FORMS OF TASTING NOTE

Every taster has his or her own way of commenting on a wine verbally or of making a written tasting note; and what is said depends very much on the object of any given tasting exercise. It also depends on the audience or readers to whom the comments are addressed. Furthermore, not all wines are discussed in the same way; some wines lend themselves to very little descriptive elaboration and they can be summed up in a couple of words; others merit precise, detailed notes. Thus, depending on the wine in question, comments will be more or less descriptive, more or less explanatory, and the conclusions more or less detailed. An analytical tasting, for example, requires a long written account, whereas when comparing wines simply to rank them for quality all that is necessary is to highlight the features which distinguish them. Nor is it always necessary to describe all the aspects of smell and taste; sometimes it is enough to limit a judgment to whichever individual aspect matters.

Among professionals verbal comment is normally the rule. It is direct, concise, summed up in a single phrase, and should only be voiced after all the tasters have made up their minds. The discussion which follows will conclude with a common viewpoint, sometimes a compromise. Making comments as one tastes should be forbidden, to avoid influencing the other tasters.

Notes on wines being presented to wine buffs or those for use in teaching are necessarily more complete. There are rich, complex wines of distinguished origin which raise so many interesting questions that a fluent speaker can talk about them for a quarter of an hour.

Writing a note forces one to make an effort to be clear and precise. For this reason it is desirable, at least in certain exercises, for the taster to make a written report, the detail of which will vary according to the circumstances. The text of a formal, written assessment or one for publication will obviously be more elaborate than one made purely for personal use. As the following example shows, a wine can be described in a few words, a few lines, or in a whole page. The one-line comment is forceful but too telegraphic and hence distorting, and a whole page note involves lengthy descriptions which reduce one's interest.

It is an excellent discipline to limit the written description of a wine to four or five lines, and I have given a few examples of this below. In each case, whatever the length of the note, its order follows that of the tasting sheet shown on page 176. The chronological order of sensations is a good mnemonic for the order of a tasting note, and, using this system, appearance and color are described first, then smell, followed by taste and length before a final judgment is made.

Beaujolais-Villages 1974

Nine-Word Note
Dark red; ripe fruit, raspberry; vinous; firm, attractive finish.

Forty-Seven-Word Note
Fine dark color. Very clear-cut nose with an aroma of very ripe fruit, crushed raspberry, and a hint of licorice. A warm attack, almost as though sweetened; firm finish with a little bitterness. Medium length. A good-quality Beaujolais-Villages which will keep well in bottle.

Three-Hundred-Word Note
This Beaujolais-Villages, bottled at the property and tasted in the spring after the vintage, is remarkable for its richness of both aroma and flavor. Regarded as a **primeur** wine, it has the characteristics of a wine for keeping. Its deep ruby appearance has the hue and liveliness typical of Beaujolais, but its color is deeper than is usually produced by the Gamay grape. Particularly brilliant, its strong alcoholic vinosity shows on the sides of the glass.

Its smell is clean, forthright, and very distinct; the aroma is of medium intensity, pleasant, and fruity in style with recognizable varietal character. It is reminiscent of ripe fruit, crushed raspberries in particular, against a background of licorice where the tannin shows through. The nose is heavy and a bit lackluster.

On the palate the attack is alcoholic, warm, almost sweet, followed by a very agreeable development of flavors and a roundness of texture sustained up to a finish which is fresh from a perceptible level of acidity and carbon dioxide. The tannin is slightly bitter, giving a certain firmness, and the wine is marked by a high level of alcohol which makes it alcoholic and hot, but its balance remains harmonious thanks to its tannin and acid content. The palate aroma displays the raspberry character of the nose even more intensely, showing other characteristics at the same time: fatty acid esters of a soapy kind, and a woody background tasting of licorice in particular. Its aromatic persistence is moderate, not dominating those of flavor proper.

In conclusion, a good-quality bottle of Beaujolais-Villages. The wine is out of the ordinary by virtue of its full-bodied, vinous support and the attractive tannin which gives it the structure of a wine which will keep well. On the other hand, it falls a little short from lack of aroma. Scored: 17/20, graded "very good."

Notes in Four Lines on Seven Wines

Les Gradins, Dezaley 1973
(Swiss white wine.) Pale color. Fine, heavy aroma with a lactic character and a waxy smell. On the palate soft, flabby, washed out; a very low acidity gives the wine a beer-like taste. Its pleasant freshness is due to a light carbon dioxide spritz. Thirst quenching nonetheless.

Torcolato di Breganze
(Italian white made from partially dried grapes.) Beautiful golden color. Oxidized style of nose based on aldehyde and acetal. Smells at once of apples, grape juice, and fine madeira. Very sweet, very rich, very unctuous, and low in acidity. Unusual type of wine.

Rioja Alta, Viña Pomal 1948
(Spanish red.) Advanced color. Very old, *rancio* bouquet of a southern, sunny climate wine, reminiscent of port. Considerable contrast between the softness of the attack and the dry character of the finish. Very old, rough, woody tannin. A wine rich in nuance and personality. Old-fashioned.

Hermitage 1972
Deep, brown-hued color. A complex nose: crushed mulberries, black currants, licorice, resin, spices, and wood smoke, but lacking elegance. Very fleshy on the palate, with a tannic finish that is rough, aggressive, and accentuated by the woody flavor. Well structured but rustic.

Nuits-St-Georges, Perrières 1967
Beautiful orange-hued, ruby color. Generous bouquet of considerable distinction in which there is a black-currant-raspberry-vanilla blend and a discreet note of excellent wood. On the palate, long and soft, with both body and vigor. Very savory tannin. Very fine quality.

Ch. Léoville Las Cases, 1971, St-Julien, Médoc
Intense color. Strong, very subtle bouquet, smelling at the same time of fruit, spice, truffles, and vanilla. Very full bodied; powerful but not yet mellowed. Vigorous finish but neither hard nor astringent. Not yet ready; still dominated by oak. Very promising.

Ch. Grand-Barrail — Lamarzelle-Figeac, 1967, St-Emilion
Medium color. Pleasing, well-developed bouquet difficult to analyze: suggestions of wood, very ripe fruit, venison. On the palate, savory, vinous, a bit heavy, and with a nice consistency. Richly aromatic on the palate, with a curious impression of cocoa. Distinctive wine from a modest vintage.

NOTES ON SOME VINTAGE WINES

To be present each year at the birth of a wine, to follow its development from time to time until bottling, then to lose sight of it until encountered a few years later with its neighbors, in a neat row of glasses gathered before me as though posing for a family photograph—these are experiences I have had at many properties. In this way tasting becomes a sort of machine for going back in time.

It is a voyage of rediscovery. Each wine reflects the passage of time, at once a reference point and a memory. Nature stamps every vintage with an indelible mark, that of the weather during the formation and maturation of the grapes. The vintage is given a unique character by the amount of summer sunshine, by heat, drought, nocturnal cold coming off the river, morning mists, and thunderstorms. The weather during the harvest decides the final character of the vintage. Old bottles, however, are also a testimony to the taste and know-how of the men who made and raised the wine, and to an oenologist they will show traces of the techniques of their period.

Bottles of wine from an old vintage can be quite astonishing. There is something touching about the lasting character of wine. The bottle which stores and refines it gives it a personality at the same time. For the receptive amateur with something of the poet in him, such a wine becomes a message from the past, a continuation, a milestone, a trace, a memento.

To get to know an individual *cru* then, there is nothing more instructive than a vertical tasting; a comparison of successive vintages, the wine at different ages. One of the advantages of the *grands crus* is their capacity to age, offering the possibility to bear witness, so to speak, over several decades. I love this *tête-à-tête* with wines: lined up in their glasses in the tasting room, going back down memory lane. In a way these are so many renderings of the same work, at once similar and yet different; for from one year to the next nature never yields quite the same grapes, and each vintage the winemaker makes minor adjustments.

Tasting Notes on Some 1982s (Tasted in 1985)

As has often been said, the 1982s have everything going for them: a strong constitution, a profusion of flavors, and the concentrated taste of very ripe grapes. In particular, they are marked by the abundance and remarkable savor of fine-textured tannins. Never, since the start of the "modern" era of vinification, had grapes been picked that were so ripe and so sweet. This is a vintage full of charm, the archetypal example of wines from an early harvest.

Their grand-scale structure confers on them considerable vinosity; power allied to finesse, both elegance and complexity. Without doubt these are wines with a great future, yet they are already agreeable to the palate. And tasting them early on in bottle simply confirms that, unlike certain other great vintages, this is not one which is going to be "closed up" for years. 1982 is a generous, sumptuous year whose fame will carry for many decades.

1982 Ch. Petit Village (Pomerol)

It is difficult to write something original about the color of this wine: It is perfect—rich and full of nuance. To taste, it has the brilliance and complexity of flavor that characterizes great pomerols; above all great finesse. Its bouquet is redolent of all sorts of extremely ripe fruit, and the overall impression is one of succulence. Vinous, warm, flowing, smooth, and with velvet-textured tannins. This is a particularly rounded, thoroughbred wine with real length of flavor and aroma. Clearly not yet at its peak, and a wine I would love to taste and retaste frequently.

1982 Ch. Figeac (St-Emilion Premier Grand Cru)

A beautiful, luminous color with some brick hues starting to show. A wine that is still somewhat closed on the nose, though the bouquet is just beginning to evolve; a bouquet marked by Cabernet Sauvignon and by the refinement that is characteristic of one of the rare St-Emilions to be based on a gravel soil. On the palate there is an overwhelming suppleness, sweetness, and flowing texture which mask its richness in tannin. A full, ample, almost chewy wine of notable vinosity and great length. A great wine from a great vintage.

1982 Domaine de Chevalier (Cru Classé, Graves)

Powerful and abundant tannins are already perceptible from the color and nose alone. A wine which, not surprisingly considering its strong constitution, is still very backward. The tannins are what give this wine its sapid character and backbone: providing a firm development to the palate after an attack that is gentle and fleshy. There is a fine tannic astringency that persists throughout, which prolongs the flavor in the mouth and gives the wine great length on the finish. Solid and elegant at once, this is a Domaine de Chevalier which will need patience and long aging.

1982 Ch. Léoville Las Cases (Second Growth, St-Julien)

A wine marked by the magnificent tannins of the great 1982s. These can be seen in the profound color and smelled on the nose which is, for the moment, restrained but of great finesse. To taste, this is all power and concentration; full-bodied, round, and complete, but with tannin far from resolved. It is not difficult to see that this will be a wine for long keeping, which will eventually yield one of the very finest bottles from this property. A quite exceptional Las Cases.

1982 Ch. Lynch Bages (Fifth Growth, Pauillac)

Like many 1982s this wine is passing through a phase where, while maintaining its youthful fruit, it has not acquired the "bouquet" that comes with bottle age. That will come quickly enough. The attack is astonishing, for the wine is almost as sweet as if it had been sugared; and it gives an overall impression of perfect roundness, with such richness of flavor and "roasted" character that its clearly abundant tannin is almost completely hidden. Just a hint of fine wood adds to its savor. Flattering to the palate right from the start, it is full of promise for a great future. It is just a question of waiting.

1982 Ch. Cos d'Estournel (Second Growth, St-Estèphe)

In its early youth this wine was always remarkable for its aromas of both a singular intensity and great complexity. It has developed magnificently since; gaining in class and acquiring a supreme elegance which makes it one of the most distinguished 1982s. This is a wine that is full of contrasts: firm and gentle at once; very full bodied and yet also subtle; supple in texture and with a lively, spicy finish. Given time, such a profusion of flavors can but yield a rare and superb bottle.

Eleven

Training Tasters

How to Learn to Taste

For a long time most tasters learned their trade alone, at work, by dint of repetition and depending on the wines they came across. During their apprenticeship the luckiest had the benefit of advice from a professional and a model to imitate. This haphazard and disorganized approach could not possibly be the best method of learning. To start with, tasters lacked basic information and they had inadequate knowledge about the mechanism of sensations and the balance of tastes and smells. In most cases their situation meant that they had no choice in the wines tasted which were limited to one type from one region. Nor could they learn much from books. Since the first edition of this book, there has been an enormous increase in both the number of tasting handbooks and centers teaching tasting, and with various aims in mind: vinification, commerce, formal qualifications, and so on.

Realizing that the worth of a taster is a guarantee of the quality of the product, several organizations have set up various tasting courses over the last couple of decades. These ventures are run by the oenological stations, agricultural training institutes, the Technical Institute of Wine, and even the universities. An hour a week is something, but still too little. For their influence and advice to be effective, oenologists need good training in this field. I would like to see oenology based on tasting and tasting based on oenology.

The program of lectures leading to the Diplôme Universitaire d'Aptitude à la Dégustation from the Institute of Oenology at Bordeaux University consists of numerous lectures and exercises throughout the year. Since 1974 these have replaced the Lectures and Practical Exercises in Oenology which were started by the Bordeaux Oenology and Agronomy Station in 1949. At present this diploma course is the only really serious in-depth training available. Ideally, it should be accessible to all professionals; from it they would learn a different approach to understanding and talking about wine.

Tasting certainly cannot be taught in, say, five to eight sessions; reading this book is proof enough of that. Also, any training certificate which could be awarded after such a short time would not have much value. It is dangerous to lead anyone to believe that a few hours are enough to train a competent taster.

Teaching to taste is necessarily a long process because imparting concepts alone is not enough; tasting reflexes must also be acquired. Students need to be trained, educated, and in some cases reeducated because bad habits are widespread. It is not an easy thing to teach. Of course, as tasting is an art, it should be possible to teach it, but providing descriptions and formulas is not enough. Teaching material must be prepared and rules and techniques established; practical exercises need to be planned, and tests codified. And they should all be attractively presented because this sort of training requires considerable participation from the students. Lectures should also deal with vinification and the treatment of wines, because a sound technical knowledge is indispensable for interpreting taste. How can one pass judgment on a product if one knows neither how it is made nor how it is kept?

SOME THEORETICAL TASTING EXERCISES

Tasters can be helped to acquire the basic concepts of tasting by the use of appropriate exercises. Those outlined here have benefited from forty years' teaching experience, and they continue to be improved.

The first exercises are designed to inculcate a technique: how to look at wine, how to hold the glass, how to smell and taste. It is only after this that one can start the practical exercises related to three different aspects: **theoretical tasting** which studies taste mechanisms, **analytical tasting** which studies the relationships of taste and smell to the wine's constitution, and **applied tasting** which consists of precise and detailed descriptions of taste impressions; commenting on, scoring, and making written notes on wines.

Theoretical tasting includes exercises (some of which are described below) which enable one to define the physiological bases of tasting: the anatomy and mechanisms of the senses; definition of the sensation thresholds for the primary tastes and several common smells; tasting various fixed and volatile constituents of wine in water solutions; the notion of balance between the tastes and smells of these constituents. These are an introduction to learning to taste, but they are also useful exercises for the experienced taster; they are his way of practicing his scales, so to speak.

1. The four primary tastes: sweetness (sucrose solution at 20 g/l), perceived on the point of the tongue; acidity (tartaric acid solution at 1 g/l), perceived by the sides of the tongue, right around to the underside; saltiness (sodium chloride solution at 5 g/l), perceived over a wider surface of the tongue except for the central area; bitterness (solution of quinine sulfate at 2 mg/l), perceived only at the back or base of the tongue. Astringency (yielded by a tannin solution at 1 g/l) is more of a tactile sensation, a reaction of the mucous surfaces, than a taste strictly speaking.

2. The sweet taste of ethyl alcohol: Alcohol in solution at 4° (32 g/l) has a sweetish taste. This taste is perceived along with a caustic sensation, one of warmth, in a 10° solution (80 g/l).

By preparing sweet solutions of 20 g/l of sucrose at different degrees of alcohol (0°, 4°, 8°, 12°), it can be seen that alcohol considerably increases the sweet taste of a sweet solution.

3. Sweetness modifies the impression of acidity. Compare the taste of a solution that is both sweet and acid (20 grams of sucrose and 1 gram of tartaric acid per liter) with that of a solution that is only acid or only sweet. The intensity of both tastes is diminished.

Compare the taste of an acid solution at different degrees of alcohol (0°, 4°, 8°, 12°, for example). The acidity diminishes the sweetness of the alcohol and the latter, reciprocally, corrects the acidity; the two tastes are perceived alongside each other, it is just their intensity that is lessened. Note how acidity reinforces the burning taste of alcohol.

4. The taste of wine is the result of a balance between sweet, acid, and bitter tastes. This demonstration consists of the experiment described on page 200, in which a wine's alcohol is separated from its acids and polyphenols by distillation. In wine, the sweetness of alcohol counterbalances the tastes of acid and bitter substances. By way of example, compare the tastes of a perfectly balanced (supple) red wine with one where acid tastes dominate (hard), and one where sweet tastes dominate (flabby).

5. Tasting substances in wine which have a sweet taste. Compare the following solutions: ethyl alcohol at 4° (32 g/l), glycerol, glucose, and fructose (all at 20 g/l). The first three solutions have an intensity of sweetness that is relatively close, but with qualitative differences in the sweet taste. Fructose is twice as sweet as glucose and, as a consequence, at equal levels of residual sugar, white wines which are rich in fructose seem much sweeter.

6. Tasting various acids found in wine. Compare the following solutions: tartaric, malic, citric, lactic, and acetic acid (1 g/l) and succinic acid (0.5 g/l). The first three acids come from the grape and have an acid taste that is pure, clear-cut, a fruit acid taste. The others are the result of fermentations and have acid tastes which are less intense, but more complex. Lactic acid has a sourish freshness; acetic acid is sour and unpleasant; succinic acid is not clearly acidic and, at this low concentration, has a mixture of intense flavors and which certainly contributes to giving fermented drinks this type of taste which they have in common. In wine, succinic acid produces sapidity, vinosity, vigor, and perhaps sometimes bitterness. These solutions demonstrate the taste of free acids. They have different pH levels; the comparisons could also be made at the same pH. This demonstrates that the anion influences the acid taste in the same way as the hydrogen ion (H^+).

7. Sensitivity to primary tastes. Research into the sensitivity thresholds of a large group of tasters to primary tastes is very instructive. Tasters are asked to taste solutions of acid, sweet, salty, or bitter sub-

stances, in gradually increasing concentrations, and the minimum perceptible level is noted for each person.

Tasters are given three glasses in any order: Two contain water and the third the solution to be recognized. Performance is better if one starts by tasting the weaker solutions. The following solutions might be tasted, for example:

Sucrose	0.5—1—2 and 4 g/l
Tartaric acid	0.05—0.1 0.2 g/l
Sodium chloride	0.1—0.25—0.5—1.0 g/l
Quinine sulfate	0.5—1—2 mg/l

These concentrations are given in a geometric progression, doubling for example, following Fechner's laws of physiology.

8. Smelling a number of volatile and odorous constituents of wine in water solution. The concentrations indicated in parentheses are in milligrams per liter. Obviously, this list is not definitive.

Isoamyl alcohol (300) isobutyl alcohol (120)	unpleasant smell of crushed bugs
Phenylethyl alcohol (50)	smell of roses or hyacinths
Hexenol (2)	vegetal smell
Ethyl acetate (100)	the smell of pricked wines
Isoamyl acetate (3)	banana smell
Caprate, caproate, ethyl caprylate (2)	fatty smell with a soapy character
Isobutyric acid (250), ethyl butyrate (50)	putrid fermentation smells
Acetaldehyde (30)	smell of apples
Geraniol (0.4), terpineol (2), linalool (0.08)	terpenes present in the smell of Muscat
Methyl anthranylate (4)	foxy smell
Ethyl sulfur (0.1)	nauseating smell of mercaptan
Styrene (1)	smell of plastic material

In the 1960s Lousteneau de Guihem of the Institut Technique du Vin devised a collection of various natural and synthetic odors in solution. These were grouped according to type: floral, fruity, moldy, spicy, aromatic, vinous, and so on. Today these are available in sets of small vials for teaching purposes. Among the most popular are those boxed sets, in various sizes, entitled *Le Nez du Vin*, produced in Paris by Jean Lenoir.

SOME ANALYTICAL TASTING EXERCISES

These exercises enable one to study the influence on a wine's taste and smell of modifications involving the levels of alcohols, acids, esters, terpenes, polyphenols, sugars, polyalcohols, salts, carbon dioxide, sulfurous acid, etc. They sharpen one's basic perceptions and provide points of reference. The following list is a series of examples, but many other useful exercises could be devised.

1. The influence of alcoholic strength. Compare samples of the same wines, red and white, which have been artificially raised to varying degrees of alcohol. Pure ethyl alcohol without any extraneous smells is used. Begin with differences of 0.7° between each wine, taking a 10° wine to 10.7°, 11.4°, and 12.1°. An initial attempt is made to order them correctly, tasted blind. If this is unsuccessful, taste the wines again knowing what the alcohol levels are, so that the exact influence of alcohol on taste can be determined. The wines are then tasted a third time, again not knowing which is which. After some practice the differences of degree can be gradually narrowed to 0.5° or even 0.3°. Assessing the alcoholic degree in a wine is always difficult because the taste of alcohol is complex; it acts more by the indirect effect of neutralizing or reinforcing certain flavors than by its own actual taste.

A similar exercise consists of arranging a series of different wines, though of the same type, in order of their alcoholic strength. In reality, judgment in these exercises is based more on other characteristics such as body and general richness in constituents which often run parallel to the alcoholic strength.

2. The influence of glycerol. Compare samples of red and white wines which have had 3 to 6 grams per liter of glycerol added to them. The change affects the actual taste of sweetness more than it

does the richness of the wine; and if the wine is very full bodied an addition of 3 grams is barely perceptible.

3. The influence of residual sugars. Red and dry white wines, preferably young, are prepared with additions of 2, 3, 4, and 5 g/l of residual sugars, either glucose or fructose. The taster then tries to arrange them in order of their sugar content. Such exercises prepare one for detecting wines which still contain some residual sugar after vinification.

One could also try and grade a series of medium-sweet and sweet white wines according to their levels of residual sugar.

4. The influence of acidity. The taster attempts to grade samples of the same wine in order of total acidity after they have been modified by deacidification or acidification with tartaric acid. A red wine might be tasted with its total acidity altered to 3.2, 4.0, and 4.8 g/l. The margin of variation can be progressively reduced according to the taster's ability to distinguish the differences.

This exercise may be modified by making increasing additions of other acids such as citric, lactic, or succinic.

In the context of the influence of acidity, wines can also be compared before and after their malolactic fermentation.

A further exercise consists of establishing the order of a series of wines according to their acid taste. Putting wines in order of their total acidity solely on the basis of taste is not always possible; other elements influence the taste of acidity, particularly in the case of white wines with a certain degree of sugar.

5. The influence of acetic acid. Compare wines whose level of volatile acidity has been raised to 0.60, 0.75, and 0.90 g/l by the addition of acetic acid. The taster's attention should be concentrated on the finish which is sour and hard, not on the difference in smell which is minimal. In this way one observes that the hardness on the finish due to acetic acid is not the same as that due to the fixed acids, and that it is more unpleasant.

6. The influence of polyphenols. Compare red wines containing different levels of tannin as indicated by their tannin index. The samples can be prepared by blending with press wines which have a pronounced astringency. An index of 30 represents a supple wine, of 40 a full-bodied wine, of 50 and above a relatively tannic wine for

keeping. It will be seen that the hardness due to tannins, which is accompanied by astringency, is different from that due to fixed and volatile acids.

Compare white wines with a natural variation in tannin level. Tannin in white wines makes them harder. The same wines could also be compared after an addition of pharmaceutical tannin or wood tannin, oak tannin.

7. The influence of ethyl acetate. Compare wines which have had ethyl acetate added to produce samples with 100, 150, and 200 mg/l. The first level is normal and has no effect on taste; 150 mg/l produces a hardness, distinct again from that encountered in the previous exercises; a level of 200 mg/l is discernible on the nose and gives a wine the characteristics of acescence.

It is interesting to compare carefully selected red wines whose hardness is due to strong acidity, or to a high concentration of phenol compounds, or to a high level of volatile acidity, or, finally, to excess ethyl acetate.

8. The influence of sulfur dioxide. Compare samples of the same red or white wine with increasing levels of free sulfur dioxide: 0, 10, 20, 30, 50 mg/l. Sweet wines can be compared similarly with 30, 60, and 90 mg/l. At high levels, in addition to the unpleasant piquant and acrid sensation that it produces, sulfur dioxide neutralizes part of the fruit character of the aroma, as well as destroying the wine's finesse and aromatic character on the palate.

9. These exercises may be complemented by studying, in a similar manner to the other tastings, the influence of various salts (1 g/l of sodium chloride or potassium sulfate), or that of added higher alcohols such as butyleneglycol, diacetyl (the substance which gives good butter its delicate hazelnut smell), or any other wine constituent, fixed or volatile. The effect is clearer when they are added at levels which more or less double the normal concentration.

My Tasting Apprenticeship

Novels are full of stories of young people with a passionate thirst for knowledge who, having had the good fortune to work in a library, have become erudite. Imagine an adolescent, senses all fresh, coming to an exceptionally large wine library, full of hundreds of selected wines of all types and colors, constantly replenished by the commercial flow of entries and exits, dispatches and purchases. For sixteen years he remained in the service of this great Bordeaux house, absorbing by osmosis the traditions of the trade plied by those devoted to the cause of wine. How could he avoid becoming a taster? All it needed was for him to be curious, attentive, and to learn by example. The wines lay in thousands of barrels in the *chais* and the aging cellars, staying there for the two to four years necessary to acquire the qualities of age that were appreciated at the time. At any time our young man could compare up to four vintages in barrel, and not infrequently he had access to the fine collection of bottles as well. What better conditions in which to develop one's palate and enrich one's memory?

He began with white wines, easier on his young taste buds. During those years in the 1930s, medium-sweet and sweet white wines, aperitif whites, were the height of fashion. Throughout the Gironde at that time, perhaps because of yields of only 25 quintals per hectare, grapes were harvested in a raisin-like, overripe condition, yielding fat, concentrated, golden-hued white wines that gained an additional mellowness and aromatic quality in cask and in bottle. The bouquet from reduction in bottle was highly prized. Such wines are a thing of the past and cannot be revived. Later on he got to know the great red wines and became accustomed to the noble asperity of their tannin. Tasting, never drinking, he became expert in his knowledge of the wines of Bordeaux, and, later still, he discovered other forms and harmonies in his encounters with the wines of the Côte d'Or, the Yonne, Saône et Loire, the Rhône, and the Drôme and Vaucluse, all of which J. C. and Company sold through its subsidiary in Beaune. He was never partisan nor chauvinistic for this would have been limiting. Very early on he became aware of the astonishing diversity of wines and he discovered that each one is a discovery, even if it is already known, and all the more so if it is not. He immediately took to the wines made from Pinot and Chardonnay because their idiom was different from his own. In this situation the first requirement for training a taster was satisfied: the opportunity to taste often, without prejudice and with the aim of getting to know wines of different qualities and from different origins.

However, nothing of value is learned without study, without examples, without mentors. And during these sixteen years he had the most prestigious of instructors, Jean Ribéreau-Gayon, who was in the process of building modern oenology. At his side he witnessed the creation of a science and its practical application, and in order to understand it better he took part as far as he was able. Following a work program drawn up by his teacher, he had the good fortune to contribute to the understanding of wine's profundities, first by analysis of its constitution, then by analysis of the various phenomena and transformations associated with it. In order to explain taste it was necessary to understand the anatomy of wine, determine the quantity of certain constituents more precisely, discover new ones, recognize the taste and smell of the measured substances, and learn what part they played in taste at the levels at which they were present. For if one does not know the exact influence of the constituents on flavor, then extensive listing of them is of little interest other than to show the incredible complexity of wine's composition. These days wine journals are full of lists of substances present in minute quantities; but what is the use of knowing the names of five hundred constituents if one has no idea of their concentration in wine, and if one has never experienced their tastes or smells? Telephone directories are just as full of the surnames of people about whose appearance and character one knows nothing.

I often tasted with Ribéreau-Gayon, at certain periods practically every day, and first of all on the tasting bench of the little laboratory. We forced ourselves to practice tasting even though, to begin with, it seemed obscure, uncertain, and difficult to reproduce the results. Progress remains slow until one has acquired a reliable technique and a basis for comparisons.

Even in such favorable circumstances it took us years to synchronize our tastes, to acquire the necessary reflex reactions, and to agree about the meanings of words.

We used to organize tasting sessions of a new kind for ourselves. In this way we drew up the various exercises which, much later, were to form the basis for our teaching at the oenology station. We developed the theoretical exercises applied to pure tastes and odor types, to their influences on each other, to balances, to sensation thresholds, perceptible differences, etc. We examined the tastes of all the constituents which were known and had been measured at the time, in particular, the taste of the organic acids which are among the wine substances with the most flavor. It was at this time that the role of ethyl acetate was discovered as the source of the characteristic of acescence and as a taste element which dried and hardened a wine. Little by little an oenology of taste developed, with the aim of explaining taste and its variations by differences in structure and composition. A new attitude to the quality of wines was bound to arise from this. These were the first exercises in analytical tasting. They consisted of observing the change in a wine's taste as a result of experimental changes to its constitution. We added constituents and took them away and thus came to understand better the role of the manipulated element in the overall flavor.

At the same time we directed our efforts toward the description of tastes. It is difficult enough to analyze one's own impressions; it is even more difficult to communicate them to others. One feels the lack of a special language, and that there should be other, more suitable words. This obstacle can be overcome by defining words and by setting up a rational system, but the traditional vocabulary in common use should not be eschewed, however approximate it is. In this area Baroussou gave us the benefit of his wide experience as an expert taster. He was one of those cellarmasters who began to work and train in wine from a very early age and who rose through the ranks. He knew the secrets of the trade and had at the tip of his tongue, so to speak, the hierarchies of properties and appellations as well as a fund of anecdotes from both sides of the business. We tried to persuade him to write a dictionary of cellar work, alas in vain.

He knew very well how to pass on his practical knowledge during tastings, and working with him made me understand the importance for the trainee taster of a good general understanding of the trade, of the people involved, and of its wider context. This illuminating breadth of knowledge is the hallmark of the great tasters. Baroussou's vocabulary was economical, precise, colored with Bordeaux expressions, and not particularly profuse because he was a man of few words. The garrulous speaker's vocabulary is often illusory; a brief phrase from Baroussou said more. He tasted everything with the same pleasure: special wines, brandies, rums, and liqueurs. "A taster," he would say, "should know how to taste everything, and that includes the stew simmering on the barrelmakers' coals."

The taster's apprenticeship lasts a lifetime, for there are always wines to learn about. As long as one remains curious, one makes progress; it is when you think you know everything that you are actually out of date. I have since had the opportunity to meet the most famous tasters, the great wine brokers and merchants, but one certainly learns most when going abroad. It must be said to start with that our wines are not always recognizable on foreign tables; some present a rather sad face, as though they felt exiled. This is doubtless because the exporter is not aiming high enough; for export he needs to choose the type of wine which will travel and withstand the vicissitudes of distribution. On the other hand, during the course of one's travels one sometimes comes across extremely seductive wines, wines which have ripened under different skies and which have the appeal of the exotic. They are remarkable for the intensity of their aromas or for sunny climate characteristics. They sometimes arouse a bit of jealousy so that one goes home humbler and more demanding. In this way, leaving the confines of our own tasting room, you gain experience and increase your memory bank of the vast range of benchmark tastes and smells.

THE GREAT TASTING CEREMONIES

The taster who works in certain branches of the wine trade tastes practically every day. He works with close associates and tries to resolve methodically the problems posed by the succession of samples submitted to him. It is this routine tasting, humdrum but effective, that is the essential function of his art. His employers do not expect him to be a virtuoso or a spiritual medium; they expect clearly formulated opinions which enable them to make practical decisions.

Now, the public sees the taster's art in quite a different light; he is expected to give a rather more spectacular expression of his talent. He is thought to take part only in public tastings, tutored tastings, regional, national, or even international competitions. In fact, this happens rarely and only if the taster is fairly well known. These are demonstration or show tastings, and they are often covered by the specialist press. Many tasters who take part in such events are not aware, until too late, of the purely promotional character of some of them. True, this is the price of a certain renown. I myself have often participated in what I call the great tasting ceremonies. I do not disapprove of them, but I consider them to be psychosensory amusement, not serious work. Sometimes I have questioned the value of the conclusions drawn from them. However, I can well imagine that people might want to work alongside the specialists.

Recruit the services of three dozen fine palates from the French wine regions, and also from England, Belgium, and Switzerland, drawn from the cream of the restaurateurs, *sommeliers,* merchants, brokers, and oenologists. Group them in teams of three around an upturned barrel serving as a table in a Parisian cellar, subject their noses and taste buds to some four dozen classed growth Bordeaux, from all the appellations, and ask them to score, rank, and make notes on the wines. Each team tastes only one vintage, but this is already a considerable number. Obviously, the tasters cannot see the wine labels, nor do they know the list of wines included. If you have followed my instructions so far, you will have just organized "the comparative tasting of the century," the biggest ever tasting show and the most extraordinary tasting lottery ever witnessed, as well as the most futile gathering of all time. And it concerned no less a dispute than that of the official classification. The Bordeaux equivalent of the May 1968 demonstrations was carried out by winetasters with an admixture of journalists. It was the moment to give vent to the accumulated rivalries between the tail end of the Crus Classés and the vanguard of the Crus Bourgeois impatiently snapping at their heels. Each taster went to work, compared and compared again, and lost both saliva and any sense of direction confronted by so many wines; he classified, then declassified, and the glasses just kept on coming. The tannin from the Merlot and Cabernet Sauvignon continued to build up, there was too much wine to taste, the whole thing was excessive. The laws of chance, errors of calculation, blood-alcohol level, and the effect of such number was bound to be explosive in its effects. And the explosion did indeed take place, several days later, across ten pages and four charts. However, when the sound waves had died down, the original classification was seen to be still standing.

There are many possible ways of classifying wines into a hierarchy. The Syndicat des Crus Bourgeois du Médoc, for example, organizes an annual competition based on classification by elimination. Over a hundred wines compete in successive pairs, proceeding through numerous "rounds" in a similar fashion to tennis or football championships, ending up with quarterfinals, semifinals, and a pair of finalists. And year after year very much the same names appear among the winners.

I have had many experiences which have taught me that identification at blind tastings is only possible if one has encountered the wines previously, if one knows them personally, in other words, if they are familiar. If all you have to go on is a description and you have to imagine the wines' identities without ever having come across them, then there is little chance of recognizing them, even if their vintage and origin are revealed.

The gathering I attended one evening, in a manor house hidden within the boundaries of the vineyards, was a memorable occasion. Now distance give it the indefinable sense of a dream and the impression in my memory is of a moment of perfection. The place, the people, the food, and the wines were all in harmony, something rare and precious. I sat between Bernard Pivot and Paul Bocuse. The hostess, officiating in a priestess's robes, made the ritual comment: "Rigorously selected and raised with care according to our traditional methods, the 1964 wines have fulfilled their promise. Here they are mature, ready to reveal the secrets and mysteries of their soil, a soil with such personality that it will prove itself again and again down the years." That evening I was confronted by strange puzzles. The glasses, all filled with *premier crus*, were offered in groups of eight, first Volnay and Pommard, then Beaune and Corton, Vosne-Romanée and Nuits St-Georges, finally, Chambolle-Musigny and Gevrey-Chambertin, the cream of the Côte de Beaune and the Côte de Nuits. Each group of eight had to be divided into two groups of four, for which you could score eight points. If, in addition, you could give each glass its appellation and distinguish, for example, Pommard-Epenots, Grands-Epenots, and Rugiens, you would earn extra points. The quality of these wines reached heights that I had never before encountered. In their harmonious complexity I discovered the widest variety of Pinot perfumes. I would have had to be Chauvet himself to describe them, but for me these unknown wines all mingled into the same perfection. How can one properly evaluate works of art from a private collection which one can admire but once, on one single evening? Fortune did not favor me that evening and prevents me from revealing my score. The winners on this occasion were the great chefs of the Saône-Rhône axis. Admittedly, they were on home ground, but underneath their chef's hats they showed themselves not only geniuses of the culinary art but steeped in Burgundian lore as well.

There are no greater snobs than American wine lovers. They collect bottles in the way others collect great masters or rare stamps. I know some who have five thousand bottles in air-conditioned cellars (which are too cold), but only of first-growth wines. One Texan surgeon serves only Latour, Margaux, Haut-Brion, Cheval Blanc, Ausone, Pétrus, Yquem, and their Burgundian equivalents. His collection of Mouton-Rothschild starts only in the year when it became a first growth, 1973. When I spied a case of Figeac in the corner, he apologized saying, "That's nothing, it's for my wife's parties." I led a tasting for him that was the longest of my career: twenty vintages of Château Haut-Brion, drawn straight from his own stock, and tasted over a four-hour period without a break.

Twelve people crowded around the horseshoe-shaped table on which all the glasses and bottles were lined up. In one corner of the room the Stars and Stripes put the scene in context and perhaps acted as a reminder that Haut-Brion, my neighbor in the Graves, is an American property—one more star, in short. The years ran back one by one from 1972 to 1945, like so many memories of vintages past. I was responsible for introducing the wines. I recalled the weather pattern of this or that year on the gravelly outcrops: the spring rains, August thunderstorms, the miraculous Indian summers. I also recounted the hopes and fears of Delmas father and son; I described their skill in maintaining Haut-Brion's place among the first growths, and my words had a certain depth of feeling. What is so good about the Americans is that they listen. Michael Buller, who can reproduce the Bordeaux style of my impromptu remarks, translated them phrase by phrase.

Shortly afterwards I had the privilege of conducting the same tasting among friends, in the surroundings of the Haut-Brion fermenting room; on this occasion I found my attitude was different. My comparative analysis of the vintages was the same, but my notes were shorter and more precise. The oenologist in me had resurfaced, rigorously critical, and whereas he had a cause to plead in Texas, in Pessac he was once again the demanding judge.

Many properties have been tempted to put on this type of vertical tasting. The comparisons are always instructive, if only to follow the development of the wines. The technician may discover some aspect which can be improved, and this is the way in which great quality is obtained, by continual refinement and small corrections from year to year.

A point of particular interest in Château Lafite, owned by the Rothschilds for over a hundred years, is the possibility of going way back in time and looking at vintages from the last century. Here are some notes made by Odette Kahn on one-hundred-year-old wines.

1892: Powerful, concentrated nose; still young and firm, long on the palate, quite beautiful. Inky and licorice aromas. Made by Mortier and the cellarmaster Laumonier who described the wine as "respectable." Very early harvest, starting on August 25.

1888: A wine which lacks elegance, vegetal but nicely cut, solid, firm, and remarkably young. After the miserable mildew years, Bordeaux mixture finally managed to save the vintage; harvest started on October 11.

1873: Still a fine color, a brilliant tile red; sweet and fruity, having thrown a considerable deposit; excellent wine, a miracle of youth. Small vintage as a result of April frosts; harvest started September 20, one of the last vintages made by Goudal and the cellarmaster Tourteau.

1869: Brown in appearance, but the wine is round and seductive, similar to the 1953. An abundant and forward year, right from the start the wines were judged to be "remarkable and complete."

The world of wine is infinite and here I have only described several wines which are geographically close to me. How could I possibly commit to memory the thousands of wines that I have tasted from all over the world, wines from Chile, Greece, Switzerland, Austria, Mexico, Italy, Spain; those from the Rhine and Palatinate or from California, the Finger Lakes, and so many others? The rate at which I taste now has gone beyond the limits of memory; it is wasteful in effect. Nonetheless, I still have the notes of all my tastings and every now and again I leaf through them; the experience is like looking at the pages of a travel album which can take me back in time and space.

TASTING SPIRITS

It could be said that the rules given for tasting wine also apply to tasting spirits, but in practice they are very different. A spirit is not drunk like a wine, nor do professionals taste spirits in quite the same way. Whatever the distilled drink one is tasting, whether it be fruit brandy, grain alcohol, distilled young wine, or spirits which have softened in barrel, from the first sip ethyl alcohol masks all other sensations. It hinders the taster and rapidly fatigues the palate because of the burn in its flavor. The level of alcohol in young spirits to be tasted may be as high as 70°. Above this the sensation is painful, similar to an inflammation or sore on the lips. Thus the whole technique consists of finding a means of avoiding this very strong taste, whose dominant presence completely overwhelms any aromatic substances as well as any other flavors, the very smells and flavors one actually wants to perceive. Examining the olfactory phase by itself is not enough; the nose can perceive numerous qualities and faults, but one needs to experience the aromas in the mouth, too, for it reveals other less volatile nuances, and there are certain faults which can only be detected on the palate.

Every group of tasters has its own way of resolving this problem, dependent on the type of alcohol and their habits. Some people lower the alcoholic degree to 30° or 40° by adding either distilled or lightly mineralized water, cold or warm according to choice. However, this sort of dilution, the only means of tackling spirits of 85° or 90°, is not always suitable for other sorts where water weakens and alters the aromas as well as destroying the body and balance. Another method is for the taster to pour a little of the spirit into the palm of the hand and then rub it so as to make it evaporate. With his nose buried in the palm of his hand, he then follows the evolution of smells given off, perceiving them one after another as a function of their volatility; those which stick to the skin longest being the heaviest, the fattest.

However, it is not possible to examine many samples in this manner. Nor is the practice very widespread in Cognac, though I have seen it used on a callused palm at Plaisance-du-Gers in the Armagnac region. Another solution is to rinse a glass with the spirit, empty it, and cover the mouth of the glass with a flat sheet of paper. After sufficient time is allowed for the excess alcohol to evaporate, the odorous contents of the glass can be smelled.

After an initial phase of smelling from a half-filled and then briskly agitated glass, the best procedure is to work very rapidly with a very small quantity of the spirit. The taster takes a tiny sip between his lips and spits it out within a couple of seconds. The rapidity with which the alcohol spreads over the mucous surfaces leaves little time for it to become aggressive and so renders it bearable. While the liquid goes no further than the mouth, the aromas that have vaporized therein literally explode in a multiodorous and many-flavored bouquet. Rid of the encumbrance of alcohol, one can experience all the impressions of body, richness, weight, lightness or heaviness, suppleness or hardness; and the whole range of aromas with their evolution and persistence can be perceived.

Tasting spirits is a very clean business and the tasting room is often a comfortable, carpeted office. It would not be possible to taste seriously on the premises of the distillery or the aging cellars. You should see the Fillioux, the Renards, the Frugiers, the Guirauds, and the Dumons at work buying young spirits or studying a variety of glasses containing old spirits in order to arrive at a commercial blend of cognac, which will remain absolutely consistent in style and quality. By comparison with winetasting one gets the impression of a mini-tasting. They work with tiny samples in small narrow bottles with miniature labels on them. Little tulip glasses are used or smaller versions of the standard INAO glasses (see page 130), and only a few drops are used for tasting. Spirits being stable and almost insensitive to air, the reference samples can be stored standing up on cupboard shelves, stoppered with corks but not necessarily full. The spirit taster has an enormous advantage over the winetaster in that he has at hand, practically immune to spoilage, his whole collection of comparative samples as well as the reference styles he needs to match by blending. As one of the advertisements says, there may be eighty different brandies in a cognac.

It seems that the spirit taster uses a much narrower range of descriptive terms than the winetaster. His comments are briefer; qualities and defects are simply outlined in a few words, and description of tastes is limited. What counts most in a young brandy is the absence of faults, what is called cleanness or frankness; for it is aging in wood which will produce the essential qualities. Among the common defects a distinction is made between those due to some taint in the distilled wine: one that is pricked or slightly acetic, moldy, sulfured or having a lees smell, putrid, stale; tasting green or woody, of green boxwood, with an earthy taste, a bitter one, or the piquant taste of acrolein; and, on the other hand, those defects due to complications or problems during distillation or aging: a cooked or burnt taste, the taste of bronze or copper, of fat (also described as "seconds"), of grease, a rancid flavor, or one of rubber, plastic material, hydrocarbons, or a casky taste. The qualities which are sought are those of fruit and finesse. A light aroma of herb tea or dried flowers develops well during the course of aging. Brandies can be described as acid (a not too excessive acidity gives body), flat, dry, short, harsh, or, alternatively, round. A palate aroma is appreciated when it is discreetly reminiscent of fine soap, fatty acids or when it smells subtly of fruit kernels, plum, or violets. Brandies aged in wood become more supple and acquire the vanillic odors known as wood or oak *rancio*.

The art of drinking spirits is similar to the art of tasting them in that the same attempt is made to overcome the purely alcoholic taste. For this reason fruit brandies are drunk cold or iced. Their alcohol seems less caustic as a result and their smells more aromatic. Ponthier writes: "Place an ice cube in a balloon glass, and roll it around until the crystal is frosted. Then, empty the glass, pour a small quantity of the spirit into the bottom and run the liquid slowly round the cold walls. Now you can bring the glass close to your nostrils and smell the fruit's perfume before drawing the first drop of icy liquid on to your tongue." This is how the finest fruit brandies should be drunk, for example, raspberry and pear or even Danziger Goldwasser, a grain alcohol with tiny gold flakes in it, both a refinement and a curiosity. More rustic examples such as cherry, plum, sloe, and juniper brandies are drunk as an accompaniment to regional dishes, and used in cakes and to lace coffee.

Vodka at 40° or 50° is drunk in one gulp. It is swallowed quickly as it reaches the throat before its harshness and lack of refinement can show. Neutral and with no aromatic length, it leaves no memory; one drinks it to forget and it is quickly forgotten itself. There are additional reasons for drinking schnapps as quickly as possible and without drawing breath to stop it revealing traces of its origin. The lover of old brandies aged for years in oak behaves quite differently. The mellowing that comes with age renders their alcohol less aggressive, and they are drunk at temperatures of 20°C to 22°C in small sips, at intervals and in a careful manner so as just to wet the palate which slowly becomes used to the alcohol and so less sensitive to it. Quite the reverse of gulping. Very quickly the taster tastes only their sweetness and softness, renewing the astonishing burst of aromas at each sip. Armagnac, cognac, and old calvados are sipped in this manner; but I know of old Spanish brandies which have gone through all the criadera stages, which merit the same treatment.

Basically, there is nothing like water for stretching alcohol, and the long drink of whisky, bourbon, or light brandies diluted with water almost makes one believe that alcohol is thirst quenching. However, heed the saying: "When I drink a whisky I become another man, and this other man needs a whisky."

Finally, one can always neutralize alcohol with sugar, letting a sweet tooth compound one's indulgence. Thus we have the sugar lump dipped in brandy, West Indian punch, and an endless series of cocktails and liqueurs.

Out of sheer curiosity, I have drunk numerous spirits throughout the world, ranging from Arrack with the *mezze* in Beirut, to Ouzo in the Greek tavernas, Pisco, the cold Muscat grape brandy in Peru and Chile (which both lay claim to its invention), and saké, a rice-based spirit, from tiny cups in Tokyo. It is in Mexico, however, that I came across the most original way of enjoying alcohol. Mexican tequila is a brandy obtained by distilling the fermented juice of the agave plant; it has little aroma and its taste is particularly sharp; its fiery character is therefore avoided by a contrast of flavors. Just before downing the spirit you bite into the segments of a lime and lick a few grains of salt off the back of your hand, and the tequila, thus tamed, tastes softer and sweeter.

As you can see, man has contrived all sorts of ways of making his favorite poison attractive and inoffensive.

Twelve

Quality in Wine

HOW TO DEFINE QUALITY

To talk about the quality of wines, we often use a whole collection of expressions and aphorisms. We speak of a "quality" wine, meaning a high-quality product; but an ordinary wine can be good quality and a so-called quality wine may be mediocre. Thus, somewhat confusingly, the word quality describes the nature of something, that is to say, its particular properties; or it indicates superiority and excellence. There are *vins de qualité supérieur* (but this so-called superior quality is inferior to that of Appellation Contrôlée wines!) and *vins de qualité produits dans des régions determinées* (quality wines produced in specific regions). There are different properties to be distinguished in a wine: organoleptic, hygienic, pharmacodynamic, etc. We speak of a policy of quality, and use clichés such as "the constant search for quality," "preoccupation with quality," "an obligation to produce quality," "the health of viticulture lies in quality," and if one is a merchant or a buyer then one talks about a "quality-price ratio."

Much has been written about quality, first and foremost in an attempt to define it. The same ideas are found coming from different pens: "Quality is something perceived more than defined" (Pisani); "The quality of a wine is easier to experience than to demonstrate" (Poupon); and the Americans and the Italians express the concept similarly: "Quality in wines is easier to recognize than to define"

(Amerine), and "The quality of a wine is difficult to define in an entirely unequivocal way." (Paronetto)

A very simple, obvious, and very clear definition is this: "The quality of a wine is the totality of its properties, that is to say, the properties which render it acceptable or desirable." In effect, it is the totally subjective pleasure provided by drinking the wine which conditions judgment.

Behind each definition lies hidden the person who, in the final analysis, actually judges the quality, the wine drinker. Quality only exists in relation to this individual and then only in as far as he has the ability to perceive it and approve it. Quality will depend on his judgment, that is, on his taste, his preferences, and the pleasure he derives from the wine. It is easy to understand the relativity of the notion of quality, something which is often stressed: "Quality is not an object, by itself it does not exist. . . . It is a mental concept which tries to establish a hierarchy and a classification." (Roubert) "Quality is a concept which simply indicates the consumer's preference regarding a product, preferences created by fashion or advertising." (Larrea) "Quality itself is a theoretical notion which signifies nothing in practical terms. It depends on numerous factors among which the consumer's environment plays a preponderant role. . . . The quality of a food is defined by its power to satisfy an organism (to give something extra, or supplementary). . . . Quality is a notion that is both positive and relative; positive because the food satisfies the body's needs, relative because this satisfaction depends on the organism in question and its particular requirements." (Debry)

In a way it is the quality of the consumer which determines the quality of the wine he drinks. Everyone drinks the wine he or she deserves. Without well-informed consumers there would be no great wines. Some people have pushed the paradox even further: The quality of wine has no existence on its own since it is dependent on the quality of the consumer! Perhaps, but there is a quality potential in wine which is all the more real because it is recognized by more connoisseurs; it is they who make reputations. Certainly, informing and educating consumers, by making them more demanding, are effective means of improving the quality of wines indirectly.

The conditions for obtaining quality wines have been defined for a long time now. Olivier de Serres had already outlined them at the beginning of the seventeenth century: "The climate, the soil, and the

vines." Sometimes the work of man was added to this list. The first
three conditions would correspond to natural factors, to nature's gift,
to the elements of **innate quality**, with man's intervention providing the **acquired quality**. All this is fair enough, but I would like to
point out that nothing is completely innate in a processed product of
agricultural origin. So-called natural conditions are only potentially
so: in effect, everything has had to be acquired, discovered, or invented. Of course, this work has taken generations of vines and
winemakers, so that today it is difficulty for us to imagine the conditions in which our viticultural heritage was created. The climate and
the soil represent the general location and particular vineyard from
which a wine comes; it should not be forgotten that they have been
chosen by man from thousands of different locations, that the soil has
had to be constantly worked and maintained, and that without
drainage and improvements there would be no good soils for wine,
no production of quality grapes, and no quality wines.

It is man who has chosen the grape variety best adapted to the
soil and the climate, who has also judiciously mixed several varieties
and who has thus managed to create from the soil a wine of quality
and individuality. Grape varieties have been improved by selection.
In order to maintain the vine, one of the most fragile and vulnera-
ble of plants, and to make it productive, man has had to create complex methods of cultivation, of pruning, and of protection. Basically,
in terms of its shape and production there is nothing less natural
than a vine in a quality vineyard. Can it really be right to say that the
science of viticulture, something so complex, so diverse, so refined
and the result of such a considerable sum of knowledge and work, is
simply a gift of nature?

As for the wine itself, it is a direct product of man's labor. Wine
is not made from the whole of the grape; it is obtained from a partial extraction of soluble substances contained in different tissues.
The quality of the wine depends on the choice of a method of vinification and on how this is carried out. The grape's acids, its mineral
salts, and its aromatic constituents are not all retained in the wine:
In white wine vinification generally avoids dissolving the tannins; in
red vinification only 20 to 30 percent of the tannins in the skin and
pips are extracted. The type of wine obtained and the quality within
this type are directly related to the manner in which this partial extraction is realized. The way in which alcoholic fermentation is con-

ducted influences the finished product, and the option of allowing malolactic fermentation to take place or not is also a choice affecting quality, as are the conditions and period of aging before bottling, and the methods of clarification and stabilization, all of which can improve a wine. Another example of quality potential is that some wines only express the uniqueness of their character and appeal after sufficient aging in barrel and then in bottle. Essentially, quality only exists if it is desired, sought after, patiently waited for; it is not a free gift. I cannot agree with the view that "one accepts human intervention (in vinification), as long as it allows the natural characteristics to remain intact," since it is precisely human intervention which has created and highlighted these so-called natural characteristics! On the other hand, I agree wholeheartedly with Baron Le Roy's fine sentiment: "Quality can be endlessly improved because it is essentially the work of man."

Quality is also relative because in order to judge a wine, its type, class, age, and place in the hierarchy have to be taken into account. All wine is regulated by a system of laws drawn up to avoid confusion between wines of different merits. The classification system also takes into account conditions of production and commercialization, and it is necessarily different from one country to another. It is not based solely on geographical location, and the sacrosanct appellation of origin is not the only formula for expressing quality. Other details may also serve as quality criteria. Examples include grape variety (wines labeled Riesling, Chardonnay, Cabernet Sauvignon, and so on, are now common), method of harvesting (the Auslese and Spätlese wines of Germany), method of vinification (rosé wines, sparkling wines, fortified wines), age (in certain countries *fino* wines are those with at least a year's aging, and *reserva* wines those which have been aged for five years), and, finally, the brand and/or the winemaker's name.

Top-quality wine can only be made in conditions where there are the benefits of a high technical level of viticulture, vinification, cellar care, and distribution; and where there is a sufficiently informed clientele capable of appreciating better quality and prepared to pay for it.

The principal obstacle to promoting quality in any given region is the fact that it frequently does not pay. And yet it is logical that a better wine should sell for more, otherwise there would be no point in making it better. It is a mistake to imagine that quality can be obtained without investment and without any additional effort. Besides, by restricting the product to an elite of demanding connoisseurs, the high price put on quality contributes to a wine's prestige and erects a barrier against bad taste, whereas excessive availability leads to a devaluation of its currency. A high price protects fine wine and, by imposing on it an obligation to excellence, prevents it from compromising its quality.

THE QUALITY OF WINE IS THE DOMAIN OF OENOLOGY

The aim of oenology is to help the producer obtain the best possible wine, with all the qualities latent in the grapes from which it is made. This problem is the more readily solved the better one understands wine, its constituents, and the transformations they undergo; that is to say, the more advanced the science of wine, the more effective will be its application. This presupposes studies based on sound oenological theory, correctly adapted to various types of wine, and this in turn requires a diffusion of knowledge through education.

It is all the more necessary to insist on this point because there are still people who tend to think that quality is independent of technology, who minimize man's role in order to underline the natural qualities of wine.

According to this view, oenology can provide the means of avoiding mishaps during fermentation and conservation, but it can neither explain the finer qualities of great wine, nor create the conditions necessary to their production, conditions which are linked to subtle and indefinable circumstances. And yet, the history of recent decades shows that it was by improving the finest wines that oenology began its transformation to a modern science. The Bordeaux classed growths were the most receptive to the new doctrines and were the first to benefit.

Quality criteria have often been studied. A distinction is made between the **negative** aspect which is the absence of faults and corresponds to a minimal quality threshold, and the **positive** aspect which concerns real qualities: pleasure, appeal, complexity, personality, purity. Defects are more readily perceptible than qualities. Consumers cannot always appreciate a wine's qualities but they are very capable of recognizing its faults. They are often happy with a wine of little quality providing it has no apparent defects.

Two categories of quality criteria have been mentioned. First, there are the **objective** criteria. These are essentially statutory, subject to increasingly detailed and stringent standards and regulations. Since the beginning of the century successive steps in setting up these criteria were the official definition of wine, the control of production, and measures for protecting quality by codifying the practices of vinification, conservation, and treatment, as well as by various prohibitions and restrictions.

The **subjective** criteria ("quality, like truth, is above all subjective" according to Quittanson) are those which are not measurable, or at least not yet. They are often the results of balances which are difficult to quantify, and they are measured principally by consumer satisfaction. They are the organoleptic characteristics of smell and taste, and can only be evaluated by tasting.

It is worth pointing out that in matters of quality, the distinction between what is objective and what is subjective is always difficult, because these characteristics overlap. The quality of any object is determined in relation to the subject making the judgment. Objective qualities are said to be true, real, and measurable, whereas subjective ones are unreal. However, quality in a wine as perceived by tasting is a notion which is real enough. In effect, there are greater and lesser degrees of objectivity when evaluating the quality of taste, depending on the quality of the taster.

In any case, the essential role of technical intervention by man is implicitly recognized by the regulations. It is realized that quality is not an automatic consequence of origin because controls are based more and more on a tasting test. This takes place several months after the harvest when the wine is far from finished; it can change, often profoundly, in one way or another subsequently, and some regions have introduced a tasting test just before bottling.

These various controls have done much to improve quality, certainly more by technical developments which they encourage, than simply as a result of selection. Obliged to present a well-constituted and correctly made wine very quickly, the producer finds he must look to technical advice and analysis.

As fast as knowledge of wine and the complex phenomena involved in its making progress, and the means of obtaining quality are better understood and implemented, so ever stricter regulations are imposed. This is effective to the extent that it closely follows the developments of oenological knowledge and remains consistent with them. Changes in vinification technique have meant a change in the requirements for certain composition standards; for example, the limits for dry extract in a red wine take into account the extent of maceration during vinification, as represented by an index of tannin compounds. The sulfur dioxide limits now depend on the type of wine, and they are being progressively lowered as the properties of this antiseptic and the laws relating to its combination with elements of the grape are defined more accurately.

In short, regulations define and guarantee a minimal quality and they are an incentive to improve this minimum level. It is oenological technique which provides the means. However one argues, one always comes back to the preeminent role of technique; technique holds the keys to quality. Everyone agrees that at present there is no hope of defining the quality of a wine analytically. However detailed the analysis, it cannot distinguish between an ordinary wine and a fine wine. Besides, as we have seen, quality is not due to a certain level of this or that taste or odor constituent, but to complex balances in its constitution.

Even if chemical analysis cannot quantify quality, it is very well able to measure defects, thus enabling limits to be fixed for certain constituents contained in grapes (diglucoside malvoside, of hybrid grapes), for bacterial spoilages (volatile acidity, ethyl acetate), for additives (citric acid, sulfur dioxide, sulfates, sodium), and for contaminants (arsenic, cyanide derivatives, boron, bromium, fluorine, lead, etc.). Analysis can also investigate the relationships between normal constituents or between certain indices and so reveal any anomalies.

Consumers are very sensitive to notions of what is pure, clean, natural, and authentic, even if qualities of taste normally take precedence over nutritional and hygienic qualities which are more difficult to perceive. A wine should first of all be good, but it has also to be *hygienically* good.

The oenologist has a duty to monitor the hygienic qualities of a wine by eliminating, or at least reducing to a minimum, any chemical additives or treatments. Giving preventive oenology priority over curative oenology is what I wish to convey in the words: "Vinify in such a way that the wine will have to undergo no treatments other than clarification."

Quality control is being developed at all levels and is becoming increasingly stringent, whether it concerns production or sale in bottle, especially for export, where the requirements of increasingly exigent foreign consumers must be taken into account. At this stage quality control also includes some aspects of product presentation: design and resistance to wear of the bottle dressing (labels and capsules), cork quality, and the effectiveness of the stopper. Stability tests, which consist of placing the wine in extreme conditions (at high or low temperatures, exposed to oxygen or light), enable the potential risks of haze or deposits to be measured. Current tests also involve more precise determinations of limpidity: the number of particles, the number of live yeasts and bacteria which have escaped clarification, and possibly the identification of these microorganisms. This test for microbiological stability requires clarification procedures that are increasingly effective, and antiseptic measures for bottling materials that are increasingly rigorous. Quality control is a factor for progress in the sense that it constantly forces the producer to improve his techniques.

All aspects of quality are the proper province of oenology. Even today the quality of wine is not what it should be, because some people have no idea of the possibilities of oenology in this respect, and they are insufficiently utilized even in the best conditions. There are still too many wines which owe nothing to the principles of oenology and which pervert the consumer's taste and thus provide unhealthy competition for the production of good wines.

According to the formula of one leading viticulturist: "Quality is a state of mind, a constant concern and determination to do better." The first priority for progress of this kind is the best possible knowledge, and the same argument can be used for the consumer whose palate must be educated and reeducated. If fine wines refine the consumers' taste, they in turn contribute to progress in wine quality by their better-informed choice. Making wine better known in order to make it better appreciated is just one more of oenology's many functions.

ON THE CONCEPT OF CRU

Siloret goes back to the sources of the word *cru*: "We have gathered this old French word in the same way that one picks up a pebble from the river bed, formed from hard and ancient stone, which has changed its shape and meaning several times under the influence of various very different currents (popular, linguistic, scientific, administrative, and legal)."

It is true that dictionaries offer little explanation of the word *cru*: "Soil considered as something which makes vegetables and their produce grow" (Littré); "Soil considered from the point of view of its special products and the qualities they draw from it" (Larousse); "What grows in a given region and, by substitution, the region itself." (Robert) The word *cru* can be applied to anything that has grown; plants and animals or processed products: brandies, fruits, vegetables, wood, honey, butter, cheese, etc., even meat.

In the area which interests the taster, *cru*, in its widest sense, means "viticultural produce." In reality, it is a complex notion because it combines a whole group of activities that are essentially different: agricultural, in part industrial, always involving processing, and even commerce. For example, it is generally said that Beaujolais or Juliénas are famous *crus*, thus including in the one word all the wines of Beaujolais, which is a region, or all those of Juliénas, which is a commune. This is the geographical use of the word defined as: "A zone within which all the products share unique characteristics, or are different from those of neighboring soils." (Vedel)

In Bordeaux the usage is very specific. The *cru* is a more restricted entity; it is the wine-producing property, the château, different from its neighbors, having an individual production within the confines of the same appellation. Its wine is harvested and raised on the one site, more and more often right up to its final commercial form, the bottle. The Bordeaux *cru* thus combines the three activities of production, processing, and marketing. Deeply rooted in a small geographical location, in an appellation of which it is promoter and exemplar, and whose reputation it helps create, it has also become a commercial brand. In some regions the brand eclipses the *cru*; in Bordeaux they are one and the same. "The *cru* has the value of an individual brand, supported by a tradition of quality and the owner's particular care, both of which have enabled his brand to stand out among the other properties of the region." (*Dictionnaire du Vin*)

One wonders why there is no equivalent of the word *cru* in other languages. Spanish, Italian, and Portuguese translators generally keep the word *cru*; similarly, neither "growth" in English nor "Gewächs" in German have quite the same meaning, and each pronounce *cru* in their own way. The Americans transcribe if phonetically as "crew," the Germans as "Krü."

The concept of *cru* has often been analyzed. It includes a number of fundamental elements: site, soil, climate, grape varieties, techniques, quality, and reputation; if only one of this roll call were missing there would be no *cru*. Nor could there be any *cru* which was not the creation of and exploitation by man. A *cru* is the result of making the most of natural conditions, as we saw in the human factors in quality.

The importance of the combination of site and soil (*terroir*) is well known, it is the whole basis of the vineyard; it depends on the surface soil, the subsoil and its water content, and exposure. Wines can be classified according to the topology of their vineyards, so distinguishing river wines, coastal wines, mountain wines, plateau wines, foothill wines, valley wines, and wines of the plain. Each of these sites and localities corresponds to a particular type of wine. Vineyards of repute are situated on poor soils, generally halfway up a hillside or on the top of sand and gravel banks and outcrops. The balance between the vine and its available water sources also characterize the *crus*. The ripening grapes have more to fear from too much water than too little. The quality of the grapes will differ according to the permeability of the soils, the depth of the vine roots, and the state of permanent moisture at root level. We do know for a fact that soils which retain moisture produce higher yields, larger grapes, later maturity, higher acidities, less intense colors, a lower level of tannins, less attractive grape aromas, and wines that are more neutral.

The part played by grape varieties is also well known; while there are a hundred-odd different grape varieties grown in France, only seven red and nine white varieties are called noble, according to Orizet. The hierarchy of the appellations and those of the *crus* are also well known; in the case of the *crus* it is a classification within a classification for it would be inaccurate to say "the *cru* is the appellation of origin." In Bordeaux as in many other regions the *crus* (or brands) both divide and dominate the appellation.

I will conclude with Gatheron's fine definition: "The *cru* is the most useful, most attractive, and most durable expression of man's relationship with his natural surroundings."

ABOUT VINTAGES

A definition of *millésime* (vintage date) that I found in the work of the very serious Conseil Internationale de la Langue française appealed to me on account of its historical precision: "Figures indicating the year in the Gregorian calendar which are put on bottles as a guarantee of the year of production." However, no definition is ever thorough enough and one sort of precision calls for another; personally, I would have added "since 1582."

The vintage is a wine's birth year, and there are at least two reasons for putting this date on its identity card, its label. First, it certifies the age of a wine that needs laying down and, depending on his taste and circumstances, it enables the drinker to choose a young or an old wine. Second, with the harvests being so different in quality from one year to the next, in Europe at least, the vintage gives some idea of the possible quality of the wine without opening the bottle.

Each vintage has its own style, development in bottle, reputation, and market value. For these reasons all fine wines bear a date. The character of the vintage is part of the wine's personality. It is sometimes said to dominate the *cru*, meaning that there is a greater similarity between wines of the same vintage but different properties, than there is between wines of the same property but different years. On current price lists and in the shops one can find excellent nonvintage wines, but these are generally drunk young. Their consistency of style over a long period is the result of the merchant's judicious blending of vintages.

It is the chance factor of climatic conditions which creates a different vintage each year; there are no two vintages which are identical. I can confirm that in a lifetime of winemaking one never makes the same wine twice. Climate seems to have a more decisive effect on grapes than on other fruits, no doubt because they take forty-five days to ripen and because they remain on the vine right up to the end. Ripe grapes are very sensitive; bad weather during the harvest can spoil everything, sunshine, on the other hand, can produce a beneficial overripening. Good and bad years follow each other without apparent rhyme or reason, quite unpredictably. Whatever anyone says, there is no discernible cycle. The chart of good Bordeaux vintages shows just how haphazardly they are distributed. Some decades have produced only two good years and other more favorable ones such as the 1980s have yielded up to seven.

Of the thirty vintages on the following chart there are fifteen odd years and fifteen even years. Sometimes two good years follow each other. The most celebrated pair are 1928 and 1929, since when we have had 1970 and 1971, 1975 and 1976, 1978 and 1979, 1982 and 1983, 1985 and 1986, 1989 and 1990; curiously, the younger vintage is usually more supple in style and ready to drink first.

The best Bordeaux vintages.

1930–1939				34			37		
1940–1949					45		47		49
1950–1959	50		52	53		55				59
1960–1969		61	62		64		66			
1970–1979	70	71				75	76		78	79
1980–1989		81	82	83		85	86		88	89
1990–1995	90				94	95				

The winetaster cannot escape the need to classify vintages, however arbitrary such a classification may appear. This is as much part of a professional's knowledge as knowing about appellations. In effect, a wine cannot be given an absolute rating, but only one that is relative to its peers of the same vintage. The league table of vintages is difficult to establish fairly because the idea of vintage is a subjective one, abstract in nature. The problem is that of comparing the average qualities of a given year for wines of different ages. How, for example, should one compare the 1995s today, as represented by an imaginary synthesis of all the appellations in this vintage, with the

1975, 1970, or 1961 archetypes which have been in bottle for several years, and which have developed in different ways? Either one has to make a retrospective judgment on these wines as imagined at the start of their careers, or else extrapolate and project an image of the young wines as they will be when mature. It is easy to see how such classifications give rise to endless discussion. The surprising thing is that, given time, there is a large measure of agreement among tasters.

Other aspects such as the homogeneity of quality over the whole range of wines produced, ease of vinification, regularity of success, and the commercial climate also need to be taken into account in the image of a vintage. There are some years when the *grands crus*, being better situated, manage an excellent quality, whereas the harvest in the lesser appellations lacks ripeness. The Merlot in the Libournais may be more successful than the Cabernet Sauvignon in the Médoc or vice versa. Thus, in contrast to the Médoc, 1952 has a better reputation than 1953 in St-Emilion, and 1971 is recognized as being particularly successful.

Moving to a different region, the quality of the vintages is completely different. 1975, a fine year in Bordeaux, is very ordinary in Beaune. Exactly the reverse is the case for 1969 and 1972. The ratings for the Rhône, Rhine, and Loire valleys would be different again. It is rare for all the wines in France to be similarly successful; this happened only in 1929, 1961, and 1990 and, to a lesser extent, 1959 and 1989.

Every wine lover knows the vintage charts produced by various companies, wine academies, and viticultural organizations, and reproduced in the trade press. There is an enormous amount of information on the subject; it is even found in pocket diaries. Vintages are marked out of twenty or graded with stars. The ratings do not always agree with each other; there are nonconformists everywhere. The Bordeaux Academy's vintage chart is unique in not attempting to class the vintages, no doubt on the principle that all the wines are good to drink providing you drink them at the right time. This avoids one problem only to encounter others which are just as serious, such as the schematic representation of numerous subjective qualities. In this system each year is defined by a symbol which represents the general character of the wines, more or less light or full-bodied, more or less well structured or delicate; the consistency of quality in the vintage, or whether advice should be sought in choosing bottles; and, finally, the state of development of the wines, so that they may be drunk at their best. The Academy brings out a new chart each year, corrected and updated in the light of the development of each vintage.

To divide vintages into just two categories, the good and the bad, would be an oversimplification. Reality is not as clear-cut. Besides, as one concise saying puts it: "There are no longer bad years, only difficult ones," meaning that modern techniques enable one to get the best out of material that is sometimes inadequate and, in difficult years, enable one to make wines which, if not of really top quality, are, by dint of selection, at least always satisfactory.

A year with a poor reputation will always produce some good bottles. Some wine buffs, with little imagination, limit their drinking to great wines from great vintages, unaware of the clever buyer's maxim: "Lesser *crus* from great years; *grands crus* from lesser years."

The frequent appearance of the expression "vintage of the century" has given rise to many jokes; but each generation needs at least one! For myself, I know of only one vintage of my century, and that was the result of both exceptional weather conditions and modern technology: 1961. As for 1928, 1929, and 1945, these are now extremely rare bottles. In any case, I never found them entirely satisfactory. The faults they had are something which oenology has battled against for a long time now. Recent years which lay claim to "vintage of the century" are 1982 and, possibly, 1990. Only time, their development in bottle, and future contenders for the title will be able to decide.

WINE AS A MIRROR OF OUR CIVILIZATION

Wine is a very old product whose origins merge into the origins of civilization itself. Hemingway said "Wine is one of the most civilized things in the world," something that we do not always take much notice of today. And yet, like bread, it is charged with meaning and mysticism, intimately linked to our way of life and thought, and it forms part of a very old and very respectable heritage. Bread was the basic and indispensable nourishment; wine was something more, pleasure and joy as well.

We ourselves are part of the civilization of the vine; the roots of this climbing plant can no longer be separated from our own historical roots. The Greeks and Romans spread philosophy and viticulture at the same time, a taste for wine as well as a taste for art. France has kept this heritage. As Professor Dion said: "France is a country where the history of wine and the vine shed light on the history of the French people."

In fact, wine is both a reflection of the people who make it and of the region that produces it, for it is not one of nature's free gifts. Everyone seems to think of wine as a natural product; but it is a processed product, subject to deterioration, man-made and surviving only as a result of constant care. Nature alone does not make wine, even less does it produce good wine and it certainly does not make the best possible wine. The reality is that man has to intervene at every stage of its production. Wine is effectively the product of man's labor and the product is only as good as the man who makes it. Quality wine is not obtained fortuitously but as the result of a constant effort toward quality.

Wine develops, as does our civilization, primarily in terms of taste but also in terms of technology. The wines of today have nothing in common with those that the ancients preserved by various artificial means with such ingredients as resin, pitch, and spices; nor do they have anything in common with those of the Middle Ages which were sold very young, during the months immediately following the harvest, because they would not keep any longer than that. And doubtless they bear little resemblance to the wines of the last century which, although they made the reputation of our appellations, were nonetheless green, astringent, low in alcohol, kept badly, and frequently turned sour. Having had the privilege of analyzing sixty vintages of one Médoc *grand cru* from the last century and up to 1920, I was surprised to find that in only fourteen out of the sixty wines was the alcoholic strength more than 10°, the current minimum for the Médoc appellation. Only nine wines had less than 0.8 grams per liter of volatile acidity, and half of these great wines would no longer be legally saleable as table wines under current regulations.

It is well known that the way in which we eat is constantly changing, reflecting our way of life. The same goes for what we drink; so that over a period of several decades we can see a continual change in the taste of our wines. In this respect each region goes its own way, but what is clear is that they are changing. Whether as a result of passing fashion or some deeper reason linked to our way of life, these trends cannot be ignored. The statement "Tell me what you drink and I will tell you who you are" is still valid. After the great vogue for sweet white wines, the public sought lighter, drier wines that are in some ways less nourishing. At one time, aged, almost maderized white wines were much appreciated; what people look for in white wines now are freshness, youth, and the flavor of the grapes themselves.

Similarly, for red wines, the customer prefers wines that are less astringent, with less color and tannin, as well as being lower in acidity and higher in alcohol; what the professionals call supple wines, wines which are ready to drink sooner. In some regions the taste for old wine is gradually being lost and this is a pity. Lastly, the present fashion for rosé wine is a consequence of the attempts to preserve the freshness and fruit of ripe black grapes in wine.

It is sometimes said that wine is no longer made the way it used to be, the way our grandparents made it, and that this is a matter of regret. In reality, it should be admitted instead that our grandparents' wines would no longer please us, any more than would the living conditions of their times.

Wine should be a friend for life and also a reflection of our civilization. We live in an era of productivity, profitability, concentration of production, and use of industrial equipment. That cannot be changed. For vinification we use new means which are more powerful and more reliable, provided by the science and technology of oenology. As with viticulture, winemaking depends less and less on the hand of man, but we should never lose sight of the principal goal, that of making the healthiest and most attractive wine possible. The character of wine, as the most interesting because the most diverse of drinks must be preserved; modern methods of vinification cannot be a threat so long as they remain subject to our traditional respect for wine.

In the end, the most important thing for us wine lovers is that the civilization of wine survives. Because wine, today as yesterday and tomorrow, continues to symbolize dual communion: on the one hand, with nature and the soil, through the mystery of plant growth and the miracle of fermentation, and, on the other with, man, who wanted wine and who was able to make it by means of knowledge, hard work, patience, care, and love; for nothing worthwhile is achieved without love.

EXHILARATING VIRTUES OF WINE

Brillat-Savarin claimed that coffee was an exhilarating drink; Larousse says the same thing; but it is a long time since coffee made us smile.

Wine, however, has always been considered enlivening, a drink to raise the spirits. Hundreds of quotations attest to this down the centuries. Is wine really full of good cheer which it spreads through our veins? And is it the alcohol which engenders the sense of optimism? No; alcohol dulls the senses, distorts perception, and makes us lose our sense of identity; I cannot accept the notion of euphoria, dreamy or noisy, being linked to a blood-alcohol level of 70 milligrams per liter. To be merry from too much alcohol is a sad business. What interests me is the effect on the emotions, the happy state of mind that wine causes even before it is drunk. The prospect of wine is so pleasant that it relaxes the face muscles and makes one's eyes light up. Even before the cork is drawn, a good bottle induces a festive atmosphere of good humor and relaxation. The liveliness of flowing wine is infectious. It inspires wine writers to describe wines imaginatively as frivolous, funny, amusing, roguish, chic, jokey, laughing, naughty. In contrast, some wines are said to be serious; I wonder which these are? Wines that are simply dull, or those few rare and expensive bottles whose prestigious image makes even the lighthearted serious?

The most exhilarating of wines is without doubt sparkling wine. The very way of serving it has a promise of fun: the ice bucket, the napkin draped like a scarf around the bottle, the popping of the cork, and the burst of streaming bubbles which make pouring awkward as they spill over the rim of the flute. As an aperitif champagne immediately sets the tone and breaks the ice, something which no other drink can do. If champagne has a happy image, the image of a wine that can be drunk even when one is no longer thirsty, then this is because it is the wine par excellence for happy events.

Wine does indeed have an aura of conviviality. It is enough for a wine professional to identify himself as such for the person he is talking to, to say "So, you're a winetaster are you!", along with a knowing wink, implying an appreciation of the supposed delights of the job as he thinks to himself: "Work is obviously no problem for you!" He is clearly unaware of the pressure on a taster during tasting, of how tiring repeated tests can be, of the discipline required, of the constant availability and good health that the job demands. Even if he is a teetotaller all he can think of is the jovial aspect of wine.

The journalist Jean Ferniot experienced this when interviewing French people, so he knew what he was talking about when he said: "Stop someone in the street, it does not matter who, and ask what the name Burgundy means to them. They will reply wine. And generally their faces will break into a big smile."

One morning I was walking along a crowded pavement in Mexico City. The previous evening I had appeared on Mexican television. My interview with Jacobo Zabludosky, the Mexican Léon Zitrone, had covered the civilization and the humanity of wine, the preferred drink of Latin races, and the possibilities of wine production in Mexico. The average annual per capita consumption of the Mexicans is barely more than a quarter of a liter of wine (they make up for this with other alcoholic drinks: beer, brandy, cocktails, and tequila). Afterwards, still in front of the cameras, I had managed an improvised tasting of the wines of five different countries fairly well. So, that morning I was recognized among the crowd and addressed in a familiar way accompanied by a broad smile: "Hey! Are you the Frenchman who was tasting wines on the television yesterday?" I had spoken about the pleasures of tasting to people who had perhaps never drunk a drop of wine, and wine had already created a sense of complicity between us. Wine's happy image had shone from their screens and lit up their faces.

I know a country where the beneficial effect of wine is well understood. It is drunk as a tonic, a stimulant, or simply because one is happy. No, it's not France, it's Austria.

Right in the middle of Mozart's C minor Mass, the devout lady in front of me fainted, collapsing onto the flagstones of Salzburg's baroque cathedral. There was nothing surprising about this unhappy incident; the heat of that July Sunday was suffocating and the sound of choir and orchestra of the Mozarteum made the whole building as well as one's eardrums resonate. The crowd of people standing in the naves and chapels of the church filled it to bursting. A few of them moved aside and tried to help the woman up, to sit her down, and give her room to breathe. She had fainted during the powerful hallelujahs. The sacristan, tapping his staff on the marble, forced his way through, bent over the woman, diagnosed the problem, and set off toward the sacristy. He came back carrying on a plate a goblet and a flagon of altar wine. He carefully made the woman drink a few sips of the beneficial liquor, and she opened her eyes at the moment when the last bars of the Ite Missa Est were reverberating around the vaulted roof. She already felt better. All that was needed to revive her spirits were a few drops of Gumpoldskirchner. Lucky parishioners whose sacristans know that there is no more delicious and effective first aid for fainting than a little local white wine!

Café Winckler is famous; it dominates the town of Salzburg. You reach this viewpoint via a lift tunneled in the rock. Night or day the view is unique and spectacular. One evening I dined there. Quite late on a whole group of happy young couples burst into the room. The young men and women sat down at table and ordered wine. No doubt they would be brought some of the toothsome pastries which are Austria's specialty, and they would have chosen a few bottles of Steiermark Traminer to accompany them. Not at all. They were brought only wine, many bottles of it; and which wine? Beaujolais! This group of Salzburgers knew that a few glasses of wine shared would warm their hearts and faces, and that was all they needed for a celebration.

I thought to myself one day, wine is still the best utilization of solar energy that we have found. Millions of vine leaves per hectare absorb the sun's rays, turned first toward the morning sun, then heated by the midday sun, and finally following the setting sun in the evening. The vine stores this energy in the tastiest form, in its ripening grapes, and not only as sugars. In fact, it is the formation of substances other than sugars which is of more interest to us: the anthocyanins of coloring matter, the tannins with their savory astringency, and the aromatic essences concentrated in the cells of the skins.

Later on, in the vat, fermentations will liberate this unstable energy. Then one day, several months or several decades later, the product obtained, purified, refined, and settled, will reconstitute those beautiful rays of summer sunshine in your glass in an explosion of smells and flavors. Old wines are always a reminder of fine days, the past regained. Popular wisdom is right: Wine really is bottled sunshine; that is why it is a cheerful drink, warmth to the heart and soul.

THE PRIMACY OF FRENCH WINES

The civilizing power of wine is conquering the world. There are few peoples who can escape the attractions that this drink exerts. The Americans have recently discovered the humanity of wine, and across the Atlantic there is a body of enthusiastic and informative wine literature giving serious coverage to the history and geography of wine, and treating the art of drinking as an art of living. The Japanese imitate the Anglo-Saxons; full of curiosity and earnest application, they are making praiseworthy efforts to absorb this refinement of Western culture. There is also a potential group of converts in Asia, non-Muslim Africa, and Central America. The consumption of wine is rising in many countries along with the rise in incomes. In contrast, the consumption in traditional wine-drinking countries is falling because people are drinking more quality wine and less ordinary wine. In France they are drinking less by drinking better.

At the same time the vine is spreading and covering the globe's surface wherever there is enough sunshine to ripen its fruit. By following the Europeans it emigrated to countries throughout the world. It has been planted for a long time in South Africa, Argentina, Chile, and Australia; and, having given up the Nordic fringe where it did not exactly flourish (though one can find remarkable bottles of white wine from England and even from Holland), it is now growing in the tropics and subtropics thanks to antiparasitic treatments and the advances that have been made in viticultural biology. Vineyards for wine can be found in Peru, Venezuela, Ecuador, Columbia, and Mexico. I have tasted wines from China, Japan, India, Iran, Turkey, Brazil, Jamaica, and New Zealand. Thousands of hectares of vines are being planted annually in Mexico.

It is noticeable that wine and the vine have been propagated by strong nations. This is Dumay's thesis. He demonstrates that the great wines have always been the privilege of great nations, those who could afford the necessary capital investment, and who had the requisite means of transport as well as a mastery of commerce. The vine developed in the West at the time of the Roman Empire and retreated during the Dark Ages.

The wines which were famous during the sixteenth and seventeenth centuries, at the time of the conquistadors and the "empire on which the sun never set," were Spanish wines; in Paris people drank wine from Alicante or the Canaries. It was France's supremacy in the eighteenth century which then gave her wines pride of place. We started by exporting wines from Bordeaux, Champagne, and Burgundy. At the same time the great maritime powers, the Netherlands and England in turn, traded in wines and helped create the great vineyards.

What is the place of French wines in this world of viticultural expansion and in the present commercial climate, and what are their chances against the competition? The reputation of our wines is very old and continues to be the best. This is the comforting observation that the traveler abroad can make. Our ancestors worked prodigiously to make our wines known throughout the world; this heritage is intact. French wines, above all French red wines, are benchmarks for quality and models to imitate everywhere. Our grape varieties, which adapt so well to different climates, are used and, thanks to enviable installations and irreproachable technology, wines are made abroad which are copies of our appellations, occasionally somewhat exaggerated, but often quite admirable.

I belong to those who consider that good wines, wherever they may come from, promote the cause of other good wines, and that no country can become a serious importer unless the indigenous consumer has been prepared by the production of good-quality local wine. However, by the same token, the competition from foreign wines is becoming more and more lively, and is an increasing threat to our interests.

There is only one possible strategy for us in the wine war which is just beginning: to produce wines that are better and better, whose quality is unquestionable and also unattainable by foreign producers. The competition is at the level of quality; we will only survive if we remain the best.

Thirteen

The Art of Drinking

THIRST

Thirst is defined as an internal sensation of the need to drink water. Our body, more than half liquid, consists of 50 to 70 percent water; and every day we lose two or three liters, more in exceptional circumstances, depending on our weight, activity, and the ambient temperature. In order to compensate we have to replace the same quantity.

Thirst is generally described as a sensation of dryness in the mouth, that is, of inadequate saliva, making it necessary to drink. One licks dry lips, has a bitter taste in the throat, and one's saliva feels thick; but these criteria are not exclusive to thirst, a dry mouth can be due to other reasons, illness or just emotion, for example. A lack of saliva is not always the result of a simple thirst.

In reality, from physiological thirst to gourmand thirst, one drinks to satisfy various needs, and various types of thirst can be distinguished. In the case of extreme privation thirst becomes an unbearable pain. This is the burning thirst of travelers lost in a desert, a thirst which leads to death in a few days.

Physiological thirst is the daily experience which balances our water requirements, ensuring that intake matches loss. The centers which regulate thirst are located in the region of the hypothalamus. They are regulated, on the one hand, by the osmotic pressure in the blood as a result of the concentration of blood plasma, and, on the other, by the decrease in blood volume. Two glandular systems are involved in these mechanisms: the adrenal and the posterior pituitary. The hormone liberated by the latter regulates the outflow of water from the body by the kidneys.

Brillat-Savarin called this type of painless thirst "which is always with us and which is, as it were, part of our existence" latent or habitual. Under normal circumstances man does not wait to drink until he is thirsty, he drinks out of habit and generally at fixed times, thus meeting his future needs by anticipation. On the whole he follows Rabelais' advice to the letter: "Always drink before you are thirsty and you will never experience thirst."

Alimentary thirst is that which accompanies eating. It is true that some people do not drink with all their meals, but they get liquid from moist foods such as soups, sauces, and boiled meat. One drinks while eating in order to moisten and soften foods, dilute their juices, and facilitate swallowing; the mouthful of liquid draws down the food with it. There is a quantitative relationship between the intake of liquid and the amount of food one eats: the bigger the meal is and the drier the food, the more one drinks, instinctively.

A little observation will reveal that one normally drinks after the last mouthful of any dish and when moving on from one dish to another, when changing tastes, that is. This satisfies a sort of physical need to rinse one's palate. The thirst one feels after a dish flavored with a lot of garlic, salt, or spices has been called a rinsing thirst. The fiery sensation of pepper, and even more that of chilies, which goes on getting stronger after the initial contact until it actually becomes painful, is assuaged immediately, albeit temporarily, by a mouthful of liquid. This is the real sense of quenching thirst. It is not a true thirst which is being quenched, but drinking refreshes and relieves the burning on the mucous lining of the mouth. There are foods which prompt one to drink, a fact well known to drinkers.

Similarly, one feels a need to drink, as though to cleanse the palate, after an unpleasant, bitter, or astringent flavor. Thirst is a physical pleasure very close to the pleasant sensation of touching a liquid and of the same order as washing or taking a bath. In addition to the pleasure of refreshing the mucous lining of the mouth and throat, there is the pleasant sensation of swallowing, of liquid flowing into the body—and there are also the delights of flavor and aroma. This gourmet thirst does not prompt one to drink just any liquid, it requires taste sensations. There are times when one very much wants to drink, not any old drink though—not plain water, for example—but a more attractive drink; and then one will not drink unless one can satisfy this desire.

This somewhat artificial, physiologically useless thirst, is acquired as a result of inclination and habit. It responds more to a desire for pleasure than to any natural need. And wine, it must be admitted, belongs to this "luxury" thirst category, for by itself wine cannot satisfy our daily physiological water needs, at least not without some danger.

The calculation is simple. Man needs to drink as many milliliters of water as he burns up calories, that is, two or three thousand a day. He can reckon to find half of this in his food, and he makes up the rest with drinks. However, he cannot be expected to consume two bottles of wine every day, some 120 to 140 grams of alcohol.

Besides, above a certain strength, alcoholic drinks do not really satisfy one's thirst; it is as though drinking them actually increases the need for water since alcohol is a diuretic. If, in place of pure water, rats are given free access to water mixed with alcohol, they regularly drink a greater quantity, no doubt because they like the taste of alcohol but also because their need for water is greater. Alcohol fuels the fire it is supposed to quench. Thus the inveterate drinker cultivates a constant and inextinguishable thirst; "the drinks he takes to slake his thirst have the inevitable effect of reviving it."

The real point of wine is to satisfy the thirst that comes with eating. This is how it is drunk by those working in the vineyards; during mealtimes, as an accompaniment to food, an additional flavoring, a liquid condiment. Wine is not drunk out of necessity but to give satisfaction. It is the indispensable complement to all good fare; I would even go so far as to say, though I am biased, of course, that without the taste of wine there is no true gastronomy. Fine wines were created to be drunk with food. The fresh acidity of white wines and the tannic character of reds, their aromas and bouquets, all harmonize with and enhance the flavor of the dishes they accompany. Tasting wine at table accentuates and heightens the combined pleasure of eating and drinking.

The use of wine to satisfy a gourmet thirst is, however, quite acceptable, indeed to be encouraged. Certain wines were devised with this in mind: sparkling wines, sweet wines, dessert wines, fortified wines. And there are also wines which are drunk without food, at any time, on any occasion. This is why the Anglo-Saxons, among others, prefer light wines; wines which are supple, off dry, easy to drink. The new vogue is for aperitif wines which whet the palate and appetite just as effectively as more complicated preparations.

SERVING WINE: UNCORKING THE BOTTLE

It is a pity that Anatole France did not leave us a complete set of Father Jerome Coignard's memoirs; he was someone who not only understood the art of drinking well but who also knew how to talk about it. Did he not once say, having emptied his glass: "This wine spreads a warm and healthy glow throughout the human frame"? One of his stories deals with opening bottles and flagons. ("What is the difference between a bottle and a flagon? Considerable: a bottle is sealed with a cork and a flagon with a screw top." So wrote Rabelais long before the invention of the crown cap.) Jerome Coignard wonders, "Which was invented first, the cork or the corkscrew?" It could not have been the corkscrew; who could have dreamt up the idea of a corkscrew without the prior existence of a cork? However, how could the first bottle have been uncorked if the corkscrew had not already been invented? Father Jerome concludes that cork and corkscrew must have been invented at the same time by the same inspired person.

Having made this historical point, how do we open a bottle and serve a wine at its best today? When you get down to detail nothing is more complicated than these simple operations. Everything has already been said on the subject and to repeat it is necessarily to confirm the opinions of some and to reject those of others. We all agree on certain points: If a bottle which has been lying in a rack shows no signs of deposit on the lower side or in the neck when it is stood upright, then there is no need for any prior preparation of the bottle, whatever its vintage. It is brought to the desired temperature, uncorked, and served immediately. If, on the other hand, generally because of its age, the bottle has a deposit, a trail of colored matter, a lozenge of sediment in the shoulder, an accumulation of tartrates at the bottom, then it should be stood upright without being shaken and left to stand for twenty-four (or better still forty-eight) hours before being served. In this way its deposit will slide down the side of the bottle without clouding the wine.

Everyone thinks they know how to open a bottle. You begin by removing the upper part of the capsule, cutting it off with a knife *below* the collar so as to reveal the top of the cork. This is often the least presentable part, the weak point in the "cork-capsule" system. What happens is that putting on the capsule at a later date shuts in tufts of mold that have developed on the cork while in the cellars. The surface of the cork thus smells of fungus or shows signs of acetic moisture. Even worse is that the end of the cork is sometimes attacked by tiny woodworms which bore holes in it. The places where the bottles are stocked may be infested with tiny members of the moth family which, like clothes moths in the home, deposit their eggs on the surfaces of wet corks. One can get rid of them by a judicious use of aerosol insecticides, and their depredations can be avoided by using temporary plastic capsules. When capsuling follows immediately after corking, it also sometimes happens that, as a result of expansion, the wine sweats between the cork and the neck of the bottle and it can then attack and corrode the capsule. In such cases this area should be carefully wiped with a clean cloth or paper tissue *even before the cork is withdrawn* to remove the whitish traces of lead salts sticking to the lip of the bottle; in this way much less will fall into the glass of the first to be served.

At this point the corkscrew comes into play. There are numerous types, few of which are practical. The fault lies mostly in the form of the spiral which is badly designed for the task; it has a pitch which is too small, or edges which cut like a drill, or else it is too thin and bends and stretches out of shape when used. Few are designed to extract long (5.5 centimeter) corks and, being too short, they break the corks and only remove the top part.

The standard manual T-bar corkscrew is best left in its drawer as an athletic method of extraction, since a pulling power of up to 40 kilograms may be required to make the cork yield! This would be an extreme example, of course (a dry cork, unparaffined, stuck to the glass), but everyone has had the experience of struggling with a cork that remains recalcitrant even when pierced right through. These types of corkscrew have only one advantage: By creating a sudden vacuum in the neck of the bottle, they make an attractive implosive pop as the cork is pulled out. There are also lozenge-shaped concertina corkscrews which reduce the effort of removing the cork. Avoid the gadget with a hollow needle and carbon dioxide under pressure; it is brutal, explosive, and stirs up the wine and its deposit. I must confess that I have never succeeded in using the device with two parallel blades which is inserted between the cork and bottle, and which is twisted to extract the cork. However, there are cellarmen with sufficient skill to extract the corks with it, unpierced, with their markings intact and ready to be used again.

For preference choose a lever corkscrew; there are simple versions in the form of a pocket knife, or more complicated ones with two levers and a double spindle. Even better, use a corkscrew with a screw mechanism. One I know of is telescopic with a double screw mechanism, a hollow tube rotating around a spindle whose thread reduces the effort. I used to own a very efficient wooden model, but at present I use a precision tool, in stainless steel, solid yet gentle and easy to use, which no cork can resist.

After many years' contact with the wine, the cork loses its impermeable cellular texture and moisture from the wine penetrates it progressively. The cork then seals the bottle less effectively and tends to disintegrate when a corkscrew is used on it; sometimes it even has to be withdrawn in bits and pieces. To avoid the inconvenience of this, it is advisable to change the corks of old bottles after twenty years or so. The collections of old vintages in Bordeaux châteaux are periodically recorked in this way. White wines, in particular sweet white wines, attack corks more than red wines do. The latter, on the other hand, clog the section of cork with which they are in contact and color it a reddish brown. This deposit is known as the *velours du bouchon* (cork velvet); it is made up of colored tannins which, in the case of richly constituted wines, felt the end or "mirror" of the cork. Learn to read the cork drawn from a bottle; it is full of information. A deeply colored mirror indicates an old, full-bodied, tannic wine; if the wine has not stained the cork, it is young or light in constitution.

Did you know that very old vintage port is not opened with a corkscrew? The French (and many others apart from the English) know nothing of these sublime bottles. They are made in the best years and sold under their brand name and vintage date. In contrast to standard port, these wines spend little time in wooden casks; their aging takes place out of contact with oxygen. They keep all their fruit in bottle and they are examples of rare longevity. Beneath their wax seals or lead capsules the cork is practically decomposed by the alcohol. The neck of the bottle is snapped with the help of a pair of special tongs which are first heated on an open flame; they are then simply applied to the neck of the bottle in order to obtain a clean break. The bottle is then decanted.

Champagne bottles are opened by hand, of course. The foil capsule is removed, followed by the wire muzzle, and the bottle is held in a tilted position and gently turned. The cork is eased with the thumb and forefinger to help it yield to the twisting movement, and it is held onto in order to prevent it flying out under the pressure. The *mousse* will not overflow if the bottle is kept tilted. If the cork sticks a pair of special flat champagne pliers can be used to help; they are part of every professional's tool kit. The shape retained by the cork indicates how long it is since the champagne was "disgorged" and received its *dosage*. If the cork is still elastic and resumes its original shape, this means it was bottled very recently. After six months to a year the cork loses its elasticity, it stays compressed, and resembles a straight-sided plug. The bottle's history is inscribed in the cork.

One question always arises when discussing the serving of wines: Should the bottles be opened well in advance as is recommended by some, or just before being served, as this is the simplest and seems the most logical? The wine merchant Chaudet voices a widespread opinion without, however, justifying it: "How far in advance to open a bottle before serving is essentially a question of how old the bottle is. For wines that are five or six years old, opening them half an hour before drinking is quite enough. For very old bottles of some twenty-five or thirty years, one should reckon on two or three hours at least."

I do not know the precise origin of this advice. Perhaps it is thought that cooling or warming are more effective when the bottle is open? Perhaps this procedure was justified at a time when technical knowledge was limited, when the wines continued to ferment to some extent in bottle and so formed a little carbon dioxide? Perhaps again they were the consequence of Pasteur's misunderstanding of the direct role of oxygen in the aging of wine, so that, having been confined in the bottle for so long, wine was seen as finally being able to breathe when the cork was drawn? The practice is all the more remarkable because usually a bottle opened in advance is immediately restoppered with it own cork, and it will just be a matter of luck that the cork has not been turned around so that the outer end, always a bit dirty, is pushed back into the bottle!

In reality, *it makes no difference whatsoever whether a bottle has been opened three hours before being served or a few moments before.* In these conditions nothing happens physically or chemically in two to three hours. There can be no evaporation and oxidation is infinitesimal. The amount of oxygen which penetrates the wine under these circumstances is barely measurable: It is about a tenth of a milligram per liter. Just how negligible this is can be judged from the fact that twice as much is dissolved in the wine as it is poured into the glass, and more than three times as much after fifteen minutes.

Thus there is only one sensible way to go about opening a bottle: just before sitting down at table or just before drinking the wine. This enables the host to check the wines he is offering or the wine waiter to open the bottle in front of the guests, both of which seem to me to be a minimum courtesy.

WHEN TO DECANT

Decanting is an operation which consists of separating the clear wine from the lees it has formed and is a very old practice. In the past it was certainly indispensable. I can remember the time, between the wars, when all wines threw an abundant deposit because methods of clarification were not as advanced as they are now. In the *chais* they used to say that there was something both to eat and to drink at the bottom of the bottle. Certain red wines would stain the bottle glass with a clinging layer of tannin, while white wines contained flakes, floating particles, "fliers" or "beeswing," and traces of fine brown sediment. Such bottles could not be served without being decanted.

How to prevent deposits was not known at the time so it was left to the consumer to separate them from the wine. This gave birth to a rite which still exists even if, in the absence of any sediment, it no longer serves a purpose. The phenomenon is akin to habit replacing reason or the letter of the law replacing its spirit. However, the idea has been taken further: I know one producer who vinifies in the old-fashioned traditional way, old fashioned in the worst sense to be sure; and who, to placate his dissatisfied and complaining customers, has had to put a label on the back of the bottles to try and persuade them that there were good reasons for the presence of sediment in young bottles. The ruse fools only the ignorant.

From the numerous investigations conducted periodically by newspapers and trade magazines, it would seem that there is considerable confusion in the minds of professionals, restaurateurs, wine waiters, and wine lovers over the subject of decanting. I would like to try and clarify this complicated situation, to outline several rules, and to rationalize the matter in terms of the science of oenology.

The formation of deposit is a natural phenomenon for red wines; it is one of the signs of aging in color and of the slow flocculation of colloidal matter. It is therefore quite normal for a red wine to throw a deposit after four or five years, for example, when it is tannic, and this cannot be completely avoided. However, sediment is unacceptable in a younger red or in a white wine.

It is a fact that if the deposit is mixed up with the wine, or poured into the last glasses served, then, however natural the deposit, it will give it a poor taste. Anyone can confirm this by trying. The smallest of particles in suspension can be felt by the tongue; they change the wine's structure, lessen the aroma in the mouth, and make a red wine rough and bitter. Thus the first rule of decanting would appear simple to remember: **Only bottles which have a deposit need to be decanted**, whatever the nature of the deposit and whatever the age of the bottle. Consequently, a bottle which has no deposit can be served immediately.

That is one point settled. However, matters become more complicated when one moves on to consider the effects of exposure to air, the slight dissolving of oxygen which inevitably accompanies decanting, and how these effects are interpreted. For some, aeration is always beneficial and necessary. According to them, the bouquet of old wines, hermetically sealed inside the bottles by the cork, is liberated and develops as a result of contact with air. Such people do not hesitate to decant all wines, well in advance, simply in order to let them aerate. Allowing a wine to breathe when it comes out of its bottle is a recommendation which is generally well received. One day the *sommelier* at the Auberge Saint-Vincent had just served a 1969 Monthélie with the usual skill and care, even adding a little something extra: He took the glasses of wine and one by one he rolled them round and round in the palm of his hand for at least twenty seconds. Intrigued by this operation, I asked him why he did it. "It is to lower the acidity of the wine and bring out its bouquet," he replied. There may be something to be said for the second reason, but air has never reduced greenness in a wine! Besides, in spite of the roundness of his gestures the wine itself remained hard, as is sometimes the case in this appellation.

For others, aeration is always harmful, and, if prolonged, affects the intensity and finesse of the bouquet. These people are prejudiced against ever decanting, however much sediment there may be. I know some people who pour very skillfully directly from the bottle into the glasses, filling them from a single pouring action, but at the risk of wasting ten to fifteen centiliters of wine.

Such clear-cut views are difficult to justify. They are based on limited experience and ill-considered generalizations. These are empirical positions which confuse the factors involved and ignore the relevant circumstances. I am more interested in opinions which are somewhat more flexible. Let us consider those who alter their method of decanting according to age and origin of the wine.

"Generally speaking very old bottles should be tasted immediately after the cork has been drawn.... Very young wines have nothing to gain by being left in a decanter. The length of time t of aeration before drinking, according to the wine's age, can be represented by a bell-shaped graph." This is an interesting and original idea, but the advice is imprecise and I doubt whether the graph used to illustrate the argument is of much help in solving our problems. Other views suggest that it is inappropriate to handle clarets and burgundies in the same way: "If prolonged, the oxidation due to decanting is harmful to burgundies but beneficial to clarets, enabling them to show at their best. Consequently burgundy is decanted just before being served and only if it contains a deposit. Claret should always be decanted one or two hours before drinking." Obviously, the responsibility for these comments is that of their authors, not mine.

I have carried out dozens of controlled decanting experiments on wines of all ages and all origins. The wines were either handled under inert gas so as to avoid any influence from oxygen, or, alternatively, I varied the amount of dissolved oxygen and the length of contact with air. The resulting conclusions are those given in our *Traité d'Oenologie:* "It is definitely incorrect to decant old wines (wherever they come from) several hours before they are drunk because, following even a light aeration, their bouquet, fruit of the reduction process slowly achieved in the absence of air, weakens with varying rapidity, depending on the wine." Edouard Kressmann, who combines tradition and experience, does as I do; he always decants at the last moment, all the more so where old wines are concerned as they are "more delicate and sensitive than their younger counterparts." I have come across wines within an ace of senility which were nonetheless very drinkable, but which could not stand being decanted and which turned to vinegar in the decanter.

J. R. Garrigo, an American wine lover, has carried out many experiments himself and has arrived at the same conclusions. He states that outstanding wines, very good wines of reserve quality, and varietal wines (appearing in California under the name Cabernet Sauvignon or Zinfandel, for example) lose bouquet, body, and personality when decanted a couple of hours in advance. The wine softens and loses the character acquired through aging. On the other hand, wines with faults on the nose or which have certain foreign tastes are improved by contact with air. This observation tallies with that of numerous impartial observers. He quotes the opinion of one cellarmaster which I find very sensible: "Uncorking and decanting one or two hours in advance serves only to dissipate eventual faults; there is no justification for airing quality wines." I have already written: "Prior aeration can only be considered acceptable in the case of wines which have become slightly gassy in bottle as a result of a trace of fermentation. In these cases their bouquet, which has become spoilt, as though suffocated, may develop and become finer after decanting and aerating. There are also wines which smell a bit too **reduced**, which may improve with aeration."

The following recent experience is worth recounting. The bottles of the 1962 Médoc Cru had been standing on the sideboard since the previous day, and Madame B, who had invited people for lunch, had, as it were, beaten her husband to it in preparing the wines. Toward ten o'clock they had been decanted into carafes: "One thing less to do—if you wait until the last moment when the guests have arrived, there is no time to do it properly." While enjoying this fine '62 at table, the guests began to discuss methods of decanting, and everyone praised the virtues of letting wines breathe. I took the opposite view to that generally expressed, and surprised everyone by explaining the harmful effect of air in this operation and how detrimental a sojourn of several hours in a decanter was to the bouquet, as was the case with the wine we were drinking. Those present applauded this oenological paradox but did not believe a word of it. Now there were still some unopened bottles on the sideboard. At my request they were opened, carefully poured into fresh glasses, and one could compare the wine as it had been before decanting and as it had become over a period of almost four hours. The strong, estery bouquet of the undecanted wine filled the glasses with a floral, truffle-like refinement, while the other appeared totally faded by comparison. On the palate the undecanted wine was livelier, fresher, less thick but also less fleshy. Everyone agreed that decanting had made the wine lose finesse and elegance though it had made it seem fuller. It had made a lively and refined wine seem rather common and lackluster.

Two last rules suffice to guard against any mistakes in decanting. First: **If it *is* necessary to decant, it should be done at the last moment, just before sitting down or just before serving, *never* in advance.** Finally (in exceptional cases): **Only wines suffering from some fault (for example, a lack of cleanness on the nose, the presence of some gas, a little thinness in constitution) warrant decanting sufficiently in advance to allow for plenty of contact with air.**

How Should One Decant?

It was Jean Bouteiller, one of the luminaries of the Bordeaux region, who introduced me to the wines of the Médoc. It was he who, at the end of the 1940s, introduced me as more than just a visitor to cellars which were very difficult to get into. There, by word of mouth, I learnt the secrets of vinification; and I discovered besides, that they were the same from one property to the next, that they were not in fact secrets at all.

The first time I lunched in the huge dining room at his Scottish-style château he asked me before the meal: "Do you prefer Médocs young or old?" "Old . . . of course. . . ." Used to working in a *négociant*'s, any wine older than three or four years was old for me. He felt that I had not quite understood the sense of his question and he clarified it: "When I say old Médocs, obviously I mean those from the last century. If I say young, they would be vintages of this century, but nevertheless before 1920." He realized that my education was still to come and decanted in front of me a bottle as old as my grandfather. Since its birth it had lain on the slats in a bin and, along with its neighbors, had become covered in the same "impalpable black fur" of *Cladosporium cellare*. My host grasped it gently and carried it horizontally to the decanting table in the same way as one would carry a spirit level without moving the bubble. The decanting table was a little bench furnished with a cradle into which he put the bottle without jarring it. He lit a candle, skillfully drew the cork, rinsed the decanter with several centiliters of wine, and decanted the bottle. These memories of Jean Bouteiller officiating in the play of light and dark in his cellar were awakened recently by reading the following words of Edouard Kressmann: "Decanting my wine at the last minute, I keep the bottle in the position in which it has slumbered for so long and I decant as much brilliant wine as possible. . . . Decanting should be done gently: pour slowly, hold the decanter at an angle so that the liquid runs down the insides instead of tumbling in a stream to strike the bottom, which would tire the wine. Watch the clarity across the shoulders of the bottle and, as soon as sediment gathers and begins to be drawn into the clear wine, bring the bottle back up quickly so as to hold it back." This is called decanting on the spot. We have seen that the bottle can also be stood up several days in advance and decanted in the room where it is going to be drunk. Without question a crystal decanter sets off the wine that it contains, and yet, deprived of its label and identity, even the best of wines attracts less interest and retreats into anonymity. I realize that the branded cork can be hung across the shoulders of the decanter with the little chain designed for this purpose, but some people prefer to present a wine in its own labeled bottle and so decant the wine back into its original bottle after emptying it of its lees and then rinsing it well. While this is not necessarily prejudicial, the practice effects a double aeration nonetheless. Professionals use a decanter only when tasting blind at table.

There are one-and-a-half-liter decanters for decanting magnums. With larger bottles, right up to imperials which contain eight bottles (about six liters), and which one only ever sees at banquets, the wine is poured back into the original container after having been decanted.

There is even a machine which has been designed for decanting six bottles, or more, at once. It is not a simple gadget, I have seen it being used in a cellar. After uncorking, the bottles are locked in position at a gentle angle, neck uppermost. A geared ratchet system with a crank means the bottles can be tilted very slowly. As the wine begins to flow into the receptacles below, the bottles are tilted more rapidly. They are lit from below by spotlights which enable one to follow the movement of the sediment. The flow of wine is stopped by reversing the mechanism before the deposit escapes. The receiving bottles may be filled with inert gas beforehand in order to avoid oxidation.

The siphon method has more to recommend it. I often use it in my tasting room. The bottle is placed upright against a well-lit background so as to make the deposit visible around the punt. The wine is decanted practically without aeration with the aid of a transparent glass and plastic siphon whose transfer tube reaches right to the bottom of the receiving bottle, and the flow is stopped by a glass tap before it sucks up the first impurities. Siphoning is an old method. Among the little cellar accessories that were produced a century ago, one finds thin copper siphons designed for the same purpose. I have come across them in secondhand shops, but they are not to be recommended, as the wine attacks the copper.

Traditional burgundy houses decant old bottles before shipping them, not by transferring the wine but by sucking up the sediment concentrated in the bottom of the bottle. This method has the great advantage of not aerating the wine and thus causing the minimum damage. Here again the implement is a siphon with a tap. The extremity of the tube is moved all along the groove around the bottom of the bottle and the deposit is removed by suction. Only a few centiliters of wine are lost and the bottle can then be topped up and recorked.

I have a great admiration for the inventors of these highly refined techniques without which the finest bottles could not be served to perfection. They illustrate the importance of the final preparation of wine, right up to its being poured into the glass, the last obstacle to cross before the pleasure of consumption.

The Art of Bringing Wine to the Right Temperature

The right temperature in this case is the right temperature for drinking a wine. In some cases this will mean cooling the wine, in others warming it, what the French call *chambrer*. To chill a wine, on the other hand, would be to bring it down to a temperature below 8°C, something not to be recommended, any more than warming a wine until it is tepid or above 20°C.

These days to *chambrer* wines no longer means bringing them to the ambient temperature, for this is often above 20°C. The appeal of even the best wine cannot withstand such a test; 18°C is a maximum which should rarely be exceeded.

The art of serving wines at the correct temperature demands great precision and a technique that is by no means easy. With the means available at present it is perhaps easier to cool a wine to the exact degree than to warm it.

The prudent advise raising or lowering the temperature very gradually. There is the well-known story of the meticulous wine lover who brought his bottle from cellar to dining room literally step by step from Friday to Sunday! Artificial means are considered brutal, no doubt because they exceed the limits of what is desired. Ideally, the bottle would be placed in surroundings of the recommended temperature for several hours, but during the various seasons the chances of having a room at 16°C to 18°C for a red wine, or an external temperature of 8°C to 12°C for a white wine are slim. All things considered, it would be better to bring a wine rapidly to 16°C to 18°C, than to bring it carefully to a fatal 22°C.

Gyllensköld, a Swedish architect, has provided a rational solution to the problems posed by the art of serving wine at the correct temperature. He has determined by experiment the development of temperature in 75-cl bottles which have been warmed in ambient air, in hot air, in warm water, and in hot water. The curves and diagrams that he has drawn enable one to calculate the exact time required to bring a wine to whatever temperature may be desired.

Heating a bottle in hot water or in the hot air of an oven, close to a stove, on a radiator, or in front of a fire is not advisable, because part of the wine will exceed the required temperature; it will be overheated.

Rapidly changing the temperature of a standing bottle produces marked differences in temperature between the top and the bottom; the top becomes warmer, as though it alone had been heated.

Warming in the ambient temperature is the best solution but it needs a lot of time; on the other hand, warming in water adjusted to a temperature close to that required gives good results much more quickly; the disadvantage is the moisture and the possibility of the label coming unstuck.

The latest fashion is to warm a bottle in a microwave oven. Generated by high-frequency currents, the microwaves produce heat within the body of a solid or liquid, and 25 seconds is enough to warm a bottle from 10°C to 18°C, evenly and without any hot spots.

A fairly common misconception is to think that a bottle cannot be warmed or cooled unless it is uncorked. The changes in temperature are thought to take place solely via the small surface area of wine in the neck, whereas they obviously occur via the glass, in spite of its low thermal conductivity, and they occur at the same rate whether the bottle is capsuled or not, corked or uncorked.

If a bottle of old wine has a deposit and needs to be decanted, it should be warmed to the appropriate temperature in advance, standing up. It could also be stood up in advance in the cooler temperature of the cellar.

As for cooling a bottle, there has been a lot of discussion as to the relative advantages and disadvantages of the ice bucket, a brief period in the freezer, or a longer one in the refrigerator. Careful experiments show that with the same bottles of white wine or champagne, providing they are within a degree of the same temperature, there is no significant difference in taste between these three methods. The ice bucket is prompt and practical, but the upper layer of wine in the part of the bottle out of the iced liquid needs to be mixed with the colder layers lower down; otherwise the first glass served, that of a guest, will not have been cooled. In the refrigerator it is best to lay the bottle down so as to avoid any unevenness in temperature. The practice of chilling the glasses alone (as is sometimes done for eaux de vie) generally produces an unsatisfactory result in the case of wine, because of the amount that is normally poured into a wineglass.

It is not as absurd as it may seem to consider cooling a red wine that is too warm (some bottles are displayed in restaurants at criminal temperatures) by the same methods, or, alternatively, by wrapping the bottle in a wet cloth in advance. The *sommelier* should look upon such an eccentric request from clients as a reprimand. In summer, red wines to be drunk at "cellar temperature" (14°C) will benefit from being placed in a bucket of cold water during the meal. In addition, it is interesting to know the change in temperature that takes place as soon as a wine is poured into the glass. If a red wine is poured at 18°C into a glass at the ambient temperature of 23°C, a thermometer dipped into the wine will read 19°C almost immediately. A white wine, cooled to 8°C and served in the same conditions, would similarly read 11°C. This should be taken into account as part of the difficult art of serving wines at the ideal temperature.

MATCHING WINE TO FOOD

To enable the wines one is serving to be shown at their best, there are certain rules one needs to know. Knowing which wine to serve with which dish is part of the art of eating and drinking.

A mistake in this area is an error of taste, a blunder that good wine does not deserve. Much has been written on this inexhaustible subject and I would direct the reader to the numerous lists of gastronomic combinations which can be found in cook books and wine guides. Besides, as an oenologist I would be venturing somewhat outside my field. What interests me here is to discover, leaving aside personal preferences and habits, and God knows they are certainly varied, the rationale which underlies the established conventions.

It is easy enough to understand that during the course of a meal we instinctively look for a certain harmony between the tastes of what we are eating and of what we are drinking. These alternating and overlapping taste impressions should neither clash with nor dominate each other; they should go well together, match, and, if possible, set each other off. The harmony between them should be based on their intensity, their character, and their quality. A richly flavored drink would not go well with something neutral. Conversely, an insipid drink cuts short the pleasure of a flavorsome dish. Only in the case of too highly flavored dishes might simple, cool drinks be preferred, drinks which would quench the thirst that such food gives rise to.

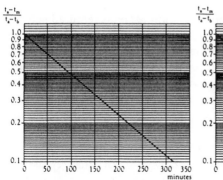
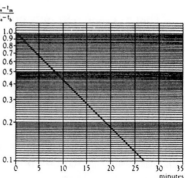

Diagram 1 relates to changing a bottle's temperature in still air, that is, bringing it to room temperature inside the room, or chilling it in a refrigerator (after Gyllensköld).

t_a = ambient air temperature
t_m = the desired temperature for the wine
t_b = the wine's initial temperature

Example 1: The dining room temperature is 22°C, that of the cellar 16°C; the desired temperature is 19°C.

$$\frac{t_a - t_m}{t_a - t_b} = \frac{22 - 19}{22 - 16} = \frac{3}{6} = 0.5$$

The graph shows that it would take 95 minutes for the wine to reach 19°C in the bottle.

Example 2: The wine is warmed by placing the bottle outside on a hot summer's day in a temperature of 30°C. The bottle comes from the cellar at 10°C and the desired temperature is 18°C.

$$\frac{t_a - t_m}{t_a - t_b} = \frac{30 - 18}{30 - 10} = \frac{12}{20} = 0.6$$

In these conditions the calculation and graph show that the time required to reach 18°C would be 70 minutes.

Example 3: A bottle of white wine at 23°C is put into a refrigerator at 4°C, and the desired temperature for the wine is 10°C.

$$\frac{t_a - t_m}{t_a - t_b} = \frac{4 - 10}{4 - 23} = \frac{-6}{-19} = 0.316$$

In this case the time needed would be 155 minutes. The required time for half bottles and magnums can be calculated by multiplying the calculation results by 0.75 and 1.5, respectively.

Diagram 2 relates to a bottle being warmed in water or chilled in a bucket of ice and water (after Gyllensköld).

t_a = water temperature
t_m = desired temperature for the wine
t_b = the wine's initial temperature

Example 1: A bottle of red wine at 13°C is placed in a bucket of water at 22°C, the desired temperature is 17°C.

$$\frac{t_a - t_m}{t_a - t_b} = \frac{22 - 17}{22 - 13} = \frac{5}{9} = 0.56$$

Calculation and graph show that 7 minutes would be long enough here.

Example 2: A bottle of white wine at 18°C is placed in a bucket of iced water at 4°C; the desired temperature is 12°C. In this case 8 minutes would be needed.

$$\frac{t_a - t_m}{t_a - t_b} = \frac{4 - 12}{4 - 18} = \frac{-8}{-16} = 0.5$$

That a certain harmony of aromas and tastes is required between solid and liquid goes without saying; it is offensive to see really good cuisine accompanied by mass-produced flavored drinks. There is also a quality relationship to be observed. A heavy, rustic style of cooking calls for a thirst-quenching drink on the same level; a fine wine in this case would be unwelcome and would not show well. A carefully prepared and delicate dish would similarly be ruined if accompanied by a coarse wine.

On analyzing the basic principles underlying this harmony, they can be seen to depend on one of three conditions: analogy, association, and unity of sensory qualities. The appeal may, however, lie as much in complement as in contrast. Thus certain chefs or writers take the opposite view as to what is considered normal, often out of a desire to be original or else out of a horror of the conventional. When this is just a question of a pleasing fantasy in a context where something too strict or formal would be unsuitable, then I would be the first to applaud the occasional audacity. One can always try something once. However, one should remember that repeated extravagances rapidly border on bad taste.

Thanks to the astonishing diversity of wine styles, one can always be sure of finding one (even several) that will go with a given dish, with a few exceptions. Vinegar is the best known of these, even sherry vinegar: It spoils the wine, and salads with salad dressings should also be avoided, at least when tasting if not from a dietary point of view. Nor are the little cube of gruyère and a fresh green walnut enough to make an exception. Also to be avoided are chocolate desserts, chocolate mousse above all, and ices, all of them.

There are both psychological and physiological reasons for allotting white wines their particular place in our meals. In my view, the qualities which make white wines appreciated as an accompaniment are the following: their pale color, their grapy aroma, their light and thirst-quenching flavor, their fresh acidity, their sweetness if they contain sugar, and, finally, the fact that they are drunk cold. The way we drink them derives from these properties. Besides, many of them, those that are the most supple and the most aromatic, can be drunk by themselves and have no need of any food to go with them.

Only those who ignore the role that color plays in the appeal of food will be surprised that, in general, white wines go best with dishes that have little color: white flesh (meat, offal, fish, or poultry), white or yellow sauces.

The association of colors prepares one for an association of tastes. In addition, their fruity aromatic qualities, their lightness of constitution, and their fluidity mean that they are better suited to the finest dishes, less so to strongly flavored food. However, white wines are known above all as the best partners for seafood. Their flavor both masks the saltiness as well as being heightened by it. White wines are nicely described as "shellfish wines," crustacea wines," and "fish wines" in order of their constitution from firmest to fleshiest, youngest to oldest, and driest to softest. Who has not noticed the successful combinations of Muscadet Sèvre-et-Maine or Entre-Deux-Mers with a dozen oysters, a glass of *amontillado* with langoustines from Sanlucar de Barrameda, Laville Haut-Brion or Bâtard Montrachet with *sole meunière*? The thirst-quenching properties of white wines are also put to good use when drunk with certain spicy specialties or cold meats, with cooked green vegetables, full-fat cheese, and goat's cheese.

In matters of taste it would be wrong to be categorical. In the previous paragraph dry white wines could be replaced by rosé wines, or even, I admit, though their color annoys me, by light red wines, young wines with little tannin, that is, providing they are drunk cold enough.

White wines have another dimension which one needs to know how to exploit, and which tends to be neglected today, in France at least: They also exist in medium-dry, sweet, and dessert (*liquoreux*) versions. Many people either do not know of this range of sweet partners, or forget about them when planning a menu or reading a wine list. Moderately sweet and sweet white wines go well with all gently flavored dishes: with chicken vol-au-vents, sweetbreads, quenelles, béchamel sauces, fine fish and poultry dishes, blue cheeses among others. Only an old dessert wine (Barsac, Banyuls, Maury) can stand up to a sweet-and-sour dish, to duck with orange or cherries. Everybody knows the combination of Sauternes and foie gras served as an entrée, a perfect marriage and the high point of a meal. Less often seen is the combination of a dessert wine with blue cheese or other strong cheeses, and yet this makes for a remarkable harmony of contrasts; the wine's silky sweetness is a perfect foil to the intense flavors of the cheese, and it softens their piquancy in a way that a dry white cannot.

The rich constitution of red wines and their complexity of taste make them a more appropriate accompaniment for heavier food with stronger flavors. Their dark color already blends with that of red meat, gravies, and wine sauces; but it is their particular tannic flavor, bitter and astringent at once, which is the determining factor. It also means that the wines can be divided into two categories which are used differently: light red wines (with a tannin index of around 30 to 35 in oenological terms) and full-bodied reds (with a tannin index of around 40 to 50). The tannin reacts with the proteins found in meats and their juices, in the saliva provoked by chewing them, in sauce bases, and hard or semi-hard cheeses. Their nitrogenous content also masks the bitterness of tannin. A wine's taste is enhanced by food. A fine red wine only really shows at its best with appropriate food. One sometimes hears that such and such a wine tasted better or less well three months ago, for example, and one tends to forget that the difference is often due to the food being eaten with it.

Very old or light red wines should be drunk with young meat such as veal or lamb, with poultry or small game birds. Tannic wines in vigorous middle age or, as Jacquelin says, which are very aromatic on the palate, can stand up to red meat such as beef or mutton, and the dark meat of game, wood pigeon, and woodcock. Their bouquet of fruit, truffles, and aromatic spices goes well with this type of food, whereas it clashes with the odors of fish. Only where a dish is prepared in red wine, as in the case of fish stew, Bordeaux-style lampreys, or the *nouvelle cuisine* sea bass stew, can one serve a young and fleshy red wine (the wine used for the sauce, a purist would say). Likewise the tannin in red wine means that it should not be drunk with food that is salty or sweet as both these flavors make it appear even harder and more bitter.

During the course of a meal one's sensory sensitivity diminishes, the senses become progressively dulled, whence the need, if one is offering several wines, to serve them in a flavor-based progression. The rule is to start with the lightest or the youngest and finish with the most full bodied, that with the finest bouquet or the most prestigious. Therefore, one would begin with the white wines and finish with the richest reds. Another useful rule is to avoid competition between wines of the same type and the same quality level. Nor should one start too high, serving the best wine too early; a fine wine is better preceded by one which will set it off by comparison. Finally, and contrary to normal practice, with each change of course I suggest waiting until the food has been served before pouring the wine. This seems important to me, for it enables guests to eat before tasting the wine, and therefore to be in a better position to judge it.

The greater the wine, the more its service demands care and ritual. A simple wine is drunk simply, but when a great vintage is served, the guests should have been given some discreet hint of its coming. In this lies the whole art of serving wine, so that the guests will wonder why the wines seemed so wonderfully harmonious on that particular evening.

ON THE PROPER USE OF WINE

I have borrowed this heading from a paper produced by the Vin et Nutrition group, led by Jean Trémolières when he was director of the Laboratoire de Nutrition humaine à l'Institut national de la Santé et de la Recherche médicale (Human Nutrition Laboratory at the National Institute of Health and Medical Research). I would like to have been a student of his; he understood wine better than the wine specialists.

Everyone who has studied the history of alcoholic drinks agrees on the universality of their production, once, that is, a society has reached a certain technical level and progressed from an economy based on gathering food to one based on culture of the soil and the processing of natural products. Before this stage man either smoked, chewed, or infused vegetable substances which had stimulant, narcotic, or dream-inducing effects. This constant search for calming or hallucinatory substances suggests that they meet a need and perform a social function common to mankind regardless of time or place.

Most ancient societies showed a very lively attraction to fermented drinks. The fermented product is often in a more stable form for keeping, but storing fruit- or grain-based food in this form was not the point. Nor was its appeal based solely on flavor; indeed, one sometimes had to accustom oneself to this; its attraction lay in a search for intense pleasure linked to the sensations of exaltation, transcendence, and light-headedness brought about by drunkenness and its approach. In a state of alcoholic euphoria man feels a sense of split personality, with the impression of being able to stand outside himself. For these reasons drunkenness had a sacred character for primitive peoples. There were no feasts without drinking, important matters were negotiated cup in hand, and the ability to drink was also proof of virility and valor.

Later, with the advent of monotheism, drunkenness lost its religious associations and a civilization of wine began to develop gradually. Not that habits changed very quickly. In the middle of the eighteenth century Sallengres had no hesitation in writing a panegyric in praise of drunkenness. After all, he said, eulogies had been written in praise of folly, lying, idleness; vice had never lacked for support. All the same, he defined the rules which made drunkenness acceptable to him: No one should be forced to drink and he only approved of those who got drunk occasionally, in good company, with good wine, and without going too far. The drinker of the period drank to forget and there was always something that needed forgetting: grief, insecurity, deception, the injustice of fate, old age and its ills, the drama of man's destiny, death. And then, to drink was to live, he proclaimed: "Alas, it is true then that wine lives longer than man. Let us drink, friends, wine and life are the same thing." Wine has the reputation of promoting wit and good humor, it stimulates and provokes a spirit of repartee: "A man animated by wine is wittier, friendlier, and livelier." The convivial nature of wine is legendary, one cannot drink alone: "Wine and the pleasures of the table are what foster the bonds of friendship." During the same period Jean-Jacques Rousseau wrote about drinkers with a touching indulgence: "Generally speaking they are friendly and sincere; they are almost all good, just, faithful, brave, and honest people." Two hundred years previously Olivier de Serres was wiser and more realistic when he said in talking about wine: "Drunk in small quantity, it stimulates and revives those who are dying from a failing heart; drunk in quantity it drugs and kills the drunkard: on the one hand, becoming an instrument of intemperance for those who dissolutely abuse it, and on the other enlivening the wit of those who use it wisely."

In reality, the art of drinking wisely took a long time to develop and one cannot even pretend that it is particularly widespread today. Instead there is a different form of vanity: that of resisting the drunken state, of being able to hold one's drink, of drinking without adverse effect. It is astonishing to discover this stupid failing in otherwise eminent people.

With a very childish chauvinism, Brillat-Savarin gives the title of "National Victory" to the story of a fight to the finish against two Englishmen, which ends in their defeat by the forces of "claret, port, madeira, punch, and spirits." This was how he gained his reputation as a heavy drinker. Balzac himself, better known as a coffee drinker, boasted that he gave wine no quarter, "whatever quantity my stomach can absorb." He relates with satisfaction that, challenged by one of his friends, he triumphed, if not in very good shape, at the seventeenth bottle and finished the evening off at the Théâtre des Italiens. Even today many consumers say of a good wine: "See how it warms one up." The effect produced by wine is of more interest to them than the pleasure to be had from its taste.

The relationships between man and wine can be divided into three:

1. **The pleasure of the taste sensations** that it produces, and this book has enabled them to be better understood and more easily discovered.
2. **Its physiological, nutritional, and pharmacodynamic effects.** There are not simply those of alcohol; the alcoholic base confers on wine certain unique biological effects: increased tolerance, antiseptic properties, effects on the vascular system. In addition, alcohol is not just a poison. "Today's scientific, economic, and technical society is willfully Manichean in spirit. It needs to classify people and things into 'good' or 'bad,' whence its difficulty with alcohol which is neither one nor the other. On the one hand, they see truth, reason, and good; on the other, passion, folly, and evil. As though everything, ourselves included, were not at one and the same time good and bad, desire and reason. Thus alcohol is at once a choice drink and a dangerous food, a benefit as well as a curse, something which can both discover and destroy a personality." (Trémolières)
3. **Its psychological, social, and cultural value.** Wine, first a drink of the Latin people and then of Christians, remains charged with symbolic value; it appears as a cultural element closely linked with Western civilization.

The words of Trémolières once again, "Contemporary science has established why wine, consumed in sensible quantities (for men not more than half a liter daily, a liter in exceptional circumstances; for women a quarter of a liter less) is a food which may be consumed profitably and without risk to the body. It also calms one down and produces a sense of euphoria, and one day science hopes to be able to explain why. Its toxicity is not in the wine itself but rather in the way it is abused. Alcoholism is thus clearly a problem to do with one's way of life; it is maladjusted behavior attempting to cope with a situation of anxiety. It is the sickness of escapism, flight from both external and internal reality."

The art of drinking, like the art of eating, is thus part of the art of living. More so perhaps because it is easier to abuse drink than food. The limits of one's appetite stop one eating, whereas alcoholic saturation does not always stop the drinker. What makes man drink is first of all the desire for pleasure and it needs a strong will to remain a sensible drinker. If I had to define the art of drinking I would say that it conforms to two rules: moderation and good taste, which can be summed up in two simple formulas: "Drink little, but drink well," or else "Drink little so that you can continue to drink for a long time." It is certainly good wines which will enable one to follow these precepts most easily. They teach self-restraint to whoever wants to listen to their message. It is by tasting wine with care that man can learn to drink in a civilized way.

Bibliography

Amerine M. A., Pangborn R. M., and Roessler E. B., 1965. *Principles of Sensory Evaluation of Food*. Academic Press, New York.

Amerine M. A. and Roessler E. B., 1976. *Wines: Their Sensory Evaluation*. Freeman and Co., San Francisco.

Brillat-Savarin A., 1839. *Physiologie du goût*. Charpentier, Paris.

Broadbent M., 1975. *Wine Tasting*. Christie Wine Pub., London.

Buffin C., 1987. *Le Vin—Pratique de la dégustation* .

Buffin C., 1988. *Le Vin—Votre talent de la dégustation* .

Cadiau P., 1987. *Lexivin/lexiwine*.

Chatelain-Courtois M., 1984. *Les mots du vin et de l'ivresse*. Belin.

Chauchard P., 1970. *Les messages de nos sens*. Collection *Que sais-je?* Presses Universitaires de France, Paris.

Chauvet J., 1950. *L'arôme des vins fins*. Mâcon.

Chauvet J., 1951. *La dégustation des vins. Son mécanisme et ses lois*. Mâcon.

Chauvet J., 1956. *La physico-chimie des surfaces et l'arôme des vins fins* . Cahiers techniques I.N.A.O.

Cloquet J., 1906. *L'art de la dégustation des vins*. Lebeque, Brussels.

Cottet J., 1976. *La soif*. Collection *Que sais-je?* Presses Universitaires de France, Paris.

Enjalbert H., 1975. *Histoire de la vigne et du vin. L'avénement de la qualité*. Bordas, Paris.

Fauré A., 1844. *Analyse chimique et comparée des vins du département de la Gironde*. Bordeaux.

Got N., 1955. *La dégustation des vins*. Perpignan.

Got N., 1958. *Le livre de l'amateur de vins*. Perpignan.

Gyllensköld H., 1967. *Att temperera vin*. Wahlström and Widstrand, Stockholm.

Jullien A., 1826. *Manuel de sommelier*. 4th edition, Paris.

Klenk E., 1950. *Die Weinbeurteilung*. Eugen Ulmer, Stuttgart.

Léglise M., 1976. *Une initiation à la dégustation des grands vins*. Défense et Illustration des Vins d'Origine, Lausanne.

335

Le Magnen J., 1949. *Odeurs et parfums.* Collection *Que sais-je?* Presses Universitaires de France, Paris.

Le Magnen J., 1951. *Les goûts et les saveurs.* Collection *Que sais-je?* Presses Universitaires de France, Paris.

Le Magnen J., 1962. *Vocabulaire technique des caractères organoleptiques et de la dégustation des produits alimentaires.* Centre national de Coordination des Etudes et Recherches sur la Nutrition et l'Alimentation.

Le Magnen J., 1965. *Les bases sensorielles de l'analyse des qualités organoleptiques.* Annales de la nutrition et de l'alimentation, volume 19.

Lesgourgues J. J., 1993. *Le vin émoi.*

Lopes Vieira A., 1971. *Prova de vinhos.* Editorial Noticias, Lisbon.

Lurton S., 1991. *VOCAVIN.* Media Vins.

MacLeod P. and Sauvageot F., 1982. *Bases neuro physiologiques de l'evaluation sensoreille des produits alimentaires.* Lavoisier–Tec Doc.

Ninio J., 1989. *L'empreinte des sens.* Odile Jacob.

Olhoff G. and Thomas A. F., 1971. *Gustation and Olfaction.* Academic Press, New York.

Mazenot R., 1973. *Le tastevin à travers les siècles.* Editions des Quartre-Seigneurs, Grenoble.

Peynaud E., 1981. *Connaissance et travail du vin.* Dunod, Paris. Trans. 1984 as *Knowing and Making Wine.* John Wiley and Sons, New York.

Pijassou R., 1974. In: *La seigneurie et le vignoble de Château Latour.* Fédération historique du Sud-Ouest, Bordeaux.

Poupon P., 1957. *Pensées d'un dégustateur.* 1975. *Nouvelles pensées d'un dégustateur.* Confrérie des Chevaliers du Tastevin, Nuits-Saint-Georges.

Poupon P., 1973. *Plaisirs de la dégustation.* Presses Universitaires de France, Paris.

Puisais J., Chabanon R. L., Guiller A., and Lacoste J., 1969. *Précis d'initiation à la dégustation.* Institut Technique du Vin, Paris.

Raboudin J. *Vocabulaire international de la dégustation.* Elvire.

Ribéreau-Gayon J. and Peynaud E., 1961. *Traité d' oenologie.* Tome 2. Berenger, Paris.

Ribéreau-Gayon J., Peynaud E., Ribéreau-Gayon P., and Sudraud P., 1975, *Sciences et techniques du vin.* Tome 2, Dunod, Paris.

Sarfati C., 1981. *La dégustation des vins—Méthode pédagogique et exercises pratiques.* Université du Vin Suze la Rousse.

Sauvageot F. *L'evaluation sensoreille des denrées alimentaires.*

Serres M., 1985. *Les cinq sens.* Grasset.

Torres P., 1985. *Le plaisir du vin.* Jacques Lanore.

Trémolières J., 1975. *Diététique et art de vivre.* Seghers, Paris.

Vedel A., Charles G., Charnay P., and Tourmeau J., 1972. *Essai sur la dégustation des vins.* Société d'Edition et d'Informations viti-vinicoles, Mâcon.

Vincens J., 1906. *L'art de déguster les vins.* Toulouse.

Index

Index